Special Makeup Effects for Stage and Screen: Making and Applying Prosthetics

Special Makeup Effects for Stage and Screen: Making and Applying Prosthetics

Todd Debreceni

ELSEVIER

AMSTERDAM • BOSTON • HEIDELBERG • LONDON
NEW YORK • OXFORD • PARIS • SAN DIEGO
SAN FRANCISCO • SINGAPORE • SYDNEY • TOKYO

Focal Press is an imprint of Elsevier

Focal Press

Focal Press is an imprint of Elsevier
30 Corporate Drive, Suite 400, Burlington, MA 01803, USA
Linacre House, Jordan Hill, Oxford OX2 8DP, UK

Library of Congress Cataloging-in-Publication Data
Debreceni, Todd.
  Special make-up effects for stage & screen : making and applying prosthetics / by
Todd Debreceni.
       p. cm.
  Includes index.
  ISBN 978-0-240-80996-0 (pbk. : alk. paper)   1. Theatrical prosthetic makeup.   I. Title.
  PN2068.D43 2009
  792.02'7--dc22
2008034231

British Library Cataloguing-in-Publication Data
A catalogue record for this book is available from the British Library.

ISBN: 978-0-240-80996-0

For information on all Focal Press publications
visit our website at www.elsevierdirect.com

09 10 11 12 13 5 4 3 2

Printed in China

Contents

CHAPTER 1 • The Industry

CHAPTER 2 • Anatomy and Design

CHAPTER 3 • Making the Lifecast

CHAPTER 4 • Sculpting the Makeup

CHAPTER 5 • Breakdown of the Sculpture

CHAPTER 6 • Casting the Appliances

CHAPTER 7 • Applying the Makeup Appliance

CHAPTER 8 • Hair and Wigs

CHAPTER 9 • Other Makeup Effects

Contents

What does it take to be a good makeup artist? There really are no formal qualifications. It's not like training to be a doctor or a pilot, where you're not able to work without hard-earned certificates and by passing rigorous exams.

Sure, there are various diplomas, degrees, and certificates you can get from the numerous schools and colleges worldwide that state that you've passed some sort of test of their devising to "qualify" you as a makeup artist, but, in my opinion, those bits of paper are all fairly meaningless.

My wife has a joke about this. She points out to me that she's put on makeup every single day for the past 20-some years, so this must qualify her to call herself a makeup artist, right? You know what? In a way, she's right. Anyone can call him- or herself a makeup artist. The question becomes, What kind of makeup artist are you?

In my experience there are several kinds of makeup artists, and I'm not talking about different categories of makeup artists such as prosthetic makeup artist, beauty makeup artist, or bridal makeup artist. What I'm talking about are the categories that makeup artists fall into defined by their attitude toward their craft. I was about to type *job* at the end of the last sentence, but of course not everyone who will read this book and practice the techniques they've gleaned from these pages will earn a living doing makeup. Some do it as a hobby. Some do it for fun at their local community theater, but however you practice makeup, you'll still fall into one of these three categories.

THE PERFECTIONISTS

I have a lot of respect for the perfectionist, especially as I'm *not* one. The perfectionist will strive to make every detail of his or her makeup...well, perfect! Though there's a lot to be admired about the perfectionist, and I know and admire a lot of them, they also have a habit of driving people nuts. Makeup is often a collaborative medium; actually, it's nearly always a collaborative medium as it involves a subject, often an actor, who participates by being the canvas for the makeup, but the perfectionist doesn't consider anyone or anything other than his or her own work.

When makeup artists keep an actor tied to the chair for five hours and push the makeup to the extremes of wearability and comfort to perfect a masterpiece, they're neglecting to consider the job of the actor who then needs to perform while wearing their creation. When this happens it's no longer collaboration. There's so much more to the job of the makeup artist than the makeup itself, but the perfectionist is often simply too consumed by his or her own interests to give a fig. Sadly, it's always for naught anyway, since nothing can ever be perfect and they spend a career chasing their tails.

THE LAZY ONES

These people are easy to spot. Their kit is often dirty, old, and made up of the cheaper products. Their attitude is slap it on, whip it off, and cash the check as soon as possible. They gossip too much on set, don't do enough checks on the makeup, and their real interest tends to lie in finding out how much everyone else is getting paid.

The lazy ones usually get into makeup because it looked interesting and a bit glamorous and frankly, they couldn't think of anything else to do with their lives. I could even name names right here, safe in the knowledge that they would never be read by those lazy individuals simply because they're never likely to read a new book on makeup, never mind buy one, because, frankly, they're not that interested.

THE PASSIONATE ONES

The passionate ones do it because they love it, pure and simple. The financial rewards, if any, aren't that important to them because they just love what they do. They're often not the most talented to begin with, but their passion and dedication to learn their craft drive them to improve with everything they do. Given the choice of hiring someone with great talent and an indifferent attitude or someone with mediocre talent and a burning passion, I'd hire the latter. There's no substitute for passion.

The passionate artist will listen and learn and strive to improve everything he or she does. The passionate artist will pore over every page of this book, learning new techniques and sucking up the information. But that passion can easily transform into one of the above, and it only takes passion to fizzle out a little for the passionate to become lazy. Equally, with just a nudge, passion can go the other way and become perfectionism.

You can probably tell that I'd consider myself passionate about makeup. My particular niche is prosthetics, and I've had the pleasure of a 20-year career in my chosen field. Sometimes the passion for it wanes—usually around 3:00 a.m. on a night shoot; it's cold and raining and I've forgotten to bring waterproofs—but mostly I maintain my passion. More recently I've found a way to keep that passion for makeup alive through teaching. Having a passion is great, but having the opportunity of sharing it is wonderful, and seeing other passionate people develop and improve through that sharing is, frankly, magical. Maybe one day one of my former students will have the honor, after their own 20-year career, to be writing the foreword to another book on makeup written by another passionate man.

—Neill Gorton, 2008

Acknowledgments

For the better part of my adult life I've been working in music, theater, film, and television; I've worn numerous hats, worked on some terrific shows with very talented people, and loved almost every minute of it. All in all, I've been very fortunate. Special makeup effects are the most fun I've had professionally, in large part because of the incredible artists and craftsmen (both male and female) who work in this astonishing field. I have never met or gotten to know more amazing, open, sharing, and supportive artists, and I want to express my deepest gratitude and appreciation to them as well as to my family and friends who supported, encouraged, contributed to, and assisted with the writing and compiling of this book.

I'm sure I could have gotten it done even without their help—*eventually*, and probably not nearly as well—but I'm sure glad I didn't have to try to write this book this without the incredible counsel and contributions of Neill Gorton, Dave Parvin, Matthew Mungle, and Mark Alfrey. I am deeply indebted to you guys. Thank you, thank you, thank you, thank you!

I am no less thankful and indebted for the support, friendship, and contributions of (in no particular order) Christopher Tucker, Dave Elsey and Rebecca Hunt, Miles Teves, Jordu Schell, Todd McIntosh, Mike Smithson, Alison and Will Chilen, Diane Woodhouse, Christien Tinsley and Tinsley Transfers, John Wilbanks, Robert Hubbard, Pixologic, Inc., Elliot Summons, Kris Martins Costa, Jamie Salmon, John Schoonraad, Brian Landis Folkins, Brian Wade, Nicole Feil, Kelly Rooney, Russell Pearsall, Kevin Kirkpatrick, Mark Garbarino, Vittorio Sodano, John Vulich and Optic Nerve Studios, Thea and FX Warehouse, Dr. Eugene F. Fairbanks, MD, Ed McCormick and EnvironMolds, Phyllis Brownbridge-Somers and WM Creations, Sharon Britt and Whip Mix Corporation, Justin Neill and the lads at Mould Life, Diana Ben-Kiki, Rob Whitehead, Matt Pilley, Chris Guarino, Brad Frikkars and Smooth-On, Tom Savini, Claire Greene, Ron Root, Jordan McDonald, Tess Fondie, Nick Sugar, Brian Walker Smith, Gernot Minke, Kenny Meyers, Chase Heilman, Mike Sisbarro and Silicones Inc., Gil Mosko and GM Foam, Meredith Faragosa and Price-Driscoll, Luke Pammant, Brandon McMenamin, Janelle D'Ambrosio, Kelsey Rich, Phil Martin, Terry Milligan, Don & Ellen Long, Tom Flanagan, Lisa DiMichelle, and John Dunsmoor. A very special thank you also to Cara Anderson at Elsevier and Focal Press for getting the ball rolling for me, and to my editor Michele Cronin for her help and encouragement through some of the most difficult fun I've ever had.

To my tolerant and understanding wife Donna, thank you for being your incredible musical self, for indulging my creative bent, and for not divorcing me for my tendency to stink up the joint and leave corpses and body parts lying around the house. To borrow a line from Ralph Kramden, "Baby, you're the greatest!" Thanks also to my parents Ted and Lois and my sister Amy for their unconditional support and encouragement and for "looking the other way" all these years after their son and big brother decided to go into *show business* instead of becoming a plastic surgeon. I love you very much!

To Travis, Ryan, and Dylan: If you can dream it, you can do it. Don't ever stop believing!

COVER CREDITS

Main image: Makeup by Neill Gorton, actor/model Kurt Carley, photography by Todd Debreceni.

Top row from left: Makeup by David Elsey, actor Peter Feeney / Age sculpt of actor Brian Landis Folkins by Todd Debreceni, photography by Todd Debreceni.

Middle row: Makeup by Todd Debreceni and Alison Chilen, actor Chris Kelly, photography by Todd Debreceni / Makeup by Julia DeShong and Todd Debreceni, actress Daniella Teul, photography by Todd Debreceni.

Bottom row: Makeup by Neill Gorton, model Karen Spencer, photography by Todd Debreceni / Makeup and photography by Todd Debreceni, actor Nick Sugar.

Preface

I've been fascinated by the trappings of the entertainment industry since I was a child. Ask my parents. I think they're still wondering when I'm going to grow up and get a real job. The sets, wardrobe, props, miniatures, makeup, acting… Movie Magic. Watching Ghoulardi and *Shock Theatre* in Cleveland, Ohio, as a kid was almost a ritual. I remember watching, mesmerized, as Lon Chaney, Jr., changed from Larry Talbot into *The Wolf Man* right before my eyes. How'd they *do* that?! And Claude Raines as *The Invisible Man* was…*invisible!* I watched footprints appear in the snow and no one was making them. I had to learn how to do that! Playing make believe, and getting *paid* for it. How cool would that be?!

Of course, many years later, after countless issues of *Famous Monsters of Filmland*, *Fangoria*, and now *Cinefex* and *Makeup Artist Magazine*, everybody knows how they do it. But it doesn't matter! It's still way cool and a heck of a lot more fun way to make a living than working 9 to 5 in the corporate world. Anyway, for me it is. It's the *doing* that floats my boat.

Was this always my chosen path? No, there was another one, quite different. So how did I come to get into this field of employment? Life is full of surprises, and who knows what the future holds in store? A lot of water has flowed under the bridge between the days of watching Ghoulardi and the writing of this book, but the defining moment for me came in 2002. I had begun teaching animation and visual effects part time at an art school in Denver just a few years earlier and our department director asked me if I'd like to teach a new "special topics" class; it could be just about anything as long as it was industry related. My reply was, "I'd like to do a class on prosthetic makeup."

Coincidentally, I had just begun to teach myself this craft using a few books I'd found: one by Lee Baygan, a couple by Tom Savini, and Vincent Kehoe's *Special Makeup Effects*. I was also doing some research online and was devouring behind-the-scenes footage on DVD releases such as Tim Burton's remake of *Planet of the Apes*, which was good but didn't really provide anything terribly enlightening in the way of techniques I could use. I still had rather limited hands-on experience. Well, somebody once told me that the best way to learn how to do something is to teach it to somebody else. So I did. And I found that adage is true.

The books offered pretty good step-by-step training: Baygan's *Techniques of Three-Dimensional Makeup* and Tom Savini's *Grand Illusions* and *Grand Illusions II*, for example; great stuff, but nothing had been written less than 10 or 15 years earlier than this book, and no book was only about creating prosthetic makeup (although Paul Thompson wrote a very good makeup textbook, *Character Make-up*, that was published in 2005 by Makeup Designory).

xvii

As I started exploring, I found great retrospectives of various artists' work. I found some outstanding "how-to" DVDs, videos, and myriad online tutorials. In fact, many of the artists whose work has inspired me and from whom I have learned contributed a great deal to this textbook. I learned a lot of valuable, helpful, and insightful stuff, most of it *really* good, but it still wasn't enough for me. To me, some of it felt incomplete, merely an appetizer.

There were steps missing (I felt) from some process descriptions, or the "how" was presented clearly but not the "why." I'd see somebody do something that looked like it was important, but there'd be no explanation of what it was I had just seen. The "why" is as important as the "how." Teaching the special topics class was an incredible learning experience for me and for my students, and my techniques and skill evolved with each subsequent class. I experimented. I tested. I got better. I discovered *Makeup Artist Magazine* and the International Makeup Artist Trade Show (IMATS). Then I met Dave Parvin. And I met Neill Gorton. And Matthew Mungle and Mark Alfrey. And a host of others. My chops improved dramatically.

There is encyclopedic information available out there in hardback, on the Internet, and elsewhere if you know where to look, what to look for, and are willing to pay for (some of) it. But there is no real textbook for creating special makeup effects. Well, there are textbooks, but not like this one. But make no mistake: This is not a traditional stage makeup book. You will not learn how to apply highlight and shadow to create the illusion of age in two-dimensional makeup. There are plenty of terrific books on the market already that can show you how to do that. This book will (I hope) teach you how to design and create three-dimensional prosthetic makeup, and *only* that.

I started thinking about this book in 2002 when I couldn't find the answers to my many questions. The thing is, the more I learn, the more questions I have, and I think that's good. I believe that no matter how good you get at doing something, there will always be someone who can teach you something new. I also believe that anything worth doing is worth doing well, and I hope this book will continue to evolve as the craft, and my knowledge, evolves. Of all the crafts in the entertainment industry, I have never met a group of professionals who are more open and sharing than the artists who work in special makeup effects.

For the most part, makeup for film, television, and theater can be separated into three categories: *straight*, or *basic*, makeup, which is designed to alleviate discernable visual changes in appearance that can occur as a result of the film, television, or theater process; *corrective* makeup, akin to beauty makeup, which is designed to enhance an actor's positive features and downplay or disguise others; and *character* makeup, or transformational makeup, which includes not only ethnic and age makeup but fantasy/whimsical, science fiction, and monster/horror makeup. This book concentrates primarily on the transformational aspects of prosthetic makeup appliances. Though monster, zombie, and horror/gore makeup is undeniably fun, the main focus of this book will be elsewhere and will do no more than glimpse those aspects of makeup effects; however, the information contained here most definitely applies to creating monster, zombie, and horror/gore-related makeups as well.

The emphasis of this book is on getting from Point A ("before") to Point B ("after") and the myriad routes one can take to get there; from concept to "Action!" The subject of special makeup effects is vast and complex, as those of you who've been immersed in it for some time know, but those of you who are not yet seasoned veterans needn't be discouraged by the range of information about to be opened up before you. There are many hats worn by the creative professionals working in the field of special makeup effects, and not all of them are worn on the same head. Not a lot, anyway, and perhaps you'll soon to begin to understand why.

It's difficult to tell someone how to sculpt a face for a character makeup or how to sculpt anything, for that matter. That is, someone can *tell* you; someone can *show* you pictures in a step-by-step manner, just like the ones presented in this book, but you still have to *do* it yourself. The very nature of everything you do as a makeup effects artist is physical. You can read every article, book, or description ever written about a particular technique, or watch every videotape, DVD, or streaming tutorial ever produced, but it will never take the place of actually doing it.

My intention is that you will read this book and look at the images to gain an understanding of the concepts and steps to achieve the intended results, then go back to read it again while actually doing the work yourself. This book is for your instruction but also for your reference. It is to be used in its entirety or for only those sections that are less familiar and unclear to you. This book will never replace face-to-face training with someone who can provide immediate feedback on the physical work you are creating. This book will be best utilized in conjunction with that face-to-face interaction with a makeup effects expert.

In many ways, this is a cookbook. Inside are "recipes" you can follow (or modify and adapt to suit your own tastes) to whip up a creative makeup effects masterpiece of your own. There are plenty of accompanying images to offer inspiration. Something that you might want to consider is taking this book to your local FedEx/Kinko's and have them cut off the binding and coil-bind it so you can lay it flat and it won't flip shut. That way you can refer to it continually as you work and follow along with many of the procedures presented in these pages.

The field of special makeup effects has evolved well beyond the application of straight makeup and into a realm bounded by gray areas of industry specialization. Let's say, for instance, that you have a script that calls for a newborn infant. Does the need for this newborn infant—a preemie in a neo-natal incubator—fall to the props folks, or is it a makeup effect? Hmm...good question. Certainly prop fabricators have the skill and technology to mold and cast such objects when the need for them arises, but how do you get to the mold-making stage in the first place? Can a full-body lifecast of a newborn be made? Not likely. *Don't even try!* You probably won't get to use a real newborn for the shot, either; what responsible parent or guardian would even let you? It's a bit too risky for most people. So, how do you get from script to screen with your preemie? Sculpt it? Absolutely.

Enter today's makeup effects artist. The prop guys can sculpt, but traditionally, prop sculpture needs have leaned more in the direction of industrial design—futuristic/fantasy weapons and the like—than in the human or animal anatomy direction. "But, Todd," you might be saying to yourself, "aren't you talking about special effects, then, and not special *makeup* effects?" I did say that there are *gray areas* of industry specialization. You say "tomato," I say "tomato." But I digress...

Many of the advances in materials used in makeup effects have their origins in the field of medicine, and you almost need to be a chemist to understand the inherent properties and uses of materials such as foam latex, platinum silicone, tin silicone, urethane rubber, polymers, resins, and gelatin. In his excellent book, *Special Makeup Effects* (Focal Press, 1991), celebrated makeup artist Vincent Kehoe noted that special makeup effects can be as rudimentary as cuts, bruises, scars, burns, and tattoos. Every makeup artist needs to know how to create these, but today's demands on a well-versed makeup artist—a makeup *effects* artist—are often to create much, much more. This book addresses that "much, much more" in a way that I hope will be beneficial to aspiring makeup effects artists as well as to makeup artists who already have some experience with the effects side of the business but want to learn even more.

With tips, tricks, and techniques from a number of our industry's most gifted artists—including Neill Gorton, Christopher Tucker, Dave Elsey, Matthew Mungle, Christien Tinsley, Vittorio Sodano, Jordu Schell, Miles Teves, Mark Alfrey, Mark Garbarino, and others—many color photos, and an accompanying "how-to" DVD, may this cookbook of special makeup effects become dog-eared from use and its pages lovingly stained by the fruits of your labor. I hope this book does for others what the astonishing artists who have contributed to this book have done for me. I hope this book will feel complete (but with room for improvement in a subsequent edition). Now clear off some workspace and get cookin'!

—Todd Debreceni

Note: The information and techniques described in this text are presented in good faith; no warranty is expressed or implied, and the author, Back Porch F/X, and Focal Press assume no liability for the use of the information or techniques. Use the techniques and materials presented in this text at your own risk.

CHAPTER 1 🎭
The Industry

Key Points

- Differences between working on stage and in front of a camera
- Contributions from the field of medicine
- Workspace necessities
- Workplace safety
- Professionalism
- What should be in your portfolio
- What should be in your makeup kit

INTRODUCTION

"Plus ça change, plus c'est la même chose." The more things change, the more they remain the same. These words, attributed to French journalist and novelist Alphonse Karr from *Les Gruêpes* in 1849, could hardly be more accurate in describing the business of special makeup effects today. Despite enormous advances in CGI technology (take a look at the makeup effects in *The Exorcism of Emily Rose,* for example: extensive digital makeup effects, very little of it practical), the majority of makeup effects work in motion pictures is still very physical. Makeup effects for theater are practical by necessity; there can be no digital enhancement before a live audience. In fact, once a practical effect becomes digital, it is referred to as a *visual effect*, not a special effect. However, a great deal of design is being done digitally, which we discuss in the next chapter. In motion pictures and television, a significant amount of work is beginning to be done through the use of digitally compositing elements of *computer-generated imagery*

(CGI) with live-action footage. It can be a very effective combination, especially when you realize you can only add, not take away, with makeup appliances. An outstanding example of practical makeup effects with digital accompaniment can be seen in *The Mummy* (1999) as the High Priest Imhotep, played by Arnold Vosloo, begins to regenerate.

It certainly hasn't always been that way, but inventive, innovative, creative people have been fooling the eye with special effects and special makeup effects since before the advent of moving pictures in the 1890s. There are scads of books and web sites in which you can find ample history of film, theater, stage craft, special effects, and special makeup effects, so this chapter doesn't present a history lesson. But a few pioneers are worth at least mentioning; their contributions to our industry and our craft have been monumental.

Arguably the first great master of special makeup effects was actor Lon Chaney, who designed and applied his own makeup in the horror classics *The Phantom of the Opera* (1925), *The Unknown* (1927), and *The Hunchback of Notre Dame* (1923). Many years later, Academy Award winner Dick Smith, the recognized father of multipiece overlapping appliances, created the 121-year-old Jack Crabb for Arthur Penn's *Little Big Man* (1970), starring Dustin Hoffman as Jack Crabb. The makeup was created out of foam latex and comprised 14 separate pieces, including hands and eyelids. Almost four decades later, Smith's process of multiple overlapping appliance pieces is still the industry standard for applying complex makeup, whether in foam latex, gelatin, or silicone. It has since been adopted by and improved on by the likes of Neill Gorton (*Doctor Who, Children of Men*), Stan Winston (*Edward Scissorhands, Terminator 2*), David Elsey (*Farscape, Star Wars: Episode III—Revenge of the Sith*), Rick Baker (*An American Werewolf in London, Planet of the Apes*), Mike Smithson (*Spiderman 3, Austin Powers: The Spy Who Shagged Me*), Ve Neill (*Pirates of the Caribbean* I, II, and III, *Beetlejuice*), Greg Cannom (*Van Helsing, Mrs. Doubtfire*), Matthew Mungle (*Bram Stoker's Dracula, Master and Commander: The Far Side of the World*), Bill Corso (*Lemony Snicket's A Series of Unfortunate Events, Galaxy Quest*), and many other truly remarkable makeup artists.

2

Neill Gorton

Neill Gorton owns and operates Neill Gorton Prosthetics Studio and Millennium FX Ltd. in the United Kingdom, providing special makeup effects, prosthetics, animatronics, and visual effects for films, TV, and commercials worldwide. He is also the man responsible for creating the amazing creatures seen in the BBC's *Doctor Who* since its distinctive 2005 rebirth. Neill's impressive credits include *Saving Private Ryan, Gladiator, Tomb Raider* (I and II), *The League of Extraordinary Gentlemen, Sahara,* and *Children of Men*. Neill has been an enormous help and encouragement to me and has influenced how I approach almost everything I do in this field.

In Neill's own words, "Not many 12-year-olds know what it is they want to do with their lives and eventually

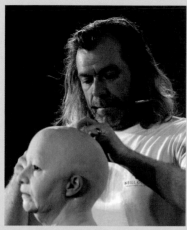

FIGURE 1.1
Neill applying one-piece silicone age makeup to Karen Spencer.
Photo by the author.

succeed at it. Frankly, I'm a bit of an oddity, and at the age of 12 I was already planning my career." This was in a suburb of Liverpool long before anyone had even heard of the Internet. Neill scoured magazines and books for any snippet of information that would help him achieve his goal. At age 15 Neill was already working with a mask maker in London; by 17 he was working on his first motion picture.

Like many artists working in the field of special makeup effects, Neill was influenced by the stop-motion animation of legendary special effects pioneer Ray Harryhausen. Ray created animated model monsters and dinosaurs for films such as *Jason and the Argonauts*, *Sinbad and the Eye of the Tiger,* and *Clash of the Titans*. At about the same time that Neill was learning about Harryhausen's groundbreaking work, films such as *Star Wars* and *ET* were bringing more lifelike monsters and aliens to the screen through animatronics and prosthetic techniques.

So Neill's attention turned from creating miniature monsters in clay to full-size mechanical beasts and prosthetic makeup. His very understanding parents realized how passionate he was and encouraged his new "hobby." By this time he'd been communicating with a number of makeup and special effects artists by post and received varying advice. Neill says, "Ultimately it watered down to 'Do practical subjects,' so amongst others I chose art, photography, and craft design and technology, which was an amalgam of metalwork, woodwork, and technical drawing."

"Looking back, craft design and technology was one of the better choices I made, because it taught the process of breaking down a product using a basic brief to determine design and function, following through to construction using a variety of skills and materials. All these things are very much a part of the work I do today, and this class gave me the fundamental skills to 'deconstruct' a project into its salient parts and follow it through from beginning to end."

3

FIGURE 1.2
Neill and an animatronic werewolf he built at age 15. Images reproduced by permission of Neill Gorton.

FIGURE 1.3
Neill's first age makeup. Image reproduced by permission of Neill Gorton.

In addition, Neill also studied drama because it gave him more time to experiment with makeup and his artistic skills to see how that role could affect the "other side of the curtain"—how the final performance is perceived by an audience.

"The last piece of the puzzle was chemistry," says Neill. "A special effects man working at the BBC, whose name, sadly, I forget, had kindly written a reply to my young enquiry telling me that chemistry was an important science in this area of work, and I'm grateful to him because he was right. I work in a world dominated by monomers, polymers, and polyesters, endothermic reactions and exothermic reactions, alkalines and solvents. My chemistry skills aren't first rate, but I learnt enough not be totally bamboozled when a rep from a chemical supply company starts waffling on about polymeric chains."

As a consequence of Neill's persistent contact with and approaches to the industry practitioners of the time, he was offered a couple of weeks' work with a makeup artist by the name of Christopher Tucker. Neill had communicated with Chris for a couple of years via post and had visited him at his studio the previous year and shown him some of his work. The offer was to come and assist for a couple of weeks working on another theatrical production and helping cast prosthetic appliances for the West End theatrical production of *Phantom of the Opera* makeup.

Neill's expertise in the field has taken him all over the world, and his travels are far from over. Neill says he wouldn't change his career path for anything, but adds, "Were I to be starting out all over again today, finding a proper vocational course in screen prosthetics which fully prepares you for a career as a workshop technician or enhances your skills as a prosthetic makeup artist for on-set work would be like manna from heaven and make the path into the industry so much easier to navigate. Hence the reason for having set up my own training studio for others who want to follow in my footsteps, but with a little less time wasted in wondering which way to turn next and bickering with well-intentioned but curriculum-bound college tutors along the way!"

FIGURE 1.4
Russell Neill in age makeup by Neill Gorton.
Images reproduced by permission of Neill Gorton.

FIGURE 1.5
Neill and Karen in finished age makeup at IMATS London, 2008.
Photo by the author.

The very first Academy Award for makeup was given to MGM Makeup Department Head William Tuttle in 1964 for his landmark work of transforming Tony Randall in *The Seven Faces of Dr. Lao*, though Tuttle's work was hardly the first notably brilliant makeup since Lon Chaney's self-applied creations some 40 years earlier. The list of remarkable, memorable makeup work continues to grow with each passing year, but some have become indelibly etched in our collective consciousness (in no particular order): Jack Pierce's work on Boris Karloff as Frankenstein's Monster in Universal Pictures' *Frankenstein* (1931); John Chambers' extraordinary work in 20th Century-Fox's *The Planet of the Apes* (1967); and Jack Dawn's Tin Man, Scarecrow, and Cowardly Lion for MGM's *The Wizard of Oz* (1939). A list of cool and favorite makeup could be as long as this book, and if you asked 30 artists for lists of their top 10, you'd probably get 30 different lists.

Jamie Salmon

FIGURE 1.6
Jamie detailing a portrait of Chris (*MEFIC Collection, Spain*).
Image reproduced by permission of Jamie Salmon.

Jamie Salmon is a British-born contemporary sculptor living in Vancouver, British Columbia. He specializes in photorealistic sculpture, utilizing materials such as silicone, rubber, fiberglass, acrylic, and human hair.

The themes of Jamie's works are varied. He says, "I like to use the human form as a way of exploring the nature of what we consider to be 'real' and how we react when our visual perceptions of this reality are challenged. In our modern society we have become obsessed with our outward appearance, and now with modern technology we are able to alter this in almost any way we desire. How does this outward change affect us and how we are perceived by others?"

Every piece of work that is created in the studio is the result of a painstaking, multistage process that is both artistic and technical. It can take anywhere from several weeks to sometimes months to create a piece, depending on its complexity and scale.

Jamie's work can be seen on permanent display in the MEFIC collection, which opened in early 2008. MEFIC is a contemporary sculpture museum showcasing work from some of the world's most influential modern contemporary artists.

Oxford art historian Steve Pulimood has written of Jamie's work, "From Picasso to Freud, painting the human form remains entrenched in the history or art making. Every foundation art education requires time with a model, and even

5

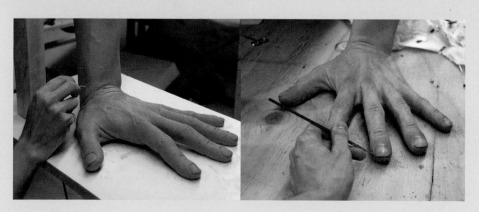

FIGURE 1.7
Hand detail. Images reproduced by permission of Jamie Salmon.

FIGURE 1.8
A work in progress. Images reproduced by permission of Jamie Salmon.

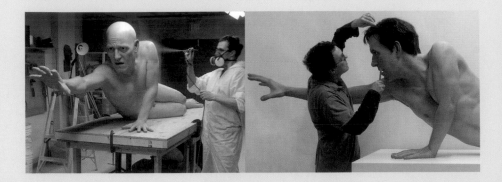

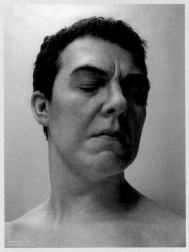

FIGURE 1.9
Self-Portrait. Image reproduced by permission of Jamie Salmon.

of the face and its extreme expressions were a science. Salmon's bronze offers to the viewer a fragmented stoicism, a portrait bust of statuesque vulnerability."

In Mueck, Salmon has a peer in modern medium and intent. Salmon has replicated the visage of the filmmaker David Lynch, earmarking a mascot for the strange, disturbing, and quietly uncanny."[1]

However, Jamie is more than just an incredible sculptor of larger-than-life realism. He is also an accomplished makeup effects artist whose film work includes *Freddy vs. Jason*, *Final Destination* 2 and 3, *Scary Movie 4*, *The Fog*, *X-Men: The Last Stand*, *Snakes on a Plane*, *Fido*, and *The Wicker Man*.

self-trained artists of masterful figuration, including Francis Bacon, no matter how fervently they denied the fact, took pencil to paper and improved with age. Giacometti, arguably the 20th century's most important sculptor of the human body, understood that timelessness could be represented in its gaunt essential form. Jamie Salmon works in a long tradition that extends from Franz Xaver Messerschmidt (1736–1783) to Ron Mueck (b. 1958). Messerschmidt was born in the age of enlightenment, when the physiognomy

FIGURE 1.10
Director David Lynch. Image reproduced by permission of Jamie Salmon.

[1]Steve Pulimood, the Saatchi Gallery, www.saatchi-gallery.co.uk, posted by editorial on August 31, 2006.

Within the industry there is some confusion about boundaries; when do special makeup effects stop being makeup, per se, and become special effects (which includes puppetry and animatronics) or the domain of prop designers? Is a severed head made from a lifecast of the lead actor's head and whose eyes blink and neck bleeds a makeup effect, special effect, or a prop? It depends on whom you ask, I guess. Legendary makeup effects pioneer Vincent J-R Kehoe said that though special makeup effects are character work in makeup, they belong to a specialized niche within the industry because creating makeup effects requires skill in painting, sculpting, mold making, and casting as well fabricating electronic controllers and articulated figure armatures used in animatronics. Therefore, he said, the work is not just makeup, but also special effects manufacturing.[2] And the field draws not only graduates from art schools but from the fields of engineering, industrial design, chemistry, and medicine as well. In fact, a cross-over between the worlds of makeup effects and the medical fields is involved in the creation of facial and somato (body) prosthetics.

STAGE VS. SCREEN

Strictly in terms of the end result, there is no discernable difference in the way 3D makeup effects are created for use on the stage or screen. Though traditional stage makeup (not prosthetic makeup) is meant to be viewed from a distance, many of today's live theater venues put actors and audience within very close proximity of one another, so makeup of any kind must read realistically from anywhere in the theater. Where the differences really begin to manifest themselves is in a particular show's makeup budget.

Typically, theater productions have relatively tiny budgets—often barely enough to break even (or slightly better) with sold-out performances for the run of the show. Traditional stage makeup is usually an expense for each actor personally. With few exceptions, theater is not a creative outlet where one can expect to become independently wealthy over a lifetime. Actors and technical craftsmen (designers) engage in theater for love, not money. That does not mean that we are willing to lose money on the endeavor, though it does invariably happen from time to time. We accept this because we are in it for the love of the craft. Only New York's Broadway theaters, London's West End, and large touring Equity (Actors' Equity in the United States and Great Britain) and perhaps a very few Equity venues elsewhere can afford 3D makeup effects on par with those regularly seen on screen.

In film and television, makeup effects are a measure of scale; in theater, they're a measure of volume. Equity shows usually run eight performances a week for several weeks, sometimes longer. Film projects often need many days' worth of appliances for various characters, but other factors can quickly come into play. When an actor is made up with prosthetics for the screen, it often happens early in the morning, and the actor remains made up throughout the day, touched up by the makeup artist between takes, after meals, and so on. If an appliance starts to come loose,

[2]Vincent J-R Kehoe, *Special Make-Up Effects* (Focal Press, 1991).

as they tend to do at high-movement areas such as the corners of the mouth, the camera can be cut, the appliance touched up, and then the camera rolls again.

When an actor is made up with prosthetics for the stage, it will happen as close to curtain time as possible, and if an appliance starts to come loose during a performance, there is likely to be hell to pay when the actor comes off stage! The same level of professionalism is required whether a performance is taking place before a camera or before a live audience; the stakes are immediately higher for stage productions for the following reasons:

- There is no possibility of halting a stage performance to repair or reapply a mischievous appliance.
- Many theaters are quite intimate, with audience members seated mere feet from the stage; if the makeup effects are not applied to perfection it will be clearly evident to those in the front rows.
- Film and television can employ additional dialogue replacement (ADR)— rerecording dialogue by lip syncing to video playback—but theater cannot; an actor must be audibly clear and succinct throughout the theater in 3D makeup, and the visible effect of the makeup must also be as effective to people seated in the last row as it is in the first row.

Other things to take into account in creating 3D makeup effects for stage are: Is there going to be a quick change for this character, either in makeup or costume? Does the actor have to put on or take off an appliance, and if so, how long will it take? Must the actor do it alone and in the dark? If clothing must come on or off past a makeup appliance, care must be taken not to damage the makeup, or time must be factored into the change to fix any damage. If it is a two-performance day, will there be time for the actor to get out of makeup and then back into it before the second show, or will the actor remain made up during the break between shows?

Probably the biggest hurdle to overcome in creating special makeup effects for theater is cost. If you're working on a major Actors' Equity production, it is somewhat less a concern, but not all Equity theaters have enormous subscriber bases to allow producers to create productions from an ideal financial situation. It becomes even more of a concern with small theater companies.

For example, special makeup effects for a Denver, Colorado, production of *Bat Boy: The Musical* can become a cost concern because not only must prosthetics be applied, they are not ones that can be easily self-applied, so a makeup artist must be taken into account for each performance.

Many times an appliance application can be simple enough that the actors themselves can be shown how to put them on and take them off without trouble. The "trouble" shows up in the form of having to have a fresh appliance for each performance. I have been working for several years to perfect a

FIGURE 1.11
The author applying prosthetic ears to actor/director Nick Sugar for a production of *Bat Boy: The Musical.* Image reproduced by permission of the author. Photo by Kelly Rooney.

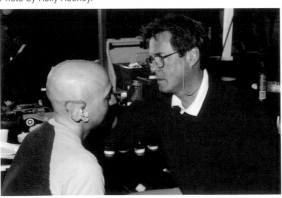

method of fabricating appliances that are soft enough for an actor to create a believable performance—to emote through—yet be strong enough to be thoroughly cleaned after each performance and used many times, thereby becoming more affordable. A few years ago I created actor-applied character appliances that lasted 40 performances for children's productions of *The Garden of Rikki Tikki Tavi* and *Lilly's Purple Purse.*

If I can do that, I'm certain I will also be able to overcome many actors' seeming inability to keep their dressing areas neat and organized and their makeup supplies clean and uncontaminated. But nah, I'm only human.

Lighting considerations are often different for makeup effects applications for the stage versus for the screen. Whether you're creating prosthetic makeup for still photography, live theater, video, or film, lighting is always crucial to the way the makeup will be perceived. The biggest makeup concern from a lighting standpoint is the use of color, which is a frequent addition to theatrical stage lighting. Colored gels have a decidedly different effect on your makeup coloring—much different than under the lighting conditions in which the makeup was applied. One way to develop makeup coloration for a stage production is to equip the dressing room with the same colored gels that will be present on stage with the makeup. Another is to do a makeup test on stage under actual lighting conditions. If the effect is negative, there should still be time to suggest makeup changes. I'd try this route before suggesting that the lighting designer change her lighting plot.

FIGURE 1.12
Actress Karen Slack as Lilly in *Lilly's Purple Plastic Purse* at the Denver Children's Theater. Photo by the author.

9

Amber gels tend to flatter makeup by adding life to flesh tones. Rosco, for example, offers several shades of an amber called Bastard Amber that are quite popular; the Roscolux color range includes four useful Bastard Amber shades—#01, #02, #03, #04—and two Rose shades, #05 and #305. Another popular Roscolux color for flesh tones is Pale Apricot #304. Surprise Pink is another color that has proved very useful for flattering makeup. There are several Roscolux shades in the Surprise Pink or Special Lavender category: #51, #52, #53, and #54. The Flesh Pink filters, such as Roscolux #33, #34, and #35, enhance the effect of most makeup by reinforcing the pink tones. But be careful of some of the other "pinks." Roscolux #37, for example, leans toward lavender and tends to warm up colors in the makeup base. It may even turn cool makeup gray or blue.

Blue filters transmit little red, so red and pink makeup appears gray and "dead" under blue light. This is an important factor since makeup normally is pink or "rosy" in tone. Blue filters are important in lighting many scenes (moonlight, for example), but care should be exercised when blue light falls on the actor, since it tends to give makeup a cold look. Even greater care is necessary when the darker Rosco blues are used, since they tend to create "holes" in the facial structure, such as hollows in the cheeks. Performers should be cautioned to use rouge sparingly. You should definitely pretest makeup when blues will dominate the stage lighting.[3]

[3]www.rosco.com/us/technotes/filters/technote_1.asp#MAKEUP.

Even rather "normal" lighting can appear to change the way makeup is seen differently by the audience than when being applied under similar lighting in the dressing room. The same production of *Bat Boy: The Musical* is a good example. Once the stage lighting was set, we did a makeup test under the lights, and coloring that was a perfect skin tone match under makeup lighting backstage made Bat Boy's enormous ears look like they were glowing several shades lighter under the stage lights. We adjusted the ear color accordingly, and the results were outstanding, though under normal lighting backstage, they were much too dark. On stage, it was impossible to tell that that actor Nick Sugar hadn't been born with those ears!

CONTRIBUTIONS FROM MEDICINE

Many developments regarding the materials used in the fabrication and coloring of makeup effects appliances as well as the adhesives used to hold them in place have come from the field of anaplastology: the art and science of restoring human anatomy by artificial means.

FIGURE 1.13
Makeup artist Kelly Rooney applying finishing touches to actor Nick Sugar for a production of *Bat Boy: The Musical* (top), and Nick in character on stage (bottom). Photos by the author.

Generally speaking, the various kinds of prostheses made by anaplastologists include facial, somato (body), and ocular (eye) prostheses.

This is exactly what makeup effects artists do. It is the job of a special makeup effects artist to create prosthetic appliances to be worn by actors that will transform their physical appearance by replicating anatomy as closely as possible, resulting in a natural and lifelike appearance while interfering with the actor's performance as little as possible.

Just as with prosthetic appliances made for use on stage or screen, even a well-made anaplastic prosthesis may be detectable under close observation. Because

FIGURE 1.14
A silicone gel prosthesis that relies on undercuts in the orbital socket for its retention; the back of the prosthesis is gel-filled to allow insertion into undercuts. Loss of orbital contents is due to malignancy. Images reproduced by kind permission of Medical Illustration Dept., UHL NHS Trust.

the prostheses are not living tissue, there are some obvious limitations: An anaplastic prosthesis might not restore normal movement, it will not blush or tan, and it must be removed for cleaning.

The process of making prostheses is the blending of art and science. There is very little difference between the methods of designing and fabricating a prosthetic device for everyday use and one created for a stage or screen character, with the possible exception of some of the materials used for the finished appliance. The result of development from silicone breast implant technology, silicone gel-filled appliances (GFAs) incorporate a tough elastomeric encapsulator—usually another silicone used as an outer skin, or envelope—over soft silicone gel that approximates the qualities of human skin over soft fleshy or fatty tissue.

Whereas special effects artists employ the use of foam latex and gelatin as well as silicone as prosthetic appliance materials, anaplastologists do not work with gelatin or foam latex. This is where the major differences stop. The results are dependent on the artistic, clinical, and technical skills of the individual professional. A well-made medical prosthesis serves to restore form whenever possible. Anatomical landmarks; facial proportion; symmetry; the direction of skin folds, skin, and tissue textures; and the coloration of the skin are all taken into account to create a convincing, lifelike appearance. This is no different from what the special makeup effects artist does. The steps in the creation of appliances are virtually identical, too.

Materials used in the creation of anaplastic prostheses include ultra-lightweight silicone and polyurethane. Furthermore, whereas special makeup effects are attached with a variety of medical-grade adhesives, craniofacial implants made of titanium have greatly simplified the daily management of facial prostheses for everyday applications. These titanium anchors do require surgical implantation, however. Some people become anxious about the possibility of a prosthetic appliance coming loose, which causes them to avoid many social activities. Craniofacial implants can give those people the confidence to participate in more activities, which, together with an improved aesthetic appearance, improves their quality of life. The use of these implants has also allowed for the development of new techniques and advanced applications of softer, more flesh-like silicones.

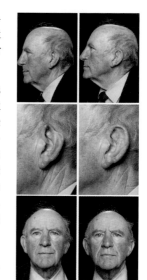

FIGURE 1.15
A partly auricular prosthesis following trauma to the pinna; retained by natural undercuts within the natural ear. Images reproduced by kind permission of Medical Illustration Dept., UHL NHS Trust.

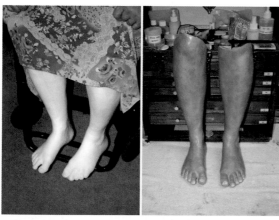

FIGURE 1.16
Nonfunctional cosmetic legs made by the author for a friend. Unpainted legs during early fitting (left), and the finished gams (right). Made of polyfoam and acrylic polymer skin. Photos by the author.

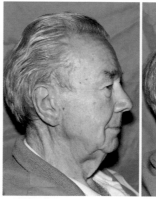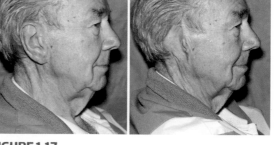

FIGURE 1.17
An adhesive-retained auricular prosthesis, constructed in medical grade silicone. This appliance must be removed and replaced each day. Loss of natural ear due to malignancy. Images reproduced by kind permission of Medical Illustration Dept., UHL NHS Trust.

High-consistency silicones with greater tear resistance can be used where edge strength is a priority. The manipulation and mold-packing characteristics of these silicones also produce deeper and longer-lasting intrinsic coloration. Nuances in pigmentation and vascularity can literally be captured with the prosthesis by layering color into the mold prior to polymerization, but this, like any painting technique, relies heavily on the artistic skills of the artist. Achieving the ideal pigment-to-polymer ratio results in a prosthesis that reflects and absorbs light similarly to the adjacent skin. Human skin is not completely opaque, and this balance between opacity and translucence produces a more natural appearance over varied lighting conditions.

The American Anaplastology Association is an organization that serves to bring together those specialties involved in anatomical restorations and to encourage acceptance and understanding of facial and somato prosthetics among health-care specialties and providers worldwide. Experts from the fields of anaplastology, maxillofacial prosthetics, medical illustration, ocularistry, prosthetics and orthotics, dental lab technology, prosthetic dentistry (prosthodontics), materials research, clinical cosmetology, biomechanical engineering, medicine, psychology, and other allied fields all participate in the task of improving patient outcomes through research and information exchange. It is through much of this activity that advancements in makeup effects technology occur. Anaplastology is an emerging global profession from which special makeup effects artists can benefit. Their annual conferences and publications offer timely topics on all aspects of restorative prosthetics, as well as conducting workshops on new and innovative developments in biomaterials, technologies, procedures, and approaches.

THE WORKSPACE

FIGURE 1.18
One of the author's workshops. Photo by the author.

Before you can begin creating makeup appliances from your ingenious designs, you need somewhere to do it. My little indie workshop is called Back Porch F/X because that's literally where it started way back when: on my back porch.

Actual square footage isn't important as long as you have sufficient room to work on whatever projects you work on and can afford. It will probably never be big enough! I have a way of filling up space rather quickly. However, whether you take up residence in your basement, garage, barn, or back porch or whether you rent or buy a studio, workshop, or warehouse somewhere convenient,

12

make sure you have adequate storage room for your materials, molds, and tools, ample electrical service to run them, and proper ventilation. *And* mellow neighbors who don't freak at the sight of various body parts being shuttled to and fro. My present office and workshop space total roughly 800 square feet, which is quite cozy; I occasionally work with my friend and fellow sculptor Dave Parvin at his studio in Denver, which is significantly larger than mine. Dave regularly conducts large workshops in his space, so there is room to move freely.

Workspace that can be dedicated to the tasks necessary for creating special makeup effects is vastly preferable to space that must be shared and used for other purposes. The very nature of the work and the materials and tools involved often all but preclude any other use. The amount of dust and potentially toxic fumes generated by a variety of fabrication processes should be reason enough to allocate a dedicated space.

Makeup rooms in many theaters or film and video studios are usually custom built with the necessary power, lighting, work surfaces, and storage areas to provide a comfortable working environment. This is often not the case when working on location. Our makeup room on location in the jungle of Belize in 2007 was a thatch-roofed, mud-walled, dirt-floored hut we shared with geckos, scorpions, doctor flies, and the occasional tarantula. Frequently when we arrived early in the morning, there would be fresh jaguar paw prints in the mud by the door. We had bare bulbs overhead for our lighting.

We may not have had air conditioning or glass in our windows, but at least we had generators for electricity and a roof over our heads. The wardrobe hut flooded every time it rained, which was daily. The point is to make the space you have functional, hygienic, and as comfortable as possible for your cast and fellow makeup artists.

Ideally, your working space will be well ventilated, including a mirror and counter space with lights for each working artist. There should also be plumbing with running water, both hot and cold. These conditions will be present in most situations, but when they're not or can't be, you must be ready to adapt to the situation at hand and make it work. You are a professional, after all, right? Or you want to be. The Boy Scouts were onto something when they came up with the motto *Be prepared*.

FIGURE 1.19
Author's location makeup hut in Central America. Photo by the author.

13

SAFETY AND HEALTH

In the application of makeup and makeup effects it is critical for you, the makeup artist, to be aware of the potential for cross-contamination of makeup and accessories. Infections such as cold sores, sties, and any number of other potentially more harmful bacterial or viral infections can be transmitted via makeup sponges, powder puffs, foundations, creams, lipstick, eyeliner, and so on. These can also be passed on via brushes and other tools that have not been cleaned or sterilized properly. Portable autoclaves for sterilizing brushes, scissors, sponges, and other tools of the trade can be purchased for less than $300. Because of this potential for contamination and because the acids in your skin could also be contaminants, you should never touch makeup products with your bare hands. Use brushes, sponges, or spatulas instead. Bulk applicator items can be purchased relatively inexpensively for just such purposes.

In the United States you can obtain health and safety regulations from the Occupational Safety and Health Administration, or OSHA (www.osha.gov); in the United Kingdom and Europe, Health and Safety Executive, or HSE, publishes the Control of Substances Hazardous to Health (COSHH) Regulations 2002 (www.hse.gov.uk/coshh). In particular, you should be familiar with the correct storage and use of cleaning agents, solvents, polymers, and the like and make certain that the storage areas are clearly marked and in compliance with your local health and safety regulations.

The tools and materials we work with are not toys. Fatalities have been known to result from improper use and storage of numerous tools and chemicals common to the creation of special makeup effects. Thankfully, that number is small. Virtually every product used in the course of fabricating makeup effects has a product Material Safety Data Sheet (MSDS) with a product overview and recommended safety precautions. In fact, MSDS information should be gathered and stored on all materials (if available) a makeup artist uses. These sheets are required when an OSHA representative requests them. Keeping them handy and in your kit, particularly when you are traveling, may actually minimize potential hassles with TSA or other security folks regarding what is in your kit and whether or not it may still be in your kit when you reach your destination.

There are enough harmful agents wafting through our daily environments already without adding to our potential health risks. Work only in areas with adequate ventilation. Buy particle masks and a respirator capable of filtering not only dust particles (even mist from airbrushed makeup foundation is not good to breathe) but toxic fumes as well, such as acetone and naphtha. Purchase boxes of disposable gloves in powder-free latex, vinyl, and nitrile. Get in the habit of wearing safety glasses. Many of the substances we can come into contact with might not be immediately harmful, but harmful levels can build up cumulatively in your system over time. Take sensible precautions and keep both your workshop and makeup room safe and clean and yourself healthy.

14

The products in your kit should be properly labeled to avoid mistaking acetone for astringent. Hazardous materials should be kept securely in lockable metal cabinets or cases. It really is easy to work safely and hygienically if you simply use common sense.

Matthew W. Mungle

FIGURE 1.20
Matthew doing finals on Drew Barrymore for *Charlie's Angels: Full Throttle.* Image reproduced by permission of Matthew Mungle.

Academy Award winner Matthew W. Mungle is regarded as one of Hollywood's premier makeup special effects artists. He has over 100 film and television projects to his credit, including *The Bucket List, Schindler's List, Ghosts of Mississippi, Bram Stoker's Dracula, Edward Scissorhands, Six Feet Under, N.C.I.S., House, The X Files, CSI,* and *Women's Murder Club*. Matthew has earned accolades and recognition as one of the industry's top masters of special makeup effects. Along with Neill Gorton, Matthew has had an enormous influence on my career and mentored me through my first feature as a makeup department head and makeup effects supervisor. I credit much of what I know to what Matthew taught me.

As a boy Matthew recalls seeing *Frankenstein, Dracula,* and *The Mummy*. He was fascinated with the makeup, often "borrowing" his mother's cosmetics to create his own version of horror. As he got older, he sent away for theatrical

makeup from New York and Dallas specialty stores—and experimented with face casts and prosthetics on willing family members and friends. Although his parents thought it was a phase he would soon outgrow, Matthew knew differently. He credits the 1964 release of *The Seven Faces of Dr. Lao*, with makeup effects on Tony Randall by the late William Tuttle, as having been his greatest influence and deciding factor in becoming a special effects makeup artist.

Matthew came to Hollywood in 1977 and in 1978 applied to and was accepted into Joe Blasco's Make-up Center, one of Hollywood's top makeup academies that is responsible for training many of the film and television industry's best makeup artists. Matthew credits Joe with his professional start in the industry. "I was a sponge, absorbing every ounce of knowledge I could," he said. "Whether learning the techniques of beauty makeup or casting molds and working with prosthetics, I wanted to be as versatile as I could." Today Matthew is a veteran voice listened to by up-and-coming artists hoping to find their own niche in the industry. Matthew says, "If you want to be a working makeup artist, you need to learn and perfect all areas of the craft."

Matthew's professional career began on low-budget projects that taught him to think quickly on his feet. His first major success was on *Edward Scissorhands* in 1990. Years later, Matthew has accumulated an impressive list of credits and an equally impressive genre of box office successes, including an Academy Award and two other nominations, as well as several Emmy Awards and continued international recognition.

Age makeup has become one of Matthew's strongest calling cards and an area of makeup effects that's definitely challenging. His fascination with artificially making someone young look old prompted him to research more viable methods, such as gelatin, first used in the 1930s but

FIGURE 1.21
Stages in application of age makeup on Christopher Walken for *Blast from the Past*. Images reproduced by permission of Matthew Mungle.

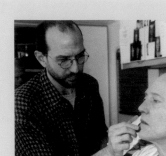

later abandoned when the hot lights caused it to melt. With today's less intense lighting and faster film, Matthew has resurrected the nearly translucent substance, which, when applied, looks and moves like real skin. "I've made it a part of my craft to see how skin moves," says Matthew. "I'm intrigued with how women and men age differently. Both get jowls and tend to get that fold of skin over the top lid of the eyes and bags under the eyes. However, men's ear lobes get longer and women's skin gets creepy and translucent."

One of Matthew's greatest challenges has been with the Broadway hit *Wicked*, creating the prosthetic face masks for the production's various characters. Balancing his film and TV projects, Matthew continues his work for the show's Broadway, U.S. tour, Japan, and Los Angeles productions.

During a rare lull in an always hectic schedule, I asked Matthew what advice he'd give someone with a desire to begin a career in special makeup effects.

TD: What advice would you give someone with little or no experience with special makeup effects to begin studying?

MM: Read as much as you can about makeup effects on the Internet and from books. Practice taking face casts, sculpting, mold making, and application of prosthetics as much as you can. Attend a makeup school, if possible. You can always learn from others, whether their techniques are time-tested or cutting-edge new.

TD: When designing a character makeup, what are important considerations to take into account?

MM: Where the character lives and the environment around them; for instance, if a person was in a cave for a long time, their skin would be very pale and translucent. How this character will move and the facial expressions they'll make are important. Most of all, how anatomically correct the facial features have to be.

TD: What is the most important skill or skills a makeup effects artist must possess?

MM: The ability to get along with actors and other crew members!

TD: What should be in a makeup effects portfolio?

FIGURE 1.22
Drew Barrymore in age makeup. Image reproduced by permission of Matthew Mungle.

MM: Beauty makeups, small and large prosthetic appliances, character and old-age makeups with and without prosthetics, and creature prosthetic makeups.

Matthew's process of fabricating bondo appliances—a combination of Pros-Aide® adhesive, Cab-O-Sil® filler and added coloring—has taken off in a big way since Christien Tinsley's success in creating 3D wound appliance transfers for *The Passion of the Christ*. The extremely soft bondo encapsulated in Matthew's alcohol-based "Soft Sealer" skinned prosthetics makes them ideal f-or use as a small to medium-sized prosthetic; he created eye bruises for Sly Stallone in *Rocky 6*, casualty wounds for *Poseidon*, and even an upper lip appliance supplied for Guy Pearce as Andy Warhol in *Factory Girl*. These appliances are great for actors who perspire a lot or have to be wet all day and are extremely easy to apply with the lightest touch of 99% alcohol.

MM: There has been a lot of use of New-Baldies® plastic-skinned Plat-Sil gel-filled silicone appliances in the last couple of years. Thanks to Ryan McDowell, we have had great success making silicone appliances with the New-Baldies skin and filled with Plat-Sil Gel 10 platinum-based silicone, which has a very low leach property when highly plasticized. However, I feel in the right circumstance that gelatin, foam latex, and even bondo appliances still have their place in our great world of creative makeup effects.

Matthew is big on not limiting himself to one particular material for casting appliances.

MM: I use all materials because they each have their own different properties. I try not to limit myself to a certain material because of the outcome of the creation.

PROFESSIONALISM

Working in the entertainment industry is supposed to be fun. We play make-believe for a living and sometimes get paid quite well for it, too. However, it is still a business, and a certain sense of decorum can and should be maintained while still having a good time. Being well prepared and well organized is a good start.

Specialty makeup cases abound in a broad price range to keep your supplies organized; there are also inexpensive cases for tools or fishing tackle that are compartmented and will work well. Rather than putting all your supplies together into one kit or even several kits through which you have to search to find things, consider organizing your kits separately: one for straight makeup; one for injury and wound effects; one for hair. I strongly suggest investing in plastic containers for your liquids, gels, and powders. Be able to store your materials so that they won't spill, break, leak, or be damaged. Keep potentially messy substances such as adhesives, artificial blood, glycerin, and dirt powders such as Fuller's Earth (Pascalite) separate from other items in your kits. Before storing liquids such as acetone in plastic bottles, be certain that these materials can be safely stored in plastic. Otherwise, stick to leak-proof glass or metal containers.

I can't say this too many times: *There's no such thing as being too prepared.* Be certain you have enough of everything in your kit to handle unforeseen circumstances, because they will arise. Do you have sufficient adhesive for your appliances? Remover? The *right* remover for the adhesive you're using? Do you have sufficient cleaning materials? Sponges? Cotton pads? Create a checklist you can use for each production and each day. Are all your materials clearly and correctly labeled?

When purchasing new or replacement stock, be sure it's what you need for the production. Do you know of any special skin-care needs of any of your cast? If you will be working out of town or abroad, make advance arrangements to ship sensitive or hazardous materials—well packed—by air or ground. Traveling by air with many items, even ones in checked baggage that nothing could possibly happen to, can create major headaches, even if you believe you are prepared for them. Trust me. I'll give you an example; I pass along this information because it is a lesson I learned and a mistake that will not be repeated if I can help it. Once, when flying to a remote location out of the country, baggage inspectors painstakingly inspected every individual crème foundation in both of my large studio kits; there must've been close to 100 of them in all. The inspectors unscrewed each lid and stuck a gloved finger firmly into the center of each crème disk and then replaced them in the drawer where they were stored, many of them upside down and all of them without the lids. Every one of them was compromised. This happened both when I left the United States and when I came back through different airports; I don't know if it happened within the United States or at my foreign destination. Nobody claimed it as their handiwork, and there were no witnesses.

Regardless of the culprit, be forewarned. Before leaving on a trip, ensure that the materials you cannot take with you are available at your destination. If they're not, advance ship them. I could do neither and was forced to use the inspected foundations, but I tossed them all when I returned home. It was an expensive lesson. Ship your kit by ground or by one of the express companies, if possible, for early arrival. This would be the most convenient choice, though not inexpensive. And it's not always possible. Since September 11, 2001, sweeping new rules have been put into play governing what can or cannot be brought on board a commercial flight, even in a carry-on bag.

Your makeup area and workshop should be sanctuaries from the anxiety and stress that often pervade a set. Models and actors need a peaceful environment. Though your workshop environment might not be exactly a model of calm, Grand Central Station during the evening rush is not what you want to emulate for your working environment. When people rush, mistakes are made and everything starts to go downhill.

Without some sort of protocol in place, a large set would be utter chaos. On smaller shoots departmental lines are often blurred, but certain rules of etiquette always apply. Every craft has its own protocol for on-set behavior, but there are some universal standards:

- Show up early for your crew call.
- Be polite. Manners you learned in kindergarten still apply when you're an adult.
- Learn and use people's names.
- Ask questions if you're in doubt about what to do.
- Pay attention to what is going on in your department.
- Make your supervisor and everyone on your team look good.
- Stay near the action. Don't leave the set, or wherever you're meant to be, unless you tell one of the assistant directors first and have permission to do so. If you can't be found when something goes wrong in your department

and someone has to go looking for you, you might well have cost the production significant money while everyone waits for you. If this happens
more than once, don't expect to be asked back.

- Remain composed. Occasionally crew members, even experienced department heads, behave irrationally or even unfairly. If someone bites your
head off about something, don't bite back; rise above it. Remain calm and
courteous and ask them how they'd like you to proceed. If it's your boss
or supervisor doing the yelling, do what they ask quickly and without getting angry or upset. If the angry one is not part of your chain of command,
check with your boss before doing anything. If you can weather the storm,
it will pass. By maintaining your composure in a confrontational situation, you've made yourself look good.
- Don't embarrass anyone, least of all your supervisor or anyone else you
directly work with.
- Unless you are just making conversation or have been given the authority
to do so, don't talk to other departments. It might be frustrating, but if you
have a problem or suggestion, talk to your supervisor about it. An obvious
exception to this rule is when safety is involved.
- Don't brag or be boastful. Ditto for arrogance. Doing good work and being
confident in your abilities are not the same as showing off. Let people find
out for themselves how good you are and how valuable you are to the department and the production. In other words: Be humble. It isn't that hard.

On-set etiquette is mostly common sense. The following list is by no means
complete, nor is it new. There are probably as many variations as there are rules.
For a makeup artist, it is generally acknowledged that you are expected to be on
the set at all times. Ideally, you will be near the camera but far enough out of the
way so as not be a distraction or blocking anyone's view of the action. When in
doubt about where to be, ask an AD.

- Dress comfortably but professionally on set. Be subtle. Remember: You're
not the star.
- Bathe! We work in very close proximity to actors. Though working with
grips who have dirt under their fingernails and don't wear deodorant
might be tolerated, it is completely unacceptable for a makeup artist to
have dirty hands and B.O.
- Brush your teeth. This is no different than not wearing deodorant. When
your face is inches away from your subject, your breath shouldn't make
them gag. At least keep gum or mints handy. As a service provider, you
should want your subjects to be comfortable and at ease as much possible
while you do your job.
- Talk to your actors; when you're applying or removing prosthetic appliances, let them know what you're doing at every stage so there won't be
any surprises via sudden movements on your part.
- Know your script, shooting schedule, and daily call sheets. Knowing how
many scenes your actor will be in will give you an idea of your application
needs. If your actor is in every shot, your application process will be different than if your actor is being shot for a small insert or short scene, and

you can adjust accordingly. The same is true of knowing what the camera setups are going to be; there is no need to do a 30-minute touchup on an actor who is partially obscured in a wide shot.

- Be able to adapt and react. Thinking outside the box is very important, from actors' allergies to certain materials or a director getting a new idea for a makeup that should take an hour to apply and you only have 15 minutes.
- You are providing a service. Your makeup is for the purpose of enhancing and supporting a performance. It's never about the makeup; it is always about the performance. Don't forget that.
- Take your time. Don't dawdle, but don't let a zealous AD or impatient actor fluster you and make you hurry. When you rush, you make mistakes, and that ultimately leads to delays, frustration, and short tempers. Don't let yourself get sucked into a situation you can't control.
- Resist the temptation to insert yourself into the middle of a discussion or rehearsal to do touchups. A director's last-minute instructions to an actor always take precedence over makeup. Wait patiently until they're done; go in for touchups only if you're certain it's okay. If it appears that you're not going to get the time you need for your finals, inform the first AD. It's the AD's job to coordinate these things; keep the AD or ADs informed of potential problems before they occur.
- If you're not sure how your makeup will read on camera or you need to double-check a detail, ask the camera operator if you can look through the camera before doing it.
- To assure makeup continuity, take notes, draw pictures, and take photographs. Polaroids or digital photos of your makeup will most likely be a necessity, and you can refer to them as you work. Keep a file on each actor and each change in his or her makeup. Every artist has his or her own way of keeping track of makeup for each actor. There is now digital continuity software called SavingFace for theater, film, and television.
- Sometimes we must be mind readers or, at the very least, intuitive; learn when and when *not* to talk to your actor. Actors might not be in a talkative mood and be getting into character when you are applying their makeup.

In a theater environment (unless you're working on Broadway or with a big touring Equity show) things will usually be a little bit different, frequently more casual, often chaotic and cramped, but the basic tenets remain unchanged.

YOUR PORTFOLIO

It is generally agreed that your makeup portfolio should contain certain things. How many of these things is not agreed, though I think it is safe to say that quality tops quantity. You might want to think twice about having only one makeup to show, though, even if it's a really, really good makeup. You need to show that it wasn't a fluke. Oscar winner Matthew Mungle believes you should have examples of beauty makeup, small and large prosthetic applications, character and age makeup with and without prosthetics, and creature prosthetic makeups.

Kevin Kirkpatrick echoes my point: "A makeup effects portfolio should only consist of your best work. Honestly, it's not about quantity, it's all about quality."

YOUR KIT

There's an adage that goes something like this: "It's not the tools that are used but the artist who uses them." Legendary photographer Ansel Adams said something similar: "The single most important component of a camera is the 12 inches behind it."[4] The materials in your makeup kit will not make you a better artist; the right materials just make it easier, faster, and more convenient for you to achieve the results you want.

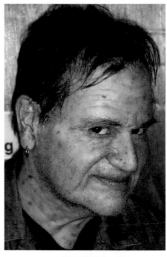

FIGURE 1.23
Matthew Mungle age makeup on Kirk Baltz in *To Serve and Protect*. Image reproduced by permission of Matthew Mungle.

If you were to ask every working makeup artist what he or she has in their kit and what they consider absolutely essential tools to have in everyone's kit, you will likely find a great many different answers, the same as trying to get a fix on what type of case or cases these tools should be carried around in. Some artists swear by Ben Nye crème foundations; others can't live without Mehron, Krylon, or RCMA products. Still others may say it's MAC or Sephora for them, or nothing. Very few, if any, artists use only one product brand for the simple reason that no one single manufacturer makes everything an artist could possibly use. The Boy Scout motto, "Be prepared," certainly applies in this instance because we makeup artists are frequently called on to come up with a makeup seemingly out of thin air— something unplanned—and if we've got a little bit of everything at our disposal, it becomes much easier to improvise on the spot and (one hopes) look like a hero. Ironically, to be good at improvising requires practice and a very broad knowledge base. Some suggested kit essentials as well as a fairly comprehensive listing of suppliers are included in the appendix.

FIGURE 1.24
Kevin Kirkpatrick age makeup "before and after" applied to Dustin Heald. Images reproduced by permission of Kevin Kirkpatrick.

CHAPTER SUMMARY

Chapter 1 shared a brief makeup effects history and introduced you to makeup effects artists Neill Gorton, Jamie Salmon, and Matthew Mungle. You also should now be aware of differences and similarities between makeup effects for the stage and those for the screen.

We discussed how advances in medicine and medical prosthetics have aided the makeup industry. We also discussed workspace and working conditions, safety and health concerns, professionalism, what should be in your portfolio, and what should be in your makeup kit.

[4]Ken Rockwell, *Why Your Camera Does Not Matter*, 2006.

CHAPTER 2 🎭
Anatomy and Design

Key Points

- Using the computer
- Elements of the design
- The human body
- Surface anatomy
- Symmetry and proportion
- Distinctions of gender, age, and ancestry

INTRODUCTION

After the script, perhaps the next most important task is designing and creating the story's physical characters. Of course, this will only apply to a story that needs physical alteration of the actors who will be playing characters. But this is where the fun begins, and having a solid understanding of human anatomy will make your job that much simpler and that much more enjoyable. Human physiology—the way the body works—is good knowledge to have also, though it's not as critical as anatomy to the success or failure of a special makeup effects artist.

The way we move and the way we look is wholly dependent on our anatomy—our bone structure, how and where muscles attach, how big or small they are, what our skin looks and feels like, how and where hair grows; everything about us right down to the dirt under our fingernails should be studied and understood. Without this knowledge, our designs, sculptures, and ultimately our finished makeups would lack the sense of genuine depth and believability that a truly outstanding, memorable character must have if we are to succeed as makeup artists.

As artists, we will never be completely satisfied with our work. Accept that as a given. Nor should we be satisfied. That is the nature of the artist. No matter how good we get, there will always be something we could have done to make it better; we might not always know what that something is, it's simply the way we are. I don't think our work should ever be "good enough" for us. That's not to say that we shouldn't recognize when something is "finished" and move on to the next project, it's just that there will always be room for improvement. In fact, I think that is a good gauge for us as artists: The moment we start thinking that there is nothing we can do improve, that is the moment for us to reevaluate what it is we're doing and why.

Our work can always improve, and no matter how skilled we become, there will always be someone who can teach us something new. Iconic dancer/choreographer Martha Graham once wrote to her dear friend and contemporary, legendary dancer/choreographer Agnes De Mille:

> There is a vitality, a life force, a quickening, that is translated through you into action, and because there is only one of you in all time, this expression is unique. If you block it, it will never exist through any other medium and [will] be lost. The world will not have it. It is not your business to determine how good it is; nor how valuable it is; not how it compares with other expression. It is your business to keep it yours, clearly and directly, to keep the channel open. You do not even have to believe in yourself or your work. You have to keep open and aware directly to the urges that motivate you. Keep the channel open. No artist is ever pleased. There is no satisfaction whatever at any time. There is only a queer, divine dissatisfaction; a blessed unrest that keeps us marching and makes us more alive than the others.

24

FIGURE 2.1
Design and sculpture by ZBrush® artist Chris Bostjanick. Image reproduced by permission of ZBrush®, Pixologic®, and Chris Bostjanick; © 2007 Pixologic, Inc.

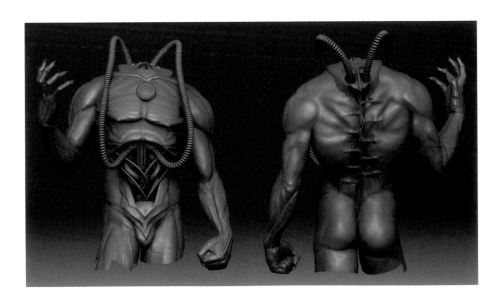

USING THE COMPUTER

Today the tools we have at our disposal to aid us in designing characters have vastly improved over the years. But human anatomy is still human anatomy. Whether you draw every aspect of a design by hand, go straight to clay and sculpt what is in your head, or enlist the aid of 2D and 3D software to model and mock up your designs, computers have become as essential a tool as Plat-sil® Gel 10, WED clay, Ultracal 30, and fiberglass. Today's 3D packages such as Lightwave,® Softimage XSI,® Maya,® and 3D Studio Max® are not merely high-end animation software but are staples among character designers as modeling tools, as are the virtual sculpting tools ZBrush® and MudBox.®

FIGURE 2.2
Design and sculpture by ZBrush® artist Kris Martins Costa. Image reproduced by permission of Kris Martins Costa.

I don't know a working artist today who doesn't have at least a passing relationship with Adobe Photoshop.® I can't imagine working without it. In fact, a great many makeup designs—age makeups or horror makeups, for example—are often initially done in Photoshop from photos of actors before being taken to a sculpture stage.

With the aid of software, the design process can be sped up considerably, though the computer is no substitute for a solid foundation in life-drawing skills and knowledge of anatomy. When asked about the skills required to be a sought-after character designer, Miles Teves (*King Kong, Interview with a Vampire, Legend*) is quoted as saying, "A good foundation in life drawing is key. You need to be able to imbue your designs with a sense of realism and nuance that you can only get from studying nature directly."[1]

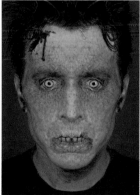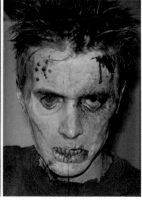

FIGURE 2.3
Design and Photoshop® image manipulation by Brian Wade; makeup test by Brian Wade. Images reproduced by permission of Brian Wade.

[1]Richard Rickitt, *Designing Movie Creatures and Characters* (Focal Press, 2006).

FIGURE 2.4
Ironman sculpt by
Miles Teves for
Ironman (2008).
Image reproduced by
permission of Miles
Teves.

Brian Wade

FIGURE 2.5
Brian Wade and
character designs.
Image reproduced by
permission of Brian
Wade.

Brian started his career in special makeup effects when he was still in high school in Studio City, California, helping makeup effects master Kenny Meyers. Continuing to work with Meyers after finishing high school, Brian got a call one day from Kenny's assistant, Erik Jensen, to work on John Carpenter's 1982 effects masterpiece *The Thing* for Rob Bottin.

"That was an amazing time in my life; working with Rob Bottin, having lunch during the week with Rick Baker and

FIGURE 2.6
Brian's first ZBrush model, 2006 (left); Baboon-Man ZBrush model, 2007 (right). Images reproduced by permission of Brian Wade.

his guys who were doing *Videodrome* at the time . . . Man, life was perfect."

Like many artists in the field of makeup effects, Brian worked for a number of makeup effects shops, each working on different projects. It was, as he calls it, the heyday for makeup effects; it was pre-CGI, so everything was live action and in camera. During those years, Brian met and worked with many of the industry's best, on projects including *The Terminator, Harry and the Hendersons, Star Trek IV: The Voyage Home, Buffy the Vampire Slayer, Blade, Bicentennial Man, Stuart Little, Van Helsing, Hellboy,* and *Chronicles of Narnia 2: Prince Caspian.*

In addition to his makeup effects skills, Brian is also exceptionally adept at Pixologic's 3D sculpting software ZBrush, as you can see from these images of his 3D work.

In 2002, pal Miles Teves lured Brian to Prague, Czech Republic, for a gig, and he's remained there, where there is quite a bit of work and the film industry is booming.

Character designer Patrick Tatopoulos (*Stargate, Independence Day, I-Robot*) agrees. "To be a good designer I think you need to have a wealth of knowledge about artistic and cultural styles, about biology, anatomy, and different types of animals. You are constantly observing these things. Then when you draw, you don't need to think about these things; they will inform your work almost instinctively."[2] The computer as a design aid is just that—an aid. Once a design has been sculpted or modeled in 3D, it can be rotated, lighting can be added or changed, textures can be applied, and images can be printed so that when a physical sculpture must be made, there are views from every angle.

27

Miles Teves

Character designer par excellence Miles Teves grew up in a suburban town near the Pacific coast of central California. An avid fan of the usual sci-fi and horror flicks shown on late-night TV as well as a huge fan of Batman, Godzilla, and *Star Trek*, Miles was a keen artist from an early age, drawing and sculpting and using the family's 8 mm movie camera to make his own stop-motion monster movies.

The release of *Star Wars* when he was in junior high school coincided with an increasing interest in art and cinema; at a science-fiction convention a few years later, Miles met special effects genius Rob Bottin, who had just completed the special makeup effects for John Carpenter's superb remake of *The Thing*. Miles showed his portfolio to Bottin and was asked to "keep in touch."

[2]Richard Rickitt, *Designing Movie Creatures and Characters* (Focal Press, 2006).

FIGURE 2.7
Miles Teves *is* Ironman. Image reproduced by permission of Miles Teves.

After high school, Miles moved to L.A. and studied illustration at Pasadena's Art Center College of Design, considered one of the best art schools there is. However, after a year he was out of funds and decided to try to get in touch with effects legend Rob Bottin, who was just beginning work on, ironically, *Legend*. Bottin hired Teves as an illustrator, and soon he was heavily involved in helping to develop the character of Darkness based on a sculpted design by Bottin's key sculptor Henry Alvarez. Miles's success on *Legend* led to more work with Bottin, first on *Explorers* (1985) and then on *Robocop* (1987).

Designing an amazing character must take into account the actor or actress who will portray that character. It all comes back to anatomy and design. Among the key characters Miles had a hand in designing are Darkness and Meg Mucklebones (*Legend*); Robocop

FIGURE 2.8
Big Momma sketch and clay sculpt. Images reproduced by permission of Miles Teves.

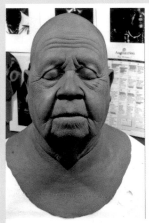

FIGURE 2.9
Miles sculpting noses for *The Passion of the Christ*. Images reproduced by permission of Miles Teves.

(*Robocop*); Lestat (*Interview with the Vampire*); Robin (*Batman and Robin*); dragons (*Reign of Fire*); Jesus (*The Passion of the Christ*); Hell Hound (*Chronicles of Riddick*); and Kong (*King Kong*). His other movie credits also include *Explorers; Hollow Man; Spiderman; Terminator 3: Rise of the Machines; Van Helsing; Pirates of the Caribbean: The Curse of the Black Pearl; Ironman; Watchmen; The Good Girl;* and *The Curious Case of Benjamin Button*. Miles designs with traditional illustration techniques as well as sculpting in clay and using Adobe Photoshop.

I think that most character designers—that is, designers creating makeups that actors will ultimately wear vs. CGI creatures or animatronics—will agree that sculpting in a 3D software package isn't the most efficient use of time and resources when designing, say, an age makeup for a specific actor. Why? Because first, a cyberscan of the actor's head needs to be taken—you can't work from a 2D photograph in either ZBrush® or MudBox®—and more often than not, the scan will be so dense and need so much cleanup work that it would make more sense to use a package such as Photoshop to create the design right from the start. Photoshop has become an indispensable tool in the artist/designer's arsenal.

Both MudBox® and ZBrush® take a little getting used to if you are unfamiliar with sculpting digitally. They work with (but don't demand) the use of a tablet and stylus pen for optimal efficiency; using a mouse for creative activities for which you would ordinarily use a brush, pencil, pen, or, in this case, a sculpting tool equates to sculpting with a brick. However, once you begin to understand the interface of each program and what the tools are capable of doing, it soon becomes really no different than sculpting with actual clay, with the added benefit of not getting little bits of clay all over everything in your work area.

FIGURE 2.10
Photo manipulation of Sharon Stone by Miles Teves. Images reproduced by permission of Miles Teves.

ELEMENTS OF THE DESIGN

Creating an effective, memorable character makeup is dependent on several things. What is the medium in which the character will be viewed? Is this a character makeup for the stage or screen? Since essentially everything in a stage production will be viewed by the audience in a "wide shot," the makeup must reflect the reality of the medium. Even makeups designed for the screen must often be bigger than life. Noted character artist Steve Wang has said that when you sculpt a character, you tend to make the detail more exaggerated than in real life because you want those details to show up. "Although we are very often inspired by nature, our aim is not always to reproduce nature—our work is very theatrical and is there to serve the movie," he says.[3]

It also has to be a design that, when fabricated and applied, will allow the actor to wear it and perform in it. For film and television, it becomes important for makeup artists to be in sync with the director of photography so that the makeup—and so the performer—will be photographed in the best possible way to achieve the storytelling objectives. In theater, lighting is the critical element with which to be in sync. How a makeup appears under certain lighting conditions can help or hurt a performance. Story and performance should always take precedence over makeup.

Crucial physical information you need to know about your character before you begin to design should include (but certainly should not be limited to) the following:

- What is the character's general physiology and body shape?
- Is the character nonhuman or animal-like? What does it resemble—a mammal, bird, reptile, amphibian, insect?
- Does the character have wings or a tail?

Body Types

There are three *somatotypes*, or body types, associated with men and women: ectomorphic, mesomorphic, and endomorphic. These body types were described by American psychologist William Sheldon, who began his research with 4,000 photographs of college-age men which showed front, back, and side views. From the study of these images, Dr. Sheldon saw that there are three fundamental elements that, when combined, made up these three physical body types.[4] No one is wholly one of the three without having at least some of the other two at the same time in varying degrees.[5]

FIGURE 2.11
Character "before and after" by Mark Alfrey. Images reproduced by permission of Mark Alfrey.

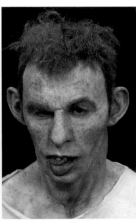

[3]Richard Rickitt, *Designing Movie Creatures and Characters* (Focal Press, 2006).
[4]Tyra and James Arraj, *Tracking the Elusive Human*, Vol. I (Inner Growth Books, 1988).
[5]Tyra and James Arraj, *Tracking the Elusive Human*, Vol. I (Inner Growth Books, 1988).

The *ectomorphic* body type is characterized by long arms and legs and a short upper body with narrow shoulders.

In addition, ectomorphs are characterized by:

- Thin physique
- Small bones
- Flat chest
- Youthful in appearance
- Lightly muscled
- Very little body fat
- High metabolism
- Tall

The literary character of Ichabod Crane (*The Legend of Sleepy Hollow*) is an example of a classic ectomorph.

The *mesomorphic* body type is characterized by a high rate of muscle growth and a higher proportion of muscle tissue. Mesomorphs have large bones and a solid torso combined with low body fat levels. They are also characterized by:

- Broad shoulders
- Narrow waist
- Overly mature appearance
- Physical strength
- Large chest
- Long torso
- Thick skin

The character Tarzan is a classic mesomorph.

The *endomorphic* body type is characterized by an increased amount of body fat. Endomorphs have wide waists and hips and large bone structure. They are also characterized by:

- Soft body
- Slow metabolism
- Round-shaped body
- Round face
- Short neck
- Low muscle mass

Santa Claus is our society's ideal endomorph.

Obviously you'll need to consider variations within each of these somatotypes when designing your character as well. Dr. Sheldon evaluated the degree to which a characteristic was present on a scale ranging from one to seven, with one being the minimum and seven the maximum of a particular somatotype.[6]

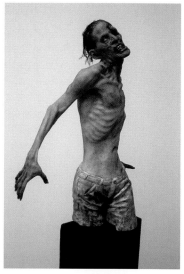

FIGURE 2.12
Maquette by Jordu Schell—an ectomorphic zombie. Image reproduced by permission of Jordu Schell.

31

[6]Tyra and James Arraj, *Tracking the Elusive Human*, Vol. I (Inner Growth Books, 1988).

In assessing a character's body type, other variables to consider may include:

- Is the character from classic fiction, popular culture, or previously unknown?
- Is the genre of the character horror, science fiction, fantasy, or reality?
- Is the character animal, vegetable, or mineral?
- What is the character's gender?
- Does the character have skin? If so, what is the color, texture, and hairiness? Are there variations of these characteristics over the body?
- Does the character have fur? Feathers? Scales? A shell or bony armor?
- How will the character's coloring affect audience perception?

What about stereotypes? Stereotypes are based in reality but tend to be a gross oversimplification of an observed or perceived trait of behavior or appearance. If you can add familiarity to your character and makeup design without becoming inappropriate or offensive, then do so. However, remain sensitive when dealing with cultural and symbolic elements that may affect your design.

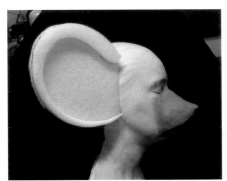

FIGURE 2.13
Design for a children's theater production of *Lilly's Purple Plastic Purse*. Photo by the author.

FIGURE 2.14
Ghost of a young girl from *The Enemy God*. Image reproduced by permission of the author. Photo by Paul Cuthbert.

FIGURE 2.15
Actor Nick Sugar from *Bat Boy: The Musical*. Photo by the author.

FIGURE 2.16
Actor Chris Kelly in foam latex character makeup. Photo by the author.

In designing special makeup effects you must remember that you can add to, but not take away from, a makeup if an actor is going to be wearing prosthetics. There must also be a basis in the reality of biology and physiology; a character with an enormous head, neck, and chest but a lower torso and waist barely large enough only for the spine and little else is not likely to have survived long enough as a species to evolve, let alone grow to adulthood with such a physique. The sheer weight of the head, neck, and upper body would topple, splintering the spine like a toothpick, not to mention the question of where the abdominal organs and digestive tract are supposed to be. In creating even a fantasy character, there must be a basis in reality, in human anatomy, *especially* if a human actor has to wear it, even if it is a nonhuman character makeup!

THE HUMAN BODY

There are 11 systems that combine to make up the human body: *skeletal* (bone, cartilage, and ligaments); *skeleto-muscular* (muscles and tendons of the skeleton); *integumentary*, or the external covering of the body (skin, hair, nails, sweat glands, mammary glands, and their products); *nervous* (brain, spinal cord, and peripheral nerves); *endocrine* (glands and hormones); *cardiovascular* (arteries, veins, and blood supply); *lymphatic* (fluid drainage and immunity); *respiratory*; *digestive*; *urinary*; and *reproductive* systems. Our skeletal system—our bones, cartilage, and ligaments—creates the rigid framework that supports and protects our bodies. But it is the study of principally three—the *skeletal, skeleto-muscular,* and *integumentary* systems—which we focus on for designing and creating special makeup effects in this book.

The Skeletal System

Our bones hold our body in its shape and are the anchor points for most of our muscles. It is the way these bones are put together as our skeleton that gives us the framework around which all other tissue forms and characterizes our species: erect posture and bipedal locomotion. Our skeleton is divided into two parts, each with clearly different functions:

- The *axial* skeleton (skeleton of the trunk, or central skeleton) includes the *cranium*, the *spinal column*, and the *thorax*. The primary function of the axial skeleton is to support and protect the internal organs.
- The *appendicular* skeleton includes the upper and lower limbs and the girdle (pelvis); the primary function of the appendicular skeleton is to enable movement and to provide support.

Of the 206 bones in our body, 29 make up the cranium, 26 make up the spinal column, 25 make up the thorax, 64 make up both upper limbs (including the hands), and 62 make up both lower limbs (including the feet). Our bones are quite strong and very elastic. Depending on their shape, bones are categorized as long, short, or flat bones. Their sizes vary considerably as well. By understanding and knowing the sizes, shapes, and purpose of each bone group, we can start to envision the way our character makeup will take shape.

Jordu Schell

FIGURE 2.17
Jordu Schell. Image reproduced by permission of Jordu Schell.

FIGURE 2.18
Brock. Image reproduced by permission of Jordu Schell.

34

Jordu Schell is widely regarded as one of the most influential creature designers in the world. Working mainly from his studio in the San Fernando Valley of suburban Los Angeles, he has been designing film and television monsters for nearly 20 years. Jordu has worked on and designed characters and creatures for numerous projects, including *James Cameron's* *Avatar*, *Cloverfield*, *Men in Black*, *Edward Scissorhands*, *The X-Files Movie*, *Predator II*, *Galaxy Quest*, *Evolution*, *My Favorite Martian*, *Alien: Resurrection*, *Babylon 5: The Series*, *The Guyver*, *Bedazzled*, *Scary Movie 3*, and many more.

As well as teaching at his own busy facility, Schell Sculpture Studio, in L.A., Jordu has also taught internationally

FIGURE 2.19
Several sculptures illustrating a foundation in real anatomy. Images reproduced by permission of Jordu Schell.

at a number of well-known shops, including Tippett Studios, Industrial Light and Magic, Blizzard Entertainment, The Monster Makers, Creature Effects, Specter Studios, Vancouver Design, Joe Blasco, Empire Academy of Makeup, and Neill Gorton's prosthetics studio in England. Jordu's work carries an innate understanding of real-world anatomy that translates into the characters and creatures

he designs, rendering his creations wholly believable when you see them in person or on screen; it's as if these beings could … do … exist. Jordu's talent and skill, plus the fact that he is a remarkably good teacher and that he's simply a really good guy, keep him in very high demand for television and motion pictures. I am thrilled to be able to include Jordu and examples of his work in this book for you.

Some basic orientation terms will help make sense of anatomical terminology and the relationship of one part to another in the descriptions that follow:

Median. The midline of the head and body.
Medial. Toward the midline and away from the side of the body.
Lateral. Away from the midline and toward the side of the body.
Anterior. Toward the front of the body.
Posterior. Toward the back of the body.
Superior. Toward the top; above; ascending.
Inferior. Toward the bottom; below; descending.

The Skeleto-Muscular System

There are three types of muscle tissue: striated, smooth, and cardiac. Of the three, striated is the one that will be influential in our makeup design. Viewed under a microscope, striated muscle appears to be striped. Striated muscle is also called *voluntary muscle* since it is under our conscious control. Over 640 voluntary muscles make up 40 to 50 percent of our body weight.[7] Voluntary muscles are grouped and arranged in two or more layers and give the human form its characteristic shape beneath layers of fat and skin.[8]

THE HEAD AND NECK

With a few exceptions, cranial muscles comprise two groups: One is located inside the head; the other connects the head to the torso. *Extrinsic* muscles originate at different points of the axial skeleton—at the shoulders, neck, and chest. *Intrinsic* muscles—the ones inside the head itself—originate and insert into the head.[9] These are the muscles that are needed for chewing, swallowing, and nonverbal communication—our ability to create various emotive facial expressions such as smiling, frowning, and grimacing.

[7]Sarah Simblet, *Anatomy for the Artist* (DK Publishing, 2001).
[8]Sarah Simblet, *Anatomy for the Artist* (DK Publishing, 2001).
[9]*Atlas of Anatomy* (Taj Books, 2002).

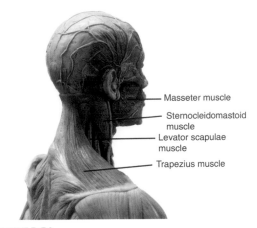

FIGURE 2.21
Posterior lateral view of head and neck muscles. Photo by the author. Anatomy model by Andrew Cawrse.

FIGURE 2.20
Head and neck muscles with shoulder and chest. Photo by the author. Anatomy model by Andrew Cawrse.

Muscles of the face, head, and neck that could dramatically affect the physical appearance of a character makeup, the surface anatomy, are the *trapezius* muscle (neck), *sternocleidomastoid* muscle (neck), *levator scapulae* muscle (neck), and *masseter* muscle (jaw).

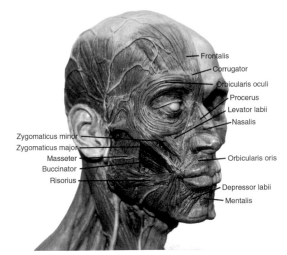

FIGURE 2.22
Facial muscles. Photo by the author. Anatomy model by Andrew Cawrse.

THE FACE

It's not so much the muscles of the face themselves that affect the way a character looks, though there are a few that can alter the face's shape; it is how the muscles affect the overlying skin as the skin ages that will create alterations. (We will look at aging later in this chapter.) The muscles of the face include:

- *Frontalis (epicranius)* muscle
- *Corrugator* muscle
- *Orbicularis oculi* muscle
- *Levator labii* muscle
- *Zygomaticus minor* muscle
- *Zygomaticus major* muscle
- *Risorius* muscle
- *Depressor anguli oris* muscle
- *Depressor labii* muscle
- *Buccinator* muscle
- *Masseter* muscle

- *Mentalis* muscle
- *Orbicular oris* muscle
- *Procerus* muscle
- *Nasalis* muscle

THE TORSO AND UPPER LIMBS

Muscles of the torso are divided into muscles of the *thorax* (upper torso or chest) and muscles of the *abdomen* (lower torso). Anterior (front) muscles of the chest and abdomen that are likely to affect the appearance of surface anatomy include:

- *Sternocleidomastoid* muscle
- Greater pectoral muscle (*pectoralis major* and *pectoralis minor*)
  - *Clavicular* part
  - *Sternocostal* part
  - *Abdominal* part
- *Deltoid* muscle (anterior and medial)
- *Rectus abdominis* muscle
- *External oblique* muscle
- *Internal oblique* muscle
- *Transverse abdominis* muscle

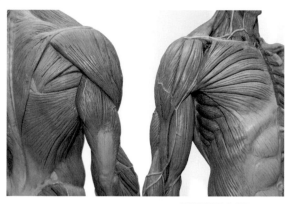

FIGURE 2.23
Anterior and posterior torso and upper limbs. Photo by the author. Anatomy model by Andrew Cawrse.

37

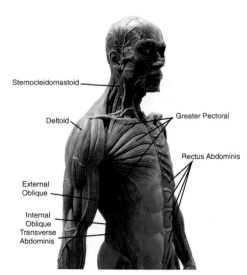

FIGURE 2.24
Anterior torso muscles. Photo by the author. Anatomy model by Andrew Cawrse.

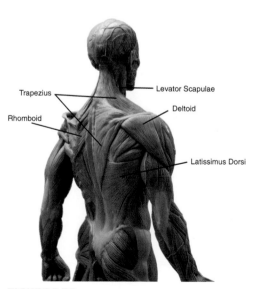

FIGURE 2.25
Posterior torso muscles. Photo by the author. Anatomy model by Andrew Cawrse.

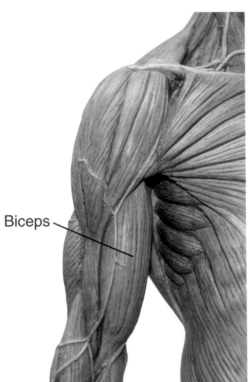

Posterior (rear) muscles of the back and lower back that are likely to affect the appearance of surface anatomy include:

- *Deltoid* muscle (medial and posterior)
- Upper, middle, and lower *trapezius* muscle
- *Levator scapulae* muscle
- *Latissimus dorsi* muscle
- *Erector spinae* muscle
- *Rhomboid major* and *Rhomboid minor* muscles

The *biceps brachii* is the muscle that shapes the front of the upper arm and bends the arm. The biceps is actually made up of two parts—*biceps* means "two heads"—that attach at separate points above the shoulder joint and converge and attach at a single point below the elbow joint.

The *triceps brachii*—"three heads"—shapes the back of the upper arm and extends it. The three heads attach separately to the humerus bone near the shoulder joint and to the scapula and then converge into a single tendon that attaches at the back of the ulna of the lower arm.

The muscles of the lower arm or forearm—more than 30 of them—consist of long extensor (extending), abductor (opposing), and flexor (flexing) muscles that shape the front and back of the forearm and pass into the hand.

Biceps

FIGURE 2.26
Anterior view showing *biceps brachii* muscle. Photo by the author. Anatomy model by Andrew Cawrse.

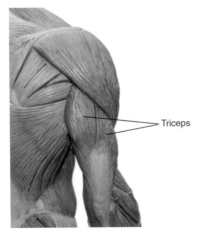

Triceps

FIGURE 2.27
Posterior view showing *triceps brachii* muscle. Photo by the author. Anatomy model by Andrew Cawrse.

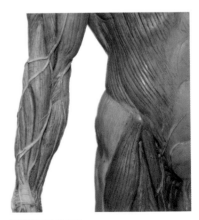

FIGURE 2.28
Anterior view of forearm muscles. Photo by the author. Anatomy model by Andrew Cawrse.

There are no muscles in the fingers, only tendons on either side of the finger bones, wrapped by lubricated fibrous sheaths. The meaty part of the fingers is fatty tissue carrying blood vessels and nerves and providing cushion for the flexor tendons as the hand grips objects. The dorsal or back side of the hand is bony and the tendons are readily visible against the skin; the palm of the hand is more muscular. These palm muscles are enclosed by a sheet of thick connective tissue called the *palmar aponeurosis*. This tissue is bonded to the skin above and bones below so that the skin does not slip when the hand grasps a surface.[10]

THE ABDOMEN AND LOWER LIMBS

Of the anterior torso muscles, *rectus abdominis* and *external oblique* are probably the most recognizable muscles, next to *pectoralis major*. Well-defined *rectus abdominis* is the classic washboard "six-pack" abdomen we've all seen on body builders.

The hip and thigh bones of the lower extremities are surrounded by some 27 muscles, comprising extensor, adductor, rotator, and flexor muscles. These large, powerful muscles are the ones that enable us to stand from a seated position, supporting almost our entire body weight. Surface definition of these muscles is frequently greater in men than in women.

Quadriceps femoris muscles flex the hip joint and extend the knee; as the name implies, it is a four-part muscle, made up on *vastus lateralis, vastus medialis, vastus intermedius,* and *rectus femoris,* that begins at the front and side of the femur near the hip joint and at base of the spine; these components converge into a single tendon that covers the knee (*patella*) and attaches at the head of the *tibia* bone, at the top of the shin. The *quadriceps* (*vastus lateralis*) and body fat beneath the skin's surface shape the outside of the thigh, while *rectus femoris* shapes the front of the thigh. *Sartorius,* the longest muscle of the human body, is both a flexor and an adductor and separates the quadriceps from the thigh's adductor muscles; it bends the knee and pulls and rotates the thigh.

The back of the thigh is shaped by the *semi-tendinosus* and *biceps femoris* muscles.

Both muscles attach near the head of the *femur* and insert, or end, at the head of the *fibula* in order to be able to flex the knee joint and extend the hip. *Gluteus maximus* is the large muscle of the buttocks; it extends and rotates the hip laterally. The buttocks are shaped by the *gluteus maximus* and by fatty tissue that covers it beneath the skin.

The bones of the lower leg and foot are accompanied by more than 30 muscles; the muscles of the lower leg are arranged in two sections, one anterior on the outside of the shin and the other

[10]Sarah Simblet, *Anatomy for the Artist* (DK Publishing, 2001).

FIGURE 2.29
Anterior lateral view of abdomen and lower limbs. Photo by the author. Anatomy model by Andrew Cawrse.

39

FIGURE 2.30
Quadriceps femoris muscles. Photo by the author. Anatomy model by Andrew Cawrse.

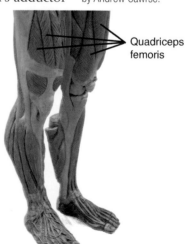

Quadriceps femoris

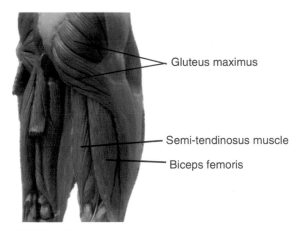

— Gluteus maximus

— Semi-tendinosus muscle

— Biceps femoris

FIGURE 2.31
Semi-tendinosus and **biceps femoris**. Photo by the author. Anatomy model by Andrew Cawrse.

posterior, giving shape to the calf.[11] These muscles are separated by the lower leg bones, the tibia and fibula. These muscles are responsible for our ability to draw our foot back, point it down, and turn it inward or outward. *Tibialis anterior* is a strong, tapered muscle that shapes the front of the leg to the outside of the shin (there is a ridge that runs along the anterior shaft of the tibia).

The *tibialis anterior* narrows into a tendon that passes over and under the instep of the foot, allowing us to flex it tightly, pull the foot back, and/or turn it inward. The superficial muscles of the posterior of the lower leg—*soleus, plantaris,* and *gastrocnemius*—shape the back of the calf; these muscles share a common tendon, the *calcaneal tendon,* better known as the Achilles tendon, which is a short, thick tendon that is clearly visible at the back of the foot as it attaches onto the upper back of the heel bone (*calcaneus*).[12]

Similarly to the muscles of the hand, the muscles of the foot are mostly beneath, on, or inside the sole. They act on the toes to collectively spread them, draw them together, pull them back, or curl them under. The sole is covered with a *plantar*

40

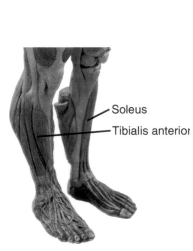

— Soleus

— Tibialis anterior

FIGURE 2.32
Tibialis anterior. Photo by the author. Anatomy model by Andrew Cawrse.

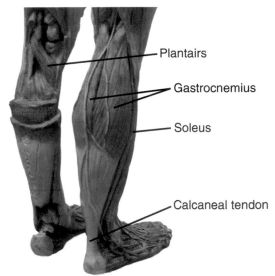

— Plantairs

— Gastrocnemius

— Soleus

— Calcaneal tendon

FIGURE 2.33
Soleus, plantaris, and *gastrocnemius*. Photo by the author. Anatomy model by Andrew Cawrse.

[11]Sarah Simblet, *Anatomy for the Artist* (DK Publishing, 2001).
[12]Sarah Simblet, *Anatomy for the Artist* (DK Publishing, 2001).

aponeurosis in tandem with the deep fascia pad of the foot. Just like the hand's *palmar aponeurosis*, it protects the foot, gives attachment to the foot muscles, and holds the skin of the foot firmly in place so that it does not slip as we stand or walk.[13]

SURFACE ANATOMY

Surface anatomy is the study of the configuration of the surface of the body, especially in relation to its internal parts. The way we are put together beneath the skin manifests itself to a great extent outwardly and is visible. Our skeletons and musculature give us our basic shape, and our skin is the covering that gives those internal structures one overall form that is each of us. From birth, as we grow and develop, our surface anatomy changes because our internal anatomy is changing as well.

The reason that understanding anatomy is so important for us as makeup effects artists is that much of what we do is based on surface anatomy being dictated by underlying anatomy. It is in the understanding of internal anatomy that we are able to know why there are bumps and hollows on the external surface of the body.[14] To create prosthetic appliances that will be believable, even if the design is somewhat stylized, we must know what people of every color, gender, size, and shape look like and how they move.

Remember also that when it comes to designing prosthetic makeup effects, you can add to the anatomy of the actor to create the new character, but you cannot take away. For example, if you are given the task of creating the makeup effects for a production with emaciated, starved, and abused concentration camp prisoners, the direction in which you can go is limited. To create a character of skin and bones requires one of the following:

- Extremely skinny actors
- CGI characters
- Shadow and highlight foundation makeup that may give a stylized impression of a gaunt appearance but will not in actuality make the actors thin

For individuals with no body fat and very little muscle mass, their surface anatomy will show much of the body's skeleton clearly defined just beneath the skin. For example, for the film *The Machinist*, actor Christian Bale was willing to lose one third of his body weight to play a character in a perilous downward spiral emotionally, physically, and mentally. And he did it.

That could not have realistically been achieved any other way than physically, and had the character been physically heavier, his impact would have been negatively compromised. Was what the actor chose to do wise and healthy? Probably not, but Christian Bale has done several films since *The Machinist* and is physically

[13]Sarah Simblet, *Anatomy for the Artist* (DK Publishing, 2001).
[14]Avard T. Fairbanks and Eugene F. Fairbanks, *Human Proportions for Artists* (Fairbanks Art and Books, 2005).

41

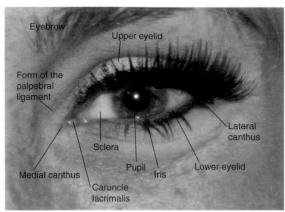

FIGURE 2.34
The eye. Photo by the author.

fine as far as I know. He is just a supremely dedicated and focused actor.

The Eyes, Ears, and Nose

If you are already relatively familiar with human anatomy and its terminology, you might notice some slight variations, perhaps even some conflicting labels, in the terminology used here compared to how you were taught. I have attempted to use the most common anatomical names from numerous anatomy reference texts.

To be consistent through out this text, we also use the labels shown here for individual facial features (eyes, nose, ears, and mouth) as well as other anatomy discussed in this chapter in the chapter on sculpting the makeup. The nose, ears, and mouth are potential problem areas for undercuts during the mold-making process.

Some people have attached earlobes, but most people's lobes are free. In fact, free earlobes are twice as common as attached lobes. As I'm sure you've already noticed, in special makeup effects, ears are nothing but undercuts—severe undercuts. For the uninitiated, an undercut is any part of a sculpture that creates an overhang that when molded will be grabbed by the other part of the mold and won't let go, making it either impossible to get the mold halves apart or breaking off part of the sculpture or mold.

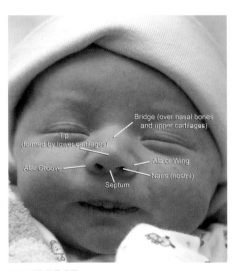

FIGURE 2.35
The nose. Image reproduced by permission of istockphoto.com.

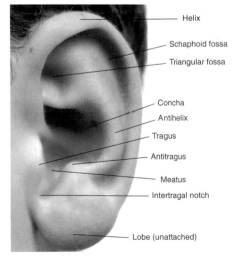

FIGURE 2.36
The ear. Image reproduced by permission of istockphoto.com.

The Mouth

The mouth becomes a potential for undercut problems, particularly if the mouth is cast partially open, which is what I recommend.

The Skin

Surface anatomy of the skin varies on different parts of the body. For example, the skin covering the shoulder and arm is smooth and very movable over the underlying muscle and bone. Over the inside and front of the forearm the skin is thin and smooth and has very few hairs. The skin on the outside and back of the arm and forearm is thicker and denser and contains more hairs. Around the elbow, the skin is thick and rough and is very loosely connected to the underlying tissue so that it falls into transverse wrinkles when the forearm is extended.[15]

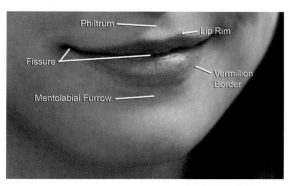

FIGURE 2.37
The mouth. Photo by the author.

THE SKIN: STRETCH MARKS

In addition to muscles and bone structure defining outward appearances, so do veins and the skin itself. Stretch marks are *striae*—furrows, stripes, or streaks in a parallel arrangement—caused when the skin is pulled by rapid growth or stretching. When skin is overstretched, the normal production of *collagen*, the protein that makes up the connective tissue of skin, is disrupted and results in scarring. But stretching alone is not the cause. It is frequently seen in pregnant women, children who experience rapid growth spurts, obese people, and body builders. These stretch marks appear first as reddish or purplish lines that may appear indented and feel different than the surrounding skin. They often feel "empty" and soft to the touch.[16] They generally lighten and fade to a silvery-white hue, almost disappearing over time.[17] Stretch marks most commonly appear on the abdomen, breasts, upper arms, underarms, both inner and outer thighs, hips, and buttocks.[18]

FIGURE 2.38
Elbow wrinkles being sculpted by Jordu Schell at IMATS 2008 in London. Photo by the author. Creature design by Jordu Schell.

[15]Henry Gray, *Anatomy of the Human Body* (Philadelphia: Lea & Febiger, 1918; Bartleby.com, 2000, www.bartleby.com/107/).

[16]Wikipedia contributors, "Stretch marks," *Wikipedia, The Free Encyclopedia,* http://en.wikipedia.org/w/index.php?title=Stretch_marks&oldid=165987535.

[17]Wikipedia contributors, "Stretch marks," *Wikipedia, The Free Encyclopedia,* http://en.wikipedia.org/w/index.php?title=Stretch_marks&oldid=165987535.

[18]Wikipedia contributors, "Stretch marks," *Wikipedia, The Free Encyclopedia,* http://en.wikipedia.org/w/index.php?title=Stretch_marks&oldid=165987535.

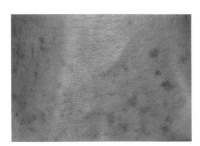

FIGURE 2.39
Age spots. Photo by the author.

FIGURE 2.40
Freckles. Photo by the author.

THE SKIN: AGE SPOTS

Age spots or liver spots are usually found on skin that is sun-exposed; despite their name, they have no relation to liver function. They're also known as *solar lentigo*. These spots represent changes in skin color associated with older age and are the result of increased pigmentation in combination with growing older as well as exposure to the sun or other UV light. They commonly begin to appear after age 40 and mostly occur on the backs of the hands, forearms, shoulder, face, and forehead—the places most apt to be exposed to sunlight. Age spots are often accompanied by other signs of sun damage, including deep wrinkles; dry, rough skin; fine red veins on the cheeks, nose, and ears; and thinner, more translucent-looking skin.[19]

THE SKIN: FRECKLES AND MOLES

Freckles are spots of melanin pigment in the skin. They are usually tan or light brown in color, flat, and very small and are usually found in people who are light skinned or have fair complexions. Freckles are often genetically associated with fair hair—blonde and more commonly red—and with light-colored eyes. Freckles are found predominantly on the face but also can appear on any skin that is exposed to sunlight. Freckles rarely are seen on infants and most commonly begin to appear on children before they reach puberty. In adults, most freckles fade with age; the people with the fairest skin often don't produce enough melanin, so freckles are always present.[20]

Moles, sometimes called *beauty marks* when found on a woman's face, are similar to freckles and are brought about by a high concentration of body pigment, or melanin, which is responsible for their dark color. Moles can be either subdermal (below the skin) or appear as a pigmented growth on the skin.[21]

THE SKIN: VARICOSE VEINS AND SPIDER VEINS

Both varicose veins and spider veins can appear almost anywhere on the body; varicose veins are most commonly found on the legs, whereas spider veins most commonly occur on the face around the nose, cheeks, and chin. Varicose veins are veins that have become twisted, bulging, and enlarged and are hereditary. Varicose veins are typically 3 mm or more in diameter and are more common in women than men. On the other hand, spider veins are small, dilated blood vessels that are near the surface of the skin and are rarely larger than a few millimeters.

[19]Mayo Clinic Staff, "Age spots (liver spots)," www.mayoclinic.com/health/age-spots/ DS00912/DSECTION=2.
[20]Wikipedia contributors, "Freckle," *Wikipedia, The Free Encyclopedia*, http://en.wikipedia. org/w/index.php?title=Freckle&oldid=166224174.
[21]Wikipedia contributors, "Melanocytic nevus," *Wikipedia, The Free Encyclopedia*, http:// en.wikipedia.org/w/index.php?title=Melanocytic_nevus&oldid=166037601.

THE SKIN: BIRTHMARKS

Birthmarks are pigment lesions on the skin—abnormal tissue usually caused by disease or trauma—that forms before birth. Some types of birthmarks even seem to run in families. There are several types of birthmarks, including these:

- Stork bite or angel's kiss
  - Pink
  - Irregular and flat
  - Less than 3 inches in diameter
  - Located usually on the neck, head, or top lip
  - Most fade or disappear by 12 months
- Mongolian blue spot
  - Bluish, bruise-like
  - Irregular and flat
  - About 4 inches in diameter
  - Located on the lower back and buttocks
  - Most common in dark-skinned people; most noticeable in East Asians
  - Might not appear until after birth and gradually fade; have been mistaken for abuse bruises
- Strawberry mark
  - Red
  - Raised and lumpy
  - Can appear anywhere on the body
  - Usually appears between one and four weeks of age; can grow rapidly before stopping and fading; 60 percent are gone by age 5, 90 percent gone by age 10
- Café au lait spot
  - Light brown, like coffee with milk
  - Oval shaped
  - Can appear anywhere on the body
  - One or two spots are common
  - These spots do not fade with age
- Congenital melanocytic nevus
  - Light brown in fair-skinned people to almost black in people with darker skin
  - Irregular shapes; usually flat, though large ones can be raised and bumpy
  - Range in size from less than ½ inch (11 mm) to about 11 inches (30cm)
  - Can appear anywhere on the body
- Port wine stain
  - Pale pink at birth, becoming darker with age and changing to a deep wine red
  - Irregular shapes
  - Usually larger than 4 inches in diameter
  - Often occur on the face
  - Occurs in three out of 1,000 births
  - The marks do not fade[22]

THE SKIN: HAIR

When designing a makeup that will need postiche in addition to the other physical characteristics and landmarks we've already discussed, it is important to have at least some understanding of the external structure of hair. *Postiche* is a French word meaning a covering or bunch of human or artificial hair used for disguise or adornment.[23] The term has come to describe any article of hair work, from false eyelashes to a full wig. I mention it because it is part of the language and vocabulary of special makeup effects.

Three types of hair are common to all humans:

- *Lanugo*, which is a very fine fair that covers nearly the entire body of a fetus
- *Vellus hair*, which is the short, fine "peach fuzz" body hair that grows in most places on the body of both males and females
- *Terminal hair*, which is fully developed hair and generally grows longer, thicker, coarser, and darker than vellus hair[24]

Different parts of the body exhibit different types of hair. From early childhood onward, vellus hair covers the entire body regardless of gender, except for the lips, soles of the feet, palms of the hands, scar tissue, the navel, and certain external genital areas.[25] At the onset of puberty, hormonal transformations cause some vellus hair on the body to transmute into terminal hair; because the hair is responding to hormonal influence, this hair is known as *androgenic hair*.[26]

THE SKIN: SCARS

After an injury and a wound heals, scars, which are areas of fibrous tissue that replace normal skin, form. With the exception of very small cuts or abrasions, every wound results in scarring to some degree. Scar tissue is quite different from the skin tissue it replaces. For example, hair follicles do not grow back in scar tissue, so that information is necessary in creating a scar effect as part of a makeup design. Scars are part of the natural healing process and as such need to be understood to create authentic scar makeup. Obviously, the greater the damage to the skin, the greater the scar will be. Most scars are flat and pale and leave a mark of the original injury.

As wounds heal, they go through changes. The initial redness that follows a skin injury is not a scar; it may take days or weeks for the redness to go away and to go from wound to scar, and if you are doing a progressive makeup, the stages of

[22]Wikipedia contributors, "Birthmark," *Wikipedia, The Free Encyclopedia,* http://en.wikipedia.org/w/index.php?title=Birthmark&oldid=164696060.

[23]Postiche; Dictionary.com, *WordNet® 3.0,* Princeton University; http://dictionary.reference.com/browse/postiche.

[24]Wikipedia contributors, "Hair," *Wikipedia, The Free Encyclopedia,* http://en.wikipedia.org/w/index.php?title=Hair&oldid=166373232.

[25]Wikipedia contributors, "Hair," *Wikipedia, The Free Encyclopedia,* http://en.wikipedia.org/w/index.php?title=Hair&oldid=166373232.

[26]Wikipedia contributors, "Hair," *Wikipedia, The Free Encyclopedia,* http://en.wikipedia.org/w/index.php?title=Hair&oldid=166373232.

a wound are important to know. Wound makeups as well as burns and skin diseases are discussed in Chapter 9.

Two types of abnormal scar result from the body's overproduction of collagen. This causes a raised scar above the surrounding skin.[27] *Hypertrophic scars* take the shape of a raised red lump on the skin but don't grow beyond the boundaries of the original wound. They often improve in appearance over time, usually a few years.

FIGURE 2.41
A hypertrophic scar.
Photo by the author.

Keloid scars are a more serious form of scarring. Keloids are capable of continuing to grow indefinitely. Both hypertrophic and keloid scars are more common on younger and darker-skinned people. Keloid scars are most commonly seen on the shoulder, chest, and abdomen and are most common among people of Asian or African descent.

Alternately, a scar can take the form of a sunken recess in the skin that has a pitted appearance. These are caused when the underlying structures supporting the skin, such as fat tissue or muscle, are lost. This type of scarring is most typical of acne scars but can be caused by diseases such as chickenpox also. Stretch marks, mentioned earlier in this chapter, are a form of scarring as well.[28]

SYMMETRY AND PROPORTION

Nature is filled with examples of balance and symmetry. The human body is one such example of proportion in nature. Phi (Φ), also known as the *Golden Ratio*, is a proportion that is found often in the natural world as well as in the structure of the human body. Perhaps our appreciation of the classical art and architecture of the Greeks and Romans is due partly to an appreciation, albeit unconscious, of dynamic symmetry.

Anatomical Planes

Before we can discuss dynamic symmetry of the human body, we need to establish a visual frame of reference for when proportions are mentioned. Anatomical planes are crucial to describing human anatomy in a way that makes it readily understandable to others. Based on a vertical figure facing the observer, let's compare planes based on a figure whose central axis is horizontal. This is like working in 3D, modeling in the X, Y, and Z axes, where X is side to side, Y is up and down, and Z is front to back.

Dynamic symmetry can be expressed in the *Fibonacci series* and in the Golden Rectangle. The Fibonacci series is a series of numbers in which any number of the series is the sum of the two previous numbers, such as $a + b = c$; $b + c = d$. It starts with 1; $1 + 1 = 2$; $1 + 2 = 3$; $2 + 3 = 5$; $3 + 5 = 8$; $5 + 8 = 13$; $8 + 13 = 21$; and so on. The

[27]Wikipedia contributors, "Scar," *Wikipedia, The Free Encyclopedia*, http://en.wikipedia. org/w/index.php?title=Scar&oldid=165002945.
[28]Wikipedia contributors, "Scar," *Wikipedia, The Free Encyclopedia*, http://en.wikipedia. org/w/index.php?title=Scar&oldid=165002945.

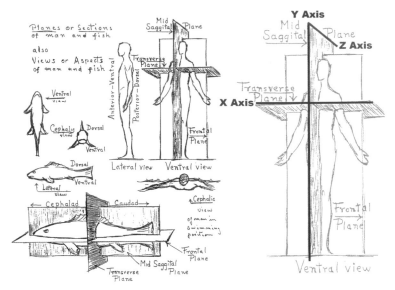

FIGURE 2.42
Anatomical planes of the human figure. Images reproduced by permission of Eugene F. Fairbanks, MD.

FIGURE 2.43
Head proportions conform to the Golden Mean, AD/AC = 1.6 = Φ. Image reproduced by permission of Eugene F. Fairbanks, MD.

48

ratio of a number of a sum divided by the preceding number approximates 1.62...; $21 \div 13 = 1.615$; $13 \div 8 = 1.625$, and so on. This number is called Phi, or Φ.[29]

For example, the ratio of the height of a human male head to its width is approximately (on average) 9 inches to 5¼ inches; $9 \div 5.25 = 1.61$. Many proportions of the human body share this ratio.[30]

Facial Ratios and Phi

As already mentioned, representative proportions and average measurements will not be found in any one person; in creating a figure for a makeup effect or perhaps as a prop, it might be best to work with a live model for truly accurate representation. Nonetheless, Phi ratios are valid and can be used to create accurate and pleasing results:[31]

Few people are aware of the significance of Leonardo da Vinci's *The Vitruvian Man* drawing and its relationship to human proportion. Quoting Vitruvius, a celebrated Roman architect under both Julius Caesar and Augustus Caesar, "Then again, in the human body, the central point is naturally the navel (umbilicus). For if a man be placed flat on his back with his hands and feet extended, and a pair of compasses centered at his navel, the fingers and toes of his two hands and feet will touch the circumference of a circle described therefrom. And just as the human body yields a

[29]Avard T. Fairbanks and Eugene F. Fairbanks, *Human Proportions for Artists* (Fairbanks Art and Books, 2005).
[30]Avard T. Fairbanks and Eugene F. Fairbanks, *Human Proportions for Artists* (Fairbanks Art and Books, 2005).
[31]Avard T. Fairbanks and Eugene F. Fairbanks, *Human Proportions for Artists* (Fairbanks Art and Books, 2005).

Vertical (Y):		Female	Male
Head height ÷ Head width		= 1.45	= 1.51
Vertex to eyes ÷ Hairline to eyes	AD ÷ BD	= 1.32	= 1.29
Eyes to chin ÷ Nostrils to chin	DF ÷ DE	= 1.59	= 1.54
Hairline to eyes ÷ Eyes to nostrils	DB ÷ DE	= 1.60	= 1.67
Eyes to mouth ÷ Eyes to nostrils	DF ÷ DE	= 1.50	= 1.56
Nostrils to chin ÷ Mouth to chin	FG ÷ FG	= 1.45	= 1.46
Transverse (X):		Female	Male
Head width ÷ Lateral eye corners	gg′ ÷ dd′	= 1.56	= 1.49
Mouth width ÷ Nose width at ala	ff′ ÷ ee′	= 1.42	= 1.34
Lateral eye corners ÷ Mouth width	dd′ ÷ ff′	= 1.59	= 1.54
Hairline to eyes ÷ Eyes to nostrils	DB ÷ DE	= 1.60	= 1.67
Eyes to mouth ÷ Eyes to nostrils	DF ÷ DE	= 2.05	= 2.00

circular outline, so too a square figure may be found from it. For if we measure the distance from the soles of the feet to the top of the head and then apply that measure to the outstretched arms, the breadth will be found to be the same as the height as in the case of plane surfaces which are perfectly square."

Whatever motivates your makeup design, there is a natural law of symmetry you can follow and adapt to the universe where your character exists, but its design must still adhere to a set of symmetrical rules; it is also imperative that the design follow

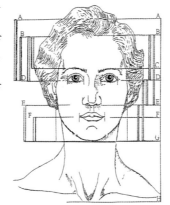
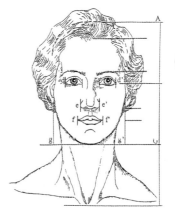

criteria set for the production, whether theater or film. Nature must give the base from which to build on a design, but since the makeup is to be theatrical and will be worn, that becomes the paramount design parameter to keep in sharp focus.

Through *anthropometry*, the study of the measurement of humans, ratios of other body proportions have been determined, all of which can be extremely beneficial in creating special makeup effects.

FIGURE 2.44
Some vertical face ratios approximate Φ, or 1.62. Images reproduced by permission of Eugene F. Fairbanks, MD.

Ratios and Body Proportions

The male and female figures in the following two drawings illustrate standing, sitting, and kneeling relationships. Both are standing at eight head heights (eight male and eight female, respectively), with kneeling height at ¾ standing height and sitting height slightly more than ½ of standing height. You'll notice that the female is a bit more than the male sitting height, since women mature physically earlier than men.

49

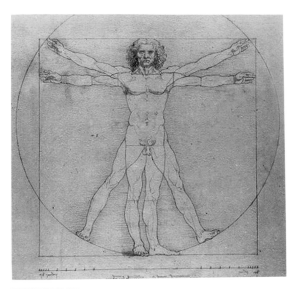

FIGURE 2.45
Leonardo da Vinci's *Vetruvian Man*, illustrating human proportion. Image reproduced by permission of Luc Viatour.

The long bones of female legs (the femur) usually don't grow as long as those in males.[32]

The shoulder width of a grown man is equal to ¼ of his height (stature) and also equals two head heights. The span of that same man's arms outstretched from third fingertip to third fingertip is equal to his height and also equal to eight head heights.

By dividing a design in half or into thirds, it could seem to lose some of its subtlety. Not so. Halves and thirds appear to be quite prevalent in studies of the human figure and of the face. The head is 1/8 of the total figure; the hair above the forehead is 1/8 of the whole of the (vertical) head. The figure minus the head is divided into thirds to reach leg length. This process establishes three main lengths: the lower leg, sole of foot to knee; the knee to the ilium crest (pelvis); and the body from the crest of the ilium to the chin.[33]

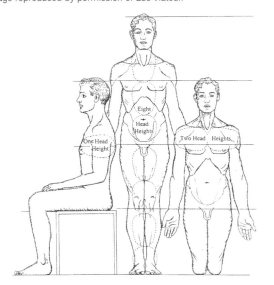
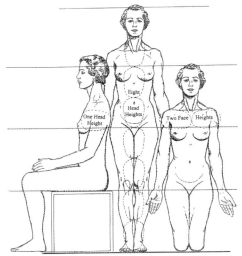

FIGURE 2.46
The male figure of eight heads is illustrated with kneeling height at ¾ and sitting height a little more than half of standing height. In the male figure the shoulders are two head heights wide. The female figure is also illustrated with stature at eight head heights. Kneeling height is also ¾ standing height, but sitting height is slightly greater than half of standing height, since maturation is earlier in females. The long bones of the legs usually don't grow as long as males. The shoulder width in females is two face heights. Images reproduced by permission of Eugene F. Fairbanks, MD.

[32]Avard T. Fairbanks and Eugene F. Fairbanks, *Human Proportions for Artists* (Fairbanks Art and Books, 2005).
[33]Avard T. Fairbanks and Eugene F. Fairbanks, *Human Proportions for Artists*, (Fairbanks Art and Books, 2005).

The head from chin to vertex is equal to the length of the foot from heel to tip of foremost toe. The face is equal to the length of the hand; from wrist to tip of middle finger equals the distance from the chin to the hairline. The neck, from chin to sternal notch, is equal to ½ the head height.

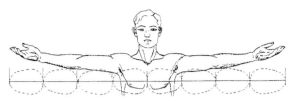

FIGURE 2.47
A man's span equals eight head heights. Image reproduced by permission of Eugene F. Fairbanks, MD.

There are also differences between the male figure and the female figure; to establish vertical measurements for a typical figure, the only measurement needed to begin modeling is the overall anticipated height of the figure. You can then determine what the body proportions will be. However, when measuring people, you'll quickly see that there are loads of individual variations. Not everyone's body will conform to a measurement norm; some people have long necks, some short. Some people have long legs and a short torso, or the like. The drawing and descriptions of human proportions shown and described in this chapter are to be considered guidelines for assistance only and should not be considered for precise measurements.

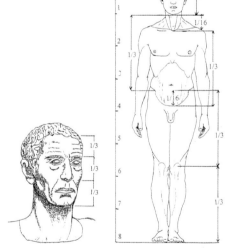

FIGURE 2.48
Body proportions are divided into thirds. Images reproduced by permission of Eugene F. Fairbanks, MD.

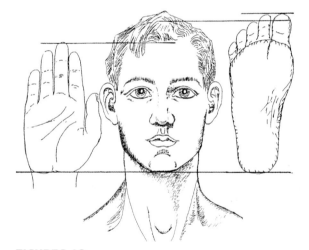

FIGURE 2.49
The male head compared to a hand and a foot. Image reproduced by permission of Eugene F. Fairbanks, MD.

GEOMETRIC ANALYSIS

It should be clear that these descriptions are a gross oversimplification of human anatomy and the proportional relationships between different segments and groupings of the body and that I am merely highlighting some areas of interest that I feel should be considered when you're designing and creating for our craft.

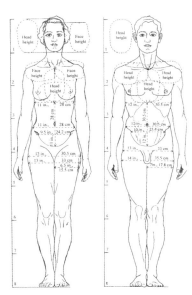

Some very interesting geometric relationships come to light when we analyze proportions of the human form. In most geometric analysis, there's a dominance of straight-line shapes and measurements, but there are relatively few such lines when looking at the human body's lines. Instead we see a preponderance of curves and arcs. For example, the *scalenius muscles* on each side of the neck give support to the vertebra laterally, much like the wires that support a utility pole. The *sternocleidomastoid muscles*, responsible for turning the head, cross the scalenius muscles, creating a triangle; the triangle shape is also visible via the *trapezius muscle* (posterior), the *sternocleidomastoid muscle* (anterior), and the *clavicle* (collar bone).[34]

In the torso, an isosceles triangle (at least two equal sides) is formed from the points of the shoulders to the navel. As you can see, there are also a number of proportions that correspond to squares and rectangles in addition to triangles.[35]

FIGURE 2.50
Male and female proportions. Image reproduced by permission of Eugene F. Fairbanks, MD.

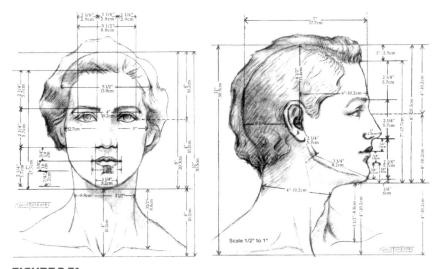

FIGURE 2.51
The female head, detailed proportions, anterior and lateral views. In the anterior (front) view the head is divided in two at the level of the eyes. One half face height equals the distance between the lateral corners of the eyes. The mouth width equals ½ distance between the lateral corners of the eyes. In the lateral (side) view the head and neck are divided into three equal proportions: sternal notch to chin, to corner of eye, and to top of head. The face is also divided into three equal proportions, commonly referred to as ***nose lengths***. Images reproduced by permission of Eugene F. Fairbanks, MD.

[34]Avard T. Fairbanks and Eugene F. Fairbanks, *Human Proportions for Artists* (Fairbanks Art and Books, 2005).
[35]Avard T. Fairbanks and Eugene F. Fairbanks, *Human Proportions for Artists* (Fairbanks Art and Books, 2005).

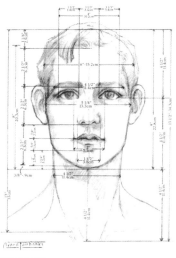
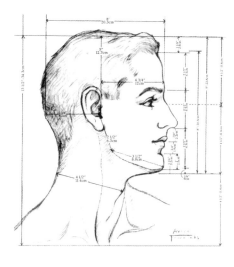

FIGURE 2.52
The male head, detailed proportions, anterior and lateral views. In the anterior view the head is also divided in two at the level of the eyes. As with the female head, ½ face height equals the distance between the lateral corners of the eyes. The mouth width equals ½ distance between the lateral corners of the eyes. In the lateral view the head and neck are also divided into three equal proportions: sternal notch to chin, to corner of eye, and to top of head. The eye is ½ the distance from the top of the head to the chin. Images reproduced by permission of Eugene F. Fairbanks, MD.

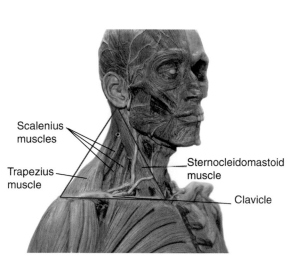

FIGURE 2.53
The clavicle, sternocleidomastoid, and trapezius form a triangle. Photo by the author. Anatomy model by Andrew Cawrse.

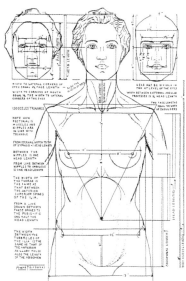

FIGURE 2.54
Geometric analysis. Image reproduced by permission of Eugene F. Fairbanks, MD.

FIGURE 2.55
Men and women are noticeably different … Image reproduced by permission of istockphoto.com.

DISTINCTIONS OF GENDER, AGE, AND ANCESTRY

In the field of forensic art and illustration there has been a great deal of research into the distinctions of age, gender, and ancestry for the creation—or *re*creation—of individuals from a variety of information sources. Whereas a forensic artist could be given the task of helping to identify an individual from composite drawings, forensic anthropologists can actually reconstruct an individual for identification from skeletal and semi-skeletal remains through sculpture. How does this apply to us as makeup effects artists? It should be fairly clear: Much of what we've just discussed regarding human proportion and surface anatomy will come into play when you create age makeups, gender change makeups, and ancestral alterations.

Distinctions of Gender

Physically, there is obvious and readily apparent *sexual dimorphism* between men and women—that is, differences in shape and size between individuals of differing gender in the same species. In many species, including most mammals, the male is larger than the female. For the most part, that's true of humans as well; on average, men are taller than women and have greater body mass and weight. The male face is more angular overall and is usually larger than the female face, and the lower half of the male's face is proportionally larger than the female's simply because the lower jaw, or mandible, of the male is bigger and stronger. The jaw angle is usually more severely defined in the male and the chin squarer and more prominent. The forehead is also often more sloping in males than in females, with a hint of a projecting brow ridge.[36]

Here are some additional outward physical differences between men and women:

- Men generally have more body hair than women.
- Men's skin is thicker and oilier than women's skin; women's skin tends to be smoother.
- Women generally have smaller waists in relation to their hips; that is, their waist-to-hip ratio is smaller than that of men.
- A man's index finger (second digit) tends to be shorter than the ring finger (fourth digit), whereas a woman's index finger tends to be longer than the ring finger.

FIGURE 2.56
Lateral view of growth pattern from one month to six years, and then to 18 years. Proportional comparison of a fetal skull (left) and an adult skull (right). Image reproduced by permission of Wes Price; © 2008.

[36]Karen T. Taylor, *Forensic Art and Illustration* (CRC Press, 2001).

- Women tend to have lighter skin coloration than men, on average, by as much as 3 or 4 percent.
- Women generally have a lower center of gravity than men—that is, shorter legs and longer torsos relative to their height—as well as a larger hip section.
- Women generally have a higher percentage of body fat than men.
- Women tend to have higher voices than men.
- Men tend to have a more prominent *laryngeal prominence*, or *Adam's apple*, than women.
- Women have enlarged, functional breasts.
- Men generally have greater muscle mass and physical strength.
- Men tend to have shoulders that are wider than their hips.
- Men's skeletal structure is generally heavier than women's.
- Men tend to collect fat deposits around the abdomen and waist (apple shape), whereas women tend to have greater fat deposits around the buttocks, thighs, and hips (pear shape).[37]

Distinctions of Age

As we grow, our bodies go through a series of remarkable physical changes of which we, as designers, must be acutely aware. The proportional change in the amount of lower face is perhaps the most fundamental aspect of facial growth. For example, as a child grows, the face grows downward and forward; the forehead becomes more upright and flat, and the lower part of the head (face) elongates downward and out.[38]

There are other outward manifestations as we grow through childhood into adolescence and puberty and then into adulthood. In fact, ossification—the hardening or calcification of soft tissue into bone—doesn't usually occur fully until around age 25.

With the exception of primary sexual characteristics—that is, having either a penis or a vagina—male and female bodies are very similar during childhood. It isn't until adolescence, when boys and girls begin to go through puberty, that noticeable differences between the sexes begin to manifest themselves. During puberty (often between the ages of 9 and 13), both boys and girls quickly begin to gain weight as well grow taller. In boys, the body becomes more muscular and the shoulders become wider than the hips; girls develop breasts and their hips become wider than their shoulders. As they reach adulthood, the secondary sex characteristics noted previously are fully developed.

You may well be asking yourself, "What does childhood and adolescent growth have to do with creating special makeup effects? I can't turn a grown man into a kid." Of course you can't. But you might be asked at some point in your career to turn a middle-aged man into a 20-something version of himself,

55

---

[37]Wikipedia contributors, "Secondary sex characteristic," *Wikipedia, The Free Encyclopedia,* http://en.wikipedia.org/w/index.php?title=Secondary_sex_characteristic&oldid=166755262.
[38]Karen T. Taylor, *Forensic Art and Illustration* (CRC Press, 2001).

FIGURE 2.57
The author at age 3, 7, 11, 13, 15, 18, 32, and 53, illustrating Gnomatic growth. Images reproduced by permission of the author's wife and mother.

something Rick Baker and his team were asked to do for several characters in the 2006 Adam Sandler movie, *Click*. You may also find yourself in the position to fabricate props—children's bodies, perhaps—for a crime show or horror movie. This information may be useful. I hope it is now and will be later.

Our faces go through a tremendous amount of growth and change from youth into old age. But at the same time, barring physically altering trauma, there is also a significant constancy of appearance. The face of a man or woman looks almost the same throughout his or her life, no matter the age. That phenomenon is known as *gnomatic growth*.

FIGURE 2.58
Karl Langer's skin tension lines go something like this. Image reproduced by permission of istockphoto.com.

Gnomatic growth is a process that leaves facial features in later years similar to those found in youth.[39] The individual's looks cannot be undermined by age. The first 20 years are constructive and growth oriented; the years after that are degenerative and destructive.[40]

Nothing will be more beneficial to your makeup designs than reference images, gobs and gobs of reference images … but a firm understanding of how the human body ages and the physical changes we go through will also aid you immensely in getting your details right. Depending on where it is on the body, aged skin wrinkles and folds in specific directions. These lines were mapped out in detail by Austrian anatomist Karl Langer in 1861.

[39]Karen T. Taylor, *Forensic Art and Illustration* (CRC Press, 2001).
[40]Karen T. Taylor, *Forensic Art and Illustration* (CRC Press, 2001).

Everyone ages differently, and factors beyond genetics also contribute significantly to the aging process. Smoking, alcohol, drug abuse, stress, fitness (or the lack of), lifestyle, the environment (sun exposure, pollution)—these can all contribute to visible aging, either premature aging or a prolonged youthful appearance. All these things, as well as the medium in which the makeup will be seen, must be taken into account when we design an age makeup. If there will be closeups, the makeup can be more subtle than if it must be seen on stage, for example. Furthermore, though you may be presented with the challenge of creating a full-body makeup at some time—perhaps a body to be used as a prop—usually at most you will be working with the face, neck, and hands and possibly part of the arms, leaving the rest of the body covered.

FIGURE 2.59
Wrinkles occur perpendicular to the stretch and pull of underlying muscles. Images reproduced by permission of istockphoto.com.

FACIAL AGING

Creating a realistic and convincing age makeup for any individual requires understanding the physical mechanics of the facial aging process, to project how a particular face will change with age. Every individual ages at a variable rate, but a fairly predictable series of changes seems to occur in a similar order in most people.[41] For example, wrinkles will first appear in certain locations, then in others, such as first on the forehead and around the eyes, then around the nose and mouth.

Terminology for the lines and grooves of the face has been published by the American Society of Plastic and Reconstructive Surgeons that is related to the degree of facial line depth, such as transverse frontal lines and nasolabial folds.

A progression of wrinkles begin as *lines*, then *grooves*, and mature into deeper *furrows* and *folds*.[42]

Here is a guideline: Wrinkles appear perpendicular to the stretch of the underlying muscles. For example, the horizontal (transverse) lines across a forehead are perpendicular to the vertical pull of the *frontalis* muscle of the face. If you understand the facial muscles, it will be easier to determine where to place age lines and wrinkles that look natural.

FIGURE 2.60
Anatomy of the face. Illustration by Wes Price. Image reproduced by permission of Wes Price; © 2008.

57

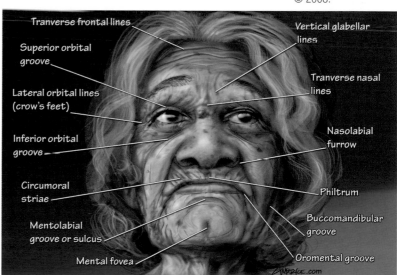

Tranverse frontal lines
Superior orbital groove
Lateral orbital lines (crow's feet)
Inferior orbital groove
Circumoral striae
Mentolabial groove or sulcus
Mental fovea
Vertical glabellar lines
Tranverse nasal lines
Nasolabial furrow
Philtrum
Buccomandibular groove
Oromental groove

[41]Karen T. Taylor, *Forensic Art and Illustration* (CRC Press, 2001).
[42]Karen T. Taylor, *Forensic Art and Illustration* (CRC Press, 2001).

FIGURE 2.61
Forehead wrinkles are perpendicular to the pull of the frontalis muscle. Photo by the author. Anatomy model by Andrew Cawrse.

58

The following breakdown by decade was created by renowned forensic illustrator Karen Taylor from research presented in *The Journal of Otolaryngology*, Craniofacial Identification in Forensic Medicine, The Combined Graphic Method (CGM) of Craniofacial Reconstruction, and the Scottsdale Artists' School.[43]

THE 20S

- Fine transverse frontal lines may appear across the forehead.
- Fine vertical glabellar lines may appear in people who frown frequently.
- Fine lateral orbital lines, or "crow's feet," may appear in people who smile often or spend a lot of time in the sun.

THE 30S

- Transverse frontal lines deepen.
- Vertical glabellar lines deepen.
- Lateral orbital lines increase in number and deepen.
- Transverse nasal lines may form across the top of the nose.
- Nasolabial lines or furrows become noticeable.

THE 40S

- The inferior orbital groove may become apparent.
- The eyebrows may descend slightly.
- An excess of upper eyelid may develop and a portion of the superior orbital groove may be obscured at the lateral side.
- The jawline becomes less firm.
- Circumoral striae become noticeable, especially in smokers.
- The lips may begin to thin.
- The oromental groove may begin, depending on facial structure.
- The mentolabial groove becomes more apparent, depending on facial structure.
- Fine lines in the neck become noticeable.

THE 50S

- The inferior orbital groove may define a developing pouch under the eyes.
- Excess upper eyelid tissue may worsen, obscuring more of the superior orbital groove at the lateral side and creating more lateral orbital lines.
- The nasolabial furrow is more noticeable.
- The oromental groove deepens.
- The lips continue to thin, especially in people who had thin lips in youth.

[43]Karen T. Taylor, *Forensic Art and Illustration* (CRC Press, 2001).

- Dental changes may become apparent, increasing lines accordingly.
- A buccomandibular groove may appear.
- The jawline becomes much less firm.
- Jowls and a double chin may appear.
- lines in the neck are more noticeable.
- Arcus senilis may begin to appear in the eyes.

THE 60S

- All the aforementioned lines become exaggerated.
- The circumoral striae may cross over the vermillion border of the lips.
- The ears appear to get larger and wrinkles appear in front of the tragus.
- The jawline is very soft and tissues under the neck sag.

THE 70S AND OLDER

- All the aforementioned lines become more pronounced and defined, accompanied by marked loss of elasticity of the skin and sagging tissue.

Arcus senilisis a cloudy grayish or whitish arc or circle around the periphery of the cornea of older adults; it's caused by fatty-acid deposits in the deep layer of the peripheral cornea. It most commonly occurs after age 50 and is most frequent in men.

Other factors can create an appearance of having aged without much passage of actual time. Hair loss and a slight weight gain can affect the appearance of aging beyond normal chronology. Keep in mind that when you're creating transverse frontal lines, they can't exist beyond the natural hairline, because they correspond to the perpendicular vertical pull of the frontalis muscle, which stops very near the hairline in most people.

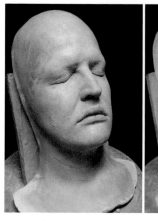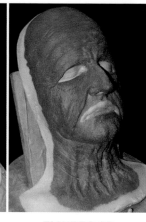

FIGURE 2.62
"Before and after" age makeup sculpt on lifecast of actor Brian Landis Folkins. Photos by the author.

FIGURE 2.63
"Before and after" age makeup on actor Ben Browder by David Elsey for *Farscape*. Images reproduced by permission of David Elsey.

Distinctions of Ancestry

As our society becomes more and more culturally and ethnically diverse, the impact of "race" is becoming more and more diluted as peoples begin to blend with one another and clearly defined descriptions blur. *Race* is a traditionally used term that describes major zoological subdivisions of humankind, regarded as having a common beginning and sharing a relatively constant group of physical traits, such as pigmentation and facial and body proportions.[44] For the makeup of today's population, *ancestry* seems to

[44]S. I. Landau, S. C. Brantley, et al., *Funk and Wagnall's Standard Encyclopedic Dictionary* (J. G. Ferguson Publishing Co., 1968).

be a more accurate term. However, as makeup artists and makeup designers, we must examine the more traditional overview of the three major racial/ancestral groups to arrive at a distinct physical appearance: Caucasoid, Negroid, and Mongoloid, or the preferred *European derived*, *African derived*, and *Asian derived*.

Of course, there is a multiplicity of physical appearances that exist with each of these groups.[45] Dr. Henry Field, in his 1946 book, *The Races of Mankind*, first described those three major racial groups—Caucasoid, Negroid, and Mongoloid—which by today's standards seem quite antiquated,[46] but regardless of how appropriate they are or not, there is no denying that physical differences in ancestry do still very much exist. I present them here as a context only for creating a particular ethnic character makeup design.

Structurally, there are immediately obvious skeletal differences (though generalized) between the European-derived, African-derived, and Asian-derived ancestral groups, visible in this illustration of facial relationships to the skull shape.

FIGURE 2.64
Lateral view showing the relationship of the face to the skull of three ancestral groups – African derived (left), Asian derived (middle), and European derived (right). Image reproduced by permission of Wes Price; © 2008.

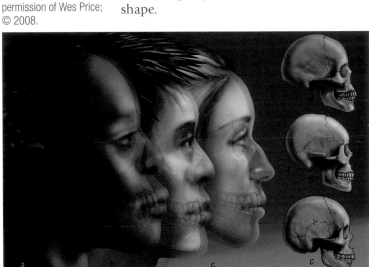

Caucasian people are referred to generally as *white*, though hardly all light-skinned people are Caucasian nor are all Caucasians light skinned. Many Caucasian skulls present a seemingly flat face in profile, with retreating or back-slanting zygomatic bones. The anterior skull shows longer and narrower nasal openings than African- or Asian-derived counterparts.[47] In his book, Dr. Field placed European-derived people into three additional groups:

- *Mediterranean*. Iberian peninsula, western Mediterranean islands, southern France and Italy, western Wales and western Ireland:
  - Short and stocky
  - Olive complexion
  - Dark hair and eyes
  - Long head; narrow, oval face
  - Small mouth

[45]Karen T. Taylor, *Forensic Art and Illustration* (CRC Press, 2001).
[46]Karen T. Taylor, *Forensic Art and Illustration* (CRC Press, 2001).
[47]Karen T. Taylor, *Forensic Art and Illustration* (CRC Press, 2001).

- *Alpine.* Central plateau of France, Switzerland, and what is now the Czech Republic; south into the Balkans and east into Russia and the former Soviet Union:
  - Round head; broad face
  - Dark complexion
  - Dark (brown) wavy hair
  - Thick eyebrows over brown eyes
  - Heavy body hair
  - Sometimes a thick neck; medium to heavy build
- *Nordic.* Scandinavia, northern Germany, part of Holland and Belgium, Great Britain:[48]
  - Tall
  - Light complexion
  - Fair hair and blue eyes
  - Long head and face
  - Prominent nose and chin

Field also wrote about Caucasian people of Africa:

The Hamites who inhabit north and northeast Africa ... possess dark brown or black hair, which is either curly or wavy in form, and the skin varies in color from reddish brown to dark brown. Their average stature varies from very tall to medium and their build is slender. The typical Hamite possesses a long head, an oval, elongated face with no forward protrusion, thin lips, pointed chin, and a prominent, well-shaped nose.

Semites ... in a measure the physical traits of Hamites resemble those of Semites. Members of the Semitic group now live chiefly in the extreme north of Africa migrated from Arabia at early dates. The Arabs, who are typical Semites in both physique and language, are usually medium in stature, are dark-haired, and generally have oval faces, with long, narrow, straight noses. There are two typical head forms among the Arabs – one is long, and the other broad.[49]

The African-derived peoples who make up the majority of the group originating in Africa are most frequently referred to as *black*, even though their pigmentation varies broadly from light brown to a very dark brown, sometimes bordering on black. Often the skull exhibits alveolar prognathism, which is a protrusion of the lower face by both the maxilla and the mandible. The anterior nasal openings tend to be wider and shorter than in Caucasians and Asians (Mongoloids), with a broader and flatter bridge. The mouth tends to be broader as well, with fuller, inverted lips. Many African-derived people also have wider-set eyes than the other groups.[50]

[48]Henry Field, *The Races of Mankind* (C. S. Hammond and Co., 1946).
[49]Henry Field, *The Races of Mankind* (C. S. Hammond and Co., 1946).
[50]Karen T. Taylor, *Forensic Art and Illustration* (CRC Press, 2001).

Field identified four African-derived groups of people:

- *West African.* Coastal West Africa:
    - Long headed
    - Medium stature
    - Well developed, with a heavy torso and massive limbs
    - Arms are long and legs short in comparison to the length of the trunk
    - Sometimes a projecting chin
    - Nose is broad, lips are thick; dark eyes and wooly hair
- *Nilotic.* Upper Nile:
    - Taller, greater stature
    - Slender build
    - Longer head in relation to width
- *Pygmies.* Ituri Forest, northern Congo:
    - Short, dark brown hair
    - Pigmentation ranges from light brown with yellow tinge to very dark chocolate brown
    - Average stature is short: 4 feet, 6 inches; both body and legs are short
    - Round head with some facial protrusion
    - Full lips; flat, broad nose
- *Bushmen.* Kalahari Desert:[51]
    - Short, frizzy hair in tufts
    - Little or no facial or body hair
    - Pigmentation ranges from yellow to olive
    - Markedly wrinkled skin at early age
    - Small head, low in the crown; somewhere between long and round head
    - Slightly protruding forehead
    - Nose very flat and broad
    - Dark, narrow, and slightly oblique eyes
    - Average male is under 5 feet tall

We ordinarily think of the Mongoloid group of people—those we think of as Asian-derived—as being Chinese, Japanese, Korean, or one of several other varied Asian groups. In actuality, this group of individuals also includes Native Americans and American Eskimos. As such, the group also exhibits a wide variety of physical features and skin colors. When we examine the facial bone structure of group members, the skull exhibits an often flattened face with a short cranial cavity—that is, a short distance from front to back. The anterior cheeks are wide, with projecting zygomatic bones. The nasal opening is somewhere between that of European-derived and African-derived features. The size of the mouth is also often somewhere in between.[52]

---

[51]Henry Field, *The Races of Mankind* (C. S. Hammond and Co., 1946).
[52]Karen T. Taylor, *Forensic Art and Illustration* (CRC Press, 2001).

Dr. Field described the following Asian groups:

- *Chinese.* China, Mongolia:
    - Represent a single racial unit, medium in stature
    - Head is intermediate, between long and round
    - Pigmentation yellowish brown
    - Eyes are oblique, with a Mongolian (epicanthic) fold
    - Hair black and straight
- *Japanese.* Emigrated from southeast Asia; two distinct types:
    1. Fine features:
        - Taller and more slender
        - Elongated face
        - Prominent, narrow, arched nose
        - Eyes are either straight or oblique; epicanthic fold may be present
    2. Coarse features:
        - Short and stocky
        - Broad face; short, concave nose
        - Rounded nostrils
        - Oblique eyes; usually with epicanthic fold
        - Darker complexion
- *American Indians*:
    - Brown skin with reddish or yellowish tinge
    - Dark eyes
    - Straight, coarse black hair
    - Minimal facial and body hair
    - Broad face with high, prominent cheekbones
    - Head is usually round; occasionally long in certain groups
    - Varied stature
    - Nose varies from flat to aquiline (curved or hooked)
- *American Eskimos*:
    - Clearly of Asiatic origin; the most Mongoloid of all American groups
    - Short, stocky build
    - Long head with very broad face
    - Massive jaw and moderately narrow nose
    - Sides of head are often flat, and a ridge may be present along the dome of the skull
    - Eyes frequently have epicanthic fold

FIGURE 2.65
"Before and after" Asian age makeup demo by Neill Gorton at IMATS in London, 2008. Photos by the author.

63

I've mentioned the term *epicanthic fold* several times in the previous descriptions of ancestral traits, but you might not know what it means. You should, because it is an immediate ancestral identifier as well as a trait of several disorders, including fetal alcohol syndrome and Down syndrome. An epicanthic fold, also known as an *epicanthal fold* or an *epicanthus*, is a skin fold of the upper

FIGURE 2.67
Asian woman exhibiting an epicanthal fold. Image reproduced by permission of istockphoto.com.

eyelid, from the nose to the inner side of the eyebrow, covering the *Medial canthus* (inner corner) of the eye.

An epicanthic fold is present in all humans in the womb; some children lose them at birth, but many children of any ethnicity may exhibit an epicanthic fold before the bridge of the nose begins to elevate.[53]

CHAPTER SUMMARY

From reading this chapter you should have gained a clearer understanding of how the computer can be put to work as a makeup design tool and how to determine what the elements of your design should be. The importance and relationship of human anatomy to character and creature design should make better sense, as should the subtlety and nuance of surface anatomy, symmetry and proportion, and ways to create believable distinctions of gender, age, and ancestry in your character or creature makeup design.

[53]Wikipedia contributors, "Epicanthal fold," *Wikipedia, The Free Encyclopedia,* http://en.wikipedia.org/w/index.php?title=Epicanthal_fold&oldid=166374872.

CHAPTER 3 🎭
Making the Lifecast

INTRODUCTION

Without intending to cause alarm, I begin this chapter with a disclaimer: *Lifecasting has the potential to be quite dangerous if done incorrectly.* Some of the materials used in lifecasting may encapsulate body hair, enclose or block orifices, cause serious allergic reactions, and create substantial heat that can cause serious burns. That being said, lifecasting is a skill that is not difficult to learn and, once learned, can be used to create myriad lifecasts of body parts, including full-body lifecasts.

Since this book is intended as both a makeup effects primer and one that also provides more advanced information, it is strongly suggested that if you have never done a lifecast before, you should take an in-person course or a workshop before attempting to go it alone. Though the information in this chapter is more than sufficient for you to make a lifecast on your own, first get some training with a professional, before venturing into this domain. If you insist on being a self-starter, may I suggest, that you begin by making a cast of someone's hand or foot rather than a head?

David Parvin

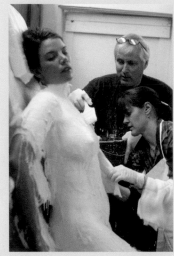

FIGURE 3.1
Dave Parvin conducting a lifecast during a workshop at his Denver studio. Image reproduced by permission of Dave Parvin.

Dave Parvin is essentially a self-taught sculptor who began carving in wood before he was 3. His primary subjects are people, and he strives to bring life to his sculptures by carefully defining the underlying muscles and bones of the human form. Unlike many of the artists who have contributed to this book, Dave didn't come to the decision to become a full-time artist until later in life, after the jet he was flying lost power to both engines while in flight, making him realize that there's no time like to present to follow your dreams.

Known mainly for his bronzes of the human figure, Dave also works in a variety of other media, including silicone, urethane, Forton MG, and raku. He became interested in lifecasting as an anatomical reference, but it occurred to him that it was very much like three-dimensional photography. Since then Dave has become one of the best lifecasters in the world and is widely recognized as one of the innovators of the form, continuing to develop new and better ways to approach the craft.

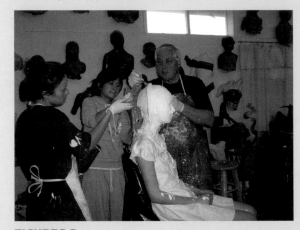

FIGURE 3.2
Dave Parvin casts subjects with hair but does not use bald caps. Image reproduced by permission of Dave Parvin.

Dave regularly presents workshops and seminars on lifecasting techniques at his studio in Denver, Colorado, and has presented internationally as well, conducting seminars at the annual International Makeup Artist Trade Show in California and England. *Art Review* magazine has called Dave "the premier lifecasting expert in Colorado, maybe in all the West." Dave is also a founding member of the Association of Lifecasters International (ALI) organization.

SAFETY RISKS

Compared to making molds of inanimate objects, lifecasting can pose some potential safety hazards. Since the mold is made directly on an actor's body, the materials must be safe and approved for use directly on the skin. There is also the potential for injury if the subject is being lifecast in a standing position and faints from holding a stationary pose for too long. Feelings of claustrophobia and anxiety can also be a reaction for some actors enclosed in a mold, and it can seem to gain weight the longer it's on the subject.

When lifecasting the face, you must take great care so that the actor can continue to breathe when a mold covers her mouth and nose; the nostrils must be kept clear but *not with straws*. There are two reasons not to use straws in a subject's nose when making a lifecast: The straws change the shape of the nose, and even the very slightest of bumps will cause a rather good nosebleed. Don't ask me how I know that. It's always a good idea to ask your subject beforehand if she generally has trouble breathing out of both nostrils; if your subject is congested and stuffed up, she will need to take measures in advance of the lifecasting session that will allow her to breathe comfortably while the alginate is covering her face. It is also possible to do a lifecast with the mouth partly open.

While most alginates used for lifecasting are considered hypoallergenic—meaning that few people (if any) are allergic—in rare instances models can have allergic reactions to a material. But far from lifecasting being a negative experience, every model finds it interesting, and most models actually find the experience to be somewhat enjoyable, not unlike getting an extended—albeit unusual—facial. Some even fall asleep!

I've lost count of how many lifecasts I've done personally or supervised—quite a few—but I have never experienced an allergic reaction or had someone faint. I consider myself very fortunate. I have heard plenty of associates' descriptions of subjects fainting. Fortunately most fainting spells are mild and brief, but they can still be awful. Not only can fainting create the very real possibility of cuts, bumps, and bruises on your subject, it can also result in vomiting; vomiting into a closed space is not good and will cause the subject to aspirate, or involuntarily inhale the vomit. That is *really* not good.

Other safety concerns to be aware of concern the lifecasting materials themselves—alginate, silicone, and plaster. The alginates used for lifecasting come as a very fine powder, and even when mixed very carefully with water they may create a substantial amount of dust. Many alginates also contain crystalline silica, which can cause silicosis—a disabling, nonreversible, and sometimes fatal lung disease caused by overexposure to respirable crystalline silica—so it is advisable to guard against breathing the dust while mixing your alginate.

Silicone that is safe for application directly to the skin, such as Smooth-On's Body Double,® EnvironMolds' LifeRite,® and Mould Life's Life Form,® should only be used in a well-ventilated room; you should also do a small test on the back of your subject's hand a day or so before to ensure that there is no allergic reaction. If you notice any type of skin reaction, do not use the product. When working with platinum silicone such as Body Double® LifeRite® and Life Form,® if you wear gloves you will want to wear vinyl or nitrile gloves, not latex gloves, as latex will inhibit if not completely prevent the cure of the silicone rubber. I'll talk about silicone at greater length in a later chapter.

There are reasons you might want to use skin-safe platinum silicone for your lifecast instead of alginate, but there is a cost difference. Just to give an example of cost between the two materials, the amount of alginate needed to cast someone's face and neck from the ears forward, across the top of the head, and down to the clavicles could cost $5.00–6.00 (£2.5–3.0); the same amount of skin-safe platinum-cure silicone can cost 10 times as much. Platinum is not cheap, and the more platinum in the silicone, the faster it will cure. Silicone won't dry out and shrink like alginate. You don't need to cast a positive immediately and you don't need to make a secondary mold from the positive, because the silicone will last a very long time and can be used many times before the silicone begins to degrade. You must weigh various factors to determine whether the cost of lifecasting with silicone is worth the benefits.

TIP

Consider doing a very thin coat of platinum lifecasting silicone—just enough to cover the body parts you need to cover—and then apply a thicker coat of tin silicone on top of that after the platinum silicone has cured. Tin silicone is much less expensive than the platinum, and it will bond very well to the platinum silicone. Be sure to use a thixotropic, fast-cure tin silicone.

There are artists who do lifecasting by applying plaster directly onto the skin of their subjects. I'm talking about faces. No offense intended to those who do, but I avoid it, and so should you, and I'll tell you why. Reason #1: Plaster heats up as it sets; the thicker the plaster, the hotter it gets— hot enough to cause real burns. Reason #2: Plaster absorbs moisture and can seriously dry out your skin. In addition, if someone is foolish enough to apply plaster directly to the skin and then fails to release the skin properly so the plaster can be removed, there is very distinct possibility that the plaster will fuse to the subject's skin and hair, making the removal of the plaster very difficult and painful. The reality of the danger of direct application of plaster to skin was illustrated in January 2007, when a 16-year-old girl in Lincolnshire, England, suffered third-degree burns after encasing her hands in plaster as part of a school art project. Why she thought she'd be able to pull her hands out escapes me, but she subsequently had both thumbs and all but two of her fingers amputated. Be forewarned!

John Schoonraad

John Schoonraad has been lifecasting for film, television, and the arts for over 20 years. Accompanied by his sons Tristan and Robin, John and his U.K. team are masters of the lifecast, having done over 1,000 of them, from hands, feet, and heads to full bodies.

Among John's many prominent models are actors Laurence Fishburne, Gary Oldman, Joaquin Phoenix, Kate Winslet, Patrick Stewart, Russell Crowe, and Tom Hanks. He has successfully brought his skills and innovative ideas to the areas of special makeup effects, prosthetics,

FIGURE 3.3
John and Sly Stallone on location for *Rambo* 4. Image reproduced by permission of John Schoonraad.

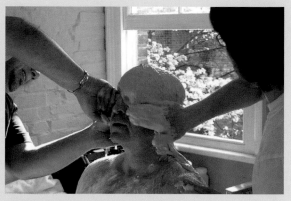

FIGURE 3.4
John and an assistant lifecasting actor Bob Hoskins. Image reproduced by permission of John Schoonraad.

and special effects and has applied them to such films as 2008's *Rambo*, the award-winning *Gladiator,* and *Saving Private Ryan*. John's also worked with pop celebrities David Bowie, Robbie Williams, and Bjork.

   Rightly considered some of the best lifecasters in the world along with Dave Parvin, John and his sons continue to make an impact on the entertainment industry as talented effects sculptors, craftsmen, and mold makers.

FIGURE 3.5
A relatively rare "eyes open" lifecast done by John Schoonraad. Image reproduced by permission of John Schoonraad.

THE MATERIALS

There are almost as many variations in the list of materials used for making a lifecast as there are artists who do them. That's a bit of an exaggeration, but there is no one set list of materials used. Most artists continue to use the materials with which they were taught the process, working from the adage: If it ain't broke, don't fix it. Other artists continue to experiment with materials to become more efficient and achieve higher quality. Dave Parvin continues to experiment and develop fresh methods for streamlining the lifecasting process for both himself and his models.

Dave is arguably one of the finest lifecasters in the world and uses procedures and materials that might not be appropriate for beginners. For example, Dave eschews the use of plaster bandages for making mother (support shell) molds and prefers instead to brush impression dental plaster directly onto the alginate mold, laying small pieces of cheesecloth onto it and painting plaster into the cheesecloth for reinforcement. Dave does this less for economic reasons (plaster bandages can be expensive; impression dental plaster is far less expensive) but because he's exceptionally good at it. Dave also says this is the best, most efficient method as well for ensuring that the resulting cast comes out flawlessly. I've tried it several times and always wind up wasting more plaster than I care to think about. Dave thinks I should just get better at it. (I'm working on it!) It is also less expensive Dave's way; one box of a dozen 6-inch plaster bandage rolls costs more than a 100-pound bag of impression dental plaster.

A number of commercially available alginates are of sufficient quality for prosthetics work, including FiberGel® and MoldGel® from EnvironMolds in Summit, New Jersey; Accu-Cast Imperial Body Gel® and Accu-Cast 390, 680, and 880 by Accu-Cast of Bend, Oregon; Prosthetic Grade Cream (PGC) by Teledyn-Getz, and Algiform® from Pink House Studios in St. Albans, Vermont. A more extensive list of suppliers can be found in the appendix at the back of this book.

Following is a list of the materials and tools you will need to create a lifecast from start to finished stone (gypsum) positive made from the alginate lifecast. As I mentioned, there is no one prescribed list of tools and materials, and the following list is in no particular order of importance nor necessarily comprehensive, but lifecasting is relatively standardized throughout the industry, so for the most part consider this list complete. After you've become proficient at lifecasting, I'm sure you'll decide to modify the list to suit your needs. This list also includes materials you may use to sculpt your character makeup appliance in clay once the lifecast has been made.

Oil-based (*non-sulfur*) clay	Spirit gum and spirit gum remover
Timer	Handle (½″ electrical conduit)
Plaster bandages (4- and 6-inch rolls)	Salt and/or terra alba (dried powdered plaster)
Polygrip® or other dental adhesive	Hair clips
Eyebrow pencil	Large and small craft sticks
Painter's rags	99 percent isopropyl alcohol (IPA)
Plastic wrap	Sculpting tools
Jiffy-Mixer®	Liquid latex rubber
Large screwdriver (flat)	1-inch chip brushes
Hair dryer	Hot-glue gun and glue sticks

1-, 2-, and 5-gallon plastic buckets
WED water clay
Scrub brushes/pads
Wood blocks (misc. 2 × 4-inch pieces)
Plastic cups (9, 12, and 18 oz.)
Rubber spatula
Petroleum jelly
Masking tape
Loose-weave burlap
Ruler
Wire cutters
Drill

Alginate
Acetone
Cholesterol cream (hair conditioner)
Plastic drop cloths
Pros-Aide adhesive
Cotton swabs
Mineral spirits or Naphtha
Algislo® or baking soda/water solution

Ultracal 30
Utility towels
Tincture of Green Soap
Sharp knife

Hammer
Krylon Crystal Clear® acrylic spray
Water
Duct tape
Pencil and notepad
Chisel
Pliers
1-, ¾-, and ½-inch router bits and a ¼-inch drill bit
Large plastic bowls
Scissors
Bald cap(s)

Sharpie marker
Cotton batting or cheesecloth
Superglue
Misc. plastic containers
Acrylic fortifier, bonder, or Acryl® 60

You might not use all the materials listed here, but these are all common to lifecasting procedures, and you may find that you prefer some over others. They are listed only as a convenience for you to decide what fits best your style.

THE PROCESS

Creating makeup effects requires a number of skill sets, including lifecasting, sculpture, mold making, and appliance casting and application techniques.

Overview

In most professional settings, the skill sets needed for creating a character makeup are most often practiced individually because each requires a good deal of concentrated expertise; however, it is not uncommon to find individuals who are adept at wearing the many hats necessary to take a project from concept to completion by themselves.

After the sculpted clay is completely removed and the two halves of the mold are thoroughly cleaned, the prosthetic material—foam latex, gelatin, or silicone—is added (poured, brushed, or injected) into the two-part mold and the mold is clamped tightly shut and the material cures, creating the beginning of a special makeup effect.

When the appliance is removed from the mold, trimmed, gently washed, and dried (only if it is foam latex), it is ready to be pre-painted and applied. Airbrush has become the preferred method (for many artists, but certainly not all) for painting appliances in the 21st century, allowing even opaque material such as foam latex to be painted with numerous layers of transparent pigment to give the impression of the translucency of human skin.

FIGURE 3.9
Front and back halves of a fiberglass matrix mold. Image reproduced by permission of Neill Gorton.

TEETH

Altering the appearance of the teeth can add a significant dimension to a character makeup, and there are several ways to change the appearance of teeth to varying degrees. The easiest way is with tooth wax; a prosthetic device that fits over existing teeth is the most difficult. Fangs, decayed and rotting teeth, and the like can be achieved commercially from kits such as Billy Bob Teeth,® Dr. Bukk,® Scarecrow,® and Toothfairy Teeth® relatively inexpensively. There is also liquid tooth enamel (Mehron,® Kryolan,® Ben Nye®) that can be painted directly onto the subject's teeth for different looks. Tooth enamel is for temporary use only.

However, if you want to have a set of truly unique and original teeth for your transformational character makeup, it will be necessary to create the teeth from scratch by first taking a cast of your subject's teeth. This is especially important for theater or film work that requires your character to speak. The results can be quite amazing, but this is a complicated process that borders on professional dental work. I don't really need to tell you this, but it is illegal to practice dentistry without a license. Common sense should also tell you that custom dental prosthetics for theater, film, and television work should never be worn for any extended period of time. They also should not to be worn while eating.

Taking impression dentals is easy enough that you can do it to yourself. It is actually not a bad idea to practice on yourself and become familiar with the procedure before trying it on someone else.

The materials for dental prosthetics are very specialized and can be purchased from dental supply companies as well as numerous makeup effects suppliers. A comprehensive list of suppliers is included in Appendix C at the back of this book.

73

Upper and lower impression
   dental trays
Dental die stone or Ultracal 30
Paper or plastic cups
Acrylic activator
Dental acrylic powder: tooth
   shade, gum shade
Petroleum jelly
Sandpaper
Water
Dental acrylic monomer

Dental alginate

Craft stick or small metal spatula
Silicone mold rubber
Minute Stain® kit
Flexacryl® clear powder

Small brushes
Dremel®
Rubber base tray mold
Sulphur-free oil clay

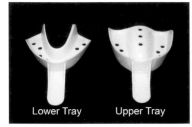

FIGURE 3.10
Lower and upper dental
impression trays.
Photo by the author.

We placed our discussion of casting teeth before casting the face because if dental prosthetics are required as part of the character makeup, they must be completed before a face lifecast can be made so that your subject can be wearing them during the lifecasting. If they are not worn during the lifecast, the appliance will not fit correctly when the teeth are in place and the prosthetic is applied.

Before you begin, determine the size of the dental trays you will need to use for the impressions. Dental trays come in different sizes: small, medium, and large. Try each to find the correct one for your subject. Next, place a cape or some sort of covering around your subject to avoid getting your subject's clothing messy.

The dental alginate that I use is Algitec® dustless alginate impression material by Patterson Dental Company of St. Paul, Minnesota. There are a number of dental alginates you can use. Follow these steps:

1. Wear gloves when casting an actor's teeth; it's a good idea hygienically, and it's simply better for your subject's confidence in you.
2. Brush a very light layer of petroleum jelly over the front of your model's teeth.
3. Begin by mixing a small amount of alginate with water. The alginate comes with specific instructions; as you use the alginate and become comfortable with it, you will be able to mix it by eye and by feel.
4. Mix for about 45 seconds or until the alginate becomes a thick paste. Then use a craft stick or small spatula to spread it into the upper plate tray. Mix the alginate thick so it won't run down your subject's throat; this will also help obtain a better gum impression.

Fill the tray completely; if it overflows, scoop the alginate back into the tray. You will have only about 2 minutes total working time before the alginate sets fully.

Your water temperature should be about 72°F (22° C). Cold water retards the set and warm water accelerates it.

It may be advisable to invest in an infrared digital thermometer, too. It will come in handy for many tasks. Radio Shack® sells one for about $75 (£40) that I have found invaluable. It's a very handy little gadget I learned about from Dave Parvin—just one of many tips I have received from a truly amazing artist and a good friend. I'm sure you can find something similar elsewhere for less money. I just happen to be a Radio Shack junkie.

FIGURE 3.11
Dental tray in subject's mouth. Very attractive! Photo by Brandon McMenamin. Image reproduced by permission of the author.

Next, do the following:

5. Once the (thick) alginate is in the tray, run the tray under water for a moment if it's handy and form the alginate into a tray-like shape.
6. Open your subject's mouth wide and press the tray gently into position; then close the subject's mouth. Carefully pull the upper lip over the tray if possible.
7. You may ask your subject to lean slightly forward in case the alginate isn't quite thick enough; this will help prevent alginate slipping toward the back of the throat.

This process can be somewhat messy, so it's a good idea to have your subject's head tilted slightly down. This will prevent runny alginate from running down the throat, and many people tend to collect a lot of saliva in their mouth during this process, creating rather excessive drool! Did I mention how much fun this is? Don't be in a hurry. Keep the mouth closed, and don't move the tray. Hold it steady until the alginate is fully set.

FIGURE 3.12
Removing the impression. Watch out for drool! Photo by Brandon McMenamin. Image reproduced by permission of the author.

Now do the following:

8. When the alginate has set, have your subject flex her lips. Ask the subject to close her lips around the tray and blow. This will introduce air between the set alginate and the teeth, making removal much easier. Have a paper towel or napkin ready for your subject to remove any residual alginate that may still be in her mouth or to wipe away saliva. Because the solidified alginate is mostly water, it is soft and rubbery and will begin to dry out quickly. You can wrap it in wet paper towels or submerge it in water to prevent shrinkage while you mix the dental stone or while you prepare to cast the lower teeth. This step is necessary only if you are going to take an impression of the lower teeth before casting the upper teeth and the alginate will be setting for a while.
9. Casting the lower teeth follows the same procedure as the upper teeth, but you must be sure to mix the alginate properly and thick because the lower tray must be upside down when it goes into the subject's mouth; you do not want the alginate to run out of the tray after you've filled it.

FIGURE 3.13
Tray with alginate impression of lower teeth. Photo by Brandon McMenamin. Image reproduced by permission of the author.

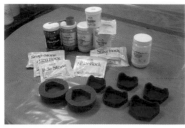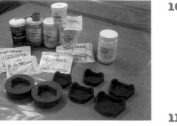

FIGURE 3.14
Some of Whip Mix's dental stone and rubber base molds. Photo by the author.

FIGURE 3.15
Stone impressions laid into base molds. Photo by Tess Fondie. Image reproduced by permission of the author.

FIGURE 3.16
Showing frenum membrane in stone cast. Photo by the author.

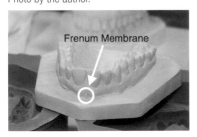

Frenum Membrane

10. Once you've got both upper and lower impressions made, it's time to make positives. You can use either dental stone or Ultracal 30. There are numerous types of dental stone available from different manufacturers. Whip Mix Corporation, one of the manufacturers whose products I use, has 22 different gypsum dental stone materials available at this writing.

11. Dental supply companies sell rubber base molds you can use to cast a nice, professional-looking stone base for your teeth to sit on, or you can make one yourself by shaping some oil clay and make a silicone mold of it. You will need this after the next step.

12. Mix enough dental stone to fill your tooth tray; with a small brush, begin to apply the stone to the alginate negative. Shake it a bit to get any small bubbles to rise. You will notice that the stone liquefies as it is shaken. This gentle shaking also helps ensure that the Ultracal 30 (let's just call it Ultracal from here on) makes its way completely into each tooth cavity. When all the tooth spaces are filled, build up the Ultracal slightly higher than the edge of the dental plate and let it sit for about an hour before demolding it.

If you want to make the Ultracal stronger, mix 50 percent acrylic fortifier (or Acryl® 60) and 50 percent water when you mix the Ultracal. You can buy cement acrylic fortifier at just any hardware store, especially the Big Box stores like Lowe's or The Home Depot. Acryl® 60 can also be purchased at most Ace Hardware, True Value, or Home Depot locations. In addition, if you cover your Ultracal cast with plastic before it sets, the plastic will help the Ultracal retain moisture as the heat builds up when it cures, making the stone stronger still. At least that's what I've been told; I have no way of proving or disproving it.

Now:

13. Remove your stone cast from the alginate and dental tray. Clean up any rough edges around your cast, and remove or patch any blemishes that are present. Mix another small batch of Ultracal, enough to fill the rubber base mold. Make it thick so that the teeth will not sink.

14. Gently tap the mold to get rid of any air bubbles or air pockets trapped inside the mold. As the Ultracal begins to set, carefully place the teeth into the wet Ultracal (with the teeth facing up, of course), being careful to leave the gum and frenum membrane visible. The frenum membrane is the thin flap of tissue that connects the upper gum to the upper lip. You can feel yours with your tongue. It important to keep this flap visible on your cast so you have a gauge of how far you can sculpt your teeth appliance later.

15. After you have done this for both the upper and lower teeth, make a silicone mold of them so that you can make duplicate positives of the upper and lower teeth. This is not essential to do, but it can be very useful for at least two reasons: You will have a clean reference model to refer to when sculpting your appliance, and if you somehow manage to break one of your positives, you won't have to start from scratch again by taking new impressions; you will already have a mold and can simply mix more stone and fill it.

16. There are a variety of silicones that you can use for this step. The procedure is the same regardless of the silicone you choose. I like to use Smooth-On's Mold Max® 30, a tin-cure (also called a *condensation-cure*) silicone simply because I'm most familiar with it, although Silicones, Inc.'s GI-1000 and Polytek's TinSil Gel-10 are very easy to work with and they can all be accelerated to *kick*, or set up, quickly.

We will get into a much more detailed discussion of silicone in Chapters 5 and 6, but for now there are two basic cure types of silicone used in makeup effects: *condensation cure* and *addition cure*. They are very different, and they are not intermixable. There are two types of condensation-cure silicones: one-part and two-part. We will concern ourselves primarily with the two-part condensation silicone, which uses tin in the curing process and is also called tin-cure silicone.

Condensation silicone needs both air and moisture in the air to cure; it will not cure in a vacuum. There is a negligible amount of shrinkage with this type of silicone. Addition-cure silicone uses platinum in the curing process and is often called platinum-cure silicone. Addition silicone cures by a self-contained chemical reaction, which means it can cure in a vacuum, if necessary, and there is virtually no shrinkage whatever. Platinum silicones cure faster, as a rule, than tin silicones which, if not accelerated, can take as long as 18 to 24 hours to fully cure. The more platinum the silicone contains, the faster it will kick. That's another reason to use it in this step (if you do this step). However, platinum is not cheap.

Next:

17. Cut two large plastic containers apart and hot-glue them to a piece of Formica® board or something similar, such as Masonite.® The containers must be large enough for the teeth cast to fit inside each one and still have at least half an inch of space between the cast and the edge of the container.

18. Mix silicone to pour over the teeth. Do you still remember your geometry from high school? To find the volume of a cylinder, which we're using here, $V = \pi r^2 h$. Translated, that's *Volume = 3.142 x radius² x height*, where the radius of a circle is half the diameter (or width of a circle), which is the distance from outer edge to outer edge through the center. The volume of silicone you'll need to mix is that

77

FIGURE 3.17
Teeth inside container ready for silicone molding. Photo by Tess Fondie. Image reproduced by permission of the author.

number minus the displacement of the teeth cast. If that seems like too much work, it's actually pretty easy to eyeball it. The thing to keep in mind here is not to be wasteful of silicone. It's your money. Or your client's.

19. Using either a triple-beam scale or an accurate digital scale, measure your silicone according to the manufacturer's recommendations and mix the components thoroughly. It's better to mix too little than too much if you're eyeballing it. Silicone sticks to silicone, so if you make your batch too small, mix up some more and pour it onto what you've already poured once it is firm; it doesn't have to be set. If you use Smooth-On Mold Max® 30, you can decrease the kick time by using FastCat® 30 instead of its regular catalyst. By increasing the amount you use in proportion to the rubber base, you can decrease the kick time to minutes and can usually demold in less than an hour.

However, accelerating the silicone like this significantly weakens it to the point that it may become brittle within days. You can use a fast-setting platinum silicone and demold in a very short time. Adding heat will also accelerate platinum silicone curing; it will also affect tin-cure silicone, but not as much. However, more air bubbles are more likely to escape and not cause problems if you let the silicone cure overnight.

Now:

20. Pour the thoroughly mixed silicone over the teeth, making sure that the silicone rises above the uppermost teeth by at least ¼ of an inch (about 6 mm). When the silicone is completely cured it will feel like hard rubber. Demold the teeth and lightly brush a very thin layer of petroleum jelly inside the molds as a release agent. You shouldn't really need it, but this will ensure that your next stone cast will pop out easily.

21. Mix another batch of Ultracal or dental stone and fill the molds. When they're filled, tap the molds to release any trapped air bubbles and make them rise to the surface. You can demold the teeth in about an hour. Remember that you can use a 50/50 mix of water and acrylic fortifier and cover the molds with plastic to get a stronger stone cast when using Ultracal. Once the teeth are demolded, you're ready to begin sculpting the teeth your character will need for the makeup.

FACE AND NECK

Face and neck lifecasts are probably the most common for creating makeup effects, since most makeups can be achieved with small appliances rather than full head and shoulder appliances. I'm sure there artists who would disagree, but face and neck lifecasts are certainly what I do more of. Here's how to do it and what you'll need to accomplish the task:

Alginate

Scissors to cut plaster bandages and burlap and trim bald cap

Pitcher of warm water

Spirit gum or Pros-Aide® adhesive. Spirit gum remover or Pros-Aide® remover (Ben Nye® Bond Off! works well)

Latex, vinyl, or nitrile gloves

1-inch chip brushes

Cholesterol conditioner, petroleum jelly, KY® Jelly

½-inch (12 mm) metal electrical conduit (about 7 inches long)

WED clay or (sulphur-free) oil clay

Cotton or cheesecloth (cut in short pieces)

Loosely woven burlap (cut into 4 × 4-inch and 3 × 6-inch pieces)

Drill with Jiffy-Mixer®

1-, 2-, and 5-gallon plastic buckets

Masking, gaffers, or duct tape

Bald cap

4- or 6-inch rolls of plaster bandages (× 2)

Misc. plastic buckets and cups

Large craft sticks

Ultracal

Eyebrow pencil

Thermometer

Comb or hair brush

Rubber kidney tool

Large plastic sheet or trash bag

Utility knife and plaster rasp

Clock or timer

It will be advantageous for you to arrange everything you will need ahead of time so that you will be able to reach it easily and work in an efficient and timely manner once you begin. It is worth noting again that there is no single way to approach lifecasting a face and neck. If you were to poll 50 artists about the way they do a lifecast, you are likely to get 25 different methods or more. I learned one way but have altered my methods several times over the years. I will probably continue to do so as materials change and advance. The description that follows is a process that works well for me, but once you've become comfortable with the process you are likely to come up with your own way to approach it.

1. Cut the plaster bandages into lengths of about 8 inches (about 20.5 cm), 10 inches (about 25.5 cm), and 12 inches (about 30.5 cm). Make several of each. Also cut several thin strips that will be used to reinforce the nose along the bridge and septum.

2. Premeasure the alginate you will be using into a plastic container. Also premeasure the amount of water you will need into one of your larger plastic containers. You might want to use the 1-gallon bucket even though we're not mixing a large batch of alginate, because the Jiffy-Mixer® is likely to cause some splatter. To minimize it even further, set the 1-gallon bucket in the 5-gallon bucket before firing up the jiffy mixer. The water temperature should be about 80°F (about 27°C).

FIGURE 3.19
Plaster bandages cut for making the mother mold. Photo by the author.

You can certainly use cooler water or warmer water. The 80°F (about 27°C) water temperature is comfortable for most people. Cooler water will cause the alginate to set more slowly; warmer water will accelerate the set time. Refer to the recommendations of the particular alginate you are using, because they could differ somewhat as to the ratio of alginate to water. With most alginates, a ratio of 5 oz. of alginate per 1 lb. of water will give you a nonrunny, workable mixture that spreads easily and stays where you put it. I strongly suggest a bit of self-experimentation before you begin putting alginate on your subject's face.

You might also want to do a pH test on your water supply. Most tap water will be just fine for mixing alginate, but some city water supplies contain chemicals that will interfere with the way alginate sets, causing partial or complete cure inhibition. It's rare, but it does happen. If you are in any doubt, use distilled water from your local grocer. Alginate also has a lifespan, and old alginate or alginate that has not been stored properly will also lose its ability to set up. It never hurts to do a test if it's been a while since you've used your materials.

For our purposes, we will be using EnvironMolds' FiberGel.® FiberGel® has a set time of 4–5 minutes (which means we will need to work quickly) and contains a matrix of tiny fibers. The fibers not only add tear resistance and strength to the alginate, they help prevent running and dripping. The fiber matrix also allows the alginate to retain moisture, thereby reducing the shrink rate and keeping your mold soft and flexible far beyond the usable time of most other alginates. This allows for delayed casting times without the loss of detail if necessary. This was one of Dave Parvin's many innovations.

We will be casting our subject seated in an upright position. I've heard that some artists like to cast a face with the subject lying flat. I've never met anyone who does it that way unless the final result requires a character to be lying flat. Lying down could be quite comfortable for the subject, but when the subject is lying flat, gravity will pull the skin and muscles of the face downward in a way that can distort the lifecast as well as prevent the resulting appliance from fitting properly when the subject is standing or sitting upright.

3. Place your subject in a comfortable chair, preferably one that can be raised and lowered. Cover your subject's body and clothing with plastic, carefully attaching it with tape at least an inch below the level of your cast.

4. Apply a bald cap to your subject. Applying bald caps properly is a necessary skill to get into the makeup guild, and we'll talk about a full bald cap application elsewhere in this book. But for lifecasting, we need only apply the cap well enough to provide us with a good cast, keeping the subject's hair out of the way. Begin by flattening your subject's hair using water and a nonoily gel or hairspray. Aqua Net® hairspray works very well. Dampen the hair with water, then spray with Aqua Net and comb flat. Gently blow dry.

You don't need to use an expensive bald cap—a regular theatrical cap will do, just make sure it's large enough to cover your subject's head. In a pinch, you can use plastic wrap tightly around your subject's head, held in place with Scotch® tape. However, I am a firm believer that anything worth doing is worth doing well, so we'll be using a bald cap made from scratch using slush latex built up in layers on a plastic head block. These can be purchased at a nominal cost and will definitely come in handy in your work. Carefully and comfortably place the bald cap snugly on your subject's head, pulling it down to cover the ears.

FIGURE 3.20
Fitting the bald cap onto my assistant Tess. Photo by Chase Heilman. Image reproduced by permission of the author.

5. Using the eyebrow pencil, lightly mark the cap around the subject's ears, and draw a line across the top of the head from the middle of one ear to the other. If the ears do not need to be included as part of the life-cast, you won't need to cut the cap to go around the ears. This will also prevent concerns of undercuts later in the process of creating your appliance.

6. Before gluing the cap down, you might want to trim the front closer to your subject's hairline; otherwise, you can carefully pull back the front edge of the cap and apply adhesive to your subject's forehead, then press the bald cap down onto the forehead. If you're using Pros-Aide,® the glue dries sticky and transparently. Press the cap down until it holds. If you're using spirit gum, wait until it is quite gummy before pressing the cap down.

7. Carefully start to secure the sides and back of the bald cap, making sure the cap is going to hold before moving on to the next section.

8. There should be no wrinkles on the head forward of the line drawn between the ears. If there are, carefully lift the cap at the edges and reposition it until the surface is smooth. Lastly, mark your subject's hairline with the eyebrow pencil. This line will transfer to the alginate and then to the Ultracal. This line is important because it shows exactly how far we can sculpt on the forehead and sides of the face without going into the hair.

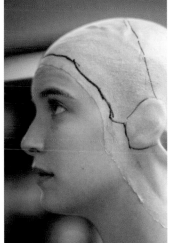

FIGURE 3.21
Lines drawn across top of head, around ears, and along hairline. Photo by Chase Heilman. Image reproduced by permission of the author.

9. Apply a small amount of cholesterol cream or petroleum jelly to your subject's eyebrows, eyelashes, and any other facial hair. Use K-Y® Jelly or petroleum jelly to lightly cover the bald cap one inch beyond the line drawn across the top of your subject's head. This will ensure that the alginate will not stick to the bald cap.

10. Before applying the alginate, explain to your subject what the procedure will entail and what the steps are going to be so that there will be

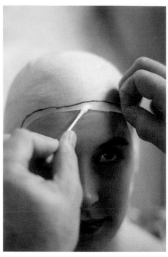

FIGURE 3.22
Final adjustment to the bald cap. Photo by Chase Heilman. Image reproduced by permission of the author.

no surprises during the lifecasting. It is very important that your subject has no trouble breathing through both nostrils, because the mouth will be completely covered with alginate. Now would also be a good time to find out if your subject is claustrophobic. If that is the case, your approach to making the lifecast must be altered to do the cast in sections. Ideally you would know this kind of information beforehand so other arrangements could be made. Last-minute changes do happen, but the less you can leave until the last moment, the better.

Make any last-minute adjustments to your subject before you mix the alginate; make sure her head is aligned straight and not tilted, turned, or cocked at an angle and that she is sitting up straight. A misalignment can result in a lifecast that might look fine overall but that will be inadequate for sculpting a makeup appliance, because it will be distorted.

If your character will have dentures, now is the time for your subject to put them in so that the lifecast can be taken with false teeth in place. This will prevent the makeup from fitting incorrectly when it is applied later.

Now:

11. It's time to mix the alginate. Look at the clock or start your timer when you begin to mix the water and the alginate powder so that you'll know how much time you have before the alginate begins to set. To do a face and neck cast, we'll need to mix 10 oz. of FiberGel alginate with 2 lbs. (32 oz.) of warm (80°F/27°C) water. Always add the alginate powder to the water and not vice versa. The alginate can be mixed with your hand, but I don't recommend it; mixing with an electric drill and a Jiffy-Mixer bit is much faster and mixes the alginate and water more smoothly and thoroughly. Be careful not to start the drill too rapidly because you will likely put a cloud of alginate dust into the air! This is not good, particularly if the alginate you use has silica in it, as some do. If you are working with another person, divide the labor so that one person is spreading the alginate and the other is keeping an eye on the subject's nostrils, making sure that they remain unblocked. Properly mixed alginate should not run, but never take anything for granted in such instances. It is also possible that you'll need to add a very small amount of water to your alginate if it is too thick. Remember to keep talking to your subject as you spread the alginate, telling her what you're doing and just letting her know that you're still there and are paying attention. It is reassuring. Lifecasting requires trust.

Every artist works a bit differently with alginate. You might want to wear gloves—latex, vinyl, or nitrile—or you might prefer to work barehanded. I suggest gloves. The reason is that you can quickly remove them to put on a fresh pair and instantly have clean hands! Keep in mind that room temperature, water temperature, and your subject's body temperature, as well as how quickly or slowly you work, will all affect the lifecasting. Ideal working conditions (for me) are a room temperature of 69–72°F (20.5–22°C), 45–45% humidity, 80°F (about 27°C) water temperature, and normal subject body temperature (98.6°F/37°C).

Next:

12. Begin to spread the alginate with your hand, starting at the top of the head where the line is drawn between the ears and move downward on the face, leaving the nostrils for last. When I say spread the alginate, I mean *spread* the alginate; you will get fewer surface bubbles when you spread rather than just blobbing it on. Be careful not to spread the alginate too thin.

13. When you get to the subject's eyes (which should be closed already), be certain—and careful—to gently press the alginate into the inner corners of the eye and under the eyelashes with your fingertips. Make sure to do the same with the eyebrows, getting alginate thoroughly into them. If you've released them properly, the alginate will come off beautifully, and when you make your stone positive, there should be no eyebrows on it at all. As you apply the alginate, make sure no air is trapped between it and your subject. Use your fingers to follow the contours of your subject's face with the alginate.

FIGURE 3.23
Spreading alginate.
Photo by Chase Heilman. Image reproduced by permission of the author.

83

> **NOTE**
>
> A note about release for your subject's eyes: Cholesterol cream may cause stinging for some people; I have never experienced it, but if you have any concerns, it is always best to err on the side of caution. Use petroleum jelly instead. *Lightly.*

FIGURE 3.24
Preparing to apply alginate to mouth.
Photo by Chase Heilman. Image reproduced by permission of the author.

14. Do the same with the sides of the face, stopping just in front of the ears, making sure to get good alginate coverage into all the lines and creases in the face. When you cover the mouth, use your fingers to work alginate into the corners of the mouth and between the upper and lower lips. If your subject's mouth is slightly open, that's fine. The goal is to have the subject's mouth in a normal, relaxed position. In fact, if your makeup design includes upper and/or lower lip pieces, having more lip exposed during the lifecast will be beneficial during the sculpture phase of your project.

15. Next cover as much of the subject's neck as needed for your makeup design. Make your coverage as even and symmetrical as possible. Lastly, cover the nose, being careful to keep the nostrils clear. You might want to use a small craft stick

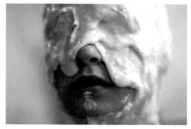

FIGURE 3.25
Save the nostrils for last.
Photo by Chase
Heilman. Image
reproduced by
permission of the author.

FIGURE 3.26
Keep the nostrils clear.
Photo by Chase
Heilman. Image
reproduced by
permission of the
author.

to spread the alginate evenly and as closely to the edges of the nostril as possible without creating a blockage.

16. If the alginate does run, carefully lift it back up over the face. Another method of getting good coverage around the nose—and the nose is a critical part to do well—is to tell your subject to take a deep breath and hold it. Then cover her nose completely with alginate, making sure to get around the nostrils, and then have your subject blow out sharply through the nose to clear the nostril openings of alginate.

17. Quickly use a craft stick to remove any dangling alginate before your subject takes another breath and inhales a bit of alginate. Your subject can then resume breathing normally, and you can further refine the alginate around the nose with your finger or craft stick. I have gotten flawless results this way, with no problems. If you choose to try this method, you might want to do the subject's nose first, while her mouth is still clear and it is possible for her to breathe through her mouth while you clear the nostrils. Then proceed with the rest of the face, taking care to keep a watchful eye on the nostrils as you work, to make sure they remain unobstructed.

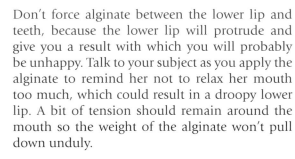

Don't force alginate between the lower lip and teeth, because the lower lip will protrude and give you a result with which you will probably be unhappy. Talk to your subject as you apply the alginate to remind her not to relax her mouth too much, which could result in a droopy lower lip. A bit of tension should remain around the mouth so the weight of the alginate won't pull down unduly.

If you work quickly, you should have no trouble covering the entire face and neck with one batch of alginate. Try to have an even layer of coverage on the face, with no thin spots. It is especially important to try to get the alginate as thick as possible around the edges, eyes, and nose. If you find you need more alginate, it is important to know that alginate will not stick to itself once it has set up, meaning that you cannot apply freshly mixed alginate to set alginate and get the two to bond. However, there is a way to make it happen.

A product called Algislo,® available from EnvironMolds, can be used as an alginate retarder, bonder, or softener. This is another Dave Parvin innovation. Algislo is a base that reacts with alginic acid in the alginate to soften it enough on the surface to create a bond between it and fresh alginate. Or if you simply need a bit more working time, you can use it per its directions when mixing the alginate to get a longer working time. You can also create a similar result by making a solution of baking soda and water. Experiment beforehand to find the right solution for your needs.

Back to work:

18. Before the alginate sets, add some fuzz—cotton from a roll—while the alginate is still sticky. The cotton fuzz will stick to the alginate, and the plaster bandages will stick to the cotton as well, making sure that your mother mold (the support mold) conforms precisely to the alginate mold. You don't need much. Press gently so you don't push all the way to bare skin.

You may opt to use cheesecloth cut into small, single-thickness pieces in lieu of the cotton for the same purpose. Make sure you get cotton fuzz or cheesecloth at the outside edges of the alginate so that the mother mold will adhere tightly at the edges. Otherwise, there is a possibility of the alginate folding in on itself when you are making the positive.

FIGURE 3.27
Algislo® slows the cure of alginate and helps alginate stick to alginate. Photo by Chase Heilman. Image reproduced by permission of the author.

19. Now that the alginate has set, it is time to apply the plaster bandages as a shell—a mother mold—to support the alginate. If you were to remove the alginate now, before the mother mold is applied, you would wind up with a floppy impression of your subject's face that will not hold its shape. To make the mother mold, you will need to dip the precut strips of plaster bandage into slightly warm water with a pinch of salt. You will definitely want to wear gloves for this process. Warm water will accelerate the cure of plaster, as will a pinch of salt. Terra alba—dried powdered plaster—will also accelerate the cure of plaster to a fraction of its normal set. If the water is too warm, however, you can actually inhibit the cure of the plaster. Fold the plaster strip in half, with the plaster side out. Dip it into the water, then carefully squeeze out some (but not all) of the water before applying it to the alginate. You want the cotton to become soaked so the plaster will stick to it. When you're finished, there should be a buildup of about four layers of plaster. Begin by creating an outside edge and work your way in toward the center of the face.

20. Make sure that your plaster strips overlap one another, with the thickest layers on the outside edges. Press gently but firmly to make sure that there's no airspace between the alginate and the plaster. If you press too firmly, you risk creating a distortion in the alginate and the resulting stone positive. Also, if your mother mold is not thick enough, the weight of the stone when you make your positive may distort the shape of the mold, also ruining your cast.

FIGURE 3.28
Cotton fuzz helps plaster and alginate stay together. Photo by Chase Heilman. Image reproduced by permission of the author.

Here is a good place to discuss in more detail the argument for brushing on plaster with a brush and laying strips of cheesecloth into it for strength instead

TIP
Terra alba will accelerate the cure of plaster; so will a bit of salt; so will warm water. However, hot water will actually inhibit or prevent the cure of plaster, so be careful with the temperature; test beforehand. White vinegar added to the water in small amounts will retard, or slow, the cure of plaster.

FIGURE 3.29
Detail showing plaster attached to gauze bandage. Photo by Chase Heilman. Image reproduced by permission of the author.

of using plaster bandages. The reason the Dave Parvin dislikes using plaster bandages—and I understand his point—is that if the first layer of plaster bandages has already started to set up when you begin to add the second layer and you accidentally press too hard and create an indentation, the plaster will not spring back. That will also cause an indentation in the alginate and will result in an indentation in the stone positive when it is cast.

It is important to note that not all plaster bandages are created equally; some contain more plaster than others. Gypsona® plaster bandages seem to be quite popular; I use them frequently. They are similar to Specialist® bandages (made by Johnson & Johnson and BSN). I also use Cliniset® bandages from EBI; they can be purchased from FX Warehouse in Florida. You'll find a comprehensive appendix of suppliers in the back of this book. There are several brands available; it is important to find one that has a lot of plaster impregnated into the fabric of the bandages. Woodland Scenics® sells a plaster bandage used for model railroad scenic construction; it has the most plaster of any bandage I have ever used and it is also by far the most expensive.

FIGURE 3.30
Applying plaster bandages as mother mold. Photo by Chase Heilman. Image reproduced by permission of the author.

Brushing on plaster as a substitute for plaster bandages can be done in the following way. Note that the logistics of this process dictate that it should be attempted only when two people are creating the lifecast, not one:

- After the cotton fuzz or cheesecloth has been pressed into the uncured alginate (the alginate should now be fully set), mix up a shallow bucket of impression dental plaster (set time 2–3 minutes) and use a 2- or 3-inch chip brush to brush on a layer of plaster over the fuzz-covered or cheesecloth-covered alginate, making sure to continue keeping the subject's nostrils open. Use a 2-inch brush on the face; a 3-inch brush is a bit too big. Rinse your chip brushes in a bucket of water before the plaster sets, to keep them viable for more than one application.

- As soon as this layer has been brushed on, the second person will begin gently applying a layer of cheesecloth to the wet plaster, matching the contours of the alginate and plaster. Repeat this step. Your plaster shell should be about 3/16- to ¼-inch (5–6.5 mm) thick. You can also add cut fiberglass fibers to the remaining plaster and spread it onto the mold by hand for added strength.
- After the plaster has heated and then begun to cool, it is cured and you can remove the mold from your subject.

Now let's resume the step-by-step application of plaster bandages for the support shell:

21. Use some of the smaller cut pieces of plaster bandage across the bridge of the nose horizontally, and the thin strips along the ridge of the nose and over the septum between the nostrils and the upper lip. Be careful to keep the nostrils unobstructed. It would be a shame to risk starting over when we're almost ready to make our positive!

22. When the plaster shell has set up – remember, plaster heats up when it is curing—that is, it is beginning to cool (about 15 minutes), it's time to remove the mold from your subject's face. I assure you, she is ready, too. Total time to this point—*including* the bald cap application—should be somewhere between 30 and 45 minutes, on average. Variables will be the alginate you use, water temperature, and so on. The actual application of plaster, whether with bandages or brushing on with cheesecloth, may take about 12–15 minutes.

23. To remove the mold, ask your subject to begin puffing out her cheeks and wiggling her face. This will help begin to break any suction between the alginate and skin, and the mold will begin to separate. Have your subject lean forward slightly and help by cupping their face in their hands while you begin to separate the mold from the bald cap at the top of their head.

FIGURE 3.31
Removing the alginate and plaster mold. Photo by Chase Heilman. Image reproduced by permission of the author.

It is possible that your subject might feel some resistance on the eyelashes and eyebrows and on any facial hair that was exposed, such as sideburns or moustache. Not to worry, unless you forgot to release them with cholesterol cream or petroleum jelly! The alginate will let go, though you could find a stray hair or two left in the alginate.

FIGURE 3.32
Sometimes the lighting can make the negative appear to be a positive. Photo by Chase Heilman. Image reproduced by permission of the author.

24. Ask the subject to keep her eyes closed because the sudden change in lighting could be uncomfortable after this much time. The lifecast should now easily pop off into your hands.

You now have a negative mold of your subject's face. Take a close look to examine it. A few minor air bubbles are nothing to be concerned about. Those can easily be cleaned up once the positive has been made. More serious imperfections may require that the entire process be repeated. Let's hope not! If all is well, we need

87

to make our positive before the alginate begins to dry. If the alginate is thin at the edges, it could already be changing color and drying. It doesn't take long. When the alginate dries, it shrinks; it is mostly water, after all. If you are working with another person, you might want to have him or her help get your subject cleaned up while you prepare to make the stone positive. If you are working alone and your subject needs your help to remove the bald cap, put some wet shop towels inside the alginate mold and around the edges to keep it moist until you are ready to make the positive.

Before you begin to mix the Ultracal for the positive, you need to plug the nostril holes in the lifecast mold, or the Ultracal will run right out of the mold. You can either use a small piece of WED clay or oil clay into the holes or mix up a small amount of dental alginate to fill the holes. Be very careful not to push whatever you use too far into the cavity or you risk deforming the nose and ruining the positive. If you don't know what WED clay is yet, I will tell you: WED clay is water-based clay that contains glycerin so it will stay moist longer. WED stands for Walter Elias Disney; it was developed for Disney sculptors to create maquettes for Disneyland attractions.

Now do the following:

1. Place the lifecast upside down, supported in a shallow box.
2. Wearing gloves, pour about a cup of water in a small plastic bucket, then sprinkle Ultracal into the water with one hand while stirring with your other hand. Continue to add Ultracal powder until it is about the consistency of a milkshake—not too thick and not too runny. (If you're interested, the official mix ratio for Ultracal is 38 parts water to 100 parts Ultracal by weight.) You are going to create a detail layer in the mold and brush it into every nook and cranny of the negative with a 1-inch chip brush. Brush the Ultracal into the negative and bring it up the sides of the mold. You can take your time with the Ultracal since it won't begin to set up for 15 or 20 minutes. Jostle and tap the mold to release any trapped air bubbles from its surface. You will notice that the Ultracal liquefies even more when it is jostled and shaken, so you will need to brush it up the walls of the mold again.

The goal of this step is to create a pure Ultracal detail layer about ¼-inch (6.5 mm) thick over the entire surface of the alginate negative. It is up to you whether or not to use Acryl® 60 or another acrylic fortifier when you mix the Ultracal. It will add strength to your stone positive, and that will be an advantage if you will be making your appliances with foam latex. (Adding acrylic fortifier will also make repairs easier when mixed 50/50 with water.)

FIGURE 3.33
Brushing Ultracal into the alginate mold.
Photo by Chase Heilman. Image reproduced by permission of the author.

If you need more Ultracal than you initially mixed, add a little more water and then more Ultracal and continue with the detail layer. When you're done with the detail layer, you might want to rinse out your chip brush in a cup of water so you can use it again. *Whatever you do,* don't *rinse it in the sink or pour any uncured Ultracal down the drain!* Ultracal will set up even under water, and if it sets in your pipes, you will help your plumber buy a lovely vacation home in Europe or the Caribbean. Any excess Ultracal you still have in a small mixing bucket can come in handy later as a mold base. Once the Ultracal has gone through its curing process, you can just pop it out of the bucket and set it aside somewhere handy.

> **TIP**
> Never pour uncured Ultracal, plaster, or any gypsum stone material into a sink and down the drain, because it will set under water and could ruin or permanently block the pipe anywhere from the drain to the main sewer line.

Now:

3. After your detail layer has cured, in about an hour . . . actually, there are a couple of schools of thought on this: One says it's better to let the Ultracal cure completely before applying a new layer to it (Ultracal will stick to itself); I find it's better to add more Ultracal before the first layer completely cures. Just make sure it's set up enough to hold its shape and not be affected by the next step. (When in doubt, and most certainly when you are getting accustomed to working with a new material, it is best to err on the side of caution until you really know the properties of the materials you're working with.) Mix another batch of Ultracal, more this time than for the detail layer; the consistency of this batch should be that of a thin milkshake. We are going to be adding the burlap pieces in this step to add strength to our Ultracal. The burlap will act like rebar in concrete, as a strengthening support. Dip a piece of burlap into the Ultracal, then press it onto the Ultracal in the negative mold, making sure to eliminate any air pockets. Do this over the entire mold, overlapping the pieces of burlap. You can even use pieces of cheesecloth or chopped fiberglass fibers. We want to build up two or three layers of Ultracal and reinforcing material and then a final layer of only Ultracal for a beauty layer. The final thickness of the positive should be about an inch.

FIGURE 3.34
Brushing the detail layer into the negative. Photo by Chase Heilman. Image reproduced by permission of the author.

FIGURE 3.35
Building up thickness of Ultracal and burlap. Photo by Chase Heilman. Image reproduced by permission of the author.

4. As the beauty layer is beginning to set, use the rubber kidney tool to smooth the Ultracal. Again, anything worth doing is worth doing well. Even though few, if any, other people will see the finished stone positive, you should want it to look good. Another reason is that if the surface is too rough, you could easily cut or scrape your hands when handling it during the other stages in your makeup creation. Try not to bleed on your mold.

89

FIGURE 3.36
Adding a handle to the positive. Photo by Chase Heilman. Image reproduced by permission of the author.

5. You need to make a handle for the positive. The handle can be added as the beauty layer is applied. There is a reason we don't just make a solid stone positive—two reasons, actually: A solid positive would be heavy, and having no handle would make it awkward to manipulate and very difficult to lift from the negative mold we will make later of the sculpted prosthetic. Take the piece of metal conduit and place it across the back of the positive; it might need to lie at an angle. Dip two of the long strips of burlap into the remaining Ultracal and wrap one around each end of the metal handle, securing it to the positive.

6. When you have finished smoothing the beauty layer and the handle, cover the mold with plastic. Remember that the plastic will help retain moisture as the Ultracal heats during its cure, adding additional strength.

7. After your positive has cooled, you can remove it from the alginate and plaster mold. Will it look good? Will there be huge air bubbles? Is the nose deformed? Will you have to start over?! It's time to find out. With your fingers, begin to gently pry the plaster and alginate shell away from your Ultracal positive around the edges. As the mold begins to pull away from your positive, it should begin to loosen more and more, to the point where you can grab the handle and pull it out of the mold.

FIGURE 3.37
Covering with plastic during cure. Photo by the author.

FIGURE 3.38
Stone positive almost ready to be pulled from the mold. Photo by the author.

There may well be some small bubble blemishes on the surface, but those are easy to chip away, and if there are any holes, unless they are enormous, they should be easy to patch and fill by mixing a bit of Ultracal with Acryl® 60/acrylic fortifier and water (1:1 ratio). There is always a bit of cleanup to do on a positive, especially at the nostrils because they were left open and then had to be plugged.

With a small chisel and hammer, you can carefully pop the Ultracal "booger" off each nostril and then clean up further with a little sandpaper or a Dremel®. If there is any edge work to clean up, you can use sandpaper or a rasp. Once the cleanup is done, you are ready to begin sculpting your makeup design.

BUST: HEAD AND SHOULDERS

Our lifecasting is going to get progressively more difficult. From here on out we will be working "in the round." We will follow many of the same steps for making a lifecast of a face and neck, but we'll include the back of the head as well as the shoulders. We'll need more plaster bandages for a full bust lifecast—about four times as many. This may be a good project to use brushed impression plaster and cheesecloth. If you want more working time for your plaster, you may try impression dental plaster or regular Plaster of Paris. This will be a lengthier process for your subject as well, so if you choose to use the brush method, perhaps it would be a good idea to first practice on something—or someone— other than your subject. We will begin by duplicating the first steps for creating a face and neck lifecast. We will also need essentially the same materials.

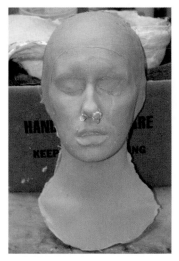

FIGURE 3.39
Stone positive ready to be cleaned up. Photo by the author.

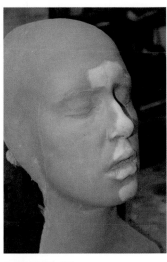

FIGURE 3.40
Cleaned-up positive. Photo by the author.

91

TIP
You should always mix a test batch of alginate when working with new material; mix characteristics may vary slightly from batch to batch. It is better to simply *stop* if something isn't working to your expectations rather than continuing and trying to fix it on the fly. This will also prevent you from wasting more money and material.

Alginate
Scissors to cut plaster and burlap and trim bald cap
Pitcher of warm water
Spirit gum or Pros-Aide® adhesive

Bald cap
4- or 6-inch 4 rolls of plaster bandages (× 2)
Misc. plastic buckets and cups
Spirit gum remover or Pros-Aide® remover (Ben Nye® Bond Off! works well)

Latex, vinyl, or nitrile gloves	Large craft sticks
1-inch chip brushes	Ultracal
Cholesterol conditioner, petroleum jelly, K-Y® Jelly	Eyebrow pencil
½-inch metal electrical conduit (about 7 inches (8 cm) long)	Thermometer
WED clay or (sulphur-free) oil clay	Comb or hair brush
Cotton or cheesecloth (cut in short pieces)	Rubber kidney tool
Loosely woven burlap (cut into 4 × 4-inch and 3 × 6-inch pieces)	Large plastic sheet or trash bag
Drill with Jiffy-Mixer®	
2-gallon plastic bucket	Utility knife and plaster rasp
Masking, gaffer's, or duct tape	Clock or timer
1 roll of plastic wrap	¾-inch (19 mm) round router bit

1. Cut the plaster bandages into lengths of about 8, 10, and 12 inches (20, 25.5, and 30.5 cm). Also cut several thin strips that will be used to reinforce the nose, just as you did for the face and neck lifecast. Premeasure the alginate you will be using into a plastic container. Also premeasure the amount of water you will need into one of your larger plastic containers. You might want to use the 2-gallon bucket even though we're not mixing a large batch of alginate, because the Jiffy-Mixer is likely to cause some splatter. The water temperature should be about 80°F (about 27°C).

Again, you can certainly use cooler water or warmer water; an 80°F (about 27°C) water temperature is comfortable for most people. If you recall, cooler water will cause the alginate to set more slowly; warmer water will accelerate the set time. Cooler water will give you more working time, but I guarantee that warmer water will be more comfortable for your subject. Again, refer to the recommendations of the particular alginate you are using since they may differ somewhat as to the ratio of alginate to water. With many alginates, a ratio of 5–5½ oz. of alginate per 1 lb. (16 oz.) of water will give you a nonrunny, workable mixture that spreads easily and stays where you put it.

EnvironMolds' MoldGel actually mixes best with a ratio of 3.5–4 oz. of alginate per 1 lb. (16 oz.) of water. We'll go with 4 oz. per pound of H_2O; so, for a head and shoulders lifecast, front and back, we will need approximately 40 oz. of alginate, which means we'll need 10 lb. of water (160 oz.). (In case you didn't know, a gallon of water weighs 8.3 lbs. It's math time again for those of you who need help: There are 16 ounces in 1 pound. If we need 4 ounces of alginate per 16 ounces of water, and we need 40 ounces of alginate, simply divide 40 by 4 to get the number of pounds of water we'll need.)

TIP
Suppose you want to use less than a pound of water or less than 4 ounces of alginate (MoldGel). How do you determine how much you need of each material? What is the ratio of alginate to water? It is 4 oz. to 16 oz., or 4 divided by 16, which is .25, or ¼; so a 1:4 ratio. Therefore, if you want to use 2.75 ounces of water, you multiply 2.75 by .25 to get the amount of alginate, or .68 ounces. (There are 28.3495231 grams to 1 ounce; .68 ounces is 19.27 grams, and 28.3495231 multiplied by .68 gives the total in grams.)

We will be using EnvironMolds' MoldGel.® We will need to work relatively quickly, but we do not want to hurry; we can work quickly and still not hurry. When you rush, you make mistakes.

2. Place your subject in a comfortable chair, preferably one that can be raised and lowered. Cover your subject's body and clothing with plastic, carefully attaching the plastic with tape at least an inch below the level of your cast.

3. The next thing we need to do is apply a bald cap to our subject. You can refer to the earlier section for more information on how to put on a bald cap for lifecasting.

4. Next, carefully start to secure the sides and back of the bald cap, making sure the cap will hold before moving on to the next section.

TIP
Cholesterol cream may irritate and sting the eye if used to release eyelashes. A very thin coat of petroleum jelly will prevent such problems.

5. Since we are doing a full head and shoulders lifecast, you need to make sure the bald cap is glued down fully around the head. If your subject has long hair, take the time to flatten it well enough against your subject's head or down the neck so it won't create a bulge that will be a problem to clean up. If hair sticks out below the bottom of the bald cap, be sure to thoroughly release it with cholesterol cream. Lastly, mark your subject's hairline with the eyebrow pencil. This line will transfer to the alginate and then to the Ultracal.

6. Apply a small amount of cholesterol cream or petroleum jelly to your subject's eyebrows, eyelashes, and any other facial hair. Use K-Y® Jelly or petroleum jelly to lightly cover the bald cap 1 inch beyond the line drawn across the top of your subject's head. This will ensure that the alginate will not stick to the bald cap.

7. Before applying the alginate, explain to your subject what the procedure will entail and what the steps are going to be so that there will be no surprises during the lifecasting. It is very important that your subject have no trouble breathing through both nostrils, because the mouth will be completely covered with alginate.

> **TIP**
> It's a good idea to wear a dust mask when mixing batches of alginate, because some alginate contains silica. Breathing silica can lead to serious respiratory problems.

8. Now it's time to mix the alginate. We will begin with the back of the head, neck, and shoulders. Look at the clock or start your timer when you begin to mix the water and the alginate powder so you'll know how much time you have before the alginate begins to set. For this step we'll need to mix half the alginate and half the water: 20 oz. of MoldGel® alginate and 5 lb. (80 oz.) of warm (80°F/27°C) water. Always add the alginate powder to the water, and not vice versa. Properly mixed alginate should not run, but never take anything for granted in such instances. It is also possible that you might need to add a very small amount of water to your alginate if it is too thick. Remember to keep talking to your subject as you spread the alginate, telling her what you're doing and just letting her know that you're still there and haven't gone out for a cup of coffee. Since you will be starting at the back, it will be rather obvious that you're still there.

I've already said that I prefer to wear gloves; I can change gloves quickly and have clean hands immediately to continue working. Keep in mind that room temperature, water temperature, and your subject's body temperature as well as how quickly or slowly you work will all affect the lifecasting. The alginate is also bound to stick to your hands, whether you're wearing gloves or not. I also like to have an extra small bucket of water handy to dip my hands into; that helps keep the alginate from blobbing too much on my hands, which makes it easier to spread.

> **TIP**
> Always start with the back of the subject's head and body so that you have face contact with your subject for the longest period of time possible to keep them engaged, involved, and aware of what is going on.

9. Before spreading any alginate, dip your hands into the water, which will allow you to spread the alginate more easily without it sticking as much to your gloves or your skin. Then take a handful of alginate and begin to *spread* it with your hand, starting at the top of the head where the line is drawn between the ears and move downward on the back of the head toward the shoulders.

10. Spread alginate behind and into the ears (if the ears are not covered by the bald cap) *but not into the ear canal.*

11. Before the alginate sets, add some fuzz while the alginate is still sticky.

12. Once the alginate has set, it is time to apply the plaster bandages to support the alginate. To make the mother mold, you will need to dip the precut strips of plaster into slightly warm water with a pinch of salt. You will definitely want to wear gloves for this task. Fold the plaster strip in half with the plaster side out, giving a double thickness of plaster bandage. Dip it into the water and carefully squeeze out most of the water before applying it to the alginate.

13. When you are finished creating the mother mold, there should be a buildup of about four layers of plaster. Make sure that your plaster strips overlap one another, with the thickest layers on the outside edges. Make your edges as clean as you can make them. Press gently but firmly to make sure that there is no airspace between the alginate and the plaster. If you press too firmly, you risk creating a distortion in the alginate and the resulting stone positive. In addition, if your mother mold is not thick enough, the weight of the stone when you make your positive could distort the shape of the mold, also ruining your cast. It's better to use too much than too little. Plan accordingly.

> **TIP**
> If too much water has been squeezed from the plaster bandage, the cotton fuzz or cheesecloth won't be soaked and the plaster might not adhere to it, causing the mother mold to separate from the alginate mold, potentially resulting in a bad cast.

14. Once the plaster shell has begun to cool, we can prepare to do the front. First clean off any plaster that got onto your subject's face, neck, and shoulders that could interfere with the alginate. Furthermore, if the line of alginate across the head, neck, and shoulders is not straight and neat, you can neaten it by carefully cutting away the offending alginate with a dull palette knife.

15. Next, brush a line of petroleum jelly over the edge of the plaster mother mold, about 2 inches (5 cm) in width. It might help to add a bit of food coloring to tint the petroleum jelly so that it can be easily seen. Since most alginate will not stick to itself once it has set, we only need to make sure that the plaster will not stick to itself and encase your subject in a plaster and alginate case. Tincture of Green Soap is also a good release you can use, as is Murphy's Oil Soap.

16. Now it's time to mix the rest of the alginate. Look at the clock or start your timer when you begin to mix the water and the alginate powder so that you'll know how much time you have before the alginate begins to set.

17. Spread the alginate with your hand; starting at the top of the head, spread the alginate up to and just beyond the alginate on the back half of your subject. Make sure that you get good contact along the edge so that there will be little or no seam between the two halves of alginate. Do this all the way around the edges and then spread alginate everywhere else, moving downward on the face and leaving the nostrils for last.

18. When you get to the subject's eyes, gently press the alginate into the inner corners of the eye and under the eyelashes with your fingertips. Do the same with the eyebrows, getting alginate thoroughly into them. As you apply the alginate, make sure no air is trapped between it and your subject. Use your fingers to follow the contours of your subject's face with the alginate.

19. Do the same with the sides of the face, stopping at the back edge of the ears (getting inside the ears, *but not into the ear canal*), making sure to get good alginate coverage into all the lines and creases in the face. When you cover the mouth, use your fingers to work alginate into the corners of the mouth and between the upper and lower lips. If your subject's mouth is slightly open, that's fine. The goal is to have the subject's mouth in a normal, relaxed position. In fact, if your makeup design includes upper and/or lower lip pieces, having a bit more of the lip exposed during the lifecast will be beneficial during the sculpting phase of your project.

20. Cover as much of the subject's neck as needed for your makeup design. In fact, you need to come down as far in front as you did in back; come straight across the chest in front. Make your coverage as even and symmetrical as possible. Lastly, cover the nose, being careful to keep the nostrils clear. You might want to use a small craft stick to spread the alginate evenly and as closely to the edges of the nostril as possible without creating a blockage. If the alginate does run, carefully lift it back up over the face.

96

TIP
Try having your subject take a deep breath and hold it on your command; cover her nostrils with alginate and tell her to blow out sharply through her nose to reopen the nostrils. Clear any obstructing alginate and then she can breathe normally again. This will result in a very good impression of the nose and nostrils.

If you work quickly, you should have no trouble covering the entire face and neck with one batch of alginate. Try to have an even layer of coverage, with no thin spots. It is especially important to try to get the alginate as thick as possible around the edges, eyes, and nose. In this case, we don't want the edges too thick, because we still have to build the plaster shell for the front half of the mold.

21. Before the alginate sets, add the fuzz or cheesecloth.
22. Now it is time to apply the plaster bandages. Do this just as you did for the back, but overlap the back with the front just up to the edge of the petroleum jelly, not beyond. We need to be able to get the two halves apart. As with the back, when you're finished there should be a buildup of about four layers of plaster. Because we are making a larger mold, you might want to add reinforcing strips of plaster in front and back and along the bottom.

23. When the plaster has begun to cool, draw marks with a Sharpie or other marker to help line up the two halves again when you pour the stone positive. Now it's time to remove the mold from your subject. You might have to wake her up! This is the lifecast during which I have the most people fall asleep because it's dark, quiet, and warm. Just as with the face and neck lifecast, ask your subject to begin puffing out her cheeks and wiggling their face. This will help begin to break any suction between the alginate and skin, and the mold will begin to separate. It will be a bit difficult for her, but have your subject lean forward slightly and help her by cupping her face in her hands while you begin to separate the mold from the back half of the mold and her body. Your subject could feel some resistance on the eyelashes and eyebrows and on any facial hair that was exposed. Not to worry, unless you forgot to release them with cholesterol cream or petroleum jelly! The alginate will let go, though you may find a stray hair or two left in it. Ask your subject to keep her eyes closed because the sudden change in lighting may be uncomfortable after this much time. When you've removed the front half of the mold, set it down somewhere safe and carefully remove the back half.

24. While your subject is getting cleaned up, mix a bit of dental alginate or grab a small chunk of WED clay and carefully plug the mold's nostril holes so as not to deform the shape of the nose. Then put the mold halves back together carefully and secure the halves with duct tape, or you can take the time to wet some more strips of plaster bandage and wrap them around the mold to hold the pieces together. Examine the seam to make sure it is tight. If you've lined up the two halves properly, the seam should be almost invisible.

> **TIP**
> You might want to create a flange and keys made of plaster for the front and back halves of the mold instead of overlapping the front and back; the two halves can then be held together with drywall screws afterward.

FIGURE 3.41
Have your subject help with the removal of the lifecast. Photo by the author.

FIGURE 3.42
When the mold halves are put back together, the seam should be almost invisible. Photo by the author.

FIGURE 3.43
It helps to support the mold so that it can be more easily filled. Photo by the author.

98

FIGURE 3.44
The finished positive (smooth base already added). Photos by the author.

25. Use a large bucket or sturdy box with foam or newspaper (or both) padding in the bottom to support the mold while the stone is poured.

26. Mix a large batch of Ultracal, enough to fill the head cavity up to the neck. It should not be too thick or too runny—about the consistency of a milkshake. There is a formula for mixing Ultracal: The mix-ratio is 38 parts water to 100 parts Ultracal by weight, but I've found—and anyone who works with Ultracal will tell you the same thing—that it's easy to judge your mixture by eye and by feel. (How much you affect the structural integrity of the stone by not following the mix ratio is arguable.) Ultracal is easy to mix by hand; you should definitely wear gloves when working with it. Though the powder is fine, it is still abrasive, and like plaster it will draw moisture from your skin, so over time your skin will dry and crack. I didn't use gloves the first several times I worked with it, and then while I was mixing a batch—for about the eighth or ninth lifecast of the day—I noticed that it was turning pink . . . *Anyway,* when you're mixing the stone, add the Ultracal powder to the water a little at a time so there will be fewer lumps to break up as you mix with your hand. You can use a mixer if you want to, but since Ultracal has such a long working time, speed won't actually gain you anything except quicker lump-free Ultracal.

27. Pour the Ultracal into the mold. With a gloved hand, reach inside and work your hand around the surface of the mold to dislodge air pockets. You can also gently bounce the bucket or box supporting the mold to dislodge air bubbles. Then, with your hand, bring some of the liquid Ultracal up the sides of the mold. We want to create a detail layer in this mold also, before adding layers of Ultracal with burlap. It should be about ⅛ inch to ¼ inch (3–6.5 mm) thick.

28. Once the detail layer has begun to cool, you can begin to add Ultracal with burlap in three or four layers. We want our cast to be hollow because if we were to make it solid, it would be very heavy, unwieldy, and extremely difficult to work with. Your finished stone cast should be no more than an inch thick.

29. Cover the mold with a plastic bag so that it will strengthen during its cure. I've heard that retaining moisture while it heats will make the stone stronger. Whether this is actually true or not, I have not been told by a gypsum expert. As long as it does not purportedly make the stone weaker, there's no reason not to give it a try. Because this is a larger stone cast than the face and neck cast, it will take longer to fully go through its cure process. In about two hours you can demold the bust.

30. With a bit of luck, when you carefully pry apart the plaster and alginate mold halves, your stone bust cast should look just like your subject, only in Ultracal.

31. A bit of cleanup with some sandpaper and a rasp is all that's left; then we'll create a smooth aesthetic base for the bust using a piece of Formica® board or Masonite® or even a piece of sheet plastic.

32. Place the bust on the nonstick and trace around the base with a marker. This line will be the guide for the batch of Ultracal that will be mixed and applied to square off the bottom of the bust, making it smooth and better looking.

33. Mix a batch of Ultracal and apply some of it around the inside of the bust at the bottom. Then place Ultracal along the inside of the traced line on the nonstick surface and put the bust down onto it. As the Ultracal begins to set, take a rubber kidney tool and scrape away the excess, and with a damp paper towel make the edge nice and clean. Once the Ultracal has completely cured, you can easily loosen the bust from the nonstick surface and remove it. A little more cleanup may be needed, and you'll be ready to begin sculpting.

FIGURE 3.45
The bust is placed into fresh stone to create a smooth base. Photo by the author.

34. To save time later, go ahead and drill keys near the base of the bust for lining up the mold. You can use a ¾-inch (19 mm) round router bit in an electric drill to create the keys. Make three in front and three in back.

HANDS, ARMS, LEGS, FEET, AND EARS

The intended end use of hands, arms, legs, and feet will determine how these body parts will be lifecast. If you need the body part in the round, you'll need to cast it one way; if you need only one side, you will cast it another way.

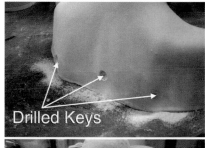

For as small as they are, it's a challenge to lifecast ears. Because of the many severe undercuts, getting a good impression of a model's ears can be difficult, but it's not impossible, obviously. Care must be taken to get the alginate into every nook and cranny of the ear to avoid thin areas and trapped air bubbles.

FIGURE 3.46
Keys drilled into the lifecast will facilitate mold registration later. Photos by the author.

Hands and Arms

More often than not, when it comes to makeup effects for hands and arms, you will find yourself working with hands more often than arms unless the makeup involves much more of the body, such as with a muscle or fat suit, in which case the entire body will likely be cast. With hands, too, unless close-ups will be involved, you might be able to create the necessary effect with nothing more than applying makeup, not prosthetics.

> **TIP**
>
> A few drops of dish soap in
> a spray bottle filled with water creates
> "wet" water; a very small amount of soap
> will remove surface tension and allow
> better surface contact between
> alginate and skin.

> **TIP**
>
> Remember the Goldilocks
> Principle when mixing alginate: If the
> alginate is too thin and runny, you'll get air bubbles;
> if the alginate is too thick you'll get air bubbles. You
> want the alginate to be *just right*. Alginate should be
> thin enough to spread easily but thick enough to
> stay where you put it, with very little or
> no downward movement.

Legs and Feet

Much of the time, you will want to cast your subject with the leg straight, in a standing position; even if you want a leg bent at the knee, the process will be the same. Your subject's comfort is very important for this process because she will need to hold the same position for an extended period of time, so you need to come up with a system in your workspace that will let you make your subject comfortable and still provide you with the room you need to make the lifecast. Even if you encase the leg in one batch of alginate and make a cut to separate the leg and alginate, you will make a two-part mother mold. Creating some sort of keys will help hold the soft mold and rigid mold together in registration.

Ears

Ears are interesting bits of anatomy, and you need to take great care to create a convincing appliance—whether it is an earlobe extension to simulate gauged piercings, ear tips for a fantasy character or alien, or a full ear prosthetic that needs to sell an audience up close.

If you cast a head and shoulders bust, casting ears separately from the head and shoulders lifecast can provide you with ears to complete the head or with base ears from which to create character ears. Let's begin by cutting the bottom off a large deli container about 4½ inches (11.5 cm) in diameter and 3 inches (7.5 cm) deep. Be careful cutting off the bottom of the container!

FIGURE 3.47
Some prosthetics for stage must sell up close. Photo by the author.

1. Cut a slit in a piece of clear plastic sheet (such as from a large lawn bag) about 10 inches by 10 inches (25 cm by 25 cm) and fit it over your subject's ear. You will need a piece for each ear. Use spirit gum of Pros-Aide® to glue the plastic at the edges around the ear for a clean casting. You might need to trim the plastic a bit first so there won't be any wrinkles. Use tape if you need to keep the outside edges of the plastic lying flat.
2. Make a thin line of nose and scar wax or use tape and place it along the larger edge of the plastic container to help prevent alginate from running out.

FIGURE 3.48
Plastic covering the subject's head to prevent alginate from sticking to the hair. Photo by the author.

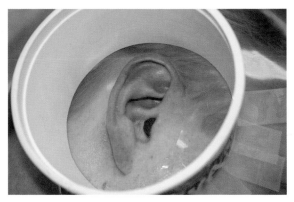

FIGURE 3.49
Ready to fill with alginate. Photo by the author.

3. Have your model's head rested on a table or against his hand so that his head and ear are horizontal, where it must remain until the alginate mold is removed. Though it is not necessary, for your model's added comfort place a piece of cotton or piece of foam earplug into his ear canal to close it.

4. Place the plastic container over your subject's ear and make sure it is centered. Press it and the nose wax down so that it sticks to the plastic. Check for gaps, and seal them with extra wax if necessary.

5. We've been using EnvironMolds alginates and will continue to do so for this task. However, you might decide to use dental alginate because it sets quickly. EnvironMolds has a dental alginate called Hollywood Impressions, and there are others that are listed in the appendix of this book. Accu-Cast® 390 alginate—which is not a dental alginate; it's just quick setting—has a working time of 3 minutes and is also a choice you might consider. Working with warm water, the MoldGel will set pretty quickly. Mix a small batch of alginate by eye—don't worry about the formula here—to a consistency that you can easily pour but not so runny that it's filled with air bubbles. When it's mixed, pour it into the plastic ring of the container until it is about ½ inch (12 mm) past the top of the ear. Use your finger to make sure the alginate gets behind, under, around, and into every bend and fold of the ear. Let the alginate set.

FIGURE 3.50
Alginate ear mold ready to remove. Photo by the author.

6. Next, gently separate the container from the plastic covering your model's face, starting from the front of the ear so that you don't damage the alginate negative. The alginate is fairly thick, so it will not dry and shrink rapidly, but if you want to cast the other ear before making a stone positive, wrap the alginate in wet cloth or paper towels. Then repeat steps 1 through 6 on your model's other ear.

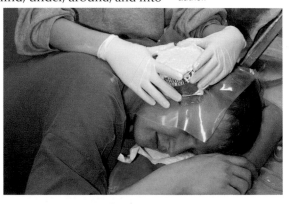

FIGURE 3.51
Thin foam wall supporting Ultracal in the alginate mold. Photo by the author.

7. When you're ready to cast positives of both ears, cut strips of craft foam about 1½-inch wider than your alginate container is thick. Wrap the foam around the plastic container to form a wall and secure it with masking tape, gaffers tape, or duct tape. There should be no gaps between the foam wall and the edge of the container for the Ultracal to seep through.

8. Mix a batch of Ultracal large enough to cast both ears and a base. Don't mix the Ultracal too runny, but you should be able to pour it. Pour the Ultracal slowly into the mold and let it fill up the ear cavity. Before it is completely filled, tilt, tap, and rotate the mold to get the Ultracal into all the spaces. You can also gently squeeze the entire mold to get rid of trapped air pockets. Then continue to fill the mold until the Ultracal is about an inch thick above the alginate. Tap it gently until the air bubbles all disappear, and then let the stone cure.

9. When the Ultracal has cooled, remove the foam wall and the plastic container, which should come off easily. With a dull knife or spatula or a slightly sharpened wooden craft stick (you don't want to scratch or otherwise damage the positive), you can begin to cut away the thickest part of the alginate.

10. When you're certain the Ultracal is fully cured, remove the rest of the alginate a little at a time from front to back so that you don't risk breaking off the Helix and Schaphoid fossa.

11. With a rasp or sandpaper, smooth out any defects or rough areas, and your ear positives are ready for sculpting.

FULL BODY

Why would you want to do a full-body lifecast? I can think of only two reasons that apply to makeup effects work for stage or screen. The first is for the purpose of creating a body or corpse, in which case the task is somewhat easier because the lifecast will most likely be done with the subject in a prone position. The second would be for the purpose of creating a body form that will be used to create a sculpted costume or body suit.

To do a full body, front and back, will require about 15 lbs. of alginate (about $120, or £61.5); to do the same job with a skin-safe silicone will require about 3 gallons of (platinum) silicone. The cost difference between alginate and silicone for a project of this size is enormous. You must know before starting what your time allotment will be to perform the task and whether or not you will need more than one "pull," or copy, from the mold. The advantage to using silicone is that you do not have to make a stone or foam positive from the mold immediately because once silicone has set, it will not dry out and any shrinkage will negligible. With alginate, a positive must be made fairly soon after the alginate mold is removed because it will begin to dry out quickly due to the water it is made with. However, if you need to make multiple copies, you can make a silicone mold from your positive using a much less expensive tin silicone.

Before we go any further, let's also discuss the materials we could use for casting our positives: oil or wax clay, Ultracal 30, plaster, Hydrocal, or urethane. Here are the characteristics of each:

- Sulfur-free oil-based clay or wax-based clay is ideal for melting and brushing into molds where additional takeaway sculpture and texturing may be needed. Often, rigid urethane foam is cast as a reinforcing element to the positive after the clay has been brushed in and allowed to cool. Rigid urethane foam is lightweight and can be quite strong.
- Ultracal 30 has the lowest expansion of any rapid-setting gypsum cement available. Ultracal was designed to give the patternmaking industry the ultimate in a gypsum cement tooling medium. It is also ideal in the makeup effects industry for its ability to withstand repeated heating and cooling, which is necessary when fabricating foam latex appliances. Since prosthetic appliances must fit precisely to sell the illusion of reality and believability, Ultracal is outstanding mold making due to its exceptional hardness and accuracy of detail.
- Impression dental plaster and Lab dental plaster are harder than regular Plaster of Paris; they set faster and have a negligible amount of expansion compared to Plaster of Paris. However, I would not recommend any plaster as a casting medium for prosthetic appliances; in fact, I would not use plaster of any kind for prosthetic fabrication except as a mother mold/shell material or as a core model that will be reworked and molded again.
- Hydrocal® from U.S. Gypsum offers higher strengths than typical plaster products (such as #1 Potter's Plaster, Impression dental plaster), though it is not as strong as Ultracal. It can be used in a variety of arts and crafts applications in addition to makeup effects work. Hydrocal is especially designed for thin sections, which require high green (early) strength to minimize breakage during removal from intricate molds.

Full Body: Prone

To create a dead body lying prone, we first need a live body lying prone. Since we will only be casting one side of a subject, we need less alginate than for a full body front and back. For this task we need about 8 lb. of alginate. Here is a rough list of what you'll need:

8 lbs. of alginate	Clock or timer
Scissors to cut plaster and burlap	4- or 6-inch rolls of plaster bandages (× 2)
Lots of warm water	Thermometer
18-quart roaster oven	Misc. plastic buckets and cups

Latex, vinyl, or nitrile gloves

1-, 2-, and 3-inch chip brushes

Cholesterol conditioner, petroleum
jelly, KY® Jelly

Cotton or cheesecloth (cut in short
pieces)

Loosely woven burlap (cut into
4 × 4-inch and 3 × 6-inch pieces)

2-gallon plastic bucket

Masking, gaffer's, or duct tape

Urethane foam – 1-gallon kit

Oil or wax clay, about 50 lbs.

At least 3 capable helpers

Large craft sticks

Ultracal

Impression dental plaster or #1
Potters Plaster

Rubber kidney tool

Paint stir stick

Utility knife and plaster rasp

1 × 2-inch wood strips, 2½ and
4 inches long (2 each)

Drill with Jiffy-Mixer®

Acrylic bonding agent (Acryl® 60)

Since this is a learning exercise, let's make it an exercise that won't frustrate you to the point of looking for another line of work. How about a corpse laid out on an autopsy table? Seems simple enough. You need a model who won't mind lying absolutely still for a while. You also need a surface large enough for your subject to be posed on, as well as a space large enough to work in comfortably without everyone running into each other like the Keystone Cops! My studio is too small, so we enlisted Dave Parvin's studio, which is quite roomy. There were six of us working, including our model Nicole Feil, one of my former students who is now a visual effects artist working in New York.

If we were to mix all our alginate at once, it would solidify way before we were done applying it to our model. Since we don't want that to happen, we will mix up a smaller amount and add to the alginate we've already applied. Remember that alginate will not stick to itself once it has set up, *unless* we do—what? We need to retard the set. We can do that in one of two ways: (1) We can use colder water, which is usually less comfortable for subjects than warm water (since this particular subject will be modeling for a corpse, we want our skin to be somewhat relaxed, not all hard and goosebumpy), or (2) We can spray our alginate with Algislo® or a solution of baking soda and water to react with the surface of the alginate and make it sticky and able to receive new alginate and stick. We will use this method to also get cotton fuzz and cheesecloth to stick to the alginate for the plaster mother mold.

The positive from this lifecasting session will be different from the ones created up to this point. Instead of making an Ultracal positive, this positive will be only another step toward a finished camera-ready piece. We will make an oil clay skin and urethane foam-core positive. We need to do substantial sculpture work on this positive if we are to have a convincing autopsy subject.

We'll do this lifecast in two stages. Stage one will be a cast of the body minus the head; stage two will be the cast of the head. When both lifecasts are completed, we will put the two molds together and reinforce the seam with plaster before we fill the mold and make our one-piece positive. When the two casts are put together, a layer of melted clay will be brushed into the alginate mold—at least ½ inch in most places, thicker in others, depending on what your ultimate autopsy corpse design entails.

After putting water in the bottom of the roaster oven, you need to put as much of the clay as you can safely put into the top of the roaster and turn the thermostat to just under 200°F (93°C); somewhere between 175°F and 200°F should be fine. It will take a while for the clay to liquefy—probably several hours, depending on which clay you actually use, so plan ahead.

1. Divide the alginate into separate containers with about 1 lb. (16 oz.) of alginate in each; set one of the containers aside for the head. We are using EnvironMolds' FiberGel.® That's eight batches. If we mix the alginate to the ratio of 5 oz. of alginate per lb. of water, we will need 3 lb. 3.2 oz. (51.2 oz.) of 80°F (about 27°C) water for each batch; for the math challenged, that's 3.2 oz. of water per 1 oz. of alginate. It would be ideal to have the water premeasured before starting. (Interestingly, a fluid ounce of water weighs one ounce, so 1 lb. (16 oz.) of water is 16 ounces by volume as well.)

2. You shouldn't need to release your subject's skin with anything—petroleum jelly or cholesterol—unless there is hair present that could get caught in the alginate. If that is the case, work cholesterol or petroleum jelly thoroughly through the hair so that it will release easily when the alginate is removed. Our model Nicole wore an old bikini bottom that she didn't care about; we thoroughly released the fabric with vegetable oil so that the alginate would not impregnate itself into the fabric and would separate easily.

FIGURE 3.52
Nicole covered with FiberGel alginate from EnvironMolds. Photo by the author.

105

3. With your subject comfortably in position, mix one of the batches of alginate and begin to apply it at the neck and work your way down the body, making sure to *spread* the alginate, not just glob it on. Even though we will be doing sculpture work on the positive, we still want to avoid air bubbles and make our cast as good as possible. Be careful to not spread the alginate too thinly. We can add more alginate if necessary, but try to do it evenly to begin with. The alginate should be between ¼ inch and ½ inch (about 6 mm to about 12 mm) thick.

4. While the first batch of alginate is being applied, a second batch should be getting mixed so that it can be applied immediately after the first one, before it has started to set up. While the alginate is being mixed and applied, someone also should be making sure the cotton and cheesecloth will be ready to apply once the alginate has been fully applied.

5. Spray the alginate with Algislo. For best results the surface of the alginate should be sprayed before it sets. This will act as a surface set retarder,

giving you time to apply cotton or cheesecloth on the surface. If that's not possible, the surface should be recently set. Spray the surface rather than using a paintbrush; the results will be more even, and you want to avoid pulling on a tacky area. Rub the Algislo on the alginate with a gloved hand to determine whether it is sticky enough for cotton fuzz and cheesecloth to stick. When it is, dab the cotton onto the alginate and pull back, leaving some of the fuzz, which will be enough for plaster to adhere to. Lightly press cheesecloth onto the alginate, especially near the edges of the alginate.

FIGURE 3.53
Cheesecloth imbedded in alginate, ready to plaster application. Photo by the author.

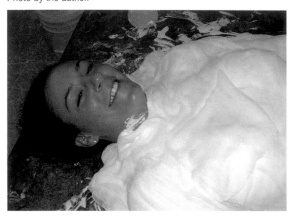

FIGURE 3.54
Wooden supports attached to the plaster shell with plaster bandages. Photo by the author.

6. For the plaster mother mold, you will want to use Impression dental plaster or #1 Potter's Plaster (with terra alba to shorten the set time) as the primary shell and plaster bandages for adhering wood supports after the shell has set. Mix a small bucket of plaster; mix only as much as you can use working fairly quickly, because you don't want the plaster to kick while most of it is still in the bucket. Brush the plaster into the cheesecloth and smooth it as you go. As you brush a layer of plaster onto cheesecloth, have another of your team add more cheesecloth on top of the fresh plaster. While this is taking place, more plaster should be mixed in a new bucket. Remember, if you mix new plaster in a container that has setup plaster in it, the hard plaster will cause the new plaster to kick much more quickly than if it had been mixed in a clean bucket.

7. When the plaster mother mold has set, the mold can be *carefully* removed. We have not built the supports yet. While the model is getting cleaned up and ready for the next step (casting the head), the supports can be attached using the lengths of 1 × 2-inch wood strips. The purpose of these supports is to prevent the mold from buckling or cracking from the weight of the clay, plaster, and alginate when it is repositioned for attaching the head and then for removing the positive once the mold has been filled. One long piece should be positioned along the torso and leg on each side of the mold. The shorter pieces are to be laid across the log pieces and screwed together. Once the four pieces of wood are attached to each other, they need to be attached to the plaster mother mold. Plaster bandages wet in 50/50 mixture of water and acrylic bonding agent can be wrapped around the wood joints and pressed onto the plaster shell to form a strong bond.

8. Mix up a batch of plaster using the same 50/50 mixture of water and acrylic bonding agent and spread it over the wood joints and plaster bandages to give the mold a really strong connection between the wood and the plaster shell.

9. Now it's time to cast our subject's head so that we can attach it to the body. Since we used Dave Parvin's studio space for this project, we'll also use one of his techniques for casting a head: no bald cap. Dave's lifecasting is almost exclusively for the cast to become artwork, so incorporating the subject's hair into the cast is usually critical when the head is involved. Since we are going to do extensive resculpting once our positive is made, it is really irrelevant whether the hair is there or not. Cholesterol is thoroughly worked through the subject's hair so that there will be no problem removing the alginate cast. Then casting the face proceeds normally. Notice the fibers in the FiberGel® that give it remarkable tear strength.

FIGURE 3.55
Nicole's face covered with alginate. Photo by the author.

10. We leave the nose for last, making sure to keep the nostrils clear before pressing cotton fuzz into the alginate and then letting it set up.

11. Plaster is applied to the alginate and cotton fuzz, just as with the body. Plaster is brushed onto the fuzz; cheesecloth is laid into it and layers built up until we have three or four layers of plaster and cheesecloth. Our mother mold is about ½ inch (about 12 mm) thick.

12. When the plaster has cured, it's time to wake up our model and remove the cast from her head. It should come right off, with marginal pull, if any, against the hair. Nicole's job is done; while she showers off and gets ready to leave, the head and body can be assembled.

13. Some minor trimming might be necessary to line up the neck seams on both molds, and then some fresh plaster can be mixed—either #1 Potter's Plaster and cheesecloth or plaster bandages—and the seams bonded.

14. After the plaster seam has cured, carefully flip the mold and support it underneath with foam, rags, crumpled newspaper, or anything you have handy to keep it level and wobble-free.

15. Open the roaster oven (someone should have been checking periodically to see how melted the clay is) and begin to brush the clay into the alginate mold with the large chip brushes. Be careful to make good contact against the alginate with the clay when it is brushed in so as to not leave gaps and air pockets. Toes and fingertips might be especially tricky to get clay fully into. Build up the clay thickness to ½ inch through most of the mold, thicker where you will do takeaway sculpting—for a traumatic wound, perhaps. We used close to 50 lbs. of clay in the mold. The next step is to fill the remaining cavity with rigid urethane foam. We used Smooth-On's Foam-It!® 5 urethane foam that is a 1:1 mix ratio by volume and expands to seven or eight times its original volume; a little goes a long way.

107

FIGURE 3.56
Cotton fuzz is attached while the alginate is still sticky. Photos by the author.

FIGURE 3.57
Properly released, the alginate mold should come off easily, even without a bald cap. Photos by the author.

FIGURE 3.58
Alginate body mold ready for melted clay to be brushed inside. Pictured are Dave Parvin, Kelly Rooney, and Elliot Summons. Photo by the author.

16. Mix small batches at a time and pour it into the mold, brushing it into the mold until you see it begin to rise. It becomes tack-free in several minutes and develops handling strength in about 20 minutes. Full cure is 2 hours; the foam goes through a heat reaction during its cure also. If you pour freshly mixed foam liquid onto risen foam that has not begun to solidify, it could collapse, so be aware of that as you work.

17. Since quite a bit of melted clay was put into the mold and the foam also generated heat during its cure, it would be a good idea to let the mold cool overnight and demold the positive the next day. At the very least, you should wait several hours before attempting to demold the clay and foam positive. If the clay is not completely cooled and back to its restive state of hardness, you could damage the positive when you begin to peel away the plaster shell and alginate.

18. You might need to do some sanding or cutting to flatten the foam backing so that your positive cast will lie flat when it is turned over to remove the mold.

19. Take your time removing the plaster and alginate. The plaster is quite hard and will require effort to cut and pull it away without damaging the positive.

Now you have a full body cast of a prone body. There is still much work to be done, but now the real fun can begin!

Full Body: Standing

Creating a front and back standing body form is not as difficult as it sounds. It can be achieved with the subject clothed or unclothed, with little difference in the end result. Much will depend on your model's level of modesty and what is required for the final product. Any clothing the model wears must be thin and form-fitting, such as a spandex bathing suit.

Lifecasting is a critical part of creating prosthetic makeup effects for theater, television, and film as well as props and animatronics. The steps outlined in the previous pages are certainly not the be-all and end-all of lifecasting techniques. As I've mentioned, there are many ways to accomplish the same task. After completing your own application of these processes, you are certain to discover a way that will suit you well.

Here are a few lifecasting tips and suggestions to keep in mind:

- Spread the alginate when applying it; you'll get fewer bubbles when spreading than when just laying it on.
- Add fuzz—cotton from a roll—before the alginate sets, while it is still sticky; cotton fuzz sticks to the alginate and gives the plaster something to adhere to.
- Try cheesecloth instead of cotton.
- To repair alginate tears or to add two coats, use Algislo or a baking soda/water solution to soften the alginate enough for new alginate to stick to it.
- Try using Impression dental plaster or Lab dental plaster with cheesecloth instead of plaster bandages.
- Use terra alba to get your plaster to set faster. A pinch of salt in the water will also help plaster set faster; slightly warm water will make plaster set faster, and *hot* water will actually inhibit the set of plaster.
- A small amount of white vinegar will slow the set of plaster.
- Use plaster-coated rolled cheesecloth along the outer edges of a mother mold to add strength.
- Mix 50 percent acrylic fortifier with 50 percent water to mix plaster for a stronger plaster or Ultracal.
- The warmer the water used to mix alginate, the faster it will set up; cooler or cold water will give you longer working time.
- Rule of thumb with most alginates (some of EnvironMolds' alginates need only 3–3.5 oz. of alginate per 1 lb. of water): 5 oz. of alginate to 1 lb. of water will prevent the alginate from running. A full torso (front) will use 40 oz. of alginate and 8 lbs. of water (1 gallon of water weighs roughly 8 lbs.).
- If you're casting with clothing, use vegetable oil as a fabric release.

FIGURE 3.59
The plaster and alginate are carefully peeled away to reveal the finished clay figure. Photos by the author.

109

CHAPTER SUMMARY

This has been a lengthy chapter with lots of information to retain. Fortunately there is considerable repetition and redundancy within the chapter. So you should now be familiar with:

- How to safely make good dental impressions
- Lifecasting using alginate vs. lifecasting with skin-safe platinum-cure silicone
- The safety risks involved with lifecasting
- The materials needed for various types of lifecasts
- Making gypsum and plaster positives
- Mixing ratios and determining material amounts
- The various methods and the overall process of creating a lifecast for special makeup effects

CHAPTER 4
Sculpting the Makeup

Key Points

- Materials
- Preparation
- Sculpting tools: Making your own
- Types of clay
- Sculpting: Blocking, refining, and finishing

INTRODUCTION

By now you should be more than ready to get some clay under your finger-nails. However, before any sculpting for a prosthetic appliance can begin, the positive that you'll be sculpting on must be properly cleaned up and prepared, and you will need to have your tools and other materials ready so that you can work without interruption and not continually be looking for something you need. Having a prepared workspace with everything you need in plain sight and within reach will maximize your efficiency. I can't do anything without music playing in the background, so there's that to consider, too.

MATERIALS

You might not need all the materials listed here, but they are all commonly used in the procedures discussed in this chapter:

Chavant® Le Beau Touché oil clay
Ultracal positive

Rotating sculpture stand
Misc. sculpting tools: wood and metal

Freeman sheet wax
Misc. small brushes
Cat or dog hair brush
Lighter fluid, mineral spirits,
    Naphtha, or WD-40®
Baby powder
Serrated scraper

Cut and uncut chip brushes
Plastic wire brush
Plastic toothpicks
Toothbrush

Reference photos
Heavy plastic sheet

 Mark Alfrey

Like a great many kids, Mark was fascinated with the stop-motion animation of *King Kong* (1976), but he switched gears with the arrival of the 1980s genre of horror films. "I was a big George Romero fan and I thought Tom Savini's work was great! I always loved magic and that was the impressive thing about Savini's effects—the magic elements. He used visual tricks to make you think you were seeing what he wanted you to see."[1]

Mark developed skill as a sculptor as a youngster and upon graduation from high school moved to California to pursue a career in special makeup effects, earning his first credits on *Critters 2* and *Demonwarp*. Mark moved back to New Jersey, where he'd grown up, and had the good fortune to meet artist John Dods, perhaps best known for creating makeup effects for the Beast in Broadway's *Beauty and the Beast*. Mark worked with John on several film, television, and theater projects and, with a heftier body of work to show, moved back to California in 1995. Since then Mark has racked up credits including *Babylon 5, Buffy the Vampire Slayer, Deep Rising, A Kiss Before Dying, The X Files, From Dusk Till Dawn, Men in Black, Dogma, Grey's Anatomy*, and *300*.

Mark has worked with and learned from some of the best artists and shops our industry has to offer, including KNB, Optic Nerve, John Vulich, Rob Bottin, and Rick Baker. He says, "Rob Bottin was great to work with because he never held my hand. He usually likes to give you inspiration; he would sit and talk for an hour about what he needed to be sculpted. Then he let you go where you could go."[2]

In 2001 Mark began producing a series of instructional DVDs to share his vast knowledge and experience with other artists, myself included. Mark is a generous artist and teacher and continues to work a very busy schedule in Hollywood as well as training new artists for work in the field of special makeup effects. Mark is one of Hollywood's most sought-after character designers and sculptors and is also an outstanding makeup artist.

FIGURE 4.1
Mark Alfrey working on a figure sculpture. Image reproduced by permission of Mark Alfrey.

[1] "The Creature Walks Among Us—Thanks to Mark Alfrey," by Daniel Roebuck, *HorrorShow Magazine*, Issue #3.
[2] "The Creature Walks Among Us—Thanks to Mark Alfrey," by Daniel Roebuck, *HorrorShow Magazine*, Issue #3.

PREPARING THE POSITIVE

Putting that first piece of clay onto a lifecast to create something new is a great feeling. But first, there is a bit of cast preparation to do. I will presume that your lifecast positive has been cleaned up—minor imperfections repaired and edges smoothed and rid of any roughness. Often it is necessary to brush a very light layer of petroleum jelly over the surface of your stone positive, then rub it into the surface; this will help the oil clay adhere to it. Make sure that there is no dust left over from your cleanup of the positive before you apply the petroleum jelly. If there is, wipe the cast with a damp cloth or paper towel to remove dust or tiny pieces of Ultracal that might mix with the petroleum jelly and make a gritty or otherwise yucky surface.

TOOLS

There is no set number or type of tools to use for sculpting your makeup. That, I imagine, is pretty obvious. What might not be obvious are the tools themselves. They could be expensive store-bought tools; they might be home-made jobs or even found objects. I'm sure Jordu Schell and Mark Alfrey have sculpted entire heads with nothing more than a Popsicle stick. In fact, I've watched character designer Jordu Schell create a creature sculpture from start to finish in less than a full day, and it looked great!

If you're interested in some DIY sculpting tools, they're very easy to make and inexpensive. Go to your favorite hobby store—mine is Caboose Hobbies in Denver (perhaps the biggest and best model railroad store on the planet!) —and pick up some 1/8-inch (3 mm) or 3/16-inch (4 mm) brass tubing (or steel, or aluminum) and some 1/32-inch (1 mm) wire; then swing by Guitar Center or Musician's Friend and buy an inexpensive set of heavy guitar strings —they can be acoustic or electric. One last stop at Ace, True Value, Lowe's, or The Home Depot for scroll-saw or band-saw replacement blades.

You will also need a few tools to help you make your new sculpting tools:

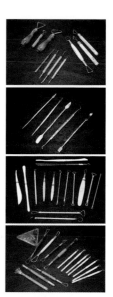

FIGURE 4.2
Numerous tools are available for sculpting. Photos by the author.

113

FIGURE 4.3
Creature designer Jordu Schell working on his Stonehenge Demon at IMATS in London, 2008. Photo by the author.

FIGURE 4.4
Homemade sculpting tools: brass tubing and guitar string. Photo by the author.

Soldering torch	Solder
Pliers	Wire snips
Dremel® with a cutting wheel	Bending pliers

1. Cut the tubing into 4½- or 5-inch (11.5 cm to 12.5 cm) lengths with the Dremel®.
2. For a rough loop, cut a length of the low E string (the fattest wound string) about 2½ inches (6.35 cm) long and bend it into a triangular shape. Cut another length the same and bend it into a U shape.
3. Fit both ends of one piece of the bent wire into one end of the 3/16-inch (5 mm) tube and make sure it's in as far as you want it; you do not want it to be so far out that you will risk bending and breaking it off at the tubing when working with it later. Crimp the tubing shut around the guitar string with your pliers and solder it in place. This will also add strength at the join point. Repeat for the other end with the other piece of E string.
4. For other loop tools, use the 1/8-inch (3 mm) tubing and the other guitar strings, repeating the process in Steps 1–3. Create whatever shapes you need for carving, blending, and shaping.
5. To create a rake tool using the saw blade, you will need to heat the blade with your soldering torch so that the blade will not snap as you bend it. Bend the blade slowly (so that it won't snap) into the curve you want for it. Then cut it with the wire snips or the Dremel. I shouldn't have to remind you to wear safety glasses when you're using the Dremel, but I will anyway. Wear safety glasses!
6. Stick the ends of the bent blade into the tubing, crimp, and solder. You might need to file down some of the blade's teeth to fit into the tube end if the blade is too big. You can do that with your Dremel.
7. Another tool that could come in handy is what I call a wrinkle rake. It consists of several pieces of guitar string stuck into the ends of a 1/8-inch (3 mm) piece of tubing, crimped, and soldered. This is a terrific tool for creating lip wrinkles, eye wrinkles, and any number of various creases and wrinkles on the skin.

The most common tools you will use for your sculpture are rakes, wires (loops), steels (scrapers), and hoggers. Rakes are serrated tools used for removing clay efficiently. Wires or loops are useful for intricate detail work and don't need much pressure to remove clay from the sculpture. Steels or scrapers are used to smooth out the sketched-in clay that has been raked. Some steels also have serrated edges and can be used as rakes to blend bits of clay, removing unwanted highs and lows on the clay surface. Hoggers are essentially large wire tools—more blade than wire—used for removing large hunks of clay. I use them mainly for cutting chunks of clay off the supply block to add to the sculpture.

Clay

I've already mentioned that I think it's a good idea to get into the habit of never using clay with sulfur in it, whether you're using silicone for your appliances or not, for the simple fact that sulfur will inhibit the cure of just about every type of silicone.

SULFUR CLAY: JUST FORGET IT

If you are intending to cast silicone appliances for your makeup...well, anything that has come into contact with the sulfur-infused clay will prevent silicone from curing. I've heard rumors that it's not even a good idea to say the word *sulfur* around uncured silicone! I hope I haven't upset the sulfur clay aficionados out there, but facts are facts, and sulfur and (uncured) silicone just do not play well together. So why do manufacturers put sulfur in clay at all if it is so bad for curing silicone? According to Chavant®, maker of Professional Plastiline, NSP, Le Beau Touché, and Da Vinci Italian Plastilina, sulfur is used in some of its clays because it is an inexpensive nontoxic filler that enhances the surface texture of the clay, giving it a unique, silky feel.

WED CLAY

Perhaps you're a water clay lover and want to use WED (for Walter Elias Disney) clay or other water-based clay for your sculpting. Just beware of the pros and cons before starting so that you don't wind up screaming bloody murder when your clay dries out and cracks into chunks or is so wet it resembles a California mudslide. Lightly spritzing your clay with a bit of water from a small spray bottle or using a mixture of water and glycerin will keep your clay nice and workable.

An advantage of water clay over oil clay is its ability to take texture stamps more easily with less pressure. You do need to be careful not to press so hard as to alter the shape of your sculpture when you press the stamp into the clay. If the clay is too wet, the stamp will simply make a smear; just when your clay starts to begin to feel leathery is a great time for carving and shaping your design and for using texture stamps. Water clay is also very easy to work with quickly because it is so soft. A design can be roughed out in a relatively short amount of time. If you are relatively new to sculpting, I suggest you practice with WED clay because it is easy to work with. Try roughing up some anatomy studies in WED before moving on to the harder, more difficult-to-work-with oil clay.

OIL CLAY

Chavant® Le Beau Touché is the oil clay I prefer to use; it is popular clay among many makeup effects artists, including Mark Alfrey and Neill Gorton. It's a firm clay, but it is easily warmed for malleability and takes texture stamps fairly easily without damaging the sculpt by pressing firmly into the clay surface. Oil clay can also be melted and poured or brushed, but I'll talk more about that later. Artists use other clays; a listing of materials is included in the appendix at the back of this book. Le Beau Touché is not the firmest clay to work with, but it's probably the firmest you will want to work with unless you are also involved in sculpting prototypes and models for props: armor, weapons, and the like. For that kind of work I suggest a material called Casteline, a wax-based clay that is very hard (some say very difficult to work with, too); it's available through The Compleat Sculptor. (See the appendix for contact information.) There are also numerous industrial design clays that are very hard and are ideal for carving, shaping, and styling extremely detailed models; some are even de-aired; entrapped air is removed, making the clay more dense, smoother, and great for achieving fine extrusions. Like the oil clays used by makeup effects designers, some of these clays can also be melted and poured or brushed into molds. Chavant® makes a very lightweight, hard sulfur free clay called Y2-Klay that is outstanding for sculpting extremely fine detail.

Reference Photos

Trying to sculpt from memory alone is difficult at best, and practically impossible if your skill level is below "expert." Maybe your ego won't let you "cheat" by looking at photos that represent portions of what you are going to create, but I don't know an artist worth his or her salt who doesn't maintain a "morgue" filled to overflowing with images of all sorts—eyes, ears, noses, lips, hands, teeth, wrinkles, scars, scabs, pimples, cleft chins, turkey necks, age spots, pores, moles, and so on. You name it. In the digital age, I suppose those magazine pages are supplemented with Googled pictures downloaded from the Internet. "Ask and ye shall receive!" It all depends on what you need to augment your memory and make your design interesting and appropriate for the character.

If you have a digital camera, you might even want to go out on your own in search of interesting faces and bodies to add to your reference library, if you aren't already doing just that. Be sure to be polite when asking if you can take someone's photograph; don't approach someone with a wonderfully weathered face full of character and say, "Ma'am, I've never seen wrinkles like that except on an elephant!" and expect to get a favorable response. But to be on the safe side, have a supply of photo releases at the ready, or snap unobtrusively and discretely from afar with a telephoto lens if your people skills need work. But as a makeup effects artist, I certainly hope that isn't the case!

TEETH

If teeth are going to be a part of your character makeup, they need to be completed first, before a lifecast is done of your actor's face. If the teeth are not done before the lifecast is taken and if they aren't worn when the lifecast is made, the makeup will not fit correctly when the teeth are put in, because the face will then deform and cause the makeup to buckle or wrinkle improperly. Completing the teeth first is a priority.

Materials

Dental articulator	Petroleum jelly
Small sculpting tools	Mineral spirits
Small fine brush	Al-Cote® dental separator

Take the upper and lower teeth positives you made in Chapter 3 and rub on or lightly brush a little petroleum jelly to help the clay stick to the stone. For this, I'll use Chavant Le Beau Touché sulfur-free oil-based clay.

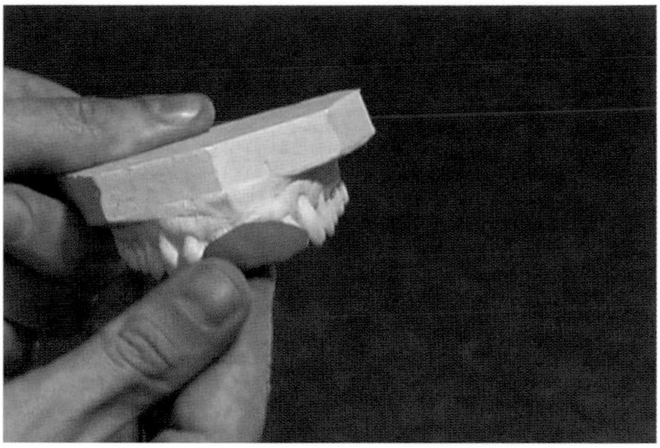

1. Place bits of tooth-shaped clay over each tooth on the positive; keep the thickness close to the thickness and shape you want the finished teeth to be. Keep in mind that your actor probably won't want to have to take speech lessons to learn to speak all over again when wearing these new choppers!

2. Anchor the clay to the positive with a sculpting tool and remember to anchor the underside, too.

3. Start creating the gum line with small sausages of clay and smooth the clay with one of your tools. We're still roughing everything in at this point.

4. Next, start defining the tooth root structure. You can even begin to do some preliminary smoothing with a small brush dipped in a very small amount of mineral spirits, WD-40, or lighter fluid to soften the clay.

5. To maintain strength in the new teeth, you might want to mark a piece of wire to show a depth of 1 mm; if your tooth sculpt is less than that, you risk breakage of the finished piece anywhere the thickness is less than 1 mm.

6. Periodically check the bite with the uppers and lowers to ensure that your actor's mouth will close correctly. The proper dental term for this is *occlusion*.

7. If you're doing lower teeth as well as uppers, your job will be doubly difficult because you want to create dentures that will be strong, will allow your actor to speak or sing, *and* will maintain normal occlusion.

8. When you've finished sculpting the new dentures, you are ready to mold and cast them, which will be covered in Chapters 5 and 6.

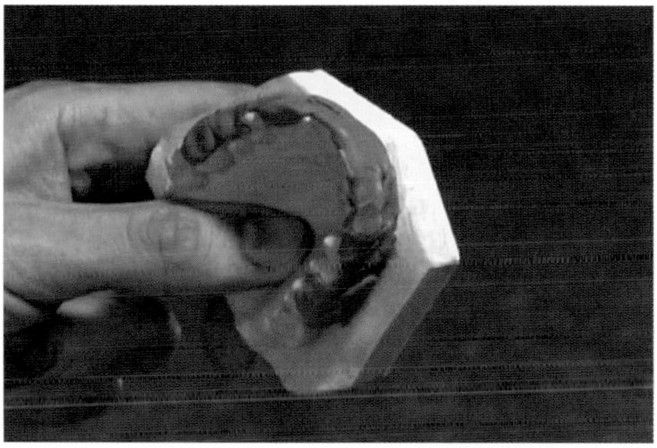

FIGURE 4.5
Beginning to sculpt new dentures on stone impression. Image reproduced by permission of Mark Alfrey.

FIGURE 4.6
New teeth being sculpted. Image reproduced by permission of Mark Alfrey

117

SCULPTING THE FACE

I don't draw nearly as much as I ought to and as a consequence my skills aren't nearly as good as I would like them to be. That's partly to do with being an artist; I don't ever particularly think my work is as good as it could be, but it's also partly because I'm not very good at saying no and there's always a lot on my plate. Anyway, the point I'm trying to make is that rather than work from sketches of a

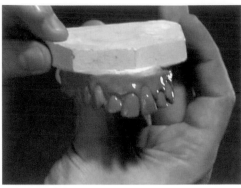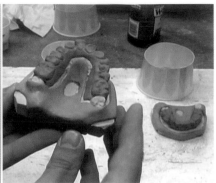

FIGURE 4.7
Finished teeth sculpt ready for molding. Images reproduced by permission of Mark Alfrey.

particular makeup design, as many artists do, I prefer to take what I see in my head and begin directly with sculpture. Whether you work from sketches, photos, 3D renderings from ZBrush,® or images printed from your mind's eye, the process is essentially the same. There's no right way or wrong way to sculpt a character makeup, but there are some steps and tips I will share that I have learned over the years, some from artists who have contributed a great deal to this book.

If you are going to be creating a multipiece, overlapping makeup, you need to coat your stone positive with two or three thin layers of Al-Cote® dental separator (and let it dry) before you begin to sculpt. Why? Because once you've decided how the sculpture will be broken up, you need to be able to get those pieces separated from the positive and from each other without destroying them. To do that your finished sculpt will need to be soaked in water to float off the clay pieces so they can be resculpted. Don't fret; this task will be covered in the next chapter. This design is a one-piece face and neck, with a separate lip piece and separate ears.

FIGURE 4.8
Lifecast ready for sculpting. Photo by the author.

Blocking the Sculpture

Follow these steps:

1. Place the positive of your actor's face, also known as a *buck*, upright on the sculpture stand so that it will be easy for you to work with. Take a good look at the cast and become familiar with the face.

This is the blocking stage, the roughing stage. Neill Gorton suggests simply picking out features and details that you want to translate from the lifecast to the sculpture. Take a pencil and lightly, loosely draw lines on the face that correspond to lines on the cast to make them more obvious for when you begin to place clay on the cast. If you sculpt lines that are counter to where the face will actually move and bend, creases in the face will not move and deform correctly and it will look wrong. It will *be* wrong.

This is an ideal time for your knowledge of facial anatomy to kick in. Remember that skin develops creases and wrinkles that are perpendicular to the direction that the underlying muscle pulls. I think it's a good idea to have a small makeup mirror nearby when you're working, so you can use your own face for additional reference. Take a moment now and look in the mirror; make an exaggerated, forced smile and notice the way wrinkles and creases appear on your face against the pull of your facial muscles. If the makeup you've decided to sculpt is of an older character, you can incorporate the way the skin will begin to sag and hold wrinkles and creases because there is less elasticity in the skin.

FIGURE 4.9
It helps to have photos for age reference. Image reproduced by permission of istockphoto.com.

2. Begin to place bits of clay on the cast where you've drawn lines. This is the roughing-in stage of the sculpture and can be done with just clay and your fingers. You might find it useful, if not absolutely necessary, to have at least one reference photo visible near your sculpture, with features similar to what you are trying to recreate on your actor's cast. You might even have several reference images to work from. Try not to have so many that you stop using your instinct, your own vision, for the sculpture. There are so many different ways skin can bend and simply be that your inspiration can become blurred and unfocused. Find one representative inspirational image if you can, and look at others only when you get stuck for a particular shape, wrinkle, crease, or fold.

3. You might want to use a small tool or two to help press the bits of clay together, but continue to place bits and pieces of clay—Neill rolls out small pieces, "sausages" of clay, he aptly calls them—along the natural lines and folds of the face where the pencil lines have been drawn, along the forehead, the cheekbone, and so on. This is a very early stage of sculpting, you're blocking it, and it will begin to take a coherent shape bit by bit, piece by piece. At this stage you can work fairly quickly because you are merely blocking out the shape, creating an overall impression of what it will eventually become.

119

FIGURE 4.10
The sculpture is beginning to take shape. Photos by the author.

4. At this point, there should be clay over most of the face, and you can use one of your wooden shaping tools to begin sketching lines in the clay where eventually you will place details in the skin: finer lines and wrinkles. Here is where, once you've built up clay on the face to create new features—the nose, cheeks, brow, and eyelids—you can begin to blend the pieces of clay together into more of a whole. You've placed the face cast on a stand that you can rotate. It is important to be able to rotate your sculpture easily so that it can be seen from different angles quickly (even upside down) to ensure relative symmetry on both sides of the face.

5. Take one of your wooden tools and begin a light crosshatch over the chunks of clay that you placed with your hands; you will "rake" the surface with the wooden tool and start to smooth and blend rough areas into more of a whole. You don't necessarily want to redefine what you've already done but to refine the rough spots, to unify your sculpt. Sculpture is about working from the outside in – creating rough shapes, then making them more and more detailed in stages until you ultimately have a finished sculpt that is ready to be molded and cast in an appliance material.

6. Continue adding clay and blending it until your entire sculpture is blocked, until all the main features and shapes have been created and clay is everywhere that it needs to be. When the sculpture is roughed in completely, you can begin to refine it further.

120

Refining the Sculpture

It can't be emphasized enough that the process of sculpting prosthetics demands that the sculpture be defined by the face underneath. Someone, an actor, must wear it and emote through it. A certain amount of the work—the *art* of sculpting prosthetics—is a *feel* when something is or isn't right, and that can only come about through practice—through the act of sculpting. A *lot* of sculpting. It should not be forced.

FIGURE 4.11
Refining the sculpture with a medium rake tool. Image reproduced by permission of Neill Gorton.

1. Since we are beginning to refine the sculpture, you need to refine your tool selection, choosing tools that will allow you to create finer nuances in the sculpt. You might want to try a medium rake tool or loop tool to go over the surface, creating areas of slightly more definition.

2. After you've gone over the sculpture to some degree, take the plastic wire brush (plastic bristles) and lightly brush over the surface where you've been working with the rake and loop tools. Essentially what you are doing is removing tool marks left by the loop and rake. Repeat steps 7 and 8; carve in some detail, then brush over it to remove tool marks. Create lines, but remove bumps and lumps and unwanted tool marks. The plastic bristle brush will likely leave bits of clay on the surface of the sculpt as you brush; you can get rid of these by lightly whisking them away with a chip brush.

FIGURE 4.12
A plastic bristle brush can be used to soften harsh lines created by a pet brush raked across the clay. Photo by the author.

FIGURE 4.13
A cut-down chip brush with talcum powder can further soften and refine skin texture. Photo by the author.

Skin texture is like skin coloration; it is multifaceted and multilayered. There is texture within texture within texture. There is depth to the wrinkles. Some are sharp, some are soft. Some are deep, some shallow. Skin wrinkles and creases are varied. Don't fall into a trap of making all the wrinkles and folds the same depth or length. The more varied and nonuniform, the better. At this stage of the sculpture, you're still using the equivalent of medium-grit sandpaper.

121

3. Pour some of the solvent into a cup and, with a chip brush, brush over the surface of your sculpture. The liquid will soften the clay; break down the surface to smooth out any blemishes. You will probably want to use a smaller-detail brush to get into tighter areas of detail on the sculpture because the partially dissolved clay becomes slurry and the chip brush could be too large to effectively get into the tighter spots and brush it out.

4. Some of the detail you created will likely soften too much with this step, so you will need to go in with one of your small loop tools and recarve that detail, then brush over it with a soft brush to take some of the hardness of the crease away.

5. Brushing lighter fluid or other softening liquid onto your clay will keep the clay soft for several hours, most likely, until all the solvent has evaporated. It might be advisable to let the sculpture sit overnight to ensure that the surface will be hard enough to work with again and not be too soft and sticky.

6. When you come back to it, brush talcum powder or baby powder over the entire sculpture where you had brushed the solvent to soften the clay. Why? Because now you're going to use the pet brush on the clay. Notice as you run the brush across the clay that it creates and leaves behind lots of tiny beads of clay that the wires of the brush have scraped up.

FIGURE 4.14
Powder causes clay to bead up when raked with a stiff brush instead of being smeared across the sculpture. Photo by the author.

If the surface doesn't have powder on it, all the tiny lumps of clay will stick to the sculpture and be nearly impossible to remove. When the clay has been powdered first, you can take one of your chip brushes and whisk them away. I've even used pieces of stipple sponge to knock away these bits of clay. The powder also acts as a very mild abrasive that will allow you to take a chip brush that's been cut down, making it a bit stiffer, and brush back over the lines created by the pet brush to soften them.

7. Some of the lines created by the pet brush might be a little too harsh, so you can go over those with the plastic bristle brush or a toothbrush and continue to refine and increase your detail in the sculpture, underlying texture. You should really be able to see the texture upon texture I mentioned after step 2. You'll be adding pore texture shortly.

The texture of human skin varies across the face. The skin of your forehead is different, thinner, than the skin on your cheeks, which is different from the skin on your nose or your neck. This is why studying surface anatomy is very important to us as artists; we must work from a foundation of reality to create a realistic, albeit often stylized believability, in our makeup design and in our sculpture.

8. You can repeat steps 6 and 7 over and over again, even using a very small amount of solvent on the clay to brush out some detail and then create even more detail by carving with a tiny loop tool, powdering, and repeating the process again until the sculpture has the look and feel you are going for. Create fine lines, coarse lines, sharp lines, and soft lines and brush them each back in succession so that you have a skin texture with layers and layers of lines and wrinkles.

FIGURE 4.15
Layered wrinkle texture. Photo by the author.

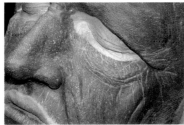

I can't tell you when your sculpture is complete; only you can know that. However, you should be getting pretty close, which would be time to add some pore texture. One way to add pores is with a texture stamp. Brushing several layers of latex over an orange peel until you have a fairly thick piece of rubber with bumps on it is frequently used as a texture stamp; its pattern is somewhat random, but in actuality, for skin pores, I think it's too uniform, and you need to do it by hand, without using texture stamps. By all means, experiment and make your own choice. There is no prescribed way to do this work; you must find methods that work for you and give you the results that you want, not what I or anyone else wants. Here I am merely presenting options and ways that I know work well.

Pores are not always uniformly round; some are deep and some almost invisible. Pores on the face are often an oval shape. They are elliptical and elongated. They also follow the direction of the skin. The same goes for facial hair or whisker follicles. These pores will all be sculpted by hand, and there's no quick and easy way to do it except as carefully and as randomly as you can.

9. Pick one of your small tools, perhaps a small loop or a small burnishing tool, and begin making small indentations across the nose with the tip. Brush them back, softening them, then make some more. You can use a sharper tool, such as a toothpick, and poke it into your thick plastic that you've laid over the clay. Create varying depths of these pores. Then brush those pores back, making them softer. Repeat this process until you're satisfied, then move on to another part of the face, such as the cheeks.

10. Because the pores need to follow the direction in which the skin is hanging, the elongated pores need to be vertical and not horizontal. Try it if you like and I think you'll see that it just feels wrong. You might want to use a narrow tool such as a dental spatula poked into the plastic that can give you a very thin pore. When you brush them with powder and a chip brush, brush in the direction of the skin and the pores, not across. If you need to add more lines, do it. At this point you are creating almost the last bits of detail. Continue to add pores until you don't need to add any more. Gently brush away any imperfections with powder and a chip brush.

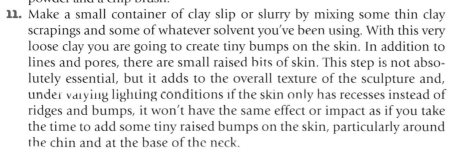

FIGURE 4.16
Nose pore texture. Photo by the author.

11. Make a small container of clay slip or slurry by mixing some thin clay scrapings and some of whatever solvent you've been using. With this very loose clay you are going to create tiny bumps on the skin. In addition to lines and pores, there are small raised bits of skin. This step is not absolutely essential, but it adds to the overall texture of the sculpture and, under varying lighting conditions if the skin only has recesses instead of ridges and bumps, it won't have the same effect or impact as if you take the time to add some tiny raised bumps on the skin, particularly around the chin and at the base of the neck.

The bumps will shrink as the solvent evaporates, and you might need to add more. The effect is well worth the time it takes to add this additional detail to your sculpture. Of course, how much of this you'll be able to do will be completely dependent on how far you are able to sculpt on the neck.

FIGURE 4.17
Bumps added with clay slurry—clay dissolved in mineral spirit. Image reproduced by permission of Neill Gorton.

12. The last step before molding your sculpture will be to make certain all your edges are as fine as you can make them. Perhaps I should have mentioned this earlier, but I think it's a good idea to turn the sculpture upside down and look at it from underneath. This is a good way to see if there is anything wrong with your sculpture that hasn't been readily evident from looking at it normally, from above. Everything is probably fine, but better safe than sorry, right?

Barring any unforeseen need to do any additional sculpting, you should be ready to make a mold of your face. That will be covered in the next chapter.

SCULPTING THE FACE, HEAD, AND NECK

The process of sculpting a full head and neck differs from sculpting the face exactly the way you think it would differ: There's more to sculpt. However, there is a little bit of preparation of the lifecast prior to beginning the sculpture. It needs to be placed securely onto a disc that will allow the sculpture to be easily rotated and looked at from different angles.

Since this sculpture will involve the entire head and neck, not just the face, clay will need to be built up around the entire cast, with care taken to leave room for the ears and surrounding tissue of the head.

Blocking the Sculpture

Just as with the face and neck sculpture, you will rough in shapes and refine them in stages, bringing out detail a little at a time until the design has been completed.

1. Loosely draw lines on the face with a pencil that correspond to facial lines on the cast to make them more obvious for when you begin to place clay on the cast, as you can see Neill Gorton doing in the accompanying photos.
2. Begin to place bits of clay on the cast where you've drawn enhancing lines. This is the roughing-in stage of the sculpture and can be done with just clay and your fingers.

Some of the areas of the face and head will be sculpted very thinly by necessity, meaning that there will be very little appliance material is some places. This is critical for the actor's performance because the thicker the appliance, the harder it will be for nuances of facial expression to translate through it and be perceptible to the audience. Never lose sight of the fact that everything we do is in support of the performance. It is never about the makeup; it is always about the performance.

Since this makeup will eventually cover the entire head, you want to make certain that there is a minimum thickness around the head to prevent over-stretching of the appliance or buckling during application, which will create serious headaches. You might find it useful to create a depth gauge by marking a piece of heavy-gauge wire, the type used in some of your loop tools, at 1/8 inch, or about 3 mm. This uniform thickness around the entire head will also give the whole head a sense of uniformity.

3. Slice off some thin slabs of clay as close to 1/8 inch as you can and begin covering the cast all the way around, except for the face and ears.

FIGURE 4.20
Neill continues to rough in the facial shape. Image reproduced by permission of Neill Gorton.

FIGURE 4.21
Refining the clay little by little. Image reproduced by permission of Neill Gorton.

4. Create some rough ear shapes that you can put on and take off simply as a point of reference and to make the head look a little more familiar.

5. Once you've covered the head with a uniform thickness, use a serrated scraper to blend the surface and then smooth it all out, tying all the pieces into one whole.

6. You might want to use a small tool or two to help press the bits of clay together, but continue to place bits and pieces of clay—those little "sausages" of clay—along the natural lines and folds of the face where you drew those pencil lines.

This is a still very early stage of sculpting, and it will start to take on the shape of your character. At this stage you can work fairly quickly because you are still just blocking out the overall impression of what it will eventually look like.

7. You can begin to use one of your wooden shaping tools to sketch lines in the clay where you will place details.

8. Take a tool and start a light crosshatch over the clay that you placed with your hands; rake the surface with the tool and start to smooth and blend rough areas into more of a whole. You don't want to redefine what you've already done, just refine the rough spots.

9. Every so often, put the rough ears on if you need a different perspective. A head without ears looks a little odd.

10. Continue adding clay and blending it until all the main features and shapes have been created and clay is everywhere that it needs to be. When the sculpture is roughed in completely, you can begin to create the detail.

11. Since we are beginning to add minor detail to the sculpture, you need to refine your tool selection, picking tools that will allow you to create increasingly finer nuances in the sculpture. Try a medium rake tool or loop tool to go over the surface, creating areas of more definition.

FIGURE 4.22
By placing ears roughly on the sculpture, you get a better overall feel for the sculpture. Image reproduced by permission of Neill Gorton.

125

FIGURE 4.23
Detail is added on top of detail on top of detail for a sense of skin depth. Image reproduced by permission of Neill Gorton.

FIGURE 4.24
Clay beads up when brushed and wipes off cleanly, leaving behind a realistic skin texture. Image reproduced by permission of Neill Gorton.

126

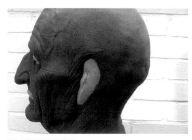

FIGURE 4.25
A view of Neill's sculpture ready to be molded and cast in silicone. Image reproduced by permission of Neill Gorton.

12. After you've gone over the sculpture to some degree, take the plastic bristle brush and go over the surface where you've been working with the rake and loop tools. Essentially what you are doing is removing tool marks left by the loop and rake. Repeat steps 11 and 12; carve in some detail, then brush over it to remove tool marks. Create lines, but remove bumps and lumps and unwanted tool marks. The plastic bristle brush will likely leave bits of clay on the surface of the sculpture as you brush; you can get rid of these by lightly whisking them away with a chip brush and a little baby powder.

13. Lightly brush solvent over the surface of your sculpture so that you can smooth out any blemishes.

14. Some of the detail you created could likely soften too much or fill in with this step, so you might need to go in with one of your small loop tools and recarve some detail and then brush over it with a soft brush to take away some of the hardness of the crease.

15. You might want to let the sculpture sit overnight or have something else you can work on while you wait to ensure that the surface will be hard enough to work with again and not be too soft and sticky from the solvent.

16. Make sure the clay is firm again when you come back to it and then brush talcum powder (baby powder) over the entire sculpture where you had brushed the solvent. Now you're going to use the pet brush on the clay. If the surface doesn't have powder on it, all the tiny bits of clay will stick to the sculpture.

17. Make a small container of clay slip or slurry by mixing some bits of clay scrapings and some of whatever solvent you've been using. With this very loose slip you are going to create tiny bumps on the skin, just as you did on your face sculpture.

The effect is well worth the time it takes to add this additional detail to your sculpture. Anything worth doing is worth doing well, and it's the little things that will help your work stand out from others who won't make the extra effort. Make sure the edges of your sculpture are as thin as you can make them, and clean off any excess clay from the sculpture. You should now be ready to make a mold of the sculpture so you can cast your appliance.

SCULPTING HANDS

Up to this point we've been sculpting for age prosthetics; everything that has been done in the previous sections can be adapted to suit any type of character sculpture. That is true of this section as well.

Blocking the Sculpture

Pull out some reference photos you have of old hands so that you won't be working from memory. You could find it necessary to only sculpt up clay on the backs of the hands and part way out onto the proximal phalanx, or first bone of each finger, including the thumb. What you don't create in clay to become an appliance you might be able to create with a wrinkle stipple technique I'll discuss in Chapter 9.

1. As with all sculpture, begin by placing small bits of clay onto the positive. You can work on both hands at the same time or do one at a time; it's up to you. If the clay doesn't seem to want to stick to the Ultracal, you can try brushing a thin layer of petroleum jelly into the stone first (if your positives are stone); then the clay should want to grab hold. This particular sculpt is on hands cast in fiberglass.

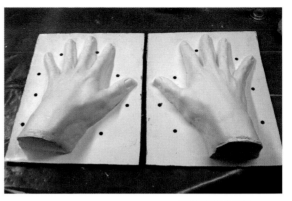

FIGURE 4.26
Fiberglass hand positives. These hands are part of finished molds, and that's why there are holes; the mold halves will be bolted together to provide a tight seal when cast with prosthetic material. Photo by the author.

2. Loosely draw lines on the hand with a pencil that correspond to tendons and veins on the hand casts to make them more obvious for when you begin to place clay onto them.

3. Begin to place bits of clay on the cast where you've drawn enhancing lines. This is the roughing-in stage of the sculpture and can be done with just clay and your fingers.

4. You might want to use a small tool or two to help press the bits of clay together, but continue to place bits and pieces of clay—those little "sausages"—on the hands where you drew those pencil lines.

5. Continue adding clay and blending it until all the main features and shapes have been created and clay is everywhere that it needs to be. When the sculpture is roughed-in completely, you can begin to create the detail.

6. You need to refine your tool selection, picking tools that will allow you to create finer nuances in the sculpture. Try a medium rake tool or loop tool to go over the surface, creating areas of more definition.

7. Take the plastic bristle brush and go over the surface where you've been working with the rake and loop tools.

FIGURE 4.27
Clay is added gradually and continually refined until the correct shape has been reached. Photo by the author.

8. Create lines, but remove bumps and lumps and unwanted tool marks. The plastic bristle brush will likely leave bits of clay on the surface of the sculpture as you brush; you can get rid of these by lightly whisking them away with a cut-down chip brush and a little baby powder.

9. After you've applied solvent to soften the clay, use a smaller-detail brush to get into tighter areas of detail on the sculpture where clay slurry may have filled it in.

10. The clay will be soft for several hours until all the solvent has evaporated.

11. When the clay is firm again, brush powder over the entire sculpture where you had brushed solvent. Just as on the face and head, you're going to

127

FIGURE 4.28
Powder is used to remove clay scraps created by using a pet brush or plastic bristle brush. Photo by the author.

FIGURE 4.29
Hand sculpts finished with flashing added; they are ready for the negative molds to be made. Photo by the author.

use the pet brush on the clay now. If the surface doesn't have powder on it, all the tiny bits of clay will stick to the sculpture and might be difficult to remove.

Make sure the edges of your sculpture are as thin as you can make them, and clean up any excess clay on the sculpture. You should now be ready to make molds of your sculpture so that you can cast your hand appliances.

SCULPTING EARS

Ear appliances can be tricky, too, mainly because parts of them can often be quite thin. As we age, our ears get longer; a study by Dr. James Heathcote,[3] a general practitioner in the U.K., concluded that our ears get bigger on average by .22 mm annually.

FIGURE 4.30
Ear appliances being roughed in with clay. Notice that natural undercuts have been minimized. Photos by the author.

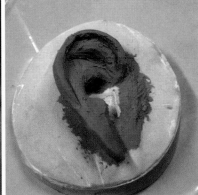

[3]Dr. James Heathcote, *British Medical Journal* (December 1995).

Blocking the Sculpture

1. Take the ears you cast in Chapter 3 and begin placing small bits of clay onto them. Have your reference images handy so that you can sculpt from them. Remember that if the clay doesn't seem to want to stick to the Ultracal, you can try brushing a thin layer of petroleum jelly into the stone first; then the clay should want to grab hold.

2. Ear skin is very thin and is textured differently than skin elsewhere on the head, at least above the earlobes. For the most part, the skin covering the ears is smooth, including the earlobes. Begin by filling in the areas around the *triangular fossa*, *schaphoid fossa*, and *meatus*, with clay to eliminate the undercuts, and sculpt a new tip onto the helix.

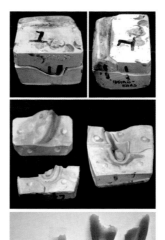

FIGURE 4.31
Multipiece molds made by Matthew Mungle for *The Indian in the Cupboard* and gauged earlobe extensions cast in flocked silicone. Photos by the author.

You might find it easier to work on both ears simultaneously than one at a time; that way you can compare as you go.

3. Decide whether you're going to create ears with attached lobes or free lobes; in Chapter 2 I mentioned that most people have free lobes by a margin of nearly 2 to 1. Will your character have gauged lobes, that is, a large hole which objects can be stuck through? That could be interesting; so would the mold. Remember that every cool design has to be moldable, and I mean moldable in a time and cost-efficient way; otherwise, the design may not work.

4. Once you have your new ear shape roughed in, you can begin to smooth the clay and blend the edges off to nothing. Use solvent to soften the clay, then smooth the clay with a soft brush. After the solvent has evaporated and the clay has hardened again, you will be able to carefully create the molds for the ears.

CHAPTER SUMMARY

Chapter 4 introduced you to methods for sculpting prosthetic appliances in sulfur-free, oil-based clay, the purpose of WED clay, and useful sculpting tools, even how to make your own tools. You also learned how to prepare your finished prosthetic sculpture for molding, which will be covered in Chapter 5.

Breakdown of the Sculpture

> **Key Points**

- Tools and materials
- Releases and sealers
- Making the negative mold
- Keys, flashing, and cutting edge
- Types of molds

INTRODUCTION

Breaking down the sculpture is the process of determining the way a complex makeup must be separated for mold making and preparing it properly for the mold-making process. Not all makeup sculpture will need to be broken down, but molds will always have to be made, and this chapter is all about preparing the sculpture for mold making and then making the molds. There are different types of molds, each with its own design concerns. I forget who told me this, and I apologize for not attributing the quote, but "Good molds aren't *made*, they're *designed*."

Kevin Kirkpatrick

Halloween aficionado Kevin Kirkpatrick has been fascinated with special makeup effects for about as long as he can remember. He received his first "professional" makeup kit as a youngster. High school found Kevin doing makeup for all his school's theatrical performances, receiving encouragement and accolades from his art and drama teachers.

In 2004 Kevin enrolled in Tom Savini's Special Makeup Effects program at the Douglas Education Center near Pittsburgh, Pennsylvania. It turned out to be a good decision. Upon graduation in 2006, Kevin got a call from Savini asking if he'd be interested in working on a project for director Joe Zito for four months in Cairo, Egypt. Kevin readily said yes and was soon on a plane bound for North Africa. Four months turned into nine, and Kevin returned to the States a seasoned veteran of makeup effects.

Shortly after returning to the U.S., Kevin moved to Los Angeles and has been working nonstop ever since. "My advice is to get your hands on any and every book that there is on the subject [of makeup effects] and try your hand at it. There's no better way to learn how to do something than to just do it. I remember when I was 9 years old and was given Richard Corson's book (*Stage Makeup*); it was like a workbook for me. I tried as many things as I could, money permitting, and I messed up horribly! But it didn't stop me. If anything, it pushed me to try it over and over until my results were successful."

Kevin's credits include *Lahzat Harega (Critical Moments)*, *The Screening*, *Staunton Hill*, *Red Velvet*, and *Black Mountain*.

FIGURE 5.1
Kevin applying drowning victim makeup to actress Nicci Wise. Image reproduced by permission of Kevin Kirkpatrick.

FIGURE 5.2
Quentin Tarantino likeness makeup applied to Dustin Heald. Images reproduced by permission of Kevin Kirkpatrick.

TOOLS AND MATERIALS

Ultracal
1- and 2-inch chip brushes
Sculpting tools
Hemp fiber
Drill and ½- or ¾-inch (12 mm or 19 mm) round router bit

Palette knife
Chavant® Le Beau Touché clay
Burlap fabric (loose weave)
Fiberglass mat, cloth, and tissue
WED clay or other water clay

Sharpie® or other marker

Solvent (whatever you used in
    Chapter 4)
Alginate
³⁄₈-inch (1 cm) foam core

Misc. containers
Formica® board or Masonite® (× 2)
Clay cutter
Coarse sandpaper
Petroleum jelly
Plaster bandages
Soft brushes
Scissors
Misc. mold keys
Safety glasses

Van Aken® nonsulfur plastalina
    (or something similar)

Hot glue gun
Misc. wood pieces of 2 × 4 and 1 × 2
    (about 6–10 inches)
Plastic wrap
Paint stir sticks
Rasp or sandpaper
2 large flathead screwdrivers
Superglue activator/accelerator
NIOSH respirator
Latex, nitrile, and vinyl gloves
Utility knife
Green Soap Tincture
Polyethylene sheet (drop cloth)

I strongly suggest you read this chapter all the way through at least once before attempting what follows. That way there shouldn't be any surprises. As I've said before, the Boy Scout motto is a good one for makeup effects artists, too: Be prepared!

RELEASE AGENTS AND SEALERS

Release agents are materials that allow you to separate cast objects from molds. There are two categories for most release agents: barrier and reactive (or chemically active) types. *Barrier* release agents work by forming a barrier between the form (the cast) and the mold. Paraffin wax is an example of a barrier release, as is Al-Cote,® which I explain in the next section. *Chemically active* release agents are releases that have an active ingredient that is usually some type of fatty acid, such as soap, that is dissolved in some sort of a carrier, such as alcohol (e.g., Tincture of Green Soap).

Sealers are liquids or sprays that are absorbed into porous surfaces to seal against moisture, making the surface essentially no longer porous; they can act as both a seal and a release for some materials. Not all materials need to be sealed and/ or released, though for some applying a mold release will make demolding easier and will most likely prolong the life of the mold. A comprehensive listing of suppliers for releases and sealers is included in the appendix at the back of this book.

MAKING THE NEGATIVE MOLD

For a makeup that may cover an entire bust—the entire head and neck, for example—it is probable that the makeup will need to be broken down so that there will likely be several overlapping prosthetic pieces, each with its own mold of two or more pieces. One very important bit of information you need to know for this chapter is this: *If you are creating a makeup that will ultimately be cast in several pieces that will overlap, the initial lifecast must first be coated with a separating agent*, such as Dentsply's Al-Cote® (liquid foil). If you don't use a separating agent between your stone positive and the clay sculpture, you will have a devil of a time getting the clay off in intact sections to create overlapping pieces—if you can get the clay off at all without destroying your sculpture.

So, let's assume that you applied two or three coats of separator to your positive before you began sculpting with your clay. You need to decide how you are going to break the sculpture apart; in doing this you will also be determining how the pieces will fit back together, overlapping so that there will be no semblance of a seam anywhere on the makeup.

1. With a thin wood tool create a separating line on the clay where you want it to part. Make the line somewhat random so that the dividing lines and subsequent edges will be less obvious. Make sure to press hard enough to reach the positive under the clay.
2. Fill a large basin or tub with water, enough to completely submerge your sculpture, and carefully place the sculpture into it.

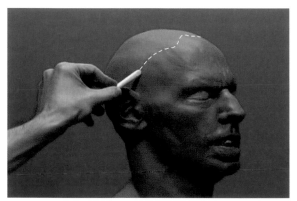

FIGURE 5.3
Dotted lines show where cut is made in clay to separate sculpture. Image reproduced by permission of Mark Alfrey.

FIGURE 5.4
Mark Alfrey submerging sculpture into bathtub filled with water. Image reproduced by permission of Mark Alfrey.

3. Let it soak for about 24 hours to be certain the water has had time to reach the Al-Cote and liquefy it. By doing this, you will be able to "float" the clay off your sculpture.
4. There will likely be Al-Cote residue left on the clay; you should carefully wash it off with water and a chip brush. You want the clay to be clean to ensure that it will adhere to the new stone cast you will be placing it on.
5. You will need to make additional positives that will be used to resculpt individual pieces that will overlap. Carefully set aside the clay you have removed from the original sculpture.
6. Blend the rough edges of the sculpture where you have removed clay, and smooth it.

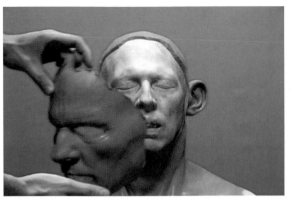

FIGURE 5.5
Lifting off the face portion after soaking it in water overnight. Image reproduced by permission of Mark Alfrey.

FIGURE 5.6
Removing residual Al-Cote from inside the clay of the face. Image reproduced by permission of Mark Alfrey.

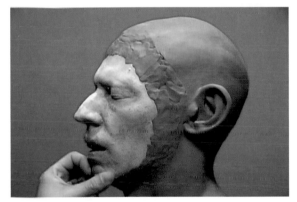

FIGURE 5.7
The clay must be extended and smoothly blended where parts will overlap. Image reproduced by permission of Mark Alfrey.

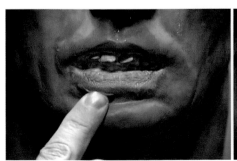

FIGURE 5.8
The clay must be extended and smoothly blended where parts will overlap. Images reproduced by permission of Mark Alfrey.

7. Now mix a batch of alginate large enough to just make a cast of the area you need to recreate, plus an inch or so beyond it.

8. You might or might not need to create a plaster mother mold of the alginate, depending on the size of the piece. When the alginate has set, carefully remove it, place it level on a support, and mix enough Ultracal to fill the alginate mold.

9. If the new piece you are making is small, such as a lower lip, you will need to create a base for it.

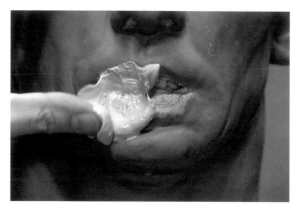

FIGURE 5.9
Carefully spread the alginate to mold the area to be recreated. Image reproduced by permission of Mark Alfrey.

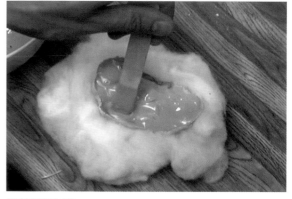

FIGURE 5.10
Carefully mix and add Ultracal to the alginate mold. Image reproduced by permission of Mark Alfrey.

FIGURE 5.11
Removing the support wall for the new base. Image reproduced by permission of Mark Alfrey.

10. You will need to create an alginate or silicone mold and Ultracal positive for each separate overlapping piece of your makeup, so repeat steps 8 and 9 as many times as necessary.

11. Place the clay you removed from the original onto the new positives and seat it well; blend and smooth the edges and finish adding skin texture detail if you haven't already done that.

KEYS, FLASHING, AND CUTTING EDGES

Now you will drill keys and flashing around the new pieces you've created. *Keys* are for precise registration of two or more mold parts so that they will fit together perfectly. Keys can be created by drilling rounded shapes into the positive (no undercuts!) or by placing clay or rubber shapes at even distances around the mold wall you will create.

Flashing is thinly placed (about ⅛ inch) over all the exposed areas of the mold and trimmed to within ⅛ to ¼ inch from the edge of the sculpture for your appliance.

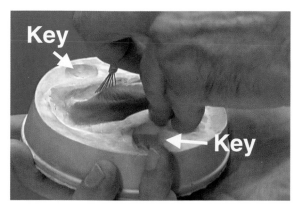

FIGURE 5.12
Drilled keys in the lip base. Image reproduced by permission of
Mark Alfrey.

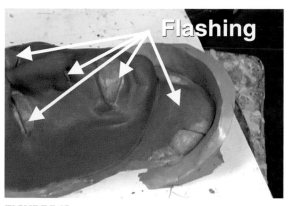

FIGURE 5.13
Flashing placed on the face sculpture. Image reproduced by
permission of Mark Alfrey.

The flashing needs to be cut away from any drilled keys. The purpose of flashing
is to create space for excess appliance material to escape when the mold parts are
clamped together to cast the appliance pieces in gelatin, foam latex, or silicone.

There is a very good reason that the flashing stops just shy of the edge of your
appliance sculpture. Do you know the reason? It's to create a *cutting edge* for
the appliance you will cast later in the mold you're about to make. A cutting edge
is the point where the negative part of the mold comes into physical contact
with the positive, creating a separation of excess material that will escape into
the space created by the flashing, and the material that is pressed into the space
created by your sculpture to make the appliance. When done properly, it will
leave you with ultra-fine edges that will be very easy to blend off onto your
actor's skin or overlapping pieces when you apply the makeup.

Building the Clay Wall

After the keys and flashing have been made, you'll divide the sculpture by creating a dividing wall along a predetermined line that will prevent creating undercuts. Traditionally in sculpture this dividing wall is created using metal shims
(thin wedges) pressed into the sculpture to create a separating line between two
mold halves. You'll use water clay instead of shims because shims will damage
the sculpture too much.

FIGURE 5.14
Dividing marks made
with a Sharpie marker.
Images reproduced
by permission of Mark
Alfrey.

1. Before cutting and placing clay, take a
   Sharpie or similar marker and mark small
   dots along the line you intend to follow
   with the clay wall—a line that will prevent
   formation of undercuts that will possibly
   damage the mold.
2. Using a clay cutting tool, either a wire
   cutter and a piece of Masonite® with paint

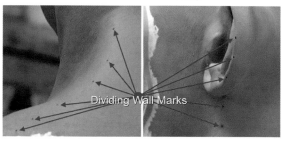

137

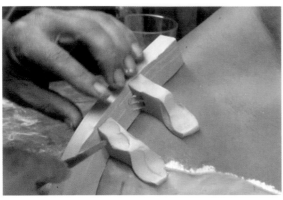

FIGURE 5.15
The dividing wall should be perpendicular to the sculpture and the edge clean and smooth; make the wall as close to 90° as it can be. Image reproduced by permission of Mark Alfrey.

138

sticks glued to each side (the width of the clay block) or an adjustable clay cutter, cut slabs of clay about ½ inch thick; lay them flat and cut strips about 2 inches wide and 4 or 5 inches long.

3. Begin to place these strips of clay along the dotted line you made along the ridge line of the sculpture, pressing down hard enough to get a good connection between the clay and the sculpture but not so hard as to cause a bulge at the contact point. You want the clay wall to be perpendicular to the sculpture and the edge to be clean and smooth; make the wall as close to 90° as you can.

A perfect wall will have no gaps where the water clay meets the oil clay. The clay in these pictures is Laguna WED clay.

4. Build the wall all the way around the sculpture. It is critical that the meeting point be closed and neat. You can use a small dental tool and a fine, soft brush dipped in water to smooth the clay in critical areas. You don't need to use much water. Alternate between smoothing and brushing until the seam where the wall meets the sculpture is perfectly smooth.

5. When the wall is finished, spray the sculpture (the side you're going to cover with Ultracal first) with a light coat of Krylon Crystal Clear.® When it's dry, spray another coat and then spray a coat of Dulling Spray over the Crystal Clear. The reason for the Dulling Spray is to prevent the Ultracal from beading up and rolling off the sculpture when you brush on your thin detail coat.

Building a Different Clay Wall

There is another way to do a wall for your sculpture: It can be done with your sculpture laid flat instead of standing upright.

1. Cut enough clay (about ½ inch—12 mm—thick) to lay your sculpture on face up. Cover the clay with plastic wrap to keep the clay from sticking to your sculpture. The clay is to prevent the sculpture from denting by being laid on a hard surface.

2. Place your sculpture on the plastic-covered clay. If you are working with just a face sculpture, you might not need or want to try this method; it works well for a full head (360°) sculpture. On the other hand, if you have only a face sculpture, it must be laid flat, facing up, because it would be awkward at best to try to mold it in an upright position.

3. So that you don't wind up using more WED or other water clay than you need to, you can first build up around the perimeter of your sculpture with precut lengths of 2 x 4-inch and 1 x 2-inch wood, or you can build platforms using pieces of ³/₈-inch (1 cm) foam core and a hot glue gun.

4. Once you've built a perimeter using either wood or foam core, proceed with your clay just as described in steps 1–5 in the preceding section, following a line around the sculpture that will prevent undercuts that would keep the front and back halves of the mold from separating.

Once you have made it through spraying Krylon Crystal Clear and Dulling Spray, you are ready to begin applying a thin coat of Ultracal for your detail layer. You should have all your supplies laid out and ready to begin, even before you start to build the clay wall around your sculpture. If you wait until you've already done the dividing wall before getting everything you need to make the Ultracal mold, the clay could already be drying out to the extent that you can see separation at the contact point on the sculpture due to shrinkage that occurs when the clay dries. You don't need to work fast, but if you have all your tools and materials handy and ready to go at each stage, you won't need to rush and won't forget important steps as a result.

FIGURE 5.16
Build up a perimeter with wood or foam core before creating the clay wall. Image reproduced by permission of Mark Alfrey.

STONE (GYPSUM) MOLDS

Stone molds, also called *gypsum molds*, are organic molds made with a base material of hydrated calcium sulfate, used for making Plaster of Paris, cement, Hydrocal, and Ultracal, among others. Gypsum has quite a few varied uses, from making drywall and fertilizer to being a major source of dietary calcium and also an ingredient in Hostess® Twinkies®! White Sands National Monument in New Mexico is a 275-square-mile expanse of white gypsum sand. Well, enough history; it's time to make your mold.

This process is exactly the same as when you made your Ultracal positive in Chapter 3 after taking your subject's lifecast, only this time we're making a negative, not a positive.

1. Spray the sculpture with a layer of Kryolan® Crystal Clear and let it dry. Then spray a layer of Dulling Spray to give the Ultracal a surface to adhere to.
2. Mix enough Ultracal to create a ¼-inch thickness that is the consistency of a thin milkshake—loose enough to brush easily with a 1- or 2-inch chip brush.
3. Begin brushing the Ultracal onto the sculpture, making sure to get Ultracal into all curves and creases such as the nose and the ears. Brush in all directions. This will help eliminate any trapped air bubbles.
4. As the Ultracal begins to thicken, dribble and brush more onto the sculpture until you have built up a thickness of about ¼ inch.

139

FIGURE 5.17
Brush on a detail layer of Ultracal, being careful to prevent trapping air bubbles. Images reproduced by permission of Mark Alfrey.

5. When your detail layer has gone through the heating phase of its cure, mix up some new Ultracal. You will add pieces of burlap fabric as you apply the next batch of Ultracal, building up a thickness of three or four layers of burlap. Thoroughly press each piece down to remove trapped air and then overlap each piece of burlap by at least 1 inch.

6. After the burlap layers have cured, add a final beauty layer of just Ultracal that will give your mold an overall thickness of about 1 inch. Artist Pedro Valdez, who is shown at work in these photos, usually leaves a textured finish rather than a smooth finish so that the mold won't slip accidentally.

140

FIGURE 5.18
Build up three or four layers of burlap for reinforcement, overlapping each piece by about an inch. Image reproduced by permission of Mark Alfrey.

FIGURE 5.19
A textured finish on stone molds makes them less likely to accidentally slip when being handled. Image reproduced by permission of Mark Alfrey.

Some folks prefer to use hemp fibers or fiberglass mat fibers instead of burlap fabric as the reinforcing material they put in the Ultracal. It is nothing more than a personal preference and whether the materials are available in your area. For me, burlap and fiberglass mat are a 3-minute ride to Home Depot, but I have to order hemp online. You'll find a list of suppliers in the appendix at the back of this book, so let's continue.

7. When this half of the mold has fully cured and is cooling down, you might begin to remove the clay wall from around the sculpture.

8. Next, carefully remove the 2 x 4s and 1 x 2s or the foam core; if you've used foam core and hot glue, spray the glue with cyanoacrylate (Superglue) activator/accelerator. It will soften the glue so that it's easier to remove. Next remove the clay base that was being supported. If your sculpture has delicate parts such as ears, be very careful when removing the clay so that you don't damage it.

9. Once the clay is removed, you can use coarse sandpaper or a rasp to remove sharp edges and smooth the edges of the mold, removing excess Ultracal.

10. When you've done this and cleaned away the clay you've already used, carefully turn the mold over, supporting it under the edges of the mold flange (the part sticking out perpendicular to the sculpture) with the wood and some of the clay you used on the other side.

11. Spray this side of the mold with Crystal Clear and Dulling Spray and then lightly brush any exposed Ultracal with a thin layer of petroleum jelly. Brush about an inch or two down the side just to be safe.

FIGURE 5.20
Add small pieces of clay about 12 inches apart all the way around the mold; they will be used as pry holes to aid you in getting the two mold halves apart. Image reproduced by permission of Mark Alfrey.

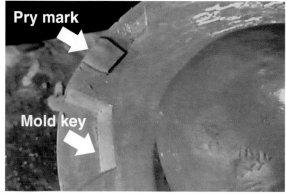

Pry mark

Mold key

12. Add small pieces of clay about 12 inches apart all the way around the mold; line them up opposite one another if you can. These will be used as pry holes to aid you in getting the two mold halves apart. You might also want to draw a mark with a Sharpie below the pry mark on the mold in case any Ultracal accidentally covers it. It will be easier to find later.

141

FIGURE 5.21
Build a 1 inch retaining wall around the flange of the stone mold. Images reproduced by permission of Mark Alfrey.

FIGURE 5.22
A box mold/plate mold made with foam core strips held together with hot glue. Photo by the author.

13. Now cut a slab of clay about 1 inch thick and trim the edges smooth. Use a paint stick to measure a width of about 1½ inches and cut the slab into strips. Begin placing the clay strips around the perimeter of the mold, and press it down onto the Ultracal so that it will hold.

14. When you've finished, spray another coat of Crystal Clear so that the clay gets coated and spray a layer of Dulling Spray.

15. Now repeat steps 1–4 for the back side of your mold. You will eventually begin to know how much Ultracal to use for certain projects, but it's easy enough to mix up a little more if you find you haven't mixed enough. Unlike plaster, Ultracal has a substantial working time—hence its name, Ultracal 30.

16. Just as with the positive you made in Chapter 3, you might choose to cover the Ultracal with a plastic bag to hold in moisture as the stone heats. It is supposed to make the stone stronger; I don't know if anyone's actually run tests, but I tend to see the glass as half full. It won't weaken your mold, and it doesn't add to the cure time. It will, however, mean that there is moisture in your mold, and if you're planning to run foam latex in it soon, you'll need to get rid of all that water or risk ruining your latex appliances. More about that in the next chapter.

OTHER TYPES OF MOLDS

Gypsum molds are not the only kinds of molds you can make that are used for special makeup effects. We'll look at them one by one and talk about their uses and how to make them. Other materials used for mold making include silicone rubber, fiberglass, urethane rubber, and urethane plastic resin. The two-piece front and back mold you just made is called a *case mold*, but there are case molds that are made in numerous pieces that must be bolted together. There are matrix molds, flood molds, box molds, block molds, and plate molds, injection molds and pour molds, and pressure molds and vacuum molds.

FIGURE 5.23
A flood or pour mold is exactly what the name implies. Photo by the author.

Some of these names might be confusing, so let me do a bit of clarifying. A *box mold* is just what the name implies—it is made by creating a box shape around the sculpture that is to be molded.

However, sometimes the shape that needs to be molded will not conform to a basic four-sided box shape without causing an inexcusable and unnecessary waste of mold-making material.

Box molds are also known as *block molds* for the same reason: their block shape. These box/block molds can be, and most often are, made with silicone rubber or urethane rubber, but they can also be made out of plaster, Ultracal, or urethane plastic resin. That material can be poured, or flooded, in, hence the names *flood mold* and *pour mold*.

If you really want to get technical, I suppose you could call the Ultracal case mold you've made a *brushed case mold* since you essentially brushed on the Ultracal to create the mold. What matters is that there be no confusion about terminology among people working together on any given project.

FIGURE 5.24
Various plate molds.
Photo by the author.

Like the other molds I've described, a *plate mold* describes what it is: a flat, one-piece mold resembling a flat plate, or a slab. Plate molds are essentially box molds.

These types of molds are frequently used for creating generic prosthetic appliance pieces such as cuts, scars, bullet holes, and the like, by sculpting the particular injury or feature on a flat surface and then creating a box mold around the sculpture and casting it in stone or plastic. Don't forget to release the surface on which you are making the mold or you could fuse them together and never get them apart. The way these molds are used is usually as follows: Gelatin or silicone is cast into the negative of the sculpted feature and excess material is scraped away with a flat scraper of some sort, leaving a piece that is flat on the back with very fine edges. I'll show you how in Chapter 6.

SILICONE RUBBER MOLDS

Rubber molds made with silicone can be quite versatile and, when made thick enough, don't require the support of a rigid support shell, or mother mold. Working with silicone doesn't require a degree in chemistry, but it sure wouldn't hurt! What I mean is, silicone is an interesting creature, and I think it is worthwhile for me to go into some of its quirks and idiosyncrasies so that you won't literally get yourself into a mess that is difficult to clean up. I will go into more detail about silicones in Chapter 6, but here are some basics.

FIGURE 5.25
A 2-gallon pressure/
vacuum chamber from
Harbor Freight. Photo by
the author.

Do you remember the silicone teaser in Chapter 3? Two basic types of silicone are used for mold making and for makeup effects: condensation cure and addition cure. The ways that these silicones cure are fundamentally different and are not intermixable. Condensation-cure silicones require moisture in the air for the reaction that's needed for them to cure. These silicones are also called *RTV silicones*. RTV stands for *room-temperature vulcanization*, which means that RTV silicones don't need the application of heat in order for them to cure.

Condensation-cure silicones used for makeup effects mix in two parts, both liquid; one part is a rubber base, the other a catalyst (activator) that triggers the reaction. There are also one-part condensation-cure silicones that are used mainly as adhesives, caulking, or sealants and are usually thick and paste-like. Of the two types of silicone, condensation cure and addition cure, condensation-cure silicone is the most tolerant of outside influence. These silicones use tin as part of the curing process and are also known as *tin-cure silicones* as well as RTV and condensation-cure silicones. Of the two main types,– condensation-cure silicone is most widely used in mold making due to its resistance to cure inhibition (not setting up because of contamination by an outside agent).

The second type of silicone, addition cure, cures by a self-contained chemical reaction. Addition-cure silicones will cure in a vacuum, and there is virtually no shrinkage, though the shrinkage with condensation silicones is also nominal. However, being able to cure in a vacuum is one of addition-cure silicone's benefits. I guess that's true if you work in outer space. Addition-cure silicones are also mixed in two parts, and when they're mixed, air bubbles get trapped in the thick liquid silicone, which is bad. The silicone must be degassed, which requires a vacuum chamber. Right now you're probably thinking, "Oh, man! Where the heck am I gonna get one of those?!" Not to worry. If you feel compelled to buy one, Harbor Freight sells a 2-gallon pressure/vacuum pot for less than $100. They're really not that hard to find. If you know what you're doing, and you will because you're reading this book, you don't have to have a vacuum chamber to get rid of the air bubbles, but it could help.

FIGURE 5.26
Cover the sculpture with a wet paper towel and then cover the sculpture with clay. Image reproduced by permission of Mark Alfrey.

A couple of rules to remember here:

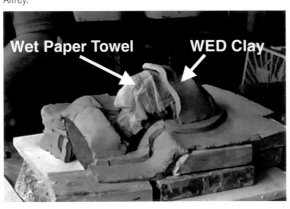

1. Mix the two parts of your silicone gently, thereby minimizing the number of air bubbles you create when you stir.
2. Many silicones take several hours to cure— some as long as 24 hours—so, the air bubbles can usually find their way to the surface of a mold in plenty of time to escape before the silicone kicks. On the other hand, some addition-cure silicones will go off in minutes. Why the huge difference? Well, addition-cure silicones are also known as *platinum-cure silicones*, and the more platinum they contain, the faster the reaction (and the more it costs).

Addition-cure silicones also come in two varieties: RTV and HTC (high-temperature cure). The HTC platinum silicones need heat to cure, and an oven or other heat source is recommended. Platinum RTVs will also cure faster with the application of heat, but it isn't a requirement.

Ordinarily, silicone will stick to silicone, but virtually nothing else will, which is why silicone is very, very difficult to paint. That topic is covered in Chapter 6.

Tin silicone will stick to tin silicone, and platinum silicone will stick to platinum silicone, with no outside help. Tin silicone will also stick to platinum silicone, but platinum silicone will not stick to tin silicone; it won't even set up. Yuk; very messy.

The biggest thing to know and remember about addition-cure silicones is that they are extremely sensitive to outside contaminants. They will not cure against or in the presence of condensation-cure silicones. They're also finicky about anything that's been in contact with sulfur, latex, foamed latex, ammonia, tin (platinum silicone *will not* set up on cured tin silicone, but tin silicone will set up on cured platinum silicone), and a variety of other substances. Just be very aware that addition-cure silicones are very sensitive to cure inhibition.

Knowing how sensitive platinum silicones are to cure inhibition is very important because of the materials you choose for your prosthetic appliances. If you make foam latex prosthetics in a mold and later decide you'd rather make a silicone version, it can't be platinum silicone, because the foam latex will prevent it from curing. Likewise, you can't cast platinum silicone prosthetics in a mold with tin silicone parts, because it won't cure either. Ah, chemistry! Gotta love it. I'll save more about silicone for the next chapter.

MATRIX MOLDS

Matrix molds are probably the best, most accurate molds you can make, but they could be overkill for some applications due to the amount of work that goes into making them. You decide. The process begins similarly to the way you make a two-piece case mold for a sculpture, with the sculpture lying horizontally on a bed of clay covered with plastic wrap. I mentioned this at the beginning of the chapter, but in case you've already forgotten, read through the following steps, then make sure you have all the tools and materials necessary before proceeding.

1. If you haven't already done so, mark the dividing line on the sculpture, taking potential undercuts into account and avoiding them.
2. Place wood blocks around the sculpture or build a foam-core structure around the sculpture to support the WED clay wall you'll build. Using wood blocks or foam core first simply allows you to use less clay in creating the wall around the sculpture.
3. Cut slabs of clay with your cutter and begin to lay them around the sculpture, conforming to the dividing line you drew.
4. Take a scraper tool and begin to smooth out the clay around the sculpture, being careful not to get too close to the sculpture and thus risk damaging it. As with all such projects, start with broad strokes and then add details once the broad strokes are completed. In this case, get rid of rough patches and lumps with a serrated scraper, then use a smooth scraper to further refine the clay wall; this wall doesn't need to be perfectly smooth right up against the sculpture, because we are going to do something we haven't done before.

5. Place a piece of paper towel over the top of your sculpture and wet it with water from a spray bottle. Cover as much of the sculpture as you can with wet paper towel, gently and carefully pressing it into the contours of the sculpture.

6. Cut thin strips of clay about ½ inch thick and place them around the sculpture, then cut thin slabs to cover the rest of the sculpture.

7. Blend the clay together and smooth it. Be very mindful of undercuts with this clay covering, and avoid making them. You should always be aware of the potential for undercuts at every stage of your projects. Remember, an undercut is any curve or indentation you can't see when looking straight down at your sculpture.

8. Once the clay is smooth, cut ½-inch strips and place them down the middle of the sculpture and across, perpendicular to the strip on the midline. These will become registration keys for the silicone and support shell.

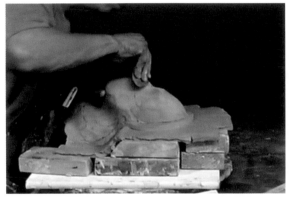

FIGURE 5.27
Blend the clay together and smooth it with a scraper tool. Image reproduced by permission of Mark Alfrey.

FIGURE 5.28
Add clay strips to be registration keys for the silicone mold and support shell. Image reproduced by permission of Mark Alfrey.

FIGURE 5.29
Add ¼-inch strips of clay around the base. Image reproduced by permission of Mark Alfrey.

9. Next, cut ¼-inch (7 mm) strips and lay them around the base. Trim them to about 5 inches long and space them around the base about 5 inches (12.7 cm) apart, all the way around.

1/4" Clay Strips

In case you haven't yet figured it out, the clay with which you have covered the sculpture and built keys will eventually be replaced entirely by silicone. A matrix mold is a precisely aligned mold with a silicone interior and rigid exterior shell. Here I am describing only one method of making a matrix mold; every artist has his or her own way of doing it—how they place keys and so on. The effectiveness of the resulting mold made by different artists remains the same despite slight differences in methodology.

10. Draw a line in the clay wall about 2 inches from the sculpture and then cut angled keys from 1- by ½-inch strips of clay and place four of them on the line, equidistant from each other.

11. Cut strips of clay ½ inch thick and a little wider than a paint stick and lay them along the line in the clay wall, flush with the keys you just placed, to create a barrier wall for the Ultracal you'll be using to create the support shell.

12. Spray the WED clay with two or three coats Krylon® Crystal Clear, then a coat of Dulling Spray. Remember, this will prevent the Ultracal from simply rolling off the Crystal Clear when you brush on the first layer.

13. Since this doesn't really need to be a detail layer—there isn't fine detail here to preserve—mix up a batch of Ultracal that is milkshake thickness: not too runny but not so thick that it doesn't flow when you brush it. Brush up a layer about ½ inch thick.

14. Let the first layer set up (begin to cool) before adding the next layer of stone.

15. With the next layer, add pieces of burlap fabric for reinforcement. Make this layer about ½ inch thick also, and remember to let each piece of burlap overlap by about ½ inch.

16. Add a bit more Ultracal if necessary, but smooth the Ultracal before it sets up. In these images you're seeing Pedro Valdez working without wearing gloves, which is okay; Ultracal is not toxic. However, it will cause your skin to dry out quickly and the Ultracal will dehydrate your skin so that it could crack and bleed—never what I would call a good thing.

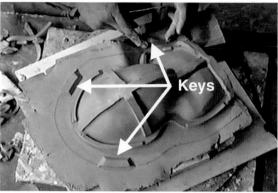

FIGURE 5.30
Cut angled keys from 1- by ½-inch strips of clay and place four of them on the line, equidistant from each other. Image reproduced by permission of Mark Alfrey.

147

FIGURE 5.31
Cut strips a little wider than a paint stick and lay them along the line in the clay wall, flush with the keys you just placed, to create a barrier wall for the Ultracal you'll be using to create the support shell. Image reproduced by permission of Mark Alfrey.

FIGURE 5.32
The back side, ready for clay. Image reproduced by permission of Mark Alfrey.

When I first began working with Ultracal I did not wear gloves. Then one time I did six lifecasts in one day, and as I was mixing the Ultracal to pour for the sixth positive, I noticed the Ultracal was turning pink... Now I wear gloves and always put lotion on my hands when I'm done for the day. You should, too.

17. You might want to put some serrations into the smooth surface for hand traction when handling the mold. The point about smoothing the outer layer is purely aesthetic. Sure, it's a mold that perhaps no one but you will ever see, but I can't stress enough that anything worth doing is worth doing well; everything you do should be done with a sense of artistic pride in the craftsmanship, even if only you will appreciate it.

18. Once the mold has fully cured and has begun to cool, remove the clay and clean up the edges of the stone mold. Next, remove the wood supporting the horizontal clay wall and remove that clay as well.

19. Carefully turn the mold over and support it with wood blocks. Remove the clay making up the dividing wall, but save any clay that was surrounding the sculpture; you will need it again. If any of the clay accidentally comes up, put it back in place. You should have something that resembles the photo.

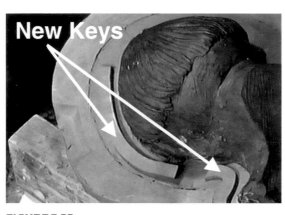

FIGURE 5.33
New registration keys must be made. Image reproduced by permission of Mark Alfrey.

20. You are going to do the same thing on this side that you did on the other. Place a piece of paper towel over the top of your sculpture and wet it with water from a spray bottle. Cover as much of the sculpture as you can with wet paper towel, gently and carefully pressing it into the contours of the sculpture.

21. Next, cut 1-inch (2.5 cm) strips of clay and lay them on top of the strips from the other side of the sculpture. Then cut thin slabs to cover the rest of the sculpture. Smooth it and place clay strips for keys.

22. Place small pieces of clay for pry holes (to facilitate removing the mold halves) and then brush a light layer of petroleum jelly over all the exposed stone surfaces.

23. Cut wider strips, about 2 inches (5 cm), and place them around the perimeter of the mold as a support wall; you might need to press the clay down onto the bottom of the mold to help hold it in place. Then spray it with Crystal Clear and Dulling Spray.

24. Mix a batch of Ultracal as you did for the first layer on the other side of the mold and brush it on. This layer will be about ½ inch thick when you are done.

25. After your first layer of Ultracal has cured and begun to cool, mix another batch of Ultracal to use with pieces of burlap. Overlap the burlap pieces to aid in reinforcing the mold. Build up three or four layers of burlap so that the total thickness of the mold will be about 1 inch (2.5 cm) overall—strong but still fairly lightweight.

26. As the Ultracal begins to set, smooth the stone so that there are no rough spots; remember, you might want to put serrations on the surface so the stone won't be too slick and possibly slip from your hands.
27. After the stone has cured and cooled, remove the clay wall and clean up the edges with sandpaper or a rasp.
28. Using a pair of large screwdrivers or some similar tools, find the pry holes and *carefully* begin to separate the support mold halves, working at opposite points on the mold. It is very important to take care not to damage the sculpture or the mold.
29. Remove the paper towel and any clay from the sculpture. Toss the paper towel, but keep the clay handy. Using a soft brush and water, clean any remaining clay from the surface of the sculpture.
30. Use a smooth detail tool to repair the clay around the edges of the sculpture, smoothing it and filling any gaps.
31. When you've done that, you can do one of two things because we need another set of registration keys. You can cut long thin strips of clay, about ¼ x ¼ inch, and lay them along the top of the embedded clay wall, with a gap about every 6 inches. *Or* you can use a carving tool and dig a ¼-inch trench in the embedded clay, leaving a gap every 6 inches or so. Then spray the clay and sculpture with another coat of Crystal Clear.
32. Remove all the clay from the inside of the mold half and, along with the clay you already removed, weigh it.
33. Clean the inside of the support case mold and scrape down any sharp edges on the keys that might have been formed by Ultracal leaking over their edges.
34. Take a Sharpie and mark several dots at low points all around the mold where you'll drill bleeder holes; these holes will allow air to escape when silicone is poured into the mold as well as provide an escape for excess silicone. Make sure to brush away any Ultracal dust so that the bleeder holes will remain clear.

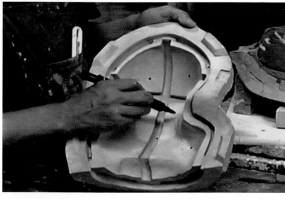

FIGURE 5.34
Use a Sharpie to mark several dots at low points all around the mold where you'll drill bleeder holes. Image reproduced by permission of Mark Alfrey.

FIGURE 5.35
Plug bleeder holes with drywall screws or clay. Image reproduced by permission of Mark Alfrey.

35. Next, drill a 1-inch hole in the case mold at the highest point of the mold. This is the point at which you will fill the mold with silicone. You will be using the mouth end of a large plastic soda bottle as a funnel that you will hot-glue into the 1-inch hole you drilled. *Or* instead of using a plastic soda bottle as a funnel, you can drill a 1¾-inch hole and use a section of a cardboard paper towel roll as your pour point, hot-gluing that in place. Whichever method you decide to use, you might find that you will have to tweak the hole size a bit to get your funnel to fit before gluing it in place.

It isn't actually important how big the hole you drill is, though it should probably be between 1 and 2 inches in diameter so that there's plenty of room for the silicone to pour at a decent rate. What's important is that the hole you make allows whatever you use for your funnel to fit.

36. Brush the interior of the mold with a light layer of petroleum jelly. The petroleum jelly acts as both a sealant and a release agent, making it far less likely that the silicone will find anything to grab onto and not want to let go.

37. The other half of the mold containing the sculpture should still be supported; carefully place the mold over the sculpture and close the mold, being careful to come straight down so the sculpture is not accidentally dinged by the case mold.

38. Clamp, tape (duct tape or gaffers tape), or strap the mold tightly shut.

39. There is still an opening at the base of the case mold. This is where casting material will be poured once the mold is completed and a casting of the sculpture will be made, but for now, we need to seal it so that silicone won't flow out of the opening once it's been poured in from the top. Cover the opening with WED clay and then use several pieces of plaster bandage to cover the clay. Don't press too hard or it could stick to the Ultracal too much. Leave a "tab" sticking out so that you have something to grab and pull when it's time to open the mold.

40. If you haven't weighed the clay yet, do it now, using either a triple-beam scale if you're "old school" or an accurate digital scale. You need to know how much silicone to mix without being wasteful. Here is a formula I got from Mark Alfrey: 100% clay = 70% silicone. Whatever your clay weighs, multiply that number by .7 to get the weight of the silicone you will need. You will most likely want to use a tin RTV silicone, not a platinum RTV silicone. Save the platinum silicones for making prosthetics, not molds; it could be too expensive.

41. Use hot glue to seal the seam of the case mold all the way around.

42. Now it's time to mix the silicone. Which silicone you use is up to you, though it should be a condensation-cure or tin RTV silicone, not an addition-cure or platinum RTV silicone.

I suggest that you do some research on your own to find a silicone that works best for your needs. I like Smooth-On's Mold Max 30 (pink), though Silicones, Inc., Polytek, and others also offer a variety of exceptionally good mold-making silicones. Things you will want to consider are shore hardness (how soft or hard the material is when fully cured), shrinkage when cured, pot life (how long you have to work with it before it begins to set up), and demold time (how long you have to wait before you can safely remove the mold when it is fully cured). You will find a listing of manufacturers in the appendix at the back of this book.

TIP

100% clay = 70% silicone
Whatever your clay weighs, multiply that number by .7 to get the weight of the silicone you will need. For example, if your clay weighs 1,200 grams, you'd multiply that by .7 and see that you will need 840 grams of silicone: 1200 x .7 = 840.

When the silicone is mixed, air bubbles are created that you do not want to negatively affect your mold. Ordinarily you would de-air or de-gas the silicone in a vacuum chamber, but that will not work here; for one thing, the mold is too big and a chamber large enough to hold the mold would be extremely expensive, not to mention the way a vacuum could affect the WED clay.

43. Pour the silicone slowly in a thin stream into the mold funnel from a height above it; this will stretch and break up most of the air bubbles.

NOTE

This could require some practice so you don't end up pouring silicone all over the place. If you're uncertain about your ability to hit a target from above, *practice first!*

You also want to be using a silicone rubber with a long cure time; that will allow any remaining air bubbles to rise in the mold, away from the surface of the sculpture, where you absolutely do not want them.

44. As the silicone fills the mold cavity, it will begin to seep out the bleeder holes. As each hole begins to leak, plug the hole with a drywall screw or a piece of WED clay.

45. The silicone cure time should be anywhere from 16 to 24 hours, depending on which silicone you used. When the silicone is fully cured, remove your funnel and cut away the excess rubber. Then remove the plaster and clay from the bottom of the mold. The hot glue may be a little trouble, but if you spray it with Superglue activator, it will soften and be easier to peel away. Then carefully open the mold with the proper tools inserted into the pry holes, just as you did before.

46. The next step is to remove the clay from the other half of the mold and weigh it, as you did for the other half. Repeat steps 33 through 40, remembering to

FIGURE 5.36
Use 99 percent isopropyl alcohol and a cut-down chip brush to clean clay from the silicone mold. Image reproduced by permission of Mark Alfrey.

> **TIP**
> Superglue activator sprayed on hot glue will soften it so that it's easier to remove.

brush a light coat of petroleum jelly over the silicone as well as the exposed stone of the case mold before clamping the mold shut; you don't want the silicone bonding to itself!

47. When this silicone has cured, you can open the mold and begin removing the clay sculpture. Be careful not to damage the silicone as you're digging out the clay. You should use dull wooden tools as you get close to the silicone.

48. After you've removed all the clay, separate the inner silicone mold from the outer rigid case mold. Cut off the little rubber protrusions (called *sprues*) from the bleeder holes so that it will be easier to reseat the silicone into the case mold. Cut them off flat by pulling on them so they stretch, and then cut them.

49. Spray 99 percent alcohol, mineral spirits, or lighter fluid—something that you can use as a solvent for the clay that will not damage the silicone—into the silicone and then brush out the remaining clay with a chip brush that has the bristles cut down.

50. Do this to both sides of the mold, and dry the solvent by patting with paper towels and a blow dryer if necessary. Then seat the silicone molds back into the corresponding case mold halves. Feel around the silicone to make sure that there are no spaces between the silicone and the stone. When you're certain the silicone and stone are seated together perfectly, put the mold halves together and strap the mold closed. When you look into the mold, you should not be able to see a noticeable seam line where the two silicone halves meet.

Your matrix mold is finished and ready for production!

FIBERGLASS MOLDS

Working with fiberglass requires safety precautions. You must wear a respirator, and there must be adequate ventilation where you work with this material. I do not say this lightly. Fiberglass gel coat and laminating resin contain proprietary polyester resin and styrene monomer, the vapor of which is quite harmful and flammable. Without adequate ventilation and a fitted National Institute for Occupational Safety and Health (NIOSH)–approved respirator, you could quickly find yourself up to your chin in floor. That being said, I *love* this stuff! But then, I have a terrific respirator and a super ventilation fan in my shop.

As a casting material and mold material, fiberglass is outstanding. You can even use it as a mold material for baking foam latex in an oven in less time than it takes using a stone mold. It is extremely lightweight and very tough. I was really leery of ever working with fiberglass until Neill Gorton convinced me that it is really easy to use. He was absolutely right, and if *I* can make it turn out well, *anybody* can!

The process is somewhat similar to making a stone mold in that a detail layer is brushed onto the sculpture first and allowed to set before adding laminate reinforced layers. However, that's pretty much where the similarities end. Compared to Ultracal, fiberglass weighs nothing. A thin (1-inch—2.5 cm), burlap-reinforced two-piece case mold made of Ultracal for a 360° head and shoulders bust may easily weigh 20 or 25 lbs. A thin (¼-inch—7 mm) fiberglass mat- or fiberglass cloth-reinforced two-piece case mold made of fiberglass for that same head and shoulders bust will weigh maybe 5 lbs., *tops!* If that much; maybe only 3 lbs. My point is that a fiberglass mold won't weigh much. This makes for far easier handling and much quicker curing times when you're making foam latex appliances, and time is money in this business.

Unlike silicone, latex, or urethane rubber molds, fiberglass is relatively inflexible. That is, it will not "give" in the way those other materials will. At least, it probably won't give as much or at the points where you want it to. In fact, compared to those materials, fiberglass is downright immobile. If you make a fiberglass mold of a hard or rigid object that has undercuts of any kind, you will find yourself with a mold that you cannot remove without breaking the mold, the sculpture, or both. Seriously, even a seemingly insignificant undercut will wreak havoc. Be very, very careful before building a fiberglass mold.

In addition, and I cannot stress this point enough so I'm saying it again: Fiberglass resin is very toxic in its liquid state. You need to work in a room with good ventilation and wear a NIOSH-approved respirator. Serious respiratory problems or death are considered to be unattractive life choices, so I suggest you try to avoid them whenever possible.

Another significant difference between making a stone mold and a fiberglass mold is the size of the dividing wall you will need to build. Because you will be creating a fiberglass flange wide enough for you to bolt the two (or more) sections of the mold together, the clay wall will need to be wide as well.

Why do the mold pieces need to be bolted together? That's an excellent question. Though the fiberglass mold you make will be very strong and stiff, it will be thin, and because it is thin and also fairly large, there will be flexibility. By bolting the pieces together around the mold flange, the flexibility is taken out of the equation, making the mold very firm and holding its shape for casting inside it.

153

FIGURE 5.37
The clay wall must be wide to accommodate the flange needed to hold the mold together. Image reproduced by permission of Neill Gorton.

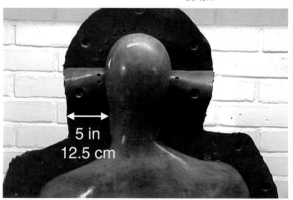

5 in
12.5 cm

To build a fiberglass matrix mold of a bust, you'll need the following tools as well as materials listed at the beginning of this chapter:

WED clay or other water clay
Fiberglass mat, etc.
Laminating resin
Water spray bottle
Clay tools
1-inch chip brushes
Utility knife
Petroleum jelly
Epoxy Parfilm or Synlube 531
Wood base
Polyethylene sheet

Misc. containers
Gel coat
Rubber gloves
Paper towels
Soft brush
NIOSH-approved respirator
Plaster bandages
PVA release
Crystal Clear, varnish, or shellac
Safety glasses

FIGURE 5.38
Fiberglass mold pieces should be bolted together for added strength. Image reproduced by permission of Neill Gorton.

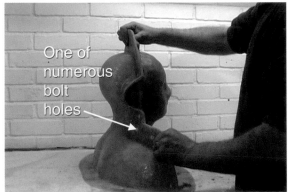
One of numerous bolt holes

Fiberglass gel coat is thicker than the laminating resin (polyester) used to apply fiberglass mat and fiberglass cloth, though some fiberglass resin is considered all purpose or general purpose. If you decide to use an all-purpose resin, you might find it helpful to thicken it with a filler such as Cab-O-Sil (fumed silica). It will need to be mixed thoroughly and left for a while to ensure that all the fumed silica particles dissolve and disperse throughout the polyester resin. Finding the right gel coat and laminating resin should not be too difficult, but the listing of suppliers in the appendix might be helpful if you cannot easily find what you are looking for locally. Most suppliers have online ordering capabilities and shipping.

Gel coat is available in different colors, so don't let color selection confuse you. Though there are differences in polyester formulation for laminating resin, mostly in terms of stiffness or surface finish after cure, those properties will not conflict with whatever gel coat is used.

A note about using fiberglass cloth vs. fiberglass mat: Fiberglass cloth is strong and is often used where it could be visible and where aesthetics are important. One of the downsides of fiberglass cloth is that because the strands are neatly woven, the layers do not intermesh as they do with the loose, disorganized strands on the fiberglass mat. Therefore the layers of cloth sit on top of one another rather than meshing together the way they do on the fiberglass mat. This might or might not be a concern for the type of mold being made, but I'm putting the information out there for you to weigh. Fiberglass tissue is very thin, very fine fiberglass mat and is sometimes referred to as *veil*. It is outstanding for reinforcing and laminating fine detail areas.

Fiberglass resin contains *styrene*, which reacts with the glass fibers in the fiberglass mat, cloth, and tissue, softening it (essentially dissolving it) so that it is easy to shape and mold around forms. Styrene is the primary reason for using proper ventilation and wearing eye protection, rubber gloves, NIOSH-approved respirator, and even coveralls.

The principal health effects due to styrene exposure involve the central nervous system. These effects include subjective complaints of headache, fatigue, dizziness, confusion, drowsiness, malaise, difficulty in concentrating, and a feeling of intoxication. The International Agency for Research on Cancer (IARC) classifies styrene as a potential human carcinogen. Acute health effects of styrene are generally irritation of the skin, eyes, and the upper respiratory tract. Acute exposure also results in gastrointestinal effects. Chronic exposure affects the central nervous system, showing symptoms such as depression, headache, fatigue, and weakness, and may cause minor effects on kidney function. Additional information about recognizing occupational hazards and health effects associated with styrene can be found at www.osha.gov/SLTC/styrene/recognition.html.

I know these warnings make working with fiberglass sound rather frightening. It really isn't. However, I would be remiss if I did not identify potential problem areas so that you can easily avoid them by working smart and being safe.

For the best step-by-step instructions for creating a fiberglass core (positive) and fiberglass matrix mold, I strongly recommend purchasing Neill Gorton's four-DVD series, *Creating Character Prosthetics in Silicone*. Neill is a great teacher and the series is terrific.

FILLERS

In casting core positives or even when making molds, it is often desirable to add some kind of filler to the polyester resin to give it added strength and longevity. Depending on the need, there are different fillers that will give different properties to the materials they're added to. For example, adding fumed silica (Cab-O-Sil®) as filler to a material such as polyester laminating resin will cause the silica to act as a thixotropic agent, making the laminating resin thicker. It also enhances tensile strength, abrasion resistance, and stiffness. Adding chopped fibers to that same laminating resin will make it stronger as well. Metallic powders can also be added as fillers. These will make a material stronger as well as heavier; heavier metal powder will add weight proportionally by volume as well as tint the material to the metallic color. Other fillers, such as certain types of microspheres, not only can add strength to a material, they can make it lighter, depending on what the spheres are. Aluminum powder added to polyester resin for fiberglass mold fabrication, for example, will increase the hardness and abrasion resistance of the surface.

RESIN MOLDS

Yes, fiberglass is a resin—a rather toxic resin in its uncured, liquid state, as is, unfortunately, the nature of most resins. Some are more toxic than others. But you've read the safety precautions discussed in Chapter 1, and you've been paying attention to them in this chapter as well, so you are well prepared for using these materials.

Forton MG (FMG), though technically a gypsum product (Hydrocal is the main ingredient), is considered a resin casting material because it incorporates plastics and fiberglass. FMG consists of a modified gypsum (hence the MG—Modified Gypsum), FGR-95, dry melamine resin powder, a hardener, a liquid polymer called Forton VF-812, and chopped fiberglass. The advantages of FMG over fiberglass are that it is odorless and nontoxic and it cures much faster. Another advantage is that it can be cast directly into an alginate mold, unlike polyester and epoxy resins. The disadvantages are that there are more components to measure and measurement must be precise, so an accurate gram scale is essential; in addition, it is heavier than polyester or epoxy resin molds. By my math, advantages outweigh disadvantages for Forton MG. (Please excuse the pun.)

You can also substitute Densite HS for the FGR-95. FGR-95 is Alpha gypsum from U.S. Gypsum, whereas Densite HS is from Georgia Pacific but is also Alpha gypsum. What *is* Alpha gypsum? Alpha gypsum is made by processing batches of gypsum under high pressure; it has a lower water-carrying capability and is used where strength is required, as in mold making. *Ahhhh*...So what's Beta gypsum? When the hemi-hydrate of gypsum (two gypsum molecules for every one molecule of water) is formed by calcining (heating to the point of burning to ash) in kettles at atmospheric pressure, it's called Beta gypsum. *Ohhhhhh*...now don't you wish you'd paid attention in chemistry class? Sources where you can get Forton MG are listed in the appendix. A similar gypsum-based resin product is called duoMatrix, from Smooth-On.

Forton MG really doesn't need fillers for strength because it already has them as part of the system. However, you can add metallic powders or marble powders to it to simulate the look and feel of foundry castings or natural stone sculpture. The surfaces can then be patinaed using foundry etching acids or be polished to a high shine.

URETHANE MOLDS

Urethane is just one more way to go in the world of mold making for special makeup effects. Actually, when we use the term *urethane* as it pertains to the work that we do and the uses we have for it, the name has been shortened from *polyurethane*. There is a specific substance called urethane, also known as *ethyl carbamate*, and the two should not be confused. For our purposes, when you see the word *urethane* in the context of special makeup effects, it means *poly*urethane.

Urethane formulas cover an extremely wide range of stiffness, hardness, and densities. These materials include low- and high-density flexible foam used in upholstery and bedding as well as in makeup effects prosthetics (known as *cold foam*), which will be discussed fully in Chapter 6; low- and high-density rigid foam used for thermal insulation; soft-solid elastomers used for gel pads, print rollers, and mold making as a substitute for some tin-cure RTV silicones; and hard-solid plastics used as electronic instrument bezels, structural parts, and mold making as well, as a substitute for epoxy and polyester resin molds. Urethanes are widely used in high-resiliency flexible foam seating, rigid foam insulation panels, microcellular foam seals and gaskets, durable elastomeric wheels and tires, electrical potting compounds, high-performance adhesives and sealants, Spandex fibers, seals, gaskets, carpet underlay, and hard plastic parts.[1] There are a number of commercial urethane foam, urethane rubber, and urethane plastic products designed for use by makeup effects artists and mold makers. These are listed in the appendix at the back of this book.

For the most part, the use of these materials is the same as their counterparts, with a few notable exceptions. The reason we use silicones for mold making is that silicones are essentially *self-releasing*; that is, almost nothing will stick to silicone except other silicone. Urethane rubbers, on the other hand, are not self-releasing. In fact, they are the opposite: Urethane rubbers are adhesive. To prevent adhesion between urethane rubber and the porous surface of a cast (made of Hydrocal, plaster, Ultracal, or the like), it must be sealed and then released. Casts made of thermoplastic, which includes urethane plastic, epoxy, and polyester resin (fiberglass), must be sealed with shellac or PVA and then released. When in doubt about what to use, manufacturers recommend a small test application to determine the proper release agent. That is a good idea, considering how much work goes into a project prior to reaching this point. It'd sure be a shame to have to start over.

All liquid urethanes are moisture sensitive and will absorb atmospheric moisture. Using water-based clays is not recommended. Mixing tools and containers should be clean and made of metal or plastic; mixing urethane with a wooden stir stick can cause problems merely via atmospheric moisture retained in the wood, even if you're working in a humidity–controlled environment. If you choose to make your mold using urethane rubber instead of silicone and you plan on building the dividing wall with WED or other water clay, it is absolutely imperative that the clay be well sealed with Crystal Clear, and dry, before applying the urethane! *I strongly suggest a test with sealed clay and a bit of urethane before trying this on a project.*

This is quite true also of urethane plastic used for a hard outer shell of a matrix mold, for example. If you are using WED clay or other water-based clay to form barriers and walls, it must definitely be well sealed to prevent moisture contact with the urethane. It will bubble and foam if there is any contact with any moisture from water. Use another material to form your walls.

Working with silicone does not require that you wear a respirator or work in a well-ventilated environment (though it's not a bad idea to have good ventilation anyway), but it is strongly recommended that you wear safety glasses and gloves to minimize the risk of contamination and irritation. However, working with urethane shares essentially the same hazardous risks of working with fiberglass resins: epoxy and polyester. Mixing should only be done in a well-ventilated

[1]Wikipedia contributors, "Polyurethane," *Wikipedia, The Free Encyclopedia,* http://en.wikipedia.org/w/index.php?title=Polyurethane&oldid=177688842

environment while wearing a respirator. Rubber gloves and safety glasses are also strongly advised. Before working with any of these materials, you should read and be familiar with each product's material safety data sheet (MSDS).

With these exceptions, working with urethane follows the same procedural steps as working with gypsum, silicone, and fiberglass. We won't repeat the step-by-step process in this book. You can easily go back and figure it out on your own.

CHAPTER SUMMARY

- This chapter describes the steps needed to break down a sculpture into the parts needed for mold making.
- You learned about the types and importance of release agents and sealers.
- Resculpting for multipiece makeup was illustrated.
- The purpose and placement of keys, flashing, and cutting edges was described.
- You were shown how to construct a sturdy clay retaining wall around your sculpture.
- You were told about different types of molds and mold materials and were given descriptions of them.
- You were told about fillers.

CHAPTER 6

Casting the Appliances

159

Key Points

- Understanding silicone (continued)
- Coloring silicone intrinsically (internally) for translucence
- Gel-filled appliances, filling the mold, and removing the appliance
- Foam latex and its properties
- Running foam latex
- Casting urethane (cold) foam
- Casting gelatin and foamed gelatin
- Casting dental acrylic
- Painting and seaming (cleaning up) appliances and teeth

INTRODUCTION

This chapter describes the methods for creating prosthetics using silicone, foam latex, foam urethane, gelatin, and foamed gelatin and dental acrylic. Rather than make a laundry list of materials needed to cast prosthetic appliances, I will add the list of materials specific to a particular type of appliance, such as foam latex, gelatin, and silicone, for each section.

David Elsey

FIGURE 6.1
Dave Elsey. Image reproduced by permission of David Elsey.

From creating fantastical creatures for the sci-fi television series *Farscape* to his plant-wrangling skills for *The Little Shop of Horrors*, Dave Elsey has demonstrated an extraordinary ability to create memorable characters using makeup and animatronics over the past 20 years. To many, Dave's résumé reads like a cult-film dream list: He created creature effects in *Alien 3*; worked as a special makeup-effects artist on *Hellraiser, Mission: Impossible, MI 2,* and *Indiana Jones and the Last Crusade*; and honed his animatronics skills in the cult classic, *The Little Shop of Horrors*. He is perhaps most well known by genre fans for his role as the creative supervisor on the sci-fi TV series *Farscape*, for which he designed and maintained up to 600 different creatures.

For his role as the Creature Shop Supervisor for *Star Wars: Episode III, Revenge of the Sith* (for which he was nominated for an Academy Award), Dave and his makeup effects team were responsible for bringing to life all the animatronics, prosthetic creatures, and characters seen in the film. Dave was at the forefront of the Creature Shop team responsible for such *Episode III* creations as the Wookies, the Utapauns, charred Anakin Skywalker, and the twisted Emperor Palpatine.

FIGURE 6.2
Dave applying Scorpius makeup to actor Wayne Pygram. Images reproduced by permission of David Elsey.

FIGURE 6.3
Applying charred makeup to actor Hayden Christensen. Images reproduced by permission of David Elsey.

FIGURE 6.4
Makeup effects from *Black Sheep*. Images reproduced by permission of David Elsey.

Since then Dave has worked on the movie *Ghost Rider* with Nicholas Cage and collaborated with Richard Taylor of Weta Workshop in New Zealand on an independent film entitled *Black Sheep*.

Most recently Dave was the co-creature supervisor as well as creating the additional creatures for Spike Jonze's *Where the Wild Things Are*. In 2008 Dave worked in London with makeup effects legend Rick Baker and fellow book contributor John Schoonraad on makeup effects for a remake of the 1941 Lon Chaney, Jr., horror classic *The Wolf Man*, starring Anthony Hopkins and Benicio Del Toro.

SILICONE: PLATINUM AND TIN RTV

I've talked at length about one of the materials commonly used for creating prosthetic appliances, but only as it applies to mold making: silicone. Appliances
made of silicone look and feel remarkably like real skin. They certainly can, anyway. And they're made mostly using platinum RTV silicone because platinum
silicone cures significantly faster than tin silicone, though both will cure in a
shorter time with the application of heat. Many platinum silicones, unlike all
tin silicones, are safe for application directly to the skin. Something else that's
true about platinum silicone is that the more platinum it contains, the faster it
will kick and the more expensive it becomes. Last time I checked, platinum was
pretty expensive.

The good news is that there are also some wonderful tin RTV silicones available for prosthetics, particularly tin silicone gels; they just take longer to cure.
They can be accelerated, but as you'll recall, a fast catalyst will weaken the
silicone. Perhaps that won't happen quickly enough to be a problem for your
application if it's immediate, but most silicones have a negligible shrink
factor. If you make multiples of a piece with the intention of storing them
over time, they may become unusable, even brittle, if the cure is accelerated.
This can happen within a matter of days, especially if you use only a fast catalyst and none of the regular catalyst. I've seen it happen with some of my tin
RTV mold rubber; I am making a presumption that it will be true for other
silicones as well. I'm sure I will be quickly corrected if I am mistaken about
that.

Silicone appliances can be cast in a number of types of molds, including Ultracal,
Hydrocal, fiberglass, Forton MG, urethane, and even silicone, provided it's supported by a jacket mold. However, remember that platinum silicone cannot be
cast into a tin silicone mold; it will not cure. Platinum into tin is not okay. Tin
into platinum is okay; tin into tin is okay; platinum into platinum is okay. But
the molds *must* be released well to prevent the new silicone from permanently
bonding to the silicone of the mold.

FIGURE 6.5
Backlighting shows the
depth and translucency
of an intrinsically colored
silicone appliance. Photo
by the author.

COLORATION

One of the great things about silicone is its simi-
larity in look and feel to human skin when it is
colored intrinsically with pigment. Human skin
is actually translucent. When silicone is colored
internally with any number and type of pigments, most notably colored rayon flocking, the
silicone color has actual depth, just like skin.

Silicone can also be colored intrinsically with
opaque pigments that significantly lessen the
sense of depth and translucence; however, if the

amount is very small, translucency can be maintained. This is something that will require experimentation on your part; there is no formula for coloring silicone. I will tell you this, though: Silicone can be very difficult to paint. Silicone is resistant to acids, bases, solvents, chemicals, oils, and water. Virtually *nothing* sticks to silicone ... except other silicone.

If you choose to forego intrinsic coloring and you color your appliance extrinsically, you will need to use a silicone-based coloring system. You can achieve decent results with a crème foundation that is not silicone based, but the moment your actor rubs his nose or accidentally brushes against something or someone, that makeup is going to wipe right off, no matter how much powder or sealer you applied to set the makeup. Fortunately, there are some terrific silicone-based airbrush paints and makeup foundations designed for use on silicone appliances. You can also color with alcohol-activated pigments, such as Premiere Products' Skin Illustrator® palettes, developed by Kenny Myers, and WM Creations' Sta-Color palettes, developed by Matthew Mungle.

Materials

We won't detail a set list of tools and materials that you'll need to cast an appliance in silicone, for the simple reason that though there are certain similarities in the process for casting any silicone appliance, each different makeup will be ... well, different. Here are several items you will most definitely need:

Two-part silicone	Mixing containers
Mixing sticks	Digital scale
Mold	Mold release
Mold straps or clamps	Powder
Screwdriver ,	Air compressor
Vacuum/pressure chamber	Syringe (at least 100 ml)

FIGURE 6.6
Stippling a thin layer of silicone into the mold as an encapsulating layer. Images reproduced by permission of Neill Gorton.

163

Silicone can be cast into a mold in more than one way. It can be poured, brushed, stippled, or injected. Or it can be cast using combination of these methods. The way the silicone gets into the mold is largely dependent on the type of prosthetic being cast. A full-head cowl appliance would be impossible to pour. A thin layer of silicone could be stippled into the mold halves first, to ensure that all details have been captured before placing the mold pieces together and then injecting the balance of the silicone into the mold.

De-airing/Degassing Silicone

Because silicone is relatively viscous as a liquid (compared to water), air bubbles easily become suspended in it when the components are mixed together. For that reason, it is often recommended that silicone be de-aired or degassed in a vacuum chamber before it goes into the mold. This might not always be possible for a couple of reasons: You don't have access to a vacuum chamber or a vacuum pump or there isn't enough time because the silicone has a very short pot life before it kicks.

If you mix the silicone components carefully it is possible (*possible* does not mean *likely*) to prevent air bubbles from occurring. It is likely that you can minimize the size and number, but you are not likely to prevent bubbles altogether. There is also an effective workaround for de-airing your silicone without investing in an expensive vacuum pump and vacuum chamber. You can eliminate air bubbles (or at least make them very, very small—almost invisible) by pressurizing the silicone instead of pulling a vacuum. You still need a pressure chamber to do it, but air compressors are far less expensive than vacuum pumps and you probably already have access to an air compressor.

FIGURE 6.7
A Venturi-type vacuum pump from Harbor Freight. Photo by the author.

Small vacuum/pressure chambers can be found rather easily online at little cost, and if you're dead-set on vacuum de-airing, for about $18(£9.66) from Harbor Freight you can buy a Central Pneumatic air-vac, a Venturi-type vacuum pump that uses air pressure to create enough vacuum to de-air your silicone in short order!

Your air compressor needs to generate at least 90 lbs. of pressure to pull 28.3 (71.9 cm) inches of mercury at sea level. From the same vendor you can also find a 2½-gallon pressure paint tank that is great for pressure or vacuum for under $100 (£53.59). Problem solved. With a little more effort you can replace the opaque metal lid with a clear Plexiglas (3/4–1 inch thick or 2–2.5 cm) replacement so you can see what's going on inside. Often, however, simply allowing the silicone to sit at room temperature until the air bubbles have risen to the surface and disappeared is all you need to do before pouring or injecting the silicone into the mold cavity provided the silicone is not fast-setting.

GEL-FILLED SILICONE APPLIANCES

If you've every held a silicone breast implant in your hand (pre-implantation), you know how soft and squishy they are, or can be. Squeeze your cheeks (gently) or feel your (or someone's) love handles … that's the consistency and softness a gel-filled appliance (GFA) should have. The best GFAs are made with a gel that has a much firmer consistency than you'd find in a silicone breast implant or breast enhancement product.

GFAs are arguably the single most difficult type of prosthetic appliance to make by reason of the steps involved in merely casting the appliance into the mold. The silicone gel must *fill* something; it is a gel-*filled* appliance. The gel is one component. The other, a silicone envelope or capsule, must be created for the gel to fill. How is that accomplished? By using an encapsulator, which can (should) be silicone or a liquid-like vinyl cap material that will cure to a solid, flexible skin. Using an encapsulator other than silicone could cause the gel and the encapsulating envelope not to bond well and to separate (since nothing sticks to silicone except other silicone), causing unwanted and largely unfixable problems with the appliance. As long as you don't try to add a platinum gel to a tin encapsulator, the silicones should cure and bond permanently to each other without a problem.

Filling the Mold

Prepping the mold is the first order of business. Depending on how long it's been since the mold was made, it might need to be cleaned again to ensure that no contaminants such as dust and stray hairs have found their way onto the negative surfaces of the mold interior.

Once the mold pieces are clean and dry (if they're stone molds) they will need to be sealed and released; if the mold is made of fiberglass or other resin, it probably doesn't need to be released, though it's never wrong to release a mold if you have any doubt as to whether the silicone will stick or not without it. If you will be casting silicone into silicone, this is very important: Tin silicone can be cast into a mold of either tin or platinum silicone (the mold must be properly released, of course) but *platinum silicone can be cast* only *into a platinum silicone mold, not a tin silicone mold.*

Injection Filling

To inject silicone into your mold, at least two holes must be drilled in the mold positive: one to inject silicone through and the other to allow air to escape as the mold fills. The syringe for injecting the silicone should be made of polyethylene or polypropylene and should not have a latex rubber end on the plunger; that would cause platinum silicone inhibition—it won't cure. Make sure the mold pieces have been thoroughly released, including the injection hole and the vent hole.

1. Release the mold pieces.
2. For creating a GFA, brush or stipple a thin coat of mixed silicone encapsulator material on both halves of the mold, positive and negative. Be careful not to stipple silicone over the cutting edge of the appliance mold.
3. When the encapsulator material begins to set, close the mold and clamp or bolt securely together.

165

FIGURE 6.8
Be careful not to stipple silicone over the cutting edge of the mold.
Image reproduced by permission of Neill Gorton.

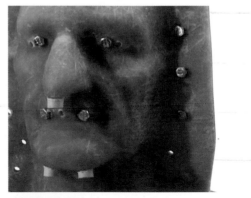

FIGURE 6.9
Hand-tighten the bolts first and then tighten them with a wrench.
Image reproduced by permission of Neill Gorton.

4. Allow the encapsulator material to fully cure inside the mold. You might want to accelerate the cure by applying heat. As a rough guide, the recommended cure schedule for a 1-inch-thick Ultracal mold is 2 to 3 hours at 200°F (93°C).

5. Allow the mold to cool.

6. Mix the gel components together and add pigment and/or flocking, then de-air them in an evacuator (vacuum chamber); or simply let the air bubbles rise and disperse on their own (only if you're using a slow-cure gel). Fill the syringe with the gel and slowly inject it through one of the holes until it begins to come out the second hole.

> **NOTE**
>
> To know how much silicone gel to mix, you need to use the weight of the clay you saved from the appliance sculpture, then mix a bit more than that so you have room for overflow. It's better to have a bit more than you need than not quite enough and need to start over.

FIGURE 6.10
After injecting as much silicone as the mold can take, remove the plunger so that the silicone will continue to fill; the photo at right shows silicone exiting one of many bleeder holes. Images reproduced by permission of Neill Gorton.

 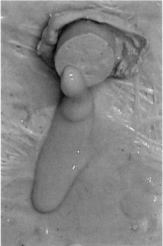

7. Carefully remove the syringe and gently tap the mold, and tilt it to work any remaining air through the holes.

8. Reinsert the syringe and top off the mold with gel if necessary.

9. Allow the gel to cure at room temperature for 24 hours (or as long as the manufacturer recommends) or place it back into the oven for 1–1½ hours at 200°F (93°C) for the gel to cure. Allow the mold to slowly cool enough to handle (90–100°F/32–37°C)—if the mold is gypsum, it may crack if cooled too quickly—and *carefully* demold the appliance. Wash off any release residue and trim the injection and bleeder sprues.

10. Cover the trimmed sprue points with fresh encapsulator material and allow it to cure. Then powder the appliance; it is ready for painting and application.

You should store your appliance in an airtight plastic bag if it's not going to be used in the near future. For painting, it would be handy to have a duplicate of the positive for the appliance to lie on or a generic positive so that the prosthetic will have the relative shape it is supposed to have.

You do not have to be making a gel-filled appliance in order to inject silicone. Injecting silicone merely ensures that you will have an easier time filling a more complex mold shape. The steps are the same, minus the encapsulator.

Hand Filling

The hand-fill method for making a GFA is similar to the injection method, though the injection hole and vent hole are not necessary.

1. Release the mold sections the same way you would if you were going to inject the silicone. Make sure the release is completely dried before the next step.
2. Brush or stipple a thin coat of mixed silicone encapsulator on both halves of the mold, positive and negative. You might want to experiment with thixotropic agents if you find the encapsulator is too runny, even when stippled on thinly. You shouldn't need to, however.
3. Mix up the silicone gel and allow it to de-air; when the encapsulator has dried (but not cured), pour the gel into the mold negative. If you are going to color the gel intrinsically, now is the time to do it!
4. Fit the positive carefully into the negative and clamp the two halves together securely, then oven cure it at 200°F (93°C). Again, the recommended length of time is 2 to 3 hours for a 1-inch (2.5 cm) Ultracal or other gypsum mold. The remaining three steps are exactly the same.

> **NOTE**
>
> The oven curing is not essential. If you do not have access to an oven or hot box, the silicone will cure at room temperature; it will simply take longer. The results will be identical.

Removing the Appliance

1. Allow the mold to slowly cool enough to handle (90–100°F)—if the mold is gypsum, it may crack if cooled too quickly—and carefully demold the appliance.
2. Wash off any release residue and trim the injection and bleeder sprues.
3. Cover the trimmed sprue points with fresh encapsulator material and allow it to cure. Then powder the appliance; it is ready for painting and application.

The steps for casting a regular silicone appliance are exactly the same—injected or hand-filled, minus the encapsulator; the oven curing is also an option and is by no means a necessity. In fact, if you use Polytek's Plat-Sil Gel-10 platinum

RTV silicone, it kicks pretty quickly (within 15 minutes at room temperature) and can usually be demolded in less than an hour with no additional heat.

Foam Latex

I *love* foam latex! As a material for making prosthetic appliances for special makeup effects, foam latex is, in my opinion, unrivaled for performer comfort. Materials such as silicone might mimic the appearance and feel of human skin more believably and realistically, but silicone does not breathe, and an active actor wearing silicone appliances will begin to perspire rather profusely beneath the silicone if it is worn for an extended period of time, as many actors must. Gelatin will probably start to melt. Don't get me wrong; the material for a given appliance should not be chosen randomly or by economy, and I have nothing against working with silicone or gelatin as an appliance material. I work with silicone quite a bit as well as gelatin and urethane (cold) foam. Appliance materials must be chosen based on numerous factors, such as climate, shot framing, performance, and budget. There are a number of foam latex systems on the market, and they are listed in the appendix at the back of this book. I am most familiar with GM foam and have been using it for a number of years.

I particularly love foam latex for its texture and feel. When it's made well, it feels better than velvet, and every subtle expression and nuance of emotion is translated beautifully through the foam from the performer; it *becomes* the performer. A nearly full-face appliance will likely weigh less than an ounce and, when applied, is almost undetectable by the actor wearing it. Foam latex breathes, so it is comfortable and an actor can wear it all day long, as is frequently the case.

FIGURE 6.11
GM foam latex components. Photo by the author.

Materials

Foam latex components (latex base, foaming agent, curing agent, gelling agent, color)

Misc. additives	Mixer and bowl
Timer	Appliance mold(s)
Digital scale	Foam latex oven
Oven mitts	Foam injector
Mold straps	

QUIRKS

However, though foam latex is extremely light, strong, breathable, and expressive, there are some qualities that could be construed as negatives by some. I must confess, to get that extremely light, strong, breathable, and expressive appliance, there are a number of hoops that must be jumped through to get there. Though every material used to make prosthetics has quirks and idiosyncrasies, foam latex is probably the most difficult material to work with overall, from several perspectives.

First, foam latex is opaque. You can't see through it. Unlike silicone and gelatin, which can be colored intrinsically to be semitransparent or translucent, just like real human skin, foam latex is naturally opaque. To create the semblance of translucency, the appliance must be painted with numerous transparent layers of pigment, usually with an airbrush, to achieve the look of real skin.

Second, foam latex requires a heat cure in an oven, and it *cannot* be the same oven you use to bake tollhouse cookies and Thanksgiving turkeys!

Why? Because third, foam latex gives off toxic fumes during the heat cure that will render your oven forever unfit for cooking. There are a few alternatives, one of which is building your own makeshift oven using infrared heat lamps in a well-insulated plywood box. I can show you how, if you're interested. I am now using an old GE consumer oven that I rewired from 220v to 110v. It's not very large, but I can fit a two-piece mold for a full-face appliance and two smaller molds

FIGURE 6.12
A rescued kitchen appliance makes a terrific foam latex oven for small to medium-sized appliances. Photo by the author.

in it pretty easily. I might be hard pressed to get a full bust mold for an over-the-head cowl in it, but it has served its purpose well, and I couldn't pass up the price—*free*—when a neighbor remodeled his kitchen and asked me if I had any use for his old oven. (On the plus side, I get pretty terrific results with it.)

Whatever you use as your latex oven, your foam latex should cure in an oven that cannot exceed a controllable/maintainable 200°F. Ideally, foam should cure no hotter than 185°F (85°C). I frequently cook it at 170°F (about 77°C) for a longer time, as I will describe a little further on.

Foam latex is time and temperature sensitive. When I was first learning how to run foam, I remember mixing the foam according to the instructions for using GM Foam and watching the foam solidify in midpour from the mixing bowl into the mold. D'oh! It was like watching a cartoon.

Foam latex shrinks. The thicker the foam, the more it shrinks. That's not to be confused with the volume of the foam; lower-volume foam (heavier) will shrink more than high-volume foam (lighter) because it has more air and a lesser proportion of foam latex components. It is *water loss* that causes shrinkage in the foam. Since higher-volume foam stretches more than denser low-volume foam, any shrinkage that does occur can usually be compensated by stretching, with little force exerted on the foam.

What the mold is made of also contributes to the shrinkage of the foam or the lack thereof. A porous mold like Ultracal will cause the foam to shrink less because it absorbs moisture from the foam.

Foam latex, being essentially a foam rubber sponge, will collapse into itself when it moves, such as with a fold of neck skin; silicone appliances displace themselves remarkably like real tissue. These are tradeoffs that you must decide on during the design (and budgeting) phase of your makeup. Foam latex is more delicate than silicone and rarely survives removal in one piece at the end of the day, necessitating fresh appliances for each performance day the actor is in makeup. Silicone, if handled and treated carefully, can be robust enough even for delicate edges to survive multiple applications.

Before I describe the process for running a batch of foam latex, let me give you a little backstory on latex itself. Latex is a natural liquid that comes from the hevea tree grown in Malaysia, Thailand, Indonesia, the Philippines, and other tropical countries. The tree is tapped and a small amount of latex (only a few ounces) is collected from each tree before the cut on the tree congeals and heals itself. Each tree is tapped only once every two days. According to GM Foam's technical information, over 95 percent of all natural latex is concentrated by a method called *centrifuging*. The result is a high-quality product containing 60–65 percent solids, used mainly for dipping compounds such as rubber gloves and condoms. The remaining latex, which is less than 5 percent of the world's production, is concentrated by another method called *creaming*, a process whereby ammonium alginate is added to the raw latex, causing separation. The watery "serum layer" is drained from the vats, leaving a higher concentration of latex.

Ammonia is then added as a preservative; this also prevents the latex from coagulating, leaving the final concentration at approximately 68 percent latex solids. Creamed latex separates over time and will continue to separate unless it is shaken on a weekly basis, to keep it mixed and fresh. This type of latex has a greater stretchiness than the centrifuged latex, so it is also considered the best latex for making prosthetic foam.

Since latex is a natural product, its composition is dependent on environmental conditions. The hevea trees and the latex are affected by how much rainfall there is in a given season, how many sunny days, how young the trees are, and so on. Thus, the quality of rubber varies from season to season, year to year, and month to month. These fluctuations can wreak havoc for artists running foam for makeup effects, because the latex will behave differently all the time. What GM Foam does when it purchases creamed latex is to calibrate its own latex base. When the company receives the latex, it first adjusts the pH balance, then conditions the latex with additives and finally makes a special blend with other types of latex. By doing this GM Foam can carefully control the cell size, foam volume, flow, and gel time. This means that if you follow the instructions provided with GM Foam latex, the foam should perform exactly as predicted, every time. In theory. Though there is significant science involved in making foam latex prosthetics, it is every bit as much an art.

Provided that you have already created your appliance sculpture, made the molds, and dried, sealed, and released them properly, you are now ready to run some foam! Basically, the operation goes like this: A batch of latex is mixed together with a foaming agent, a curing agent, and a gelling agent and maybe even a little pigment for color. It is whipped into a frothy foam at high speed in a mixer; I use a 5-quart KitchenAid, kinda like beating egg whites into meringue. Then it is poured or injected into the mold and the mold is placed in the oven and heated at 170°F (76°C) for about 4½ hours. Any temperature above 185°F (85°C) and you will risk overcooking your foam and ruining it.

FIGURE 6.13
A gypsum mold filled and ready to go in the oven. Photo by the author.

Regardless of your location, some experimentation in mixing the foam might be in order to find the right blend of mixing for your foam. Gil Mosko, creator of GM Foam, makes a point of telling people, "Don't be a slave to the schedule. All mixers run differently and many conditions can affect how the foam will rise in the mixer." A key point to remember is that *you must be able to pour the foam from the mixing bowl into the mold*. If the foam is too light and fluffy, which happens when you achieve a very high volume of foam, you may get a really, really soft-cured foam, but you are also very likely to have enormous empty cavities where the foam was unable to get into all parts of the mold due to the lightness of the high-volume foam and its nonpourable condition.

Running Foam Latex

171

A typical batch of foam latex consists of 150 grams of high-grade latex base, 30 grams of foaming agent, 15 grams of curing agent, and 14 grams of gelling agent. There are other ingredients and quantities that can be added for different foam characteristics, but this is a good place to begin. As I mentioned, this operation is time and temperature sensitive as well as humidity sensitive; optimal conditions would be in a room at 69–72°F (20.5–22°C) and with 45–55% humidity.

FIGURE 6.14
An accurate gram scale is essential for running foam latex. Photo by the author.

I am based in Colorado, so I have humidity (rather, the *lack* of humidity) to contend with as well as a lower high-elevation air pressure that also affects what I do. The above "optimal" conditions are based on mixing at sea level, so I'll stick with that, since most of you will probably be working at lower elevations.

Weigh the first three components—the latex base, the foaming agent, and the curing agent—and add them to the mixing bowl. It would be good for you to have an accurate digital gram scale.

Weigh out the gelling agent into a small cup and set it aside. We won't add that until we're almost done mixing. If you're adding pigment, put a few drops of your color into the bowl, too. Then place the mixing bowl into position and you are ready to begin. This will be a 12-minute mix. A timer that will count down is a plus, but if you can tell time and count, a clock or a watch will suffice. (Since you're reading this book, I know you're all very smart.)

1. Your mold must be sealed and released—both the positive and the negative—to prevent the foam latex from sticking and tearing when you attempt to remove it after it cures. If you are using GM Foam, follow the simple instructions for GM's release agent. If you are using different foam, do as you're instructed for that product. Price-Driscoll's Ultra 4 Epoxy Parfilm works pretty well (but only if the stone mold you're using has been sealed and is no longer porous).
2. For the first minute, mix the ingredients on speed 1.
3. For the next 4 minutes, whip the ingredients on speed 10. This will froth the foam and increase the volume in the bowl. As I've already said, Gil Mosko, GM Foam's founder, says to not be a slave to the schedule. Once you understand how foam latex works, you will be able to adapt to any situation.

What the high-speed mixing does in addition to creating high-volume foam is remove ammonia from the latex. Too much ammonia loss and your foam will gel too quickly; not enough ammonia loss and your foam might not gel at all. It might seem like you need a degree in chemistry to run foam (it certainly wouldn't hurt) but that is why there is a mixing guideline to follow, so you don't have to know specific pH values and other scientific-type stuff. Simply understanding the function of the ingredients and the stages of the process should be enough information to do some experimentation. Such as:

- The *foaming agent* bonds as a soap that bonds to the cells of the latex, lowering the surface tension of the latex and allowing it to froth and rise more easily.
- The *curing agent* contains sulfur to help vulcanize (strengthen and add elasticity to) the latex.
- The *gelling agent* creates a reaction that changes the foam from a liquid into a solid.

Record notes of what you do when you are just beginning to work with foam latex as well as when you make changes to any part of the process. Things you might want to include in your notes are:

- Air temperature
- Humidity
- Curing agent (amount, brand, date, and batch number)
- Foaming agent (amount, brand, date, and batch number)
- Gelling agent (amount, brand, date, and batch number)
- Latex base (amount, brand, date, and batch number)
- Additives: accelerators, stabilizers, etc.
- Mixing times
- Pigmentation (amount and color)
- Gel time: start and finish
- Baking time: in and out
- Oven temperature
- Mold: Ultracal, fiberglass, old, new, etc.
- Results

FIGURE 6.15
Mixing a 150 gram batch of GM Foam Latex with a KitchenAid® mixer. Photo by the author.

Prepping the Mold

Foam can be run in a variety of molds, including Ultracal to fiberglass. Ultracal is porous, so it needs to be properly sealed and released to prevent the foam latex from adhering to the mold. Every bit as important as sealing and releasing the mold is making certain that there is no moisture left in the mold before baking foam latex in it. This is important for two reasons. Residual moisture in the mold will prevent moisture from the latex being absorbed by the mold, thereby causing the foam to shrink more after curing. Moisture in the mold can also cause steam pockets to form within the mold, which can ruin the foam. Water heated under pressure (as in a clamped, sealed mold) can boil at a lower temperature than normal (212°F—100°C), such as those needed for baking foam latex (under 200°F). To prevent that from happening, your stone molds should be heated for several hours at nearly 200°F (93°C) to remove any residual moisture. This is particularly true of new molds.

The same is true of fiberglass molds—not to remove residual moisture (because there is none) but to vent off styrene remaining in the mold, which can react badly with the sulfur given off during the foam latex-curing process and transfer to the foam.

Okay, back to the process:

1. Turn the speed down to 4 for 1 minute. This stage will begin to refine the foam, breaking up the biggest bubbles.
2. Turn the speed down to 1 for the last 4 minutes to further refine the foam. When there are 2 minutes left, begin adding the gelling agent and continue mixing for 12 minutes. It is critical that the gelling agent be mixed well, and depending on what mixer you use, the methods of assuring that the gelling agent is sufficiently mixed can vary.
3. At 12 minutes, turn off the mixer and remove the bowl and you are ready to carefully fill your molds.

Once the foam has gelled (you can tell by gently pressing on the foam; it should give a little and bounce back), you can place the molds in the oven and heat them until the foam is fully cured.

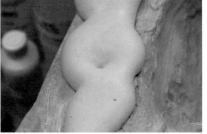

FIGURE 6.16
Testing to see if the foam has gelled. Photos by the author.

Filling the Mold

There are really only two ways to get foam latex into the mold: pouring it in or injecting it into the negative mold. For molds that are no larger than a face, pouring works very well.

If there are deep areas in the mold, such as a long nose for the character of Cyrano de Bergerac (think of Steve Martin's character in the movie *Roxanne*), you might first want to spoon or use a spatula to get some foam down into the nose tip to ensure that it fills and doesn't create an air pocket before you pour or spoon in the rest of the foam. You will learn over time

173

how much or how little foam you actually need to place in the mold to fill it; when you press the positive into the negative, the foam will spread out and into other areas of the mold. If there are deeper portions the foam needs to reach, you will want to use a spatula, craft stick, or even your hand (in a rubber glove!) to spread it into those areas to avoid trapping air.

As the foam is pressed outward by the positive, the excess needs to have somewhere to go; that is why you created an area for flashing, or runoff, when you made the mold. It might even be worthwhile to have drilled small escape holes, called *bleeders*, in the positive to help facilitate the escape of excess foam latex. Foam latex has a lot of resistance to compression, and for your appliance to have fine, ultra-thin edges, both halves of the mold must be able to close completely and touch at the mold's cutting edge.

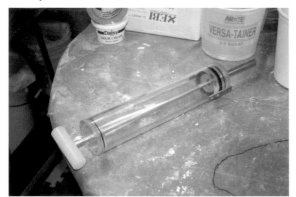

FIGURE 6.17
Foam latex injector.
Photo by the author.

It is often necessary to inject the foam latex into a mold—say, for a full head cowl piece or a large three-piece mold (one inner core positive and two front and back negatives) that would be difficult or very messy to hand-pour.

Large foam injection syringes are available for sale from several sources listed in the appendix. When foam is injected, it is fundamentally different than when you pour the foam onto an open mold. The mold is tightly closed, making it almost airtight, and the act of injecting foam into the mold will create pressure in the mold; air in the mold will need to escape. Without numerous small bleeder holes drilled or bleeder channels etched into the mold positive, foam will not be able to flow easily into those areas.

Heat-Curing Foam

Once the mold is closed and the foam has gelled, it's time to pop it into the oven. But first, you need to understand the following: (1) Higher temperatures make the foam gel faster, and (2) higher humidity makes the foam gel faster. To correct for these conditions, follow these tips: In hot and/or muggy conditions use less gelling agent into the mix and pour it sooner. Another way to extend your working time is to add extra foaming agent, which will prevent the latex from gelling too fast. GM Foam offers a product called Foam Stabilizer that is designed for use in high-humidity, high-temperature environments.

The following points are also very important to understand before embarking on a foam run:

- The cure "window" is larger at lower temperatures. At $185°F$ ($85°C$), foam can take 3 hours to cure, but at 4 hours it could be over-cured. This over-cured foam loses tear strength and in extreme cases becomes crumbly. The same foam, cured at $165°F$ (about $78°C$), could take 5 hours to cure, but even if cured for

7 hours it would still be fine. In other words, a low-temperature cure could have a 3-hour window where the cured foam would be usable. A 200°F (93°C) cure may only have a 20-minute window where the foam is usable.

- Steam lakes are areas of foam that have been pushed away from the mold surface by pockets of steam, then cured into that incorrect shape. These areas have all the detail of the sculpture, but they are depressed and too dense. This is a hazard in nonporous molds, such as epoxical and fiberglass, or molds that have not been properly predried. However, it is a problem that can be remedied:

1. The first step is mold preparation. Nonporous surfaces are to be coated with a thin solution of paste wax (such as Johnson's wax for floors) that has been cut with 99 percent alcohol. This "alcowax" should be thin and runny. Brush it into the inside of the mold, do not allow to pool, and when it's dry, brush it out with a dry brush. The mold surface will become polished and shiny. More important, the mold surface will be sealed from outgassing, which we feel causes sites for steam laking to begin.
2. Cure at a lower temperature (for a longer time). GM Foam recommends curing at 165°F (78°C) for 5 to 7 hours for this kind of mold.

Removing the Appliance

Once you determine that your foam is fully cured, turn off the oven and let the molds begin to cool. If you try to cool the molds too rapidly, they will crack and break; you do not want to rush the process! When the molds are still warm to the touch, you can carefully demold your appliances; they will come out more easily when warm than if you let the molds cool completely. Carefully pry the mold halves apart and help remove the appliance with the use of a blunt wooden tool (so you don't scratch the mold's surface detail), powdering as you go to keep the thin foam edges from sticking together. I want to stress this point: You probably went to a fair amount of trouble to ensure that your appliance would have thin, beautiful edges; if you are not careful and methodical about powdering the appliance during removal, your thin beautiful edges will fold over on themselves and become thick ugly edges that you can't separate.

FIGURE 6.18
Foam latex piece ready to be removed from the mold. Photo by the author.

After you've removed the appliance, it must be gently washed in warm water containing only a few drops of dishwashing liquid (I use either Ivory or Palmolive dish soap) to remove any residual sulfur from the curing agent. Repeat this procedure until there is no more visible residue in the water, then rinse until all the soap is gone, and gently squeeze out the water; you might want press the appliance between two towels, then allow it to dry completely on the lifecast so that it will maintain its shape.

FIGURE 6.19
Foam appliances in storage bags ready for painting and application. Photo by the author.

When the foam pieces have been washed, dried, and powdered, they should be stored resting in their natural curvature in airtight containers, away from light if possible. It is convenient to use either zip-lock plastic bags or plastic refrigerator containers that have airtight lids. These baggies or plastic containers can then be stored in a cardboard box or any other opaque container that can keep out the light. If stored like this, foam latex pieces can be kept for years without any deterioration. If a foam piece is stored or left to air out with a crease or fold in it, the piece could wind up with a permanent crease line or indentation. Store the appliances in their natural curvature.

Now the foam is ready for painting and application.

The appendix at the back of this book includes more detailed information from GM Foam about run schedules.

COLD FOAM (URETHANE)

Cold foam is urethane foam and is called *cold foam* because it is not heat-cured like foam latex; urethane foam cures at room temperature. Cold foam (Kryolan® makes a urethane foam soft enough for prosthetic work) is an alternative to foam latex and could be a good place to begin working with foam instead of with latex simply because it does not require a lengthy heat cure and can be ready to use quickly. Cold foam is not to be confused with poly foam, which is also flexible urethane foam but has a different use and density associated with it.

That said, urethane foam is *not* a substitute or replacement for foam latex. It is a different material with different properties. It is soft foam suitable for facial and body appliances, but even at its softest, it's not as soft and pliable as foam latex.

You will probably want to work with good ventilation and might actually want to wear a NIOSH-approved respirator (for the ammonia vapors), but working with foam latex does not mandate that you do so; it is not inherently dangerous to your health. Cold foam, on the other hand, contains isocynates, which are considered quite toxic. It is strongly suggested that latex, nitrile, or vinyl gloves be worn in addition to a respirator. At no time should the components of foam in its liquid state come in contact with the skin or clothing; they will adhere to most surfaces, so it is important to wear proper protection when you handle the liquid components.

Materials

Cold foam is a two-part A and B mixture, mixed in a ratio of 35A:65B, so an accurate gram scale is necessary.

Digital scale
Challenge 90 release agent
High-speed drill
Wire beater (made from wire
   hanger)
Mold clamps or mold straps
Latex, nitrile, or vinyl gloves
Appliance mold

Kryolan® two-part Cold Foam System
Food coloring
Respirator
99% alcohol (for cleaning molds)

Misc. disposable cups
½- or 1-inch chip brushes

Part A should be the color and consistency of a light maple syrup. Part B should be off-white or cream colored and the consistency of cream. The release agent (Challenge 90) should be light beige liquid and should be shaken well before using.

Quirks

The Kryolan® cold foam instruction sheet suggests working in a room temperature of at least 80°F (about 27°C). That might be a bit warm, but colder room and mold temperatures can cause the foam to fail occasionally. High humidity can also cause foam to fail; ambient room humidity and even wooden stir sticks with any moisture can cause the foam to collapse. Stone molds or plaster molds must be clean and thoroughly dried before using. New molds can be oven-dried for several hours at about 200°F (93°C); air-drying molds can take as long as several days.

FIGURE 6.20
Kryolan Cold Foam
(urethane). Photo by
the author.

177

Sometimes it is possible to reconstitute a collapsed piece by carefully crushing it; you will hear a popping sound like the noise when you crumple and twist bubble wrap. What you are doing is popping cells in the urethane, allowing the foam to return to its molded shape. Sometimes this will work, sometimes it won't.

The shelf life of cold foam is limited once the product containers have been opened. The chemicals are affected by exposure to air and light; therefore, the components should be stored in a cool, dry, dark area and used fairly soon after purchase. Keep the containers tightly sealed after each use. The manufacturer's recommended shelf life is six months after manufacturing, but I've made excellent pieces with foam components much older than that.

Prepping the Mold

If you are using a stone mold that has been thoroughly dried, it must be sealed to make it as nonporous as possible before applying the release agent. New molds or molds that have not been used in a while should receive a second coating of release. All coats of release should be thin and dry before proceeding. Care must be taken in demolding the foam to prevent tearing the skin. Stone molds can make removal of urethane foam difficult, so beware. Every surface that the foam touches must be released because of the foam's tendency to stick to anything it comes in contact with when it sets up.

Like foam latex, finding the right amount of material to pour into the mold will take some experimentation before you become adept at just "knowing." It will partly be a factor of calculating the volume of the appliance and partly knowing how much the foam will expand as the mixed liquid components turn to foam. When you mix foam latex, the volume is dependent on whipping speed and time. With urethane foam, it rises of its own accord; under the best of circumstances, the cold foam will expand seven times its original liquid volume. The molds used for urethane foam must have escape holes drilled for excess foam to get out. If too much foam is put into the mold and the mold is then clamped tightly shut, the resulting foam will be dense and less flexible than if just enough is added and expands into all the cavities of the mold.

Though cold foam can be a pain in the neck because of its high sensitivity to any moisture, what I like about it is how tough it is compared to foam latex. It isn't as soft as foam latex, though a softer foam can be achieved by increasing the ratio of part A (I'm talking mere drops for a small mold; too much A could prevent the foam from skinning at all); an appliance made of cold foam can be used repeatedly because it is less susceptible to tearing during removal. I have had pieces made that have lasted for as many as 40 stage performances, without wear noticeable from the audience. In fairness, I must attribute at least some of that success to conscientious actors.

According to Kryolan, the optimum working temperature for the foam is 113°F (45°C). You can achieve this by placing the mold halves, the positive and the negative, in an oven set on warm—about 120°F (about 49°C) in most ovens. Heat the molds until they're warm to the touch. If that's not possible, try using a blow drier on high for a few minutes.

Filling the Mold

Let me reiterate the importance of working in a room with adequate ventilation and a respirator. The release agent alone is reason enough for it. Whew! Just as for foam latex, make notes of what you do for each batch. The more you use cold foam, the better your results will be.

Before beginning, place a cup or other container on the scale and tare it (zero it out):

1. Pour Part B into a container; add food coloring to tint if needed. Experiment beforehand for color and amount. Unfortunately, food coloring choices are rather limited compared to pigment selections for other materials.
2. Pour Part A into a container (the ratio is 65:35 B:A by weight; multiply the weight of Part B by .53 to get the weight of Part A; 35 divided by 65 = .53). You can pour both parts into the same container if you are able to accurately do so.
3. As soon as the two parts have been added together, mix them quickly. The best results will be achieved by whipping the mixture with an electric

drill and wire whisk; bending a long piece of wire (such as a coat hanger) works well. If you mix by hand, stir the mixture as quickly as possible until the foam starts to increase in volume.

4. Immediately pour the foam into your mold and clamp the halves tightly closed. The setting time is usually around 8 to 10 minutes but can take longer, depending on the temperature of the molds and of the room.

5. Cleanup can be done with soap and water, but be prepared for the fact that you might not get all the foam off your tools. Definitely wear rubber gloves for this!

There is a heat reaction when the foam begins to rise; the foam might begin to rise very suddenly, so be careful to keep your working area clear of anything you care about. Urethane foam is quite unwilling to give up anything it envelops.

Removing the Appliance

The cold foam will be ready to demold in approximately 30 minutes. Because cold foam is not as soft and stretchy as foam latex, care must be taken when opening the mold so that you don't tear the appliance or separate the outer skin from the inner foam structure.

The formula for Kryolan® cold foam is designed to make it safer and easier to use and to hold up to repeated washings; it can be applied and worn immediately after demolding, though you might choose to wash it first and let it dry as you do with foam latex pieces. Cold foam takes paint and makeup well and can be used with any of the adhesives used for silicone and foam latex. From a cost standpoint, cold foam is less expensive than foam latex.

Cold foam is just another choice available to you as a makeup effects designer, and the decision to use it instead of another material should be based on a number of factors, not the least of which is skin sensitivity of the performer who will wear it. Kryolan's Research and Development department continues to refine the formula, and has stated that "one in a million people" might be sensitive to the foam and develop a rash; so far there have been no breathing or respiratory side effects. Just as with every substance you work with as a makeup artist, you should be familiar with each product; MSDS product sheets from the manufacturers are available and contain information on just about everything imaginable for their products. All you have to do is ask for them.

GELATIN AND FOAMED GELATIN

The gelatin in Jell-O® is what enables you to create all sorts of different shapes. I'm sure you've all heard of gelatin, but what exactly is it? Gelatin is a structural protein called *collagen* that is found in many animals, including humans. In fact, collagen makes up nearly one third of all protein in the human body. Collagen is a large molecule that our bodies use to make skin, bones, and tendons both strong and flexible—that is, somewhat elastic.

To manufacture gelatin, manufacturers grind up bones, hooves, and connective tissues of cows, pigs, and sometimes horses and treat these parts with either a strong acid or base to break down the cellular structure of the tissue and release the collagen and other proteins. After this treatment, the resulting mixture is boiled; during this process the collagen protein is broken down, resulting in the creation of gelatin. Yummy!

Because of its versatility, gelatin is a common ingredient in many foods and can be used in many ways; gelatin is used in foods from chewing gum to yogurt. It is even used to make capsules for medications and vitamins to make them easier to swallow.

By now some of you may be wondering, "What the heck does this have to do with special makeup effects, Todd?" Well, in addition to gelatin being used as an ingredient in foods and cosmetics, it is also one of the primary materials used in creating prosthetic appliances, along with foam latex and silicone. Gelatin has been used to create makeup effects since the 1920s.

Materials

You can find a number of formulas for making your own gelatin on the Internet, as well as purchasing pre-made gelatin prosthetic material from various industry suppliers. When describing gelatin, manufacturers refer to *bloom*. The *bloom factor* or *bloom strength* of gelatin is an industrial standard that measures the relative firmness of the gelatin in a cured state. Gelatin used for makeup effects work usually has a bloom factor of 300, whereas gelatin you can purchase from your local grocer (Knox® brand gelatin, for example) will have a bloom somewhere between 200 and 250.

This might be just fine for work you will be doing, but just be aware that the tear strength will not be as high as when using a gelatin with a bloom of 300. (The 300 bloom gelatin is also more expensive.) However, there are additives you can put into your gelatin formula that will also increase tear resistance, strength, and durability.

300 bloom gelatin (U.K. gelatine)	Microwave
Glycerin (U.K. glycerol)	Sorbitol (liquid or powder)
Distilled water	Scale
Appliance mold	Microwave-safe bowl(s)
Zinc oxide powder	Baking soda
Quick rise yeast	White vinegar
Epoxy Parfilm (for release)	Pam vegetable oil spray (for release)
Elmer's® Glue (white)	Tartaric acid (Cream of Tartar powder)
Ascorbic acid powder (vitamin C)	Witch hazel (for blending edges)
Liquid plastic sealer (alcohol based)	1-quart plastic cups
Petroleum jelly (for release)	Large craft sticks (for stirring)

There are so many formulas for making gelatin suitable for prosthetics that I've listed every ingredient I remember ever seeing in a recipe. Probably not all of them should be used in the same formula if you want to have a product that is soft, light, and strong enough to use. Fortunately, none of the individual elements is expensive; in fact, gelatin is the least expensive of the prosthetic materials used for makeup effects. Gelatin ingredients are inexpensive, and you can buy just about everything you need to create gelatin appliances at your local grocery store and pharmacy. So experiment, experiment, experiment! Or you can buy pre-made gelatin, both foaming and nonfoaming, that needs only to be heated and poured into a released mold. Several suppliers are listed in the appendix at the back of this book.

Some of the ingredients in the materials list may seem oddly out of place, so let me describe the purposes of some that might not seem obvious:

- Vinegar: foaming agent
- Ascorbic acid (vitamin C): foaming agent
- Baking soda: foaming agent
- Zinc oxide: strengthener (but will reduce translucency)
- Tartaric acid: foaming agent
- Quick-rise yeast: foaming agent
- Sorbitol: reduces shrinkage, increases strength
- Elmer's® Glue: adds strength and stability

Quirks

Gelatin is more translucent and moves better than some materials, has a very realistic texture, and doesn't take much makeup to get good cover. However, gelatin breaks down with heat and perspiration; that is, it melts and dissolves, respectively. There are several effective workarounds for sweat-related problems, but heat, such as working under hot stage lights or on location near the equator, is another matter, and there's not much you can do about that except use something other than gelatin.

Gelatin is considered to be *hypoallergenic*, that is, allergy-free for use on most people. That's a good thing. Gelatin is also considered *hygroscopic*, which means that it has a tendency to absorb moisture from the atmosphere. This is both good and not so good: Good in that it allows gelatin to be soluble—to liquefy and dissolve. With the addition of water, the gelatin particles swell and expand, actually absorbing up to 10 times their weight in water (which, in turn, can make gelatin appliances somewhat heavy); not so good in that gelatin appliances can swell in proportion to humidity changes in the air and shrink over time through evaporation.

One way to help minimize this change due to humidity is to substitute glycerin for almost all the water used in the gelatin appliance formula. This is very good for creating a variety of wounds and injuries—cuts, burns, bullet holes, swelling, and the like. This gelatin can be colored with flocking material, food coloring, or powdered cake makeup and stored in small squeeze bottles to be heated until the gelatin liquefies. This is similar to a number of gelatin effects kits that are available commercially. Just be very careful not to overheat the gelatin; because it is organic material, it can be severely damaged or ruined if heated too much (or too often), and you don't want to burn your actor by applying gelatin that is too warm. *Always test the temperature before application!*

As I mentioned, glycerin is also hygroscopic, so some formulas replace some of the glycerin with Sorbitol, which is derived from corn syrup and is less affected by changes in humidity than glycerin. Sorbitol also increases the structural integrity of gelatin formulas, making them more tear-resistant, which is critical for prosthetic work. (I've seen formulas that added Elmer's® white glue for the same purpose with good success.) Zinc oxide can also be used in small amounts to add strength and greater tolerance to temperature changes (remember, gelatin tends to melt when heat is applied). You will have to experiment when using zinc oxide because it will affect the translucency of your finished gelatin appliance. Zinc oxide powder is the preferred form, but sometimes it can be tough to find; zinc oxide ointment will work, though. Regardless of the formula you wind up using and calling your own, keep your finished appliances in air-tight plastic bags, away from the light and in a cool place. They will last much longer.

For prosthetic appliance work, the gelatin you use will need to be light and soft—foamy. So, the recipe I'll give you is for a foaming gelatin. The resulting gelatin will not be as light and soft as foam latex, but it will be substantially lighter and spongier than a solid gelatin appliance and definitely lighter than silicone gel.

Filling the Mold

A basic gelatin formula (you will notice that the following recipe does not have Sorbitol, white glue, or zinc oxide—do some experimenting—a good makeup effects artist must be part mad chemist):

> ### NOTE
>
> You can double, triple, or quadruple this formula. Very small batches aren't as easy to mix as a medium batch, which this describes; but once you've mixed a medium batch, you can take smaller amounts from it and use them in small molds.
>
> I can't for the life of me remember where I got this particular formula. Let me know if it's yours and I'll make sure you get credit in the next edition.

160 grams (1/4 cup) glycerin (U.K. glycerol)
40 grams (1/8 cup) gelatin (U.K. gelatine)
1 gram (1 tsp) quick rise yeast
3.5 grams (3.5 tsp) distilled water
Pigment color of your choice (you can also use colored flocking, food coloring, or powdered cake makeup)

1. In a microwave-safe bowl, pour the glycerin. Slowly add the gelatin granules to the glycerin. If you are adding a pigment, mix the pigment into a small amount of glycerin before adding it to the batch. Heat the glycerin and gelatin in the microwave for a minute or two, in 5–10 second increments, being careful to *prevent bringing the gelatin to a boil*. If the gelatin boils, the collagen in the gelatin will be destroyed and you will need to start over. Gelatin melts at about 70°C, or close to 160°F, depending on altitude.

2. When the gelatin has completely liquefied, pour the gelatin into a plastic quart cup. Let the gelatin cool completely (you can put it in the freezer or refrigerator; you're essentially making Jell-O®), then remelt the gelatin in the microwave three or four times—again in 5–10 second intervals so it won't boil—to ensure that all the water has evaporated from the glycerin, to minimize shrinkage of the finished appliance.

3. Before going on to the next step, apply a very thin layer of petroleum jelly, vegetable oil (PAM®), or Epoxy Parfilm onto both the positive and negative of your mold as a release agent so that the gelatin won't stick to the mold surface when you demold your appliance.

4. When you're ready to cast your appliance, mix the yeast with the water and let this mixture sit for at least 2 minutes; melt the gelatin, being careful not to let it boil, then add the yeast and water mixture, stirring it into the melted gelatin. It will immediately begin to foam.

5. Stop stirring and let the gelatin mixture rise until it stops, then stir well with a large craft stick to refine the gelatin—that is, to remove large air bubbles and to make the foam mixture consistent. It should be the consistency of meringue. If the gelatin cools too much, reheat it briefly so it is pourable. Like foam latex, foamed gelatin can be poured or injected into a mold.

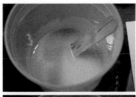

FIGURE 6.21
Foaming gelatin rising.
Photos by the author.

183

> **NOTE**
>
> Instead of using the water/yeast mixture to make the gelatin foam, you can substitute a small amount of vinegar and/or baking soda to achieve the same result. Ascorbic acid powder (vitamin C) will also cause a foaming action. You do not have to foam the gelatin to achieve an excellent appliance. It is presented as an option, albeit a good one, I believe. Gelatin can have some weight to it (though it's still lighter than silicone), and foaming the gelatin will make it lighter by using less material.

6. It is a good idea to heat the negative half of your mold in a warm oven until it is warm to the touch. This is an optional step, but it could provide a better appliance surface. The positive can be either heated or chilled prior to foaming your gelatin. If chilled, it should be cold to the touch but not frozen. The goal is to speed up the gelling time. Pouring warm foam into a frozen mold, or even a cold one, could crack it, which, as you can imagine, would be bad. Experimentation will dictate what is best.

FIGURE 6.22
Foaming gelatin going into a mold. Photo by the author.

7. When your foam is ready to pour, fill your mold; use a spatula or large craft stick to work the gelatin into the warm negative mold and close it immediately.

Be careful not to trap air bubbles when you're closing the mold. Clamp or press the mold halves together tightly to ensure a thin blending edge of the appliance, then place the closed mold into a freezer or refrigerator to gel. Depending on the size of your mold and the temperature, it could take anywhere from 30 minutes to an hour or more before the appliance is ready to be demolded.

Removing the Appliance

You can tell when the foamed gelatin has set by touching the overflow or any remainder from the mixing bowl; if it bounces back, it's ready to demold.

1. Carefully open the mold halves and find an edge; begin to remove the piece, powdering the gelatin as you go, to prevent it from sticking to itself. Place it back on the positive and it is ready for painting and/or application.

2. If the appliance piece is going to be applied to the skin, a barrier layer is recommended between the gelatin and the skin to prevent perspiration from prematurely breaking down the piece (dissolving it).

3. Apply a light plastic (such as bald cap plastic), vinyl, or acrylic layer over the areas of the appliance that will come in contact with the skin. Pieces for around the eyes—swollen bruises or eye bags, for example—should be completely sealed; you can even encapsulate gelatin in the same way you encapsulate silicone (but not with silicone as the encapsulator).

4. After sealing, powder the piece again before storing it in an airtight container. Another option is to also cover the back of the piece (but *not* the edges!) with Pros-Aide® adhesive in addition to the sealer, allow it to dry, and then powder it.

Before moving on to casting dental appliances, I'm going to share another recipe with you for gelatin appliances—a nonfoaming one—from Matthew Mungle:

- 100 g sorbitol (70%) liquid
- 100 g glycerin
- 20–30 g of 300-bloom gelatin
- Coloring: flocking, food coloring, powdered cake makeup, etc.

Here's how to prep and fill the mold and remove the appliance:

1. Mix the ingredients together and let them sit, preferably overnight, so that the gelatin has time to dissolve in the glycerin and sorbitol.

2. Heat in a microwave (in a microwave-safe container) for approximately 2 minutes (in 10–15 second increments), stirring frequently.

Do not let the gelatin boil (bubble or foam); that will burn the gelatin, causing it to change color and leave bubbles in the finished appliance.

   3. Gently swirl and jostle the mixing container to get rid of any air bubbles in the gelatin.
   4. Carefully pour the gelatin into the warmed mold, holding the container as close to the mold surface as possible.

FIGURE 6.23
Melted gelatin in a microwave-safe container. Photo by the author.

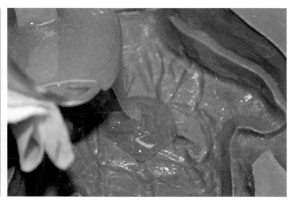

FIGURE 6.24
Slowly pour gelatin into the mold from near the mold surface. Photo by the author.

Pouring from higher up may cause the formation of air bubbles becoming trapped (with silicone, pouring from higher up causes air bubbles in the silicone to stretch and break).

   5. Tilt the mold from side to side, allowing the gelatin to coat the surface of the mold and allowing air bubbles to escape.
   6. Press the positive into the negative and close the mold tightly.
   7. Allow the gelatin to cool and set up.
   8. Carefully remove the positive, trying to keep the appliance in the negative. If there are bubbles, they will be easier to repair if the gelatin is still in the negative.
   9. Trim around the flashing at the cutting edge and powder the inside of the appliance.
   10. Carefully begin to peel up an appliance edge and gently remove the piece, powdering as you go. Powder both sides of the appliance.

I've already suggested that you take some time and experiment with gelatin because it is quick, easy, and inexpensive. What's also cool about it is that if your appliance turns out badly in the mold, you can simply clean out the gelatin, remelt it, and pour it again! There is a caveat, however: Eventually the collagen in the gelatin will begin to break down from the repeated heating, but in the learning stages, that doesn't really matter, since you probably won't be making an appliance for a major project while you're just learning how to do gelatin well (I hope).

You will notice that the two formulas/recipes for gelatin I gave you are quite different; I can't say that one is better than the other (Matthew Mungle, however, might disagree). Much of how you make the gelatin is dependent on the way it will be used. If it is going to be for a prosthetic appliance, one way could be preferable over another, but if you are making a prop body part, you could decide on a different formula to suit the project.

DENTAL ACRYLIC

I'll start this section off with another disclaimer because, next to your eyes, your teeth are the most sensitive and delicate body parts you will be working with. Now you're probably thinking, "Eyes, I can understand, but teeth? Really? They're hard. There are a lot of them. They're designed for tearing through meat and chewing food into itsy bitsy little pieces!" True, we don't always think of our teeth as sensitive and delicate … until something is *wrong* with them, and then we find out how tough (or not) we *really* are. Many of us would certainly divulge state secrets if some lunatic went to messing with our sensitive and delicate teeth. Anyone remember Dustin Hoffman and Laurence Olivier in *Marathon Man*? "Is it *safe*?" Yeeeeoowww!

For this reason alone, I caution you about the risk involved in working in and around anyone's mouth without being a licensed dental technician. *Any dental appliance that is not made by a licensed dental technician is to be considered and treated as cosmetic only, not therapeutic or corrective.* Cosmetic (theatrical) dental appliances are not suitable for chewing food. Never use force when inserting or removing a cosmetic dental appliance. I stated this in Chapter 3 and am reiterating it here in case you missed it there: It is illegal to practice dentistry without a license. (I must've been a lawyer in a past life to feel the need to say something so obvious. Sorry.) While I'm still on the subject, you should never attempt to take an impression of someone's teeth if they're wearing any kind of braces, real dentures, or removable bridge.

Materials

One of the materials used in making theatrical teeth appliances is a liquid monomer that dissolves the dental acrylic powder; you will need to wear a good NIOSH-approved respirator that is rated for organic vapors whenever you are working with monomers. This protection will hopefully help ensure that your brain continues to function properly for years to come. Never use monomers near any open flame or sparking heat source, either. Monomer vapors are heavy and will seek the lowest point; do not use monomers in any room that has floor vents that lead to a heater or furnace or you could get to see your neighborhood from the air through thick smoke and flames.

If you will be casting acrylic in a silicone mold (and you will), you need to know that all silicones will absorb monomer. So, if you cast acrylic in your silicone mold more than twice in a row (in close succession), the silicone will swell, making the dentures you are casting thinner than they are supposed to be. Using a hair dryer (on *low*) on the mold for a few minutes will evaporate much of the monomer that's been absorbed. The mold should be cool before you use it again. A spray release agent such as Frekote,® designed for molded polymers in silicone molds, will help prolong your mold life.

Flexacryl acrylic powder
Gum shade acrylic powder
Round-nosed pliers
Variable-speed Dremel®
Al-cote® dental separator
400and 800 grit wet/dry sandpaper
Mechanical pencil
X-acto® knife with #11 blades

Tooth shade acrylic powder
.028 ball clasps
Acrylic liquid monomer
Misc. Dremel® bits
Medium bowl with hot water
Dental wax
Glycerin

Filling the Mold and Removing the Appliance

The process of casting dental appliances can be rather complicated and time consuming, considering how small they can be, but considering how important our mouths and teeth are, it is important to take great care to do this task well. Sculpting and casting dental appliances is fun, but be prepared for disappointment. This job is not easy and takes much practice to become proficient; unless you are called on to do this regularly, dentures might be an aspect of makeup effects that you'll want to leave to a specialist.

> **TIP**
> Curing dental acrylic under water and at 30psi of air pressure will cause the acrylic to cure faster, denser, and with fewer surface flaws.

187

1. Place your dental positive in water and then brush it with a coat of Al-Cote® dental separator. When the first coat is dry, add a second coat. You might also opt for a thin layer of petroleum jelly instead of or in addition to the Al-Cote.®

2. Put some dental wax in the indentations between the teeth. This is fairly easy to do, but the wax must be melted; you can also use wax or oil clay instead of dental wax. This will prevent the dental acrylic from filling that space and risk breaking the stone when you remove the acrylic cast from the positive.

3. Mix a 50/50 batch of tooth shade acrylic with Flexacryl with monomer and slowly pour it into the mold when it starts to thicken, tilting it back and forth to make sure the material gets into all the cavities of the mold.

4. Press the positive into the mold, but don't press so hard that suction is created when you remove your hand; you don't want to suck air into the mold with the acrylic.

FIGURE 6.25
Dental wax in the indentations between teeth removes potential undercuts that could inhibit easy removal of the denture from the stone positive or snapping off teeth from the positive. Photo by the author.

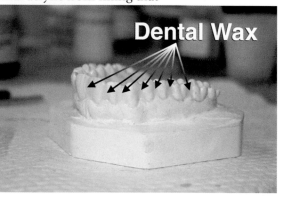

Dental Wax

5. Now you can do one of two things: You can place the mold in a bowl of hot water to cure the acrylic (it must be large enough to submerge the entire mold), or you can submerge the mold in a pressure chamber; Harbor Freight and Northern Tool & Equipment sell a 2½-gallon paint tank that is perfectly suitable for this task. You need to have an air compressor that is capable of delivering 30psi of pressure, which isn't much. This will cause the acrylic to cure faster, denser, and with fewer surface flaws. You can demold after about 20 minutes.

6. Remove from the appliance any excess acrylic that will prevent extra thickness in the finished appliance, which you don't want.

FIGURE 6.26
Simple but effective dental prosthetic appliances; upper and lower. Photo by the author.

Now, here is where I would ordinarily be done with casting dentures. All that remains is to trim away any acrylic that might be causing pressure or discomfort, paint them with Minute Stain, wash them, and wear them. What follows is more advanced, and I strongly suggest that you practice quite a bit before attempting this task for a paid gig. These next steps (7 through 23) border on the realm of a professional dental technician. *I'm providing this information as information only and do not advocate its use.*

7. Draw lines on the teeth and gums with a mechanical pencil to show where the incisal layer is; this is a translucent outer layer on all teeth. Use the Dremel® to carefully grind off some of the acrylic, leaving a thin layer around the teeth at the gums and at the base of the teeth in a somewhat jagged pattern. You will be recasting the teeth with clear dental acrylic, thereby adding a sense of depth.

8. Remove the pencil markings with a Q-tip® dipped in monomer.

9. Brush Al-cote® over any exposed stone on the positive before casting the incisal acrylic to ensure that it won't bond to it.

10. Mix 1 oz. of clear acrylic with 1 tsp. of tooth shade acrylic with monomer— enough to liquefy the powder; when it begins to thicken slightly, pour it into the mold and press the positive back into the mold. You can repeat step 5 now. After the teeth have been demolded, they need to be prepped for casting the gums. Take the mechanical pencil again and draw around the teeth at the gum line. Then take the Dremel® and remove as much of the existing acrylic covering the gums as you can, leaving a thin layer only. Then remove any remaining pencil markings with another Q-tip® dipped in monomer.

> **NOTE**
> Wear a dust mask to avoid inhaling acrylic dust from grinding with the Dremel®.

11. Since more dental acrylic is going to be added (pink gum color), we want to prevent it from bonding to the teeth.

188

12. Mix ¼ oz. of Al-Cote® separator with ¼ tsp. of glycerin. Brush four coats onto any surface you don't want the gum color to adhere to. Make sure that each coat is completely dry before adding the next.

13. Mix the gum color and when it begins to thicken slightly, pour it into the mold and then press the positive into the mold. When the excess acrylic gets spongy and bounces back when you press into it (return memory), you can demold the positive.

14. Cut around each tooth at the gum line and the vestibule area (small cavity where the midline frenum muscle attaches the upper lip to the gums) with an X-acto® knife (#11 blade).

15. Carefully remove the gum acrylic from the teeth, front and back, as well as gum material that is covering the soft palate. *Note:* This might be easier said than done. Then remove the appliance from the positive and do a rough trim with the Dremel,® grinding almost to the base of the teeth on the back side. Be careful not to grind through the acrylic and into the stone positive!

16. As an additional anchoring option, you can add a ball clasp to the appliance to help hold it in place, but it is not an essential step. Carefully bend the clasp into a curve that will fit around the back tooth of the appliance. Glue the wire in place with a drop of Superglue.®

17. Use the Dremel® to remove a section of the gums so that the appliance can be placed back on the stone positive without affecting the placement of the clasp.

18. Release the area of the positive with a bit of petroleum jelly and place the appliance back on the positive. Mix up some new pink gum acrylic and carefully rebuild the gum over the wire clasp. When the acrylic has begun to set, place it in hot water to cure.

19. Use the Dremel® to smooth out the new gum acrylic to match the rest of the appliance. Also grind down any high spots or rough areas on the inside. Be careful not to grind a hole in the appliance! Sand any rough edges with high grit wet/dry paper.

20. Use the same 400 and 800 grit paper to sand the front of the teeth and gums; then use a fine grit silicone point bit over the appliance, followed by a bristle brush bit to clean off any silicone residue. Then use a rag wheel bit with some acrylic polish to buff the appliance to a shine.

21. Use an old toothbrush and some dishwashing liquid to remove any remaining polishing compound from the appliance. The last step before painting the teeth will be to reline the inside of the appliance with a soft acrylic.

22. Brush a thin layer of petroleum jelly over the front and back of the positive. Then mix some Flexacryl (2:1) with monomer. The flexible nature of Flexacryl will make the appliance more comfortable to wear. Work quickly; this could set up rather fast.

23. Rub the inside of the appliance with a Q-tip® dipped in monomer, then place the Flexacryl evenly on the inside of the appliance before placing the appliance onto the positive. Clean up any excess with another Q-tip® dipped in monomer. Cure the acrylic in hot water and remove it. Then trim the excess, and it's ready to paint and wear!

FIGURE 6.27
Seams on Neill Gorton age appliance prior to cleanup. Photo by the author.

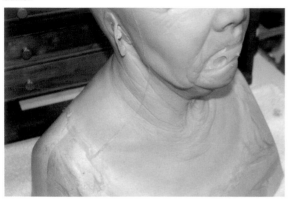

SEAMING AND PAINTING SILICONE APPLIANCES

As has already been pointed out, nothing sticks to silicone except other silicone, which can make silicone somewhat difficult to paint, especially if you want the paint to stay put. This section deals with paint options as much as (if not more so) with painting technique. Each makeup that you create will be different, so how you paint it and what you use to paint it will differ as well.

Let's begin by taking for granted that you have given your silicone appliance (or appliances) a foundation color that is at least in the ballpark of the base color you need for the overall makeup. You would have done this as you mixed the silicone prior to casting the appliance. But first we have to clean up the appliance by getting rid of seams and other surface blemishes that don't belong and should be corrected.

Seaming and Patching

The term for cleaning up seam flashing and surface blemishes is *seaming*. The process actually *deseams* the prosthetic.

Silicone

FIGURE 6.28
Starting with a small pair of sharp, fine scissors and your fingers, carefully lift the seam flashing and trim as close to the surface as possible. Image reproduced by permission of Neill Gorton.

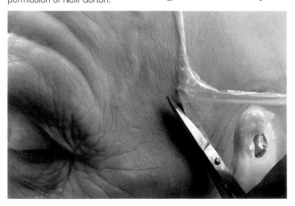

Starting with a small pair of sharp, fine scissors and your fingers (careful!) or a good set of tweezers, carefully lift the seam flashing and trim as close to the surface as possible.

Neill Gorton suggests that rather than simply trimming the flashing to the surface, which often still leaves a detectible remnant, cut a very slight channel along the seam. It is much easier to fill a small channel than to mask small bumps that could be left behind by simply trimming the seam close. These channels and indentations can be patched invisibly with small amounts of the same mixture of silicone used to cast the appliance initially.

190

After the flashing and other blemishes have been cut away, very carefully clean the surface of the prosthetic with a little isopropyl alcohol or acetone to remove fingerprints, dirt, dust, powder, mold release residue, or whatever. If the piece has been handled, you need to give it a good, gentle cleaning so that the silicone patch will grab and stick properly. Be careful to avoid appliance edges.

Using a small, accurate digital scale, mix a small amount of the silicone in the same proportion used for the appliance. Then, working in only small areas at a time on the seam—no more than 3 inches (about 7.5 cm)—it will be easier but somewhat dependent on the silicone you use. Using a platinum-cure silicone such as Polytek's PlatSil Gel-10 will allow you to work quickly. The following steps will work best if your appliance is resting on either a soft foam or rigid foam form of your model.

1. Apply a thin line of silicone along the channel cut using a small dental spatula to place the silicone.
2. Then place a piece of clear plastic wrap (cling film) over the patch and lay it down carefully to make sure there are no trapped air bubbles. It is best if you can pin it taut in place. If the patch is on the neck, you can use tools to match and follow existing wrinkles and so on. A hair dryer will also accelerate the silicone cure.

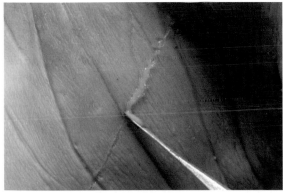

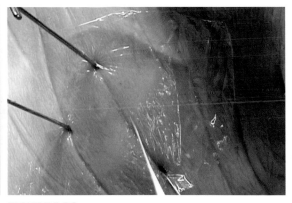

FIGURE 6.29
Apply a thin line of silicone along the channel cut using a small dental spatula to place the silicone. Image reproduced by permission of Neill Gorton.

FIGURE 6.30
If the patch is on the neck, you can use tools to match and follow existing wrinkles. Image reproduced by permission of Neill Gorton.

3. As the silicone begins to thicken and set up, indentations can be added on top of the plastic wrap. After the silicone is fully cured, the plastic wrap can be carefully peeled away (nothing sticks to silicone, remember?), leaving an invisible patch where there was a noticeable seam before. Voilà! Perfect.

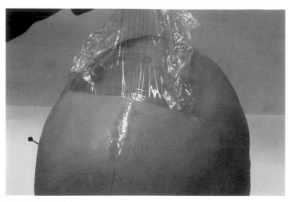

FIGURE 6.31
After the silicone is fully cured, the plastic wrap can be carefully peeled away, leaving an invisible patch where there was a noticeable seam before. Image reproduced by permission of Neill Gorton.

FOAM LATEX

Seaming and patching foam latex can be a real pain in the caboose if you actually try to seam and patch with foam latex, because it requires a heat cure again. Unfortunately, foam latex is probably the best material to use because it will be the same as the rest of the appliance. However, in many cases seams are in areas of the appliance where you may be able to get away with using a different material that doesn't move in the same manner as the foam. It probably won't really be enough for anyone to notice but you.

Pros-Aide® makes a terrific patching material, and there are two ways to use it. First, you can pour a small amount into a small cup and let it sit exposed to the air for a while; as the water evaporates from the adhesive, it will thicken up and you can then fill the seam or blemish. As the Pros-Aide® begins to dry, you can texture it carefully with a tool or a (damp) stipple sponge. When it is dry (it will be completely clear when dry), powder it, and you're good to go. You can also add a small amount of Cab-O-Sil® to fresh Pros-Aide® to thicken it into a paste and apply in the same manner. Pros-Aide mixed with Cab-O-Sil® is affectionately called *bondo* after the car body filler Bondo.® Oddly enough, the Pros-Aide® will still dry clear, even though the Cab-O-Sil® is white (unless you've added a lot of the filler). A fine brush dipped in 99 percent IPA (isopropyl alcohol) can be used to feather the edges to nothing while the Pros-Aide® is still soft.

You could even try a bit of melted gelatin as a seaming and patching material on foam latex, provided you don't apply it when the gelatin is too liquidy and seeps into the foam. A fine brush dipped in hot water can be used to smooth the gelatin. Texture the same way as the Pros-Aide;® freshly set gelatin is very sticky until it is powdered, so a light dusting of powder may facilitate texturing if the appliance needs it.

GELATIN AND COLD FOAM

If your appliance is made of gelatin, I do not recommend using gelatin as the seaming material. The reason should be pretty obvious: You must melt gelatin to apply it to a seam, and melted gelatin is hot—warm, at least—and gelatin melts when it gets too warm or wet; hence, you don't want to remelt the appliance you've just spent considerable time and effort to make. Use Pros-Aide® instead. Pros-Aide® (bondo) is also the preferred method of seaming cold foam (urethane foam).

Painting the Appliance

Painting prosthetic appliances can be handled in a variety of ways, and your method should be decided upon based on a combination of personal preference, personal style, the material of the appliance you'll be painting, and whether you'll be painting it prior to application, or after.

SILICONE

To save yourself time and paint, I suggest that your appliances be precolored at the time you cast them. Because the silicone we use for prosthetics is clear or translucent, it is an excellent material for intrinsic (internal) coloring. You can color the silicone with either a pigment that approximates the character's coloring or with rayon fiber flocking material mixed to approximate the character's coloring. Materials you'll need:

Skin Illustrator®, Sta-Color, or
   Temptu® Pro palettes
Naphtha or White Spirit

Clear RTV silicone caulk
Scissors
Misc. sponges
Wood craft sticks (for mixing)

Clear RTV silicone adhesive/sealant
Fine disposable brushes

Heptane (Bestine® rubber cement
   thinner)
1-inch chip brushes
99% IPA in a spray bottle
Mixing cups
Silicone pigments or artist oil
   paints
Hair dryer
Vinyl or nitrile gloves

An airbrush might seem to be a more practical and efficient way to paint an appliance, regardless of what material it is made of. It comes back to personal preference and how you were taught (or are being taught). For painting appliances, I believe you will be better off not using an airbrush and instead using chip brushes and cut-down chip brushes. Don't get me wrong, I love airbrushes; I have six of them ranging in size from very fine detail to big enough to paint a house. But unless you have an assistant whose job is to keep your airbrushes clean and unclogged, you will spend more time cleaning your needles and nozzles every time you change colors, even if you are using several at a time. Airbrushes clog quite easily, *especially* when you (try to) run thinned silicone through them. I was taught how to get superb results using thinned RTV silicone adhesive and RTV silicone caulk as the medium for applying color to silicone appliances.

Now:

1. Start off by thinning the silicone adhesive (sealant) in a cup with some Heptane/Bestine® so that it is a pretty thin wash of about 10 parts Heptane to 1 part silicone.
2. Of course, you have a polyfoam (soft or rigid urethane foam) form of your model that the appliance is resting on to hold its shape and facilitate easier painting.
3. Brush this onto your appliance, but be careful not to paint all the way out to the edges. Because there is a lot of solvent mixed with the silicone, you can ruin the edges; the silicone will absorb the solvent and swell.
4. Since you seamed with silicone gel, this wash will also create a thin layer of silicone over the seam patch. This wash of silicone adhesive will kick very quickly, setting up in less than an hour and resulting in a very strong bonding surface for the color you will add next.

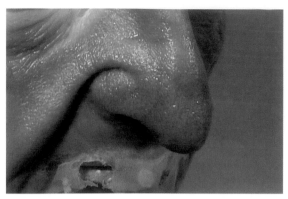

Figure 6.32
Use a wash of silicone adhesive to prime the surface for painting. Image reproduced by permission of Neill Gorton.

5. You can use either silicone pigments to make your flesh tones or whatever color you need for your appliance, or you can use artist oil paints, which will work just as well. These colors will be used as detail highlight and shadow coloring on various parts of your appliance.

6. Mix another thin wash of silicone, this time mixing Naphtha with some of the RTV silicone caulk instead of Heptane or Bestine® with silicone adhesive. The ratio is about 10:1—10 parts Naphtha to one part silicone.

7. Mix a bit of the color you need and brush it onto the appliance, getting into all the creases and folds. Dab off any excess with a piece of sponge and continue until you achieve the effect you're going for.

8. Next take one of the chip brushes and cut the bristles down about halfway. The next step is to flick or spatter paint onto the prosthetic. This can be done by alternating heavy and light amounts. Mix another batch of silicone with Naphtha in the same ratio, and mix colors to complement the complexion you are creating.

9. With your fingers (wear nonlatex gloves), flick the brush bristles so that the paint spatters randomly onto the appliance.

10. Use another chip brush with longer bristles and tap it against the handle of the cut-down brush to apply spatter in a slightly different way, with different spatter amounts.

You could be doing this with an airbrush, but even when you remove the nozzle tip and reduce the air pressure, you will get a uniform random spatter. I know

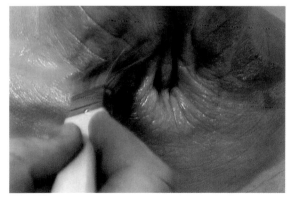

FIGURE 6.33
Mix a bit of the color you need and brush it onto the appliance, getting into all the creases and folds. Dab off any excess with a piece of sponge and continue until you achieve the effect you're going for. Image reproduced by permission of Neill Gorton.

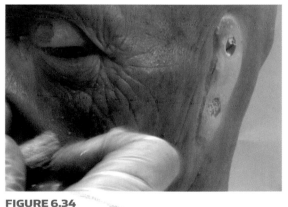

FIGURE 6.34
With your fingers (wear nonlatex gloves—nitrile or vinyl), flick the brush bristles so that the paint spatters randomly onto the appliance. Image reproduced by permission of Neill Gorton.

it's an oxymoron, but it's true, and you don't want anything that appears uniform. Be careful with the amount of color; it's very easy to overdo it, particularly with reds.

11. When you've spattered sufficiently, you can move on to adding vein color if it is appropriate to the prosthetic, dabbing with a sponge to remove excess color. Vein coloration should be very subtle.

12. You can continue to add color in the form of moles and age spots, if that is appropriate to the makeup, or you can stop and let the silicone paint cure, which will take several hours.

When the silicone has set, the appliance is ready for application. Then you can finish painting the appliance with an alcohol-activated color palette once the prosthetic is glued in place.

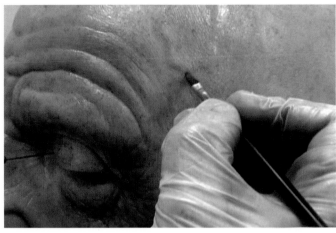

FIGURE 6.35
Vein coloration should be very subtle. Image reproduced by permission of Neill Gorton.

195

Mark Garbarino

FIGURE 6.36
Mark Garbarino (left), Jackie Chan, and David Snyder in China for *Forbidden Kingdom*. Image reproduced by permission of Mark Garbarino.

Mark has racked up a 20-year-plus career as a creator of sculptures, costumes, puppets, and special makeup effects. After moving to Los Angeles in 1987, Garbarino began specializing in the area of special makeup effects, contributing puppets for such films as *The Abyss, Nightmare on Elm Street, Hot Shots 2, Virus, Hellraiser 4*, and *Bicentennial Man*.

His makeups have appeared on Madonna and Busta Rhymes in their music videos and on Jim Carrey in print work. In the 1990s, as special makeup effects coordinator, Mark's team won Emmy Awards for the television series *Babylon 5* and *Buffy the Vampire Slayer*. Mark was honored with an individual Emmy nomination in 1997 for *Babylon 5*, for Outstanding Makeup for a Series, and again in 2003 for prosthetics on *Six Feet Under*.

Mark was also nominated for the Local 706 Hair and Make-Up Awards for Best Prosthetics, transforming John

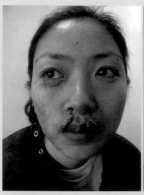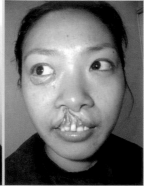

FIGURE 6.37
Actress Yi Ding wearing a silicone lip and eyelid (left) and with cleft denture appliance in place (right). Applied and painted by Mark Garbarino; designed by Stan Winston Studios. Images reproduced by permission of Mark Garbarino.

FIGURE 6.38
Mark Garbarino, actor Andy Lau in foam latex muscle suit, and makeup artist Jeff Himmell. Image reproduced by permission of Mark Garbarino.

FIGURE 6.39
Actor Greg German in progressive makeup by Mark Garbarino. Images reproduced by permission of Mark Garbarino.

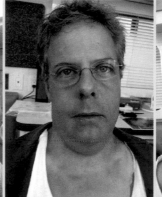

Voight into Howard Cosell for the film *Ali*. Other film makeup highlights include *The Nutty Professor 2, Pearl Harbor, Artificial Intelligence, Pirates of the Caribbean,* and *Constantine.* International film experiences in Hong Kong and China include *Home Sweet Home (Karina Lam), Running on Karma, Kiddult* starring Andy Lau, T*ak-wa, Eyes 10,* Jet Li in *Fearless* and *Ci Ma,* and Jackie Chan in *The Forbidden Kingdom.*

Mark has taught special makeup effects at the Shanghai Theater Academy but continues to maintain his home in Los Angeles. Mark's plans include working more in Asia and expanding the character makeup possibilities for China's film stars.

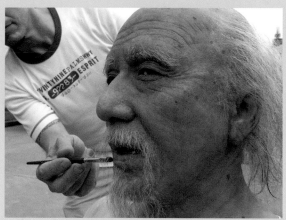

FIGURE 6.40
Mark applying age makeup to actor Jackie Chan for *Forbidden Kingdom*. Image reproduced by permission of Mark Garbarino.

FOAM LATEX

Foam latex can be tinted during the batch mixing process to approximate the character's skin tone as closely as possible, and then it can be detailed after the appliance has been washed, seamed, and patched. As you should recall, foam latex is opaque, so any sense of tissue depth will be the result of painting, not the result of intrinsic coloring.

The process for painting a foam latex appliance is essentially the same as for painting a silicone appliance (with the notable exception of needing to use silicone paint for a silicone appliance). One thing to be aware of is that foam latex is essentially a very soft sponge, so application of color should be sparing, applying just a little at a time and letting it dry to avoid saturating the foam with paint. In fact, this point alone is a good enough argument for not using an airbrush on foam latex but using the previously described spatter technique instead.

Here are the materials you will need:

Skin Illustrator®, Sta-Color, or Temptu
   Pro® palettes
1-inch chip brushes
99% IPA in a spray bottle
Artists' water-based liquid acrylic paint
Latex makeup sponges
Artists' oil paint
Plastic cups

Scissors
Fine brushes
Pros-Aide® adhesive
Airbrush and compressor
Nylon stocking

197

1. With your appliance resting on a shaped form, open your color palettes and pick your colors.
2. Spray the color you will use first with alcohol and begin to liquefy the color with a cut-down chip brush. Skin Illustrator® and Sta-Color palettes have empty compartments for mixing colors. You do not want the color too saturated or concentrated or it will go onto the appliance too rich and vibrant and will look artificial. The color should be soft and natural; add color gradually to give the appearance of depth.
3. Repeat step 2 for the other colors as well. Human skin, or any skin for that matter, is not one solid, uniform color. There are reds and blues, browns, yellows, and greens in our coloration.
4. Interchange spatter techniques by using the cut-down brush and your fingers as well as tapping the longer bristle brush against the handle of another brush or even against your hand.
5. Try getting some color on your fingers and gently dabbing your fingers onto the appliance to create age spots, if appropriate.

I shouldn't have to say this, but it's very important to have a plan before you begin painting your appliance. You should have lots of reference photos as well as an already formed idea of what you want the finished piece to look like. As artists, part of our unwritten job description is that we have to see all the things that other people, ordinary people, don't notice but that are there nonetheless— things like the way the skin at the tip of your knuckles where the digits begin is a bit pinker than the rest of the skin surrounding it, or that the color of the skin on the back of your hand is a good representation of the coloration of your face, or that the skin on the back of your arm is a different texture than the skin on the bottom of your arm … and so on.

6. Repeat steps 2–5 until you get the effect you want, and then stop. Learn to know when to stop. That's something you'll have to learn to recognize on your own.

Once the appliance is applied, you can finish up with Skin Illustrator® colors or the Sta-Color ones, or you can stipple and brush other makeup, such as Ben Nye®.

Another industry standard for painting foam latex is with PAX paint, a 50/50 mixture of acrylic paint and Pros-Aide® adhesive. The Pros-Aide® helps keep the acrylic pliant and flexible once it dries; it won't crack, which it would eventually do otherwise. PAX can be applied with a sponge-and-stipple technique, with an airbrush, or both. If you have the time to do it, airbrush is a wonderful tool, especially if you have at least two or more so that you can dedicate colors to each airbrush. If you have only one, it can become a real chore because of clogs and having to clean the brush for every color change. There are several brands available, and the choice is personal—whether you choose Iwata®, Paasche®, Thayer-Chandler®, or Badger®—but you should only consider a double-action airbrush, one that allows you to control both air and the amount of pigment. I have three Iwata and two Paasche® airbrushes and two Iwata® compressors. Two of the airbrushes I've been using since I was in college way back in the 20th century.

Applying PAX with a makeup sponge or sponges is fine and pretty simple. Running PAX through an airbrush, though doable, is asking for trouble, in my humble opinion. Here's what I suggest:

1. Apply your base foundation with PAX by hand.
2. Mix oil paint in the color or colors you want to apply next with the airbrush, and then add 99% alcohol. Stir it well, breaking up as much of the oil medium as you can.
3. Strain the alcohol/oil paint mixture through a piece of nylon hose (stocking) so that only colored alcohol filters through, leaving the oil medium in the nylon.
4. Run this through your airbrush in a stipple pattern; the alcohol evaporates almost instantaneously, leaving behind only the color. This is *much* easier to clean out of your airbrush than PAX. It is also a nice, translucent color to which you can add to achieve your skin coloration.

I don't recommend putting alcohol or oil paint directly on the skin; it can cause irritation. Reserve this method for painting appliances only.

How do you stipple with an airbrush? Airbrushing for makeup requires very low pressure to begin with and an even lower pressure to get the airbrush to spit and spatter for the stipple effect. All you need to do is lower the air pressure of your compressor (3–4psi should be all the pressure needed) and remove the needle cap (if your airbrush has one; it ought to). Your airbrush should be set to stipple. Test it first on a piece of waxed palette paper for the pattern you want before trying it on your appliance. Now you're in business.

This brings up a safety point. The very nature of an airbrush puts vapor into the environment where you're working. Even though it's not a lot of vapor and most of the pigments you will work with are nontoxic and not a health hazard, you are still breathing in foreign matter in very tiny particles. If you use an airbrush, please consider wearing a mask or respirator.

You can't very well ask an actor to wear a mask if you are applying airbrush makeup to their face, however; for this reason it might be a better idea to use a chip brush and hand-spatter technique with alcohol-activated palette colors for this application. The actor can take a deep breath and close his eyes for a moment, you can apply the spatter, and then your subject can open his eyes and breathe.

GELATIN AND COLD FOAM

Both gelatin and cold foam (soft urethane foam) will require a sealer before painting. There are a number of acrylic sealers that can be used and will work just fine. Why do gelatin and urethane foam need to be sealed before coloring? For the same reason they need to be sealed before application.

1. If you apply adhesive to gelatin without a sealer, the adhesive won't stick very well, and when gelatin gets wet it begins to lose its shape and becomes weak. If you try to paint unsealed gelatin, the wet paint will seep

into the gelatin in ways you can't control as well as weakening the gelatin by dampening it by applying a light coat of acrylic sealer: Kryolan's Fixier spray, Reel Creations' Blue Aqua Sealer, Ben Nye's Final Seal, plastic cap material (which works great), or BJB Enterprises' SC-115. I think this stuff is awesome, especially as a thin coating over polyurethane; it is water based and dries very quickly to form a very soft, stretchy skin.

2. Remember how you've been told that nothing sticks to silicone except silicone? Things we need to use really don't like to stick to the cold foam, either. However, applying a light coat of an acrylic sealer (BJB SC-115 is my preference for using with cold foam) will allow paint, or even makeup, to grab and stay. One word of caution: Apply just a small amount, a very light coat at a time, to prevent the urethane from wrinkling and collapsing due to moisture. It will return to its proper shape when all the moisture is gone. Since you are creating a watertight seal on the urethane, you want to make sure no moisture is trapped within the foam.

Once the appliances have been sealed, painting can proceed in the same manner described for painting foam latex.

You'll need the following materials:

Skin Illustrator®, Sta-Color, or Temptu
  Pro® palettes
1-inch chip brushes   Scissors
99% IPA in a spray bottle   Fine brushes

1. With your appliance resting on a shaped form, open your palettes of Skin Illustrator®, Sta-Color, or Temptu Pro® and pick your colors.

2. Spray the color you will use first with alcohol and begin to liquefy the color with a cut-down chip brush. Both kinds of palettes have empty compartments for mixing color. You do not want the color too saturated or concentrated or it will go onto the appliance too rich and vibrant and will look artificial. The color should be soft and natural; add color gradually to give the appearance of depth.

3. Repeat step 2 for the other colors as well. Human skin, or any skin for that matter, is not one solid, uniform color. There are reds and blues, browns, yellows, and greens in our coloration.

4. Interchange spatter techniques by using the cut-down brush and your fingers as well as tapping the longer bristle brush against the handle of another brush or even against your hand.

5. Try getting some color on your fingers and gently dabbing your fingers onto the appliance to create age spots, if appropriate.

6. Repeat steps 2–5 until you get the effect you want, and then stop.

Once the appliance is applied, you can finish up with palette colors or you can stipple and brush other makeup, such as Ben Nye®. You decide. It's your appliance.

Painting Teeth

Getting your prosthetic choppers looking right for the makeup you've created might be the easiest part of the whole process, but it's by no means the least important. By *easiest* I mean it represents the least amount of surface area to color. Painting teeth to look natural (for character or creature makeup) is as critical as sculpting them to look real in the first place.

Provided you've already done all the prep work to get the dentures ready to be worn, you don't need much else than what's listed below. You might or might not need or want to use the Ben Nye temporary stains on these teeth, but you will definitely want them in your kit, so in this case I think it's better to have them and not need them than to need them and not have them.

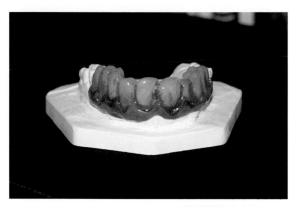

FIGURE 6.41
Acrylic dentures painted with George Taub's Minute Stain. Photo by the author.

MATERIALS

George Taub Minute Stain 7 color kit

Fine sable brushes (¼ inch)

Minute Stain Black & Violet

Ben Nye® temporary tooth stains

Using Minute Stain is really quite simple; Taub recommends the 7 color kit for effects work due to its colors for looking natural as well as darker stains such as pink and brown. The seven colors in the kit are yellow, cervical blend (kind of a toffee/tan), gray, white, pink, blue, and brown, plus a clear glaze, thinner (for colors) brush cleaner, brush, and a small ceramic mixing slab.

The following instructions for using the Minute Stain kit come directly from George Taub Products and David R. Federick, DMD, ScD:

1. Shake the Minute Stain bottles gently to disperse pigments. Shake bottles vigorously only if intense, concentrated colors are desired.
2. Dip the brush into bottle, wipe the excess off at the bottle neck, and bleed additional excess from the brush onto a ceramic or glass mixing slab. The pigments should be evenly dispersed.
3. Quickly apply the stain to the surface of the restoration using a minimum of straight, even strokes. Let the surface dry. Setting time is 10 seconds.
4. Stains must be applied thin. Clean the brush in the thinner bottle after each application and dry with a paper towel.
5. The translucent colors may be built up in intensity with multiple applications using a slight overlap of coats to create a gradual color shift.
6. Apply two (2) coats of Clear Liquid & Glaze to protect the colors and to provide a glaze-like finish. Allow each coat of glaze to completely dry between applications, cleaning the brush in thinner each time.

> **NOTE**
>
> Keep the bottles tightly sealed when not in use. Clean the bottle necks and the insides of caps to maintain a proper seal. Add a few drops of thinner periodically (or as needed) to maintain proper, thin consistency. Once colors have set on the slab, do not try to revive them. Go back to the bottle(s) for a new mix.

SPECIAL EFFECTS

Color suggestions:

- *Yellow:* To deepen shading of 66-67-69-73-77-78.
- *Cervical blend:* To deepen shading of 62-65-68-81-85; interproximal stain.
- *Blue, white:* Incisal blend, decalcified areas.
- *Gray:* To tone down shades and produce tetracycline shading; incisal stain.
- *Brown:* Tea, coffee, and tobacco stains; surface erosions.
- *Pink:* Root surfaces.
- *Color mixes:* Yellow-brown, orange (yellow-pink), purple or violet (blue-pink).
- *Technique:* Blend the colors on a slab with brush of thinner; mix well. Bleed excess on slab before applying to restoration. For reapplication of the mixed color, add some thinner to the mix on the slab, bleed excess, and reapply to the restoration.
- *Fractures:* To create a hairline fracture illusion, score the facial surface with a fine scalpel and scrape off the flashing. Place brown over the score line and wipe off the excess immediately. The brown will seep into and remain within the score line. If color does not penetrate, repeat with scalpel to make the line deeper. Do fracture lines before incisal staining.
- *Occlusal:* To highlight grooves, pits, and fissures, bleed brown onto these surfaces with a fine brush or instrument.
- *Decalcification:* Use a fine brush or instrument tip with white to create this effect. The spot should be matted and asymmetrical for best effect.
- *Tobacco and erosion-type effects:* Use brown and/or concentrated cervical blend. Layer color for the most realistic effect.
- *Incisal:* Delicately place blue or gray along incisal edge, perpendicular to the edge, unevenly in three or four strokes, to cover the entire width of the incisal area. It is best to dilute the gray with thinner for best control.
- *Root surfaces:* Use a thin pink or cervical blend to create the effect.
- *Denture base staining:* Use pink as is or concentrated for intense colors and/or blend with white or blue on a mixing slab. Add thinner to the mix. Apply in quick, even strokes.

- *Lighten shades:* Dilute white on a slab with thinner or glaze to reduce intensity. Apply one or two thin coats.
- *Tone down colors:* Dilute gray with thinner to reduce intensity and place directly over (stained) surface, or first blend with stain on initial application.

> **NOTE**
>
> To remove unwanted stains when shading is incorrect, grind it off with a rubber wheel and repolish the acrylic resin. If Minute Stain bottles solidify, fill bottles with thinner, let stand five days, and stir. Should liquid merely thicken (from solvent evaporation), just add thinner to the proper consistency. If the stain becomes too thin, add clear liquid to restore the body. Do not use monomer to dilute colors.

Shake bottles gently to produce light, translucent colors. It is not necessary to disperse all pigments in the bottle. Doing so could create an intense, concentrated, and unnatural stain.

Here are some helpful hints:

- Do not have excess stain on the brush when you apply to the resin surface. This could cause color runoff resulting in too-intense pigment buildup, visible brushstrokes, colors not drying uniformly or rippled, and grainy surfaces. Always bleed excess off onto the slab before applying color.
- In cervical areas, it is best to apply in straight, even strokes in a vertical direction from cervical to gingival or cervical to incisal.
- Apply stains quickly. Use a large (#1) brush (camel hair) for large surface areas to minimize brushstrokes. Use a fine brush for smaller, delicate areas.
- To clean the slab, use a single-edge gem razor blade and scrape the surface clean. Use thinner to clean small, loose scraps from the slab surface.
- Always clean the brush between each application of color and when finished and wipe it dry on a paper towel. If bristles have stiffened after the last use, simply dip into thinner for a few seconds to revive. Do not use inexpensive plastic brushes, since solvent will destroy them.
- Allow surfaces to dry before reapplying additional or new colors. Doing so will help you avoid creating unwanted brush marks.
- To remove excess (dried) color around small areas, such as along a fracture line or occlusal grooves and fissures, dip a clean brush in thinner, bleed the excess onto a slab, and immediately wash the affected area gently, until unwanted colors are brushed away. Wipe clean.
- For concentrated or intense pigment, dip the brush into the bottom of the bottle.
- If pigment streaks, simply blend on the slab until it is uniform.
- If colors are too intense, blend on the slab with thinner of glaze, bleed excess off the brush, and apply.

These instructions provide more information than you will need as a makeup artist, unless you suddenly decide to go to dental school.

CHAPTER SUMMARY

- In this chapter, you were given a further understanding of silicone and coloring silicone intrinsically (internally) for translucence.
- Silicone gel-filled appliances, or GFAs, filling molds, and removing appliances were also described in detail.
- Foam latex and its properties were outlined in detail, as was the process for running foam latex.
- Casting urethane (cold) foam was described, as was casting gelatin and foamed gelatin.
- Casting dental acrylic was detailed step by step.
- This chapter also detailed the steps involved in painting and seaming (cleaning up) appliances and the procedure for painting teeth appliances.

CHAPTER 7 🎭
Applying the Makeup Appliance

INTRODUCTION

The process of applying 3D prosthetic appliances has in many ways come full circle. In the days of what is considered the first modern use of foam latex prosthetic appliances, the 1940s and 1950s, the appliances were made as one piece; they were essentially masks. These one-piece foam latex appliances continued to be the norm until the late 1960s, when it is believed that iconic makeup artist Dick Smith became the first to employ the use of multiple overlapping partial appliances to create a complete makeup—on Dustin Hoffman as the 121-year-old Jack Crabb in *Little Big Man*.

That process set a new standard of prosthetic appliance application and continues to be the standard method of application. However, the one-piece appliance never went away and has begun to see a resurgence in popularity, particularly in television, where time for application is in short supply. This chapter examines each method, both one-piece and multipiece; you will most likely have occasion to use both in your career. The one-piece continuous appliance is being used with amazing results by Neill Gorton, whose silicone appliances are astonishingly real, even in tight close-up. The multipiece overlapping approach is also used to great effect by makeup artists. The chief difference between the one-piece and the multipiece approach is in the number of pieces and the time it takes to apply them. The results can be equally stunning.

Christopher Tucker

FIGURE 7.1
Christopher Tucker and the author at IMATS, London, 2008. Photo by the author.

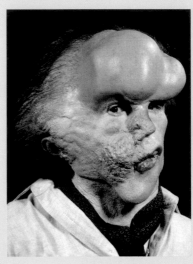

FIGURE 7.2
Actor John Hurt as *The Elephant Man*. Image reproduced by permission of Christopher Tucker.

Christopher Tucker is a legend to fans and artists alike; he certainly is to me. He was born in Hertford, England, and studied at London's famed Guildhall School of Drama and Music, and became...an opera singer. His film career began with no less than a lavish production of *Julius Caesar* starring Charlton Heston and Sir John Gielgud. He also created all the age makeup for the award-winning BBC series *I, Claudius*.

His reputation as a brilliant makeup artist led to designing and creating age, character, fantasy, celebrity look-alikes, animatronic makeup effects, and prosthetics for film, television, commercial, and stage productions in both Great Britain and abroad. Christopher has pioneered numerous techniques and the use of materials such as foam latex, silicone, and gelatin. He also designed the first animatronic eye for a television commercial.

Christopher made it possible for an American actor to turn into a werewolf in one take without use of digital effects for *The Company of Wolves*. His early men in *Quest for Fire* won both an Oscar and a BAFTA for makeup, and his work on the creature characters in the *Star Wars Episode IV* cantina scene is still a topic of conversation among

FIGURE 7.3
Neanderthal Man for the French Ministry of Culture. Image reproduced by permission of Christopher Tucker.

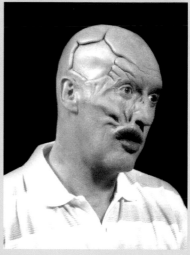

FIGURE 7.5
Actor and singer Michael Crawford in Phantom makeup for *Phantom of the Opera*. Image reproduced by permission of Christopher Tucker.

207

Star Wars devotees. His interests in science, chemistry, engineering, sculpting, and photography have greatly helped in this changing world of special makeup effects; he is also fluent in computer-created image creation and manipulation with programs such as Photoshop.

FIGURE 7.4
Actress Darryl Hannah from *High Spirits*. Image reproduced by permission of Christopher Tucker.

The Royal Shakespeare Theatre asked Christopher to create the hump for *Richard III* and the *Cyrano do Borgorac* noses for Sir Derek Jacobi. Christopher considers the peak of his career came when David Lynch asked him to save his film *The Elephant Man* and design and fabricate the Elephant Man makeup for John Hurt. No other previous makeup had been so involved; the head had 15 different foam latex and silicone rubber parts, some of them overlapping (which had never before been attempted). It took seven hours to apply and was used only on alternative days of shooting and rehearsing.

Christopher is also responsible for the *Phantom of the Opera* makeup designed for the original production starring Michael Crawford in London; he continues to be involved with *Phantom*. He has been educating makeup artists at home and abroad and continues to be highly sought as a lecturer by professionals in medicine, education, and entertainment.

SKIN TYPES

There are three basic skin types: dry, oily, and a combination of both dry and oily. Prior to prosthetic application, each of these needs to be addressed in pretty much the same manner, because what we are doing is preparing the skin to accept adhesive so that it will not adversely affect the appliance's ability to stay put.

Usually all that needs to be done is to apply a mild skin cleanser and astringent. Make sure that your model arrives wearing no makeup; any existing makeup must be removed completely and then the skin cleansed, or the adhesives will not work properly. It is also important that your model has no open sores where you will be applying prosthetics or any makeup, for that matter. You would think that this is so obvious that I wouldn't need to mention it. Wrong. I once had an extra show up on set for bodypaint makeup with a festering open infection the size of a tennis ball on his shoulder. It was amazing…and disgusting. Needless to say, I immediately went and got the first AD, who sent him straight to the hospital! Some people…

In addition to cleanser and astringent to make sure that your model's skin is clean and oil-free, there is another skin care concern I want to bring to your attention that never occurred to me before, but once it did, it fundamentally changed the way I approach every application.

I had an opportunity to be the makeup designer for a unique stage production of *The Wiz* in 2006, and for the Cowardly Lion I designed a full-face makeup in two pieces that was cast with Kryolan Cold Foam. The actor playing the lion had been working in an unpainted version of the appliance for about a week before dress/tech rehearsal. Application and removal had gone without a hitch, as I had hoped and expected, until the first night of dress.

When it came time for us to get our actor out of the appliances, *they wouldn't come off!* We had been using Premiere Products' Telesis® 5 silicone adhesive and Telesis® Super Solv® remover which is a great combination. All week long, the prosthetic had come off like putting a warm knife to butter. It was a cinch. But no, this time the prosthetic would not budge! The harder we tried, the more difficult it seemed to become. We tried a different bottle of Super Solv®—no change. Then a different remover altogether. Nothing! Then another. Aargh! My actor was getting freaked out (did I mention that he is sightless?), not to mention that his skin had become red and irritated…

I started to flop-sweat like Albert Brooks in *Broadcast News*. It was horrible! What should have taken us all of 10 or 15 minutes took almost *2 hours*. I felt like a beginner. First thing the next morning I called Premiere Products and explained what happened. The first words out of Scott Heinly's mouth were, "Does he drink?" Long pause on my end. "Well, yeah," I said, "But it's

FIGURE 7.6
Actor Don Mauck as the Cowardly Lion. Image reproduced by permission of P. Switzer.

not like he's a drunk!" Apparently, *any* alcohol in the body will exit with perspiration through the skin. Alcohol is an inhibitor to the adhesive remover. My actor was sweating profusely during dress rehearsal because he was wearing a big furry lion suit! D'oh! He hadn't been sweating noticeably in the week before dress/tech because he hadn't been in the full lion getup, and without the sweating, the adhesive and remover worked perfectly. It never, ever would have occurred to me that would be a problem. I won't make that mistake again.

So what can be done when you have an actor who wants to kick back with a cold one (or two) after a long day of rehearsal? Two words: *barrier layer*. There are a number of products on the market, but the one I used to solve my problem was the one suggested and provided by PPI, called Top Guard.® It is an acrylic resin-based that works just the way it says in the literature: It's a water- and perspiration-resistant surface primer that reduces skin irritation, increases prosthetic adhesion, and allows for easier removal. I was sold. Just a thin application of Top Guard® on the skin prior to the adhesive (let it dry first) and all was in perfect harmony again. Life was good! Top Guard® is now part of my regular application regimen, no matter what. Plus it actually makes removal and cleanup easier. That alone is worth the cost of admission to me.

ADHESIVES

There are more adhesives than there are Baldwin brothers. Many of them are fine for just about any type of application. Others are better suited for specialty applications, mostly because of cost than for any other reason.

Almost everyone is familiar with the adhesive *spirit gum*. Spirit gum is derived from mastic gum, harvested from the mastic, a small evergreen shrub or tree in the pistachio family. Widely used in theater for applying wigs, beards, and moustaches, spirit gum (also called *mastix*) tends to be a skin irritant for many people, which makes it a less than desirable choice as a prosthetic adhesive. In addition, perspiration has a tendency to weaken and dissolve spirit gum, so in situations where an actor will perspire significantly, spirit gum would not be the best choice, either. On the other hand, spirit gum is relatively inexpensive compared to other adhesives used for applying prosthetics. Spirit gum can be thinned with acetone or Hexane (if you want it to dry extremely fast).

The adhesives that are the most popular in the makeup effects business are medical-grade adhesives that are either acrylic or silicone based. Some of these (the silicone adhesives) can be rather pricey (nearing $100/£54 for 4 oz.), but fortunately a little goes a long way. They can (should) be thinned without weakening the adhesive strength, and the holding power is astounding.

Liquid latex can also be used as an adhesive, but it's not advisable to use it on appliances, because it has a tendency to build up and will come loose if the wearer perspires freely. If used regularly, a skin prep/astringent called Sweat Stop, available from Michael Davy Film and TV Makeup, will inhibit perspiration somewhat where it is applied.

APPLICATION TECHNIQUES

I've said this before and I will say it again: To be good at something requires practice. Don't expect to become sought after as an on-set master of applying makeup appliances if you aren't really good at it. You must practice, practice, practice!

Just as with most aspects of creating special makeup effects, there is no one prescribed method for applying a transformational makeup, whether it is one piece or multiple pieces that overlap to create the makeup. An obvious first step in applying a prosthetic appliance is to clean the skin using 99 percent isopropyl alcohol (IPA), regular 70% rubbing alcohol, or another skin cleanser that is non-oily. It is imperative that the skin be oil and grease free to make for better adhesion when the appliance is applied.

Whether you are applying a foam latex appliance or a silicone appliance (or gelatin or urethane cold foam) is not as important as being methodical and careful in the application. Nor is the adhesive you use as important. That being said, the appliance material and the adhesive are indeed important, relatively speaking. A few things about the adhesives you will most likely encounter: The acrylic adhesives, such as Premiere Products' Telesis® Beta Bond® and ADM Tronics' Pros-Aide,® go on white and dry clear; they also dry tacky and work best as a contact cement with the adhesive applied to both the skin and the appliance. Both surfaces should be powdered after the adhesive dries; the glue can then be reactivated with 99 percent alcohol at the time of application. The silicone adhesives, such as Premiere's Telesis® 5, go on clear and dry clear and are slightly tacky when dry, though not to the extent of Pros-Aide,® for example. Silicone adhesives work best when applied to the skin and the appliance is attached before the adhesive dries completely.

Attaching the Appliance

MATERIALS

Telesis® 5 silicone adhesive	Telesis® 5 thinner
Q-tips	Misc. makeup brushes (for adhesive)
Small cups	Pros-Aide®
Telesis® Super Solv®	Ben Nye Bond Off!® or Remove-It-All®
Isopropyl myristate	99% IPA
Powder and applicators	Pros-Aide® remover
Beta Bond®	Beta Solv

If you are doing a makeup comprising several overlapping pieces, there should be a pre-established order in which to apply the pieces:

1. Before applying any adhesive, position the piece (or each piece one at a time) and check it for a proper fit. Ordinarily, any flashing is left on the piece until application. If the piece needs to be trimmed, do it very carefully; trimming is often best achieved by hand-tearing the flashing away, keeping the blending edges thin and slightly irregular. It is easier to disguise an uneven line than a straight one.

2. After the trimming is completed, replace the appliance and check again for fit and anything that might have been missed and still needs to be trimmed.

3. With the piece in its correct position, powder along the edges with a face powder that is either lighter or darker than the natural skin color. This will show the area where adhesive needs to go.

4. It is usually best to work from the inside out when applying prosthetics; the appliance piece is more manageable that way, especially if it is a large piece, a heavy piece, or both. Sometimes a second pair of hands is advisable, so long as the application area doesn't get too crowded with fingers or the like. You will have to find what works best for you; you could decide to begin from the visible powdered edge and work your way across the piece.

5. If you're using an acrylic adhesive (e.g., Pros-Aide®), brush on a thin layer of adhesive and allow it to dry before pressing the appliance onto the sticky surface. There is a misconception that more adhesive will make the bond stronger; not so. It will only cause a buildup of adhesive, not make it stronger.

6. *Carefully* place the appliance into position, pressing gently; you could find that the foam applicator sticks or the end of a brush might be helpful in getting good surface contact between the skin and the appliance.

Trying to realign a piece after it has been set in adhesive can result in wrinkles and folds that will be difficult to fix or hide.

7. If you are working from the inside out, carefully press down and out in all directions until you reach the edges. You could find that helping to keep the thin appliance edges up can be accomplished with a good pair of tweezers and pressing outward from where glued appliance part toward the edges, letting them gently settle into the adhesive, pressing down with a powdered foam applicator.

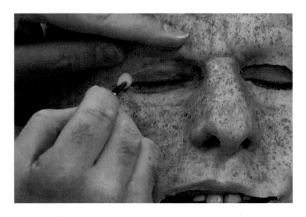

FIGURE 7.7
It is easier to disguise an uneven line than a straight one when blending edges. Image reproduced by permission of Mark Alfrey.

FIGURE 7.8
With the piece in its correct position, powder along the edges with a face powder that is either lighter or darker than the natural skin color. This will show the area where adhesive needs to go. Images reproduced by permission of Mark Alfrey.

FIGURE 7.9
You might find that the foam applicator sticks or the end of a brush could be helpful in getting good surface contact between the skin and the appliance. Image reproduced by permission of Mark Alfrey.

211

8. If you are applying a multipiece makeup with overlapping edges, work in the order necessary for the pieces to work and fit correctly. Repeat the appropriate steps.

The "Techniques" section mentioned that dry, powdered Pros-Aide® can be reactivated with 99 percent alcohol at the time of application. With the appliance piece positioned in its final location, lift a portion of the appliance and, with a brush that has been dipped in 99 percent IPA, rewet the powdered adhesive on the skin and press the appliance into place. Proceed with the application, reactivating the adhesive a little at a time until the entire appliance has been glued into place.

When applying large silicone pieces, you can employ a similar process of gluing the appliances in place. As I mentioned, Telesis® 5 dries slightly tacky and should be powdered to prevent sticking to something it isn't supposed to stick to, such as your finger or a brush, in which case it will try to ruin your life. I credit the following nifty information to Neill Gorton, from whom I learned it, though similar discoveries often happen at the same time worldwide, as has been true of many discoveries throughout history.

Silicone adhesive (chemists, please forgive this gross oversimplification) is essentially nothing more than a very thin, very soft silicone solution. When the solvent carrying the silicone evaporates, what is left behind is silicone. That makes sense, since nothing sticks to silicone except other silicone, and it sticks to us because it's…sticky.

When the Telesis® 5 adhesive begins to get warm due to trapped body heat caused by the large silicone appliance (silicone does not breathe and thereby traps heat and moisture), it gets sticky again. That tackiness, coupled with suction pressure during application, ensures that the appliance stays in place. The following example illustrates reactivating Telesis® 5 silicone adhesive using nothing more than body heat and a large silicone appliance. At the International Makeup Artist Trade Show (IMATS), January 26 and 27, 2008, in London, Neill Gorton demonstrated the application of a one-piece silicone appliance that was a full head and face appliance. Neill transformed lovely, young, blue-eyed blonde Karen Spencer into an elderly Chinese woman, including painting the appliance, in less than 2 hours! (Patching and seaming were done earlier.)

FIGURE 7.10
Makeup artist Karen Spencer in Neill Gorton's Asian age makeup, "before and after," at IIMATS London, 2008. Photos by the author.

Because Neill does quite a bit of prosthetic work for television, it was important to streamline the makeup process to suit a television timetable. Typically, a makeup of this size could be (and often is) done in several overlapping pieces, for example:

- Bald cap for wig application
- Forehead piece
- Nose piece

- Epicanthic eye-fold piece (× 2)
- Upper lip piece
- Ears (× 2)
- Lower lip piece
- Chin
- Cheeks (× 2)
- Neck piece

To achieve a makeup in that way would require numerous molds, starting with a full head and shoulders bust, from which additional casts would be made for sculpting the individual pieces. This becomes a time-consuming logistics puzzle. In truth, there could be times when the multipiece overlapping appliance makeup is the better way, but not always.

To begin, Neill and Stuart Bray quickly applied a bald cap to Karen to keep her hair manageable and out of the way. Had this makeup been for a show and not a demonstration, the piece would most likely have already been painted; in fact, for a show, it is likely that several appliances would have been created and painted to match. Since silicone is more durable than foam latex, a silicone appliance of this size could easily be used more than once if treated well and properly maintained.

1. The first step is to apply the bald cap.

Obviously, everything needed for the makeup application needs to be arranged in advance so that the operation flows smoothly and without delays while the artists look for something:

- Small scissors
- Adhesive brushes
- Chip brushes
- Skin Illustrator® palettes
- Telesis® 5 and Telesis® Thinner
- 99% IPA in a spray bottle
- Powder and applicators
- Misc. sponges

Flashing has already been removed from the eyes and ear but still remains around the mouth. The reason the flashing is left intact is to help hold the piece together and not sag under its own weight. This makeup is actually two silicone pieces: the main appliance and a small lower lip appliance. Having a separate lip piece reduces potential stress for a thin area or a large appliance and leaves a larger opening to facilitate applying adhesive inside the appliance.

FIGURE 7.11
Neill and Stuart Bray quickly apply a bald cap to Karen to keep her hair manageable and out of the way. Photo by the author.

213

FIGURE 7.12
Some of the materials needed for the application and painting of the appliance. Photo by the author.

FIGURE 7.13
Neill and Rob Mayor applying Telesis® 5 adhesive. Photo by the author.

2. Next comes application of adhesive, in this case Telesis® 5 silicone adhesive thinned about 1:1 with Telesis® Thinner. Neill is helped by Rob Mayor of Millennium FX to cover every surface of Karen's head that will come in contact with the appliance using Telesis® 5. When the adhesive is dry, it is lightly powdered to remove any tack.

3. The appliance has been resting on a rigid foam copy of Karen's head, and together Neill and Rob carefully roll the appliance up and off the form to prevent damaging the silicone GFA

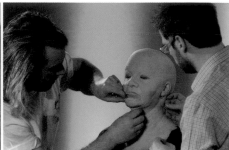

FIGURE 7.14
Adjusting the appliance and nudging it into proper alignment. Photos by the author.

FIGURE 7.15
While Neill begins to apply fresh adhesive along the jawline and under the chin (through the mouth and the ear holes), Karen's body heat is already beginning to reactivate the Telesis® 5. Photo by the author.

(did I mention that this is a silicone gel-filled appliance?). Then they place the piece on top of Karen's head, roll it back down, and reposition it, carefully nudging the appliance into place.

4. While Neill begins to apply fresh adhesive along the jawline and under the chin (through the mouth and the ear holes), Karen's body heat is already beginning to reactivate the Telesis® 5. Gently pressing and smoothing along the neck helps create suction and good surface contact between the appliance and skin.

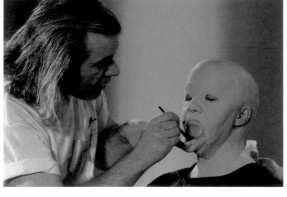

5. Neill carefully glues the appliance along the lower eyelid and blends off the edge with Pros-Aide.®

6. After the adhesive has been applied and the piece is in place, Neill places the lower lip by applying a small dab of Telesis® 5 in the middle of the lip appliance. The flashing is left on so that there is more surface area to handle while he makes sure the lip fits properly.

The lip piece is a GFA also, but the envelope is made of plastic cap material, the same blend of polyvinyl acetate that bald caps are made of. The same mixture of silicone gel (Polytek Plat Sil Gel 10 with a high percentage of softener) is encapsulated between thin layers of bald cap material. By encapsulating with cap material, we can easily blend the edges off to nothing using a small brush and 99 percent IPA.

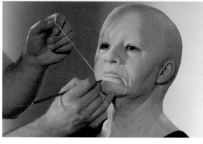

7. Working from the middle outward, the rest of the lip is glued in place and the flashing melted away with 99 percent alcohol. There is no visible seam line whatsoever.

8. While Neill has been gluing under the chin and along the jawline and gluing the lip, Rob has been using Pros-Aide® to blend the edges around the ears. (I'll talk more about concealing edges in the next section.)

9. The last thing to do before painting the makeup is to give Karen a way for heat to escape. Because silicone doesn't breathe, it retains everything, especially body heat, and since this makeup includes a lace-front wig (provided by Campbell Young), the vent hole cut in the silicone and slits in the bald cap will never be noticed when the makeup is complete.

FIGURE 7.16
The lip piece and the flashing being brushed away with 99 percent alcohol. Photos by the author.

It should be noted (here is as good a place as any) that during the casting of the full GFA appliance being applied here, a strip of mesh similar to wig lace but less stretchy—more like tulle—was placed in the mold along the top midline of the head so that there would be very little give to the appliance. On real people, the scalp is attached rather firmly to the skull, and there's not much stretch in any direction; by doing essentially the same to the appliance, the silicone on the top of the head will not over-elongate and allow the appliance to be ill fitting.

215

FIGURE 7.17
Neill cuts a hole in the silicone appliance that will be covered by a wig. Photos by the author.

Blending the Edges

Concealing appliance edges is what helps sell the believability of your makeup. If your appliances have been made well to begin with, blending off the edges is not particularly difficult. You do need to be conscious of very thin edges and not let them fold over on themselves, which can cause them to stick, and then they can be difficult to separate and even tear. If your edges are thicker than they should be or if they've torn or wrinkled, the following, or many variations, may work to conceal edges and overlaps. I will also caution you at this point that if you are working

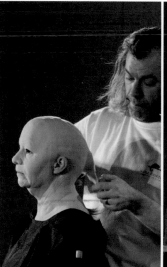

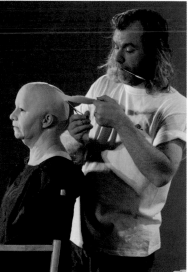

with an appliance that has previously been applied and had makeup on it, such as a Ben Nye® crème foundation, or something other than a Skin Illustrator® palette, Sta-Color palette, or Temptu® Pro palette, concealing edges might be difficult if not impossible because none of the materials commonly used for blending and concealing edges will adhere well to makeup and they will come loose. Any residual makeup must be completely removed and cleaned so that there is no residual oil left from the makeup to inhibit the adhesive used for hiding edges.

So let's assume you are applying a fresh, unused appliance for the first time:

1. Apply the piece as described previously with your adhesive of choice.
2. If the edges are thick, Pros-Aide® bondo or Cabo patch can be applied with a small brush, Q-tip®, or dental spatula to cover the edge, and smoothed with a brush dipped in water or 99 percent IPA to blend away the edge. Use a blow dryer to dry it and then powder because it will be tacky.
3. Pros-Aide® can also be applied by itself to help blend away the edges by applying with a piece of stipple sponge or latex makeup sponge. Because Pros-Aide is a water-based acrylic adhesive, if it's left out and exposed to the air the water will evaporate, making the adhesive thicker.
4. Interestingly enough, Duo® false eyelash glue also works fairly well as an edge blender, as does liquid latex, though if you use latex to blend or conceal edges you will most likely need to dab the latex with castor sealer in order for the makeup you apply next to match makeup applied to the rest of the appliance or skin.

There is really no method I can tell you that will be the be-all and end-all way to conceal edges. Obviously the best way to hide edges is for the edges to be virtually invisible to begin with and glued with care. Rushing will betray you. Do not be in a hurry at this stage of the makeup because it will come back to bite you. Redoing the makeup will take far longer than doing it well and doing it right the first time.

However, there is a method of concealing edges that can make your life easier; it involves using the plastic cap material mentioned in the preceding section about attaching the appliance. If your edges are made of the cap material (if you've created a GFA with cap material as your encapsulating material), they can be dissolved away with 99 percent IPA (isopropyl alcohol), witch hazel, or acetone.

Now, if the adhesive you are using is a silicone adhesive such as Telesis® 5, your appliance edges can be worked and reworked with a small brush dipped in Telesis® thinner. The thinner will slightly swell the silicone edge, popping it out and allowing

216

FIGURE 7.18
A bit of Pros-Aide® bondo can be applied with a small brush, Q-tip®, or dental spatula to cover the edge and smoothed with a brush dipped in water or 99 percent IPA to blend away the edge. Image reproduced by permission of Neill Gorton.

you to press the edge back into its proper position. This works very well if an edge has curled over on itself and stuck together; the thinner will allow it to come back apart and be set right. Then you can proceed to complete the application and blend all the edges invisibly.

Applying Pros-Aide® along edges can be done with a Q-tip® or cotton swab, but you must be careful not to let the adhesive begin to dry or you will risk getting fibers from the cotton tip embedded in the adhesive. There are a number of small brushes that can be purchased in bulk that will allow you to do the same thing without the risk of getting errant fibers caught.

APPLYING THE MAKEUP

The foundation you use for your appliance will largely be decided by the material the appliance is made of.

Foam Latex

If your makeup appliance is made of foam latex, a good choice for coloring after application is rubber mask greasepaint, or RMGP; Graftobian, Kryolan, and Mehron each make RMGP. RMGP is best applied with a rubber sponge and by stippling on the color over the entire prosthetic. If RMGP is only used to color the appliance and not for the rest of the makeup:

1. The greasepaint should be stippled over the edge of the appliance and onto the immediately surrounding skin and blended with your fingers, sponge, or brush to blend with the makeup used for the rest of the face or other body parts.

2. The RMGP should be powdered, pressing in as much powder as the greasepaint will absorb and then lightly brushing off the excess with a powder brush. RMGP may require periodic powdering to prevent shine.

3. To help the makeup look more natural and to help conceal the edge between the appliance and the skin, stipple additional colors (these can be RMGP or crème makeup) to add variation to the base color.

   ■ Using a stipple sponge or piece of latex sponge applicator, rubber sponge, or piece of sea sponge, apply a shade that is three or four times darker than the base color, then powder.

   ■ Next, stipple a color that is three or four shades lighter than the base, and powder.

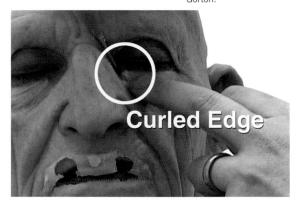

FIGURE 7.19
If an edge has curled over on itself and stuck together, a small brush dipped in thinner will allow it to come back apart and be set right. Image reproduced by permission of Neill Gorton.

FIGURE 7.20
There are a number of small brushes that can be purchased in bulk that will allow you to blend edges without the risk of getting errant fibers caught in the adhesive. Photo by the author.

217

- If you are working on a face, apply a crème pink or red (rouge)—if appropriate to the character—to the cheeks. Then powder. Do the same for the nose, if needed.

Much of this will depend on lighting conditions for the makeup and whether it is for stage or screen. Often what looks good under makeup lighting will look quite different under stage or shooting lights or even sunlight. If appliance edges are still visible, apply some detailed stippling with a small pointed brush or piece of stipple sponge.

- Where the edge is visible as a result of shadows, use a lighter stipple to counteract them.
- Use a dark stipple to offset highlights.

Crème foundations such as the ones available from Ben Nye seem to work just fine with foam latex also and can be applied in the same manner as RMGP.

Gelatin

When applying makeup on gelatin, you first need to seal it, if it hasn't already been made as part of a GFA, with the G (for *gel*) being gelatin. If you apply makeup directly onto the gelatin, the color will be absorbed into the gelatin instead of sitting on top; depending on what you are using to color the appliance, you could also begin to dissolve the gelatin if you aren't careful. You can use a number of materials as a sealer, including plastic cap material, Kryolan Fixier spray (spray a small amount into a cup along the edge of the cup, then brush it on), WM Creations' Shiny Sealer or Soft Sealer, Premiere Products' Green Marble Sēlr®, BJB SC-115 acrylic sealer, or the like.

Once the gelatin is properly sealed, makeup can be applied normally; RMGP is not recommended. You can use crème foundation color and makeup sponges, but I recommend using one of the alcohol-activated color palettes—Skin Illustrator®, Sta-Color, or Temptu® Pro.

Almost without exception, the appliances you will be putting on will have been pigmented at least basically with a foundation color at the time of casting them in their molds. So your task at this stage will be to finish the job, and that can be done quite nicely by spattering numerous layers of transparent color from one or more palettes, 99 percent IPA, and a few cut-down chip brushes.

The better-made your appliance edges are to begin with and the proper placement at the beginning of application will minimize the amount of correction the makeup will need.

Cold Foam

Makeup should be applied to cold foam the same way as for gelatin or foam latex; it should be sealed first and the sealer allowed to dry fully. Remember that urethane foam is moisture sensitive and, even after having fully cured, might wrinkle slightly when exposed to moisture in a makeup foundation or even the sealer, particularly if it is water based. RMGP, PAX crème foundation, or alcohol color palettes can all be used to color cold foam. Follow the preceding steps to apply makeup to your cold foam appliance.

Silicone

If your silicone appliance has been painted already, as described in Chapter 6, your makeup needs for the appliance should be minimal after application. If you were not the one who painted the appliance, it would be beneficial to have a color chart showing what was used. If not, you must eyeball it and mix your best match with a Skin Illustrator palette or something similar. Remember that with silicone it is important to maintain translucency of the material; that's one of the reasons that silicone is used as a prosthetic material. Work with light color application of whatever makeup you use and build up layers of depth to blend from the appliance to the skin.

REMOVING THE APPLIANCE

If handled deftly, an appliance should be reusable, no matter what material it was cast with. Even foam latex can see multiple applications if the removal is gentle and the appliance is properly cleaned and stored, though more often than not foam latex won't survive the removal. At best, the appliance will hold up, but there will be significant edge damage that will need attention if the makeup is to be reusable.

No matter what the appliance is made of, you should never attempt to simply pull it off. Depending on the adhesive used to apply the prosthetic, one of two things will happen: The appliance will tear and come off in chunks, or the appliance will come off with chunks of the wearer's face still attached to it. Either way, it will be uncomfortable, if not downright excruciating, so always use the appropriate adhesive remover to first loosen the edges and then proceed.

219

Materials

Q-tips®	Small cups
Misc. makeup brushes (for adhesive remover)	
Pros-Aide® remover	99% IPA
Telesis® Super Solv®	Ben Nye® Bond Off!® or Remove-It-All®
Isopropyl myristate	Sponges
Cloth towels	Cotton pads

Removers

There are a number of adhesive removers available, depending on which adhesive you use, though many of them will work well with different adhesives. If you have used spirit gum, spirit gum remover or mastic remover generally work better than some other removers. Residual stickiness can be removed by either applying more of the spirit gum remover or using isopropyl myristate with a piece of cloth, sponge, or cotton pad.

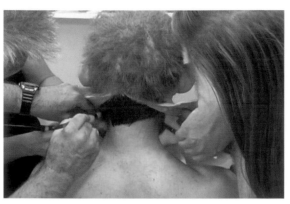

FIGURE 7.22
As the remover dissolves the adhesive, gently start to lift the appliance as you go, continuing to apply more of the remover, either with the brush or with a Q-tip® or other type of applicator. Image reproduced by permission of Mark Alfrey.

FIGURE 7.21
Gently begin to insert the brush bristles between the edge of the appliance and the skin, moving the brush to increase the size of the opening. Image reproduced by permission of Mark Alfrey.

Technique

Before starting, make sure you have everything at hand that you will need for the removal; more than likely your performer has been wearing the prosthetic for a long time and is more than ready for the appliance or appliances to come off. The trick is to work efficiently and carefully, particularly around the eyes. The last thing you want is to accidentally get remover where it should not be.

1. Dip a fairly firm-bristled brush into the remover (Telesis® Super Solv® or Ben Nye® Bond Off!® work well with most adhesives) and gently begin to insert the brush bristles between the edge of the appliance and the skin, moving the brush softly to increase the size of the opening.

2. As the remover dissolves the adhesive, gently start to lift the appliance as you go, continuing to apply more of the remover, either with the brush, or with a Q-tip® or other type of applicator.

3. Try to avoid letting the appliance flop over onto itself, adhesive to adhesive, because it will be difficult to separate and could rip or tear. If the appliance is large, another pair of hands might be useful to hold it out of your way as you work.

4. When the appliance has been removed, place it on its form until you are able to clean it properly for storage.

5. With Q-tips,® cloth, or cotton pads, use isopropyl myristate or more of the adhesive remover to gently wipe off remaining adhesive residue form the skin. The skin can be quite sensitive to irritation, especially if the performer has been in prosthetics regularly. Simply repeat step 5 until the skin is no longer sticky.

SKIN CARE

I've said before that it's never about the makeup; it's always about the performance. That includes post performance. If my actor is worried that his skin is getting more and more irritated and becomes consciously aware of discomfort, in and out of the makeup, I am not doing my job well enough. Making sure I've done everything I can to leave my subject's skin clean and feeling good will ensure that skin care is one less thing the actor has to think about and can concentrate on the performance. Skin care is part of the job description.

The first step in skin care is preventive: skin preparation. Do you recall my anecdote from the beginning of this chapter about the actor who played the Cowardly Lion in a production of *The Wiz*? Premiere Products' Top Guard® is a methacrylate-based, non-oily skin prep and surface primer that reduces skin irritation. It also increases the adhesion of prosthetic appliances *as well as* making it easier to remove them. This one product alone can make a makeup artist's post-makeup routine a relative breeze.

1. Once the adhesive residue and remover is fully removed from the skin, gently wipe the skin with isopropyl myristate using a soft cloth. This is an extra measure as a safeguard to clean the skin.
2. Apply a dedicated skin cleanser, such as Ben Nye® Hydra Cleanse® or Premiere Products' Telesis® Brisk,® which can be sprayed and wiped off with a soft cloth or cotton pad. Hydra Cleanse® is a gentle oil-free skin cleanser, and Brisk® is a skin cleanser with a peppermint oil fragrance and tea tree oil that acts also as an antiseptic, analgesic, and astringent.
3. There is no one single product choice; this is a personal preference, and you might have skin care products (cleansers, lotions, and conditioners) already in mind that you prefer. The important thing to keep in mind is comfort. Buzzwords to look for in products are:

- Emollient
- Moisturize
- Condition
- Soothing
- Refresh

Many actors have their own routine for skin care and so their own products, but it is a good idea to be involved because their skin is the foundation for our work. If the actor's skin becomes irritated, it is in your best interests and the actor's to make certain that the skin is clean before and after makeup. Since it our responsibility to restore skin to its original state when we are finished, keep a variety of cleansers, toners, emollients, and moisturizers on hand.

CLEANING AND STORING THE APPLIANCE

Whatever you do to clean the appliance and remove adhesive residue and buildup, it is important that it not be sticky or greasy (oily). If it is sticky, it will be hard to manage, could tear if it sticks to the mold form, and it won't feel clean. It also means that there is still adhesive, and adding more adhesive will add to a buildup, causing the appliance to be ill fitting.

If the appliance is oily, adhesive will not stick to it, and the appliance will not hold well after application. In addition, if the appliance is going to be reused (which is why you're cleaning it in the first place) there is likely to be a buildup on its surface where edges were concealed. Carefully work off the Pros-Aide,® bondo, Cabo patch, or whatever was used to conceal the edges. Any number of tools could be useful for this task, including toothpicks, dental spatulas, or eyelash brushes. This could take some time to do as well.

Once the appliance is clean and free of adhesive and remover, powder it and store it in an airtight baggie on a mold form so that it will hold its shape until it is ready to be reapplied.

CHAPTER SUMMARY

In this chapter you learned about:

- The three basic skin types
- Preappliance skin care
- Various adhesives
- Materials needed for appliance application
- Application techniques
- Blending appliance edges
- Applying makeup to various appliance materials
- Removing and cleaning prosthetic appliances
- Post-removal skin care
- Storing the appliance

Key Points

- Types and varieties of hair
- Tools and materials for postiche boardwork
- Wigs
- Hair attachment
- Laid-on hair
- Ventilating hair
- Punching hair

INTRODUCTION

This is one of the shorter chapters of the book because hair and wigs are not our primary focus. However, the subject is indeed important. This chapter is also more informational than practical, though it includes some "how-to" pointers that you will find beneficial. Numerous wonderful sources of in-depth information are readily available, so there is no need to reinvent the wheel for this book. Just as something as small and simple as a nose can transform a familiar face into something new and almost unrecognizable, the same can be said of hair for suggesting a particular time period, personality, or age. Merely changing one's hair color and length can often be enough to render that individual immediately unrecognizable to friends.

FIGURE 8.1
Actor Brian Walker Smith, "before" (left) and "after" (right). Photos by the author.

TYPES AND VARIETIES OF HAIR

When creating postiche for a character makeup, various types of hair are often used: human hair, animal hair, and synthetic hair. You might think that hair is hair, but there are very clear differences in hair textures, in addition to the obvious color variations. Of the human hair used for postiche, there are *European* and *Asian*. European hair is the most expensive because it offers the widest variety of natural colors and has a mild texture. Asian hair is less expensive and coarser than European hair and sometimes does not last as long, but it's readily available and can also be found in a variety of colors.[1]

Yak hair is frequently used in postiche work and because of its coarseness is particularly suited for moustache or beard work. It is naturally black, gray, or off-white and can be artificially colored. *Angora goat hair* (mohair) is a very soft hair used predominantly for fantasy character work. It colors very well, but it can be quite expensive. *Sheep's wool* (crepe wool/crepe hair) is sold in braided ropes that can be easily straightened and used for a variety of postiche, but it's used quite often for hand-laid (laid-on) hair work such as beards and moustaches. It is relatively inexpensive and is available in a broad range of colors. *Synthetic hair* is quite versatile and can be permanently curled, which is something that cannot be achieved with real hair. However, synthetic hair does not last as long as the real deal.

Tools and Materials for Postiche

There are several tools and materials that are essential for postiche boardwork if you are going to do any of the work yourself.

FIGURE 8.2
Drawing mat. Photo by the author.

- *Drawing mats and drawing brushes.* These two devices are designed to hold hair in place while you work to prevent wasting any hair by keeping it under control. When hair is placed between the brushes or mats, the longest hairs can be drawn out first.
- *Net foundation.* Foundation comes in different varieties and is used by wigmakers for ventilating hair (hand tying) into; fine, flesh-colored nylon or silk lace is used for street wear, film, television, and studio work, and heavier flesh-colored nylon lace is used for theater, though often fine lace is used to front wigs for theater as well.
- *Ventilating needle.* Also called *knotting hooks*, ventilating needles come in different sizes, all of them quite small; the size will depend on the number of hairs required in each knot. Size 00 is the

---

[1]Patsy Baker, *Wigs & Makeup for Theatre, Film, and Television* (Butterworth-Heinemann, 1993).

finest needle and is used for finishing edges, drawing one hair at a time. Sizes 01 and 02 are used for main fill areas, drawing two or three hairs at a time. Larger needles can be used for drawing even more hair for areas where more hair is required without showing the hairline. A ventilating needle is actually a very tiny fish hook and is quite sharp and should be treated carefully so as not to accidentally hook yourself or someone else.

- *Blocks*. These include *wooden blocks, malleable blocks*, and *beard blocks/chin blocks*. Wooden blocks are solid head-shaped forms for making wigs. A malleable block is head-shaped but soft and covered with canvas; these are usually used for dressing wigs. Beard/chin blocks can be made of either solid wood or soft canvas; these are chin shaped to facilitate beard work.

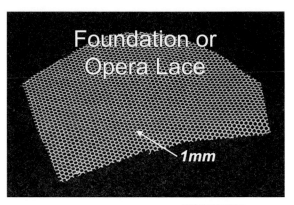

FIGURE 8.3
Various types of foundation material. Photo by the author.

WIGS

If a wig has had any hand work done to it, or if it is completely hand-made, it is going to be more valuable than one without. In general. There are also some excellent machine-made wigs. If the foundation is hand-made, the hair knotted into it is most likely going to be human hair. Synthetic hair is less likely to hold its knot in the lace foundation. The reasons for knowing what type of wig you have is so that it can be cleaned without being damaged and so you can determine the possibilities for dressing it.

FIGURE 8.4
Chin block. Photo by the author.

There are two choices for cleaning a wig: shampoo and water or dry cleaning with industrial chemicals. Human hair, whether hand-ventilated or wefted (sewn), needs to be dry cleaned. Machine-wefted hair can be shampooed, as can synthetic hair (which has most likely been machine wefted). A combination wig, such as machine-wefted plus hand-tied, must get a shampoo wash.[2]

Weft Wigs

Simple weft wigs come in different sizes and are relatively inexpensive, mass-produced wigs that are good for crowd scenes. These wigs use machine-made hair wefts that are either synthetic or real hair that has been acid-reduced (to facilitate styling). A synthetic wig cannot have its style changed, though a reduced hair wig can be styled with limitations.[3]

---

[2]Patsy Baker, *Wigs & Makeup for Theatre, Film, and Television* (Butterworth-Heinemann, 1993).
[3]Patsy Baker, *Wigs & Makeup for Theatre, Film, and Television* (Butterworth-Heinemann, 1993).

FIGURE 8.5
Hair weft being added to existing wig. Photo by the author.

A stretch weft wig is designed to fit most people; these are the kind of wigs most often found in costume shops for Halloween, are cheap, and are mostly synthetic hair, though reduced-hair stretch wigs do exist. These wigs could be suitable for a crowd scene but probably won't fool anyone up close. On the other hand, because they're so inexpensive (especially compared to hand-knotted wigs), they can come in handy when push comes to shove. I'd call these "last resort" wigs.

Another type of weft wig is more expensive: fashion weft stretch wigs. These are also known as combination wigs because the tops of these wigs have a large area of hand-tied, drawn-through parting-style work.[4] This makes the hair appear to be growing directly out of the scalp. These are stretch wigs designed to fit most people, are medium to expensive in price, and are made in a variety of hairstyles and colors.

These weft wigs are easy to care for and easy to wear, but there are disadvantages, which include:

- They're heavy to wear.
- They fade easily in strong light.
- They have a short lifespan compared to hand-knotted real hair wigs.

226

FIGURE 8.6
Hand-tied hair appears to be growing directly out of the scalp. Photo by the author.

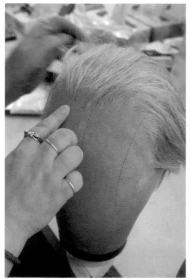

Knotted Wigs

Hand-knotted wigs are almost always made to order from specific measurements and can be quite expensive. Unless you have a money tree in your backyard, these are not Halloween wigs. They are the real deal, and they look and fit fantastic. These are fully custom wigs that are available in varying weight, color, length, and quality. Being custom wigs, knotted wigs can have hand-sewn foundations or machine-sewn vegetable (veg) net foundations with a *galloon* (silk lace ribbon) base; they can also have a hair-lace front that will allow the wigmaker to knot an actual hairline for theatrical use. The lace is so fine that with makeup it becomes invisible to all but the closest scrutiny. Even then it can be barely perceptible.

Hand-knotted wigs can have a very long life if well cared for. For stage and screen, hand-knotted lace wigs are what principal cast members wear. In researching wigs and postiche for this book, I've learned a great deal about the craft from Diana Ben Kiki, hair and wig mistress for the Denver Center for the Performing Arts. She and her work are amazing, and I'm sure glad I know her.

[4]Patsy Baker, *Wigs & Makeup for Theatre, Film, and Television* (Butterworth-Heinemann, 1993).

Hair Attachment

There are essentially six ways to attach hair—seven, actually; six of them do not involve a medical procedure:

1. To weave the hair on weaving silks to create a weft.
2. To knot the hair onto a lace net foundation.
3. To plant the hair into wax (I've never done this).
4. To punch-graft the living hair root into the scalp. This is a medical (surgical) procedure and should *never* be tried by anyone without MD at the end of his or her name. *This is not a practical theatrical application of hair and should not be attempted as such.*
5. To punch hair into a silicone, gelatin, cold foam, or foam latex appliance with a hair-punching needle.
6. To bind and sew hair (real or synthetic) to growing hair; this is called *hair extensions*.
7. To hand lay hair onto the face (or elsewhere) and secure with adhesive such as spirit gum, Pros-Aide, or Telesis 5.

In this chapter, we'll look at numbers 2, 5, and 7.

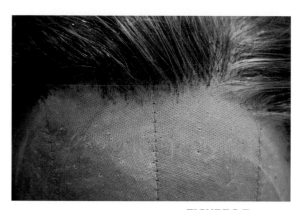

FIGURE 8.7
The lace on a hand-tied wig is so fine that with makeup it becomes invisible to all but the closest scrutiny. Photo by the author.

227

Preparation for a Wig

There are several steps to getting a head ready to wear a wig, including large elastic bands (called Alice bands in the U.K.), hairpins, combs (including a rattail comb), and a wig cap.

FOR SHORT HAIR

- Take a section of your subject's own hair from the front center hairline and braid it backward into a small tight plait (braid) if possible and secure with a hairpin or two.
- Place a large elastic hair band over the head to the neck, then comb the rest of the hair back and away from the face.
- Bring the elastic band up and around the head to hold the hair back.
- Put a wig cap over the hair; if there is any excess, tuck it in to hide it.

FOR MEDIUM HAIR

- Just as with short hair, take a section of your subject's own hair from the front center hairline and braid it backward into a small tight plait (braid) if possible and secure with a hairpin or two.
- Divide the hair into small sections and pin-curl each section flat to the head, using crossed hairpins to hold the curls in place. To make the pin-curls, twist the hair around two of your fingers.

- Place a large elastic band around the head and over as many of the sections as you can.
- Put a wig cap over the hair and tuck in any excess.

FOR LONGER HAIR

- Take a section of your subject's own hair from the front center hairline and braid it backward into a small tight plait (braid) if possible and secure with a hairpin or two.
- Make a ponytail and hold the hair tightly at the base with a small elastic band.
- Roll the ponytail into a flat chignon, or bun, and secure it firmly with hairpins.
- Use a large elastic band to keep short hairs in check, particularly those at the back of the neck.
- Put a wig cap on the subject, being sure to tuck in any excess.

Obviously these steps are useless if the makeup you are creating requires your subject to be in a bald cap as part of the makeup. (Bald cap application is described in detail in Chapter 9.) So, if your subject is in a bald cap, why do you need a wig? Perhaps the character is going bald but still has hair—perhaps an "outer rim" or "comb-over," or perhaps the hairline is receding or the hair is simply getting thinner. For whatever reason, there is visible scalp and hair, hence the need for a wig—and not just any wig. A wig for any of these situations requires a hand-ventilated lace wig. In the case of a bald cap and lace wig, it is important to know where the imagined hairline would be prior to wig placement. But I digress.

How do you place a wig onto someone's head? Funny you should ask.

How to Put on a Wig

Before the wig can be placed on your subject, it is important to know where the center front of the wig is.

- Standing behind your subject, place the center front of the wig onto the forehead just below the hairline.
- Carefully set the wig down onto the head and gently shift it into place.
- Use the sides of the wig by the ears as a hand-hold to adjust the wig, making sure that it's properly placed—centered and even.
- Secure the wig with hairpins, medium pins along the front hairline, and large pins toward the back. Until you get adjusted to the feel of a pin pushing through the wig cap nylon mesh, ease your hand under the wig at the spot where you are placing a pin, and push until the pin touches your hand, then remove your hand and gently push the pin into the hair (pincurl). If pinned properly, the wig should be secure and not come off until you take it off.

To remove the wig, first remove all the hairpins, then take the back nape of the wig in both your hands and carefully lift the wig up and forward. To store it until the next application, place it on a wig form or malleable wig block.

How to Put on a Lace Wig

Okay, so your makeup requires a lace wig or, to be more exact, a lace-front wig. Your subject could have a full bald cap, full-head cowl, or a forehead extension that covers the head to about the midline of the head. How to you apply a lace or lace-front wig? If your subject is in full bald cap or full-head cowl, the job of applying the wig is relatively simple. I'll describe that first:

1. Place the wig on your subject's head in the normal way. The lace wig should go on before makeup has been applied, because the lace must be carefully glued in place. Spirit gum can be used, but it is preferable to use either Pros-Aide® (or Beta Bond®) or Telesis® 5.
2. Make sure that the wig is seated properly, then apply the adhesive *thinly* along the hairline under the lace and down the temples to the ears on both sides. If you are using Pros-Aide®, let the adhesive get tacky; if you are using Telesis® 5, you can press the lace into the fresh adhesive. Use a damp makeup sponge to press the lace down firmly to the head. When the adhesive is dry, lightly powder to remove tackiness, and then apply makeup over the hair lace.

Removal of a lace wig takes the kind of care and finesse needed to remove a prosthetic appliance that you plan to use again:

1. Dip a medium flat brush into some Super Solv® (gel or liquid) or Pros-Aide® remover and gently brush along the glued hairline of the lace.
2. When the adhesive becomes soft, carefully begin to lift the lace edge with the brush or a pair of tweezers.
3. When the hairline lifts without resistance, lift the nape of the wig at the back and pull it up and forward, with the lace coming off last.
4. Clean the lace carefully to remove all traces of adhesive from the lace. You can use more of the adhesive remover or acetone.
5. When you're done, place the wig on a wig form for storage until it is ready to be worn again.

BEARDS, MOUSTACHES, AND EYEBROWS

There are really just two ways to apply hair to the face: by hand or by applying a knotted lace piece. Beards, moustaches, and eyebrows can easily be glued to the face as ready-made appliances but can be less comfortable than hand-laid hair simply because the hair is knotted into a lace foundation that is then glued in place. While fronting lace—which is what most tied beard, moustache, and eyebrows are ventilated into—is very fine and lightweight, it has very little flexibility and might have the ability to hamper a performance

FIGURE 8.8
Lace beard with hand-laid blend on cheeks. Applied by John Blake. Photo by the author.

by inhibiting movement. If that is the case, hand-laid hair might be preferable. All considerations must be weighed around the performance. Even when using a lace beard piece, the edge should be hand laid to blend hair into a more realistic look.

Laid-on Facial Hair

Hand-laid hair is difficult to match on a daily basis and takes considerably longer to do than applying a lace piece. For that reason it is not often used in many screen productions. Hand-laid hair is still used fairly extensively in some circles—theater and low budget shows—though it does appear to be lessening. It's not hard to do, but it is time consuming, and lest it becomes a lost art, I'm going to do my part to describe how to do it. Paul Thompson of the Makeup Designory does a terrific job describing and showing the process step by step in his book, *Character Make-up*, and so does master wigmaker Patsy Baker in her book, *Wigs & Make-up for Theatre, Television, and Film*.

I've had mixed results (more bad than good, really) laying on real hair vs. crepe wool. The problem with real hair is threefold: Crimping it is critical because facial hair does not grow straight; real hair is expensive, far more expensive than crepe wool; and real hair is not particularly fond of any kind of adhesive. Facial hair is not usually straight, either, and real hair would need to be kinked rather substantially to be believable.

FIGURE 8.9
Crepe hair/crepe wool.
Photo by the author.

Crepe Wool (Hair)

Crepe wool is ordinarily sold by the yard, but at most places you can buy it in whatever length you want; they'll just cut it to order. The wool is braided, so when it is straightened it will almost double in length. To hand-lay hair, you'll need the following stuff:

- Adhesive
- Various colors of crepe wool
- Scissors
- Drawing mats
- Hackle
- Rattail comb
- Adhesive remover
- Setting powder

There are a few ways to straighten the crepe before you lay it on the face. It can be dampened slightly and ironed (on the wool steam setting) or held in front of a clothes steamer or even a boiling tea kettle. Either of the last two options comes with this caveat: Watch your fingers! I've found that placing a section of the crepe wool into a bowl of water and microwaving it for a minute or so will take the curl right out of it. Then the wool needs to be dried before it can be separated. The straighter the crepe wool, the easier it is to work with, but completely straight facial hair doesn't look realistic when applied to the face, the exception being Asian facial hair, which is often quite straight. For a character makeup of African ancestry, you might want to forego straightening the crepe at all, since the facial hair tends to be quite curly.

PREPARATION

1. Unravel some crepe wool from the braid, but be careful not to pull too far and tangle the hair and strings. Cut away the string from the braid.
2. The goal is to remove most of the curl from the crepe hair, but not all; keep about 30–40 percent of the curl.
3. Put the cut length of hair in a microwave-safe bowl of water and nuke it for about a minute; keep an eye on it to make sure you don't lose too much curl.
4. If you are going to mix hair to get a specific color, repeat step 3 for each color you intend to mix.
5. When the hair is dry (you can pat it almost completely dry in a towel), pull the straightened braid of crepe hair apart by gently pulling one end while holding the other end. You could use a wide-toothed comb, but that tends to waste a lot of hair.
6. As you pull, the hair should separate into 6–8-inch lengths (15–20 cm). Now is when you should mix in other colors if necessary.
7. Pull several strands of each color and put them together until you have a pile of hairs the color you want. From here, continue to pull the hair apart, put it back into a bundle, and repeat until you have a bundle of crepe hair that looks fluffy and even. If you are not going to use the hair right away or if you have more than you will need immediately, you can wrap any excess hair in a paper towel, tape the roll, and put it in a plastic zipper bag.
8. The next step, if you have one, is to run the hair through a hackle.

If you've never used one before, get some Band-Aids® and antiseptic and keep them close. A hair hackle looks like a small medieval torture device but is actually used to detangle hair. When it's not in use, a cover should be placed over the hackle pins to prevent accidental impalement. I put a big chunk of Styrofoam over mine.

FIGURE 8.10
Hair hackle. Photo by the author.

9. Clamp or tape the hackle to the edge of a table or other work surface. Slowly and carefully place a small amount of hair about 1 inch (2.5 cm) into the hackle. Hold the hair firmly and pull it toward you through the pins. Repeat this process a few times, adding an inch or so more hair as you pull it through the hackle.

FIGURE 8.11
Cover your hackle to avoid injury. Photo by the author.

10. Now repeat this process with the other end of the bunch of hair you just pulled through the hackle.

11. Do this with all the hair you will be laying on. As hair is pulled through the hackle, short hairs and tangled wads of hair will build up in the pins. When the buildup of crud hair begins to interfere with your hackling, carefully remove the hair buildup and set it aside. You can pull and separate that hair later to put through the hackle again.

12. Cutting or trimming the crepe hair before laying it on is critical to a good application, as is how and where you hold the hair. The amount of hair sticking out from your hand as you hold it in your fingers is directly related to how thick the hair will be when applied. The more the hair is sticking out, the thinner the application (note how the hair fans out, away from your fingers).

FIGURE 8.12
The amount of hair sticking out from your hand as you hold it in your fingers is directly related to how thick the hair will be when applied. Photos by the author.

FIGURE 8.13
The face is broken into sections for laying hair by hand, with the foremost sections being applied last. Illustration by the author.

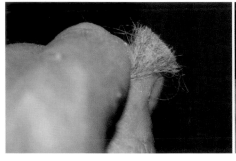 

The closer the end of the hair is to your fingers, the thicker it will be. Be careful, because with facial hair, there should be a little daylight visible between the hairs, not an impenetrable carpet. Hair will be thickest under the chin and getting thinner as you go toward the side edges on the cheeks, where the hair will be the thinnest.

13. The hair ends should be cut at an angle that will mimic the direction the hair should be growing in. Be careful when cutting so clippings will not fall into the hair and get caught.

When laying on hair by hand, the idea is to work in sections, with the hair furthest back and underneath being applied first and the foremost or top-most hair being laid on last. With that in mind, you need a plan. The hair can't simply go on. For a full beard and moustache application, the hair will be applied in 15 or 16 sections.

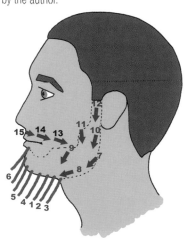

APPLICATION

Hand-laying hair is not a particularly difficult skill to master, relative to some other aspects of special makeup effects, but it does take repetition to become good at it. And this is definitely a skill to be good at. I mentioned before that hand-laying hair is becoming a lost art, but there's no reason that it should disappear. It's your makeup that the hair is going to be part of, so you should be the one putting the hair on. Enough said. It's time to apply the hair:

1. Do a position test before applying adhesive by holding the hair up to your subject's face, under the chin, because under the chin will be the first section to fill.
2. The hair under the chin should appear to grow somewhat forward, so the hair ends should be cut to make sure the application of the hair will be in the right direction.

> **NOTE**
>
> Don't use too much hair, and you want the hair to stand on end, with only the ends of the hair stuck into the adhesive.

Now that you know where adhesive will go first, mix some Telesis® 5 (thinned 1:1 with Telesis® Thinner) or Pros-Aide®. Your choice; crepe hair will adhere well with either of these adhesives. Just remember that Pros-Aide® needs to dry (clear) before you apply the hair.

3. Once you've applied the adhesive, gently press the ends of the crepe hair into it and hold until it's dry. Telesis dries pretty quickly—even more quickly when it's thinned. If necessary you can use the back of an applicator swab to press the hair into the adhesive.
4. When the adhesive is completely dry, use the tail end of a rattail comb to pick through the hair and remove any hair that isn't glued down. There will be some. The resulting hair glued in this section should be pretty thin.
5. The next section will go right in front of the last one. Comb through it and hold it the way you held the last bunch of hair. Combing will make sure the hairs are going in the right direction and will also remove any small, extraneous hairs.
6. Apply adhesive to the next area, being careful not to get adhesive in the first section of hair. Press the hair into the adhesive and hold until it's dry. Make sure the hairs look like they're growing out of the skin and not just lying on the surface.
7. When the adhesive is dry, pick or comb gently through the hair to remove loose ones.
8. Continue this process through each section, back to front, bottom to top, until all the hair has been applied.

233

FIGURE 8.14
Hair being laid on for a moustache. Work from the outside in, from the outside corner of the mouth toward the nose. Photos by author.

FIGURE 8.15

FIGURE 8.15
Press hair into the adhesive and hold until it's dry (left); use the tail end of a rattail comb to pick through the hair and remove any that isn't glued down (right). Photos by the author.

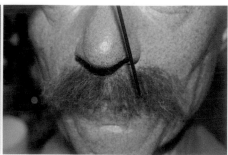

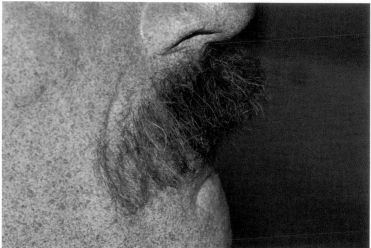

234

FIGURE 8.16
When done properly, the crepe hair should appear to be growing out of the skin. Photo by the author.

Once the hair has all been laid on, it must be neatly trimmed into a normal beard. Begin with the moustache and trim the hair back to the edge of the upper lip. Then trim the hair over the corners of the mouth in a downward direction (cutting away from the nose) with the scissors almost parallel to the skin. Continue to trim, forming the shape of the beard along the edges; use a comb to lift sections of hair and continue to keep the scissors parallel to the skin beneath the hair you're cutting to avoid lopping off too much hair.

When you've finished trimming and shaping the beard and moustache, use a pair of tweezers to pick off stray bits of hair from the beard and from the skin.

If you have a lifecast of your actor's face, it is possible to create a hand-laid beard that can be used multiple times. In the same way that you would create a bald cap from scratch on a plastic bald cap form, you can build up latex on your subject's lifecast, too, provided that it has been sealed to make removal of the latex easy.

1. With a pencil, draw a pencil line for the outline of the beard and moustache.
2. With a small piece of sponge, stipple a thin layer of latex over the beard/moustache area. When the first layer is dry, repeat, building up as many as three layers of latex to provide a good base.
3. When you are ready to apply the hair, stipple another layer of latex over the first section, then immediately press the hair ends into the latex. Just as with the Telesis, hold the hair still until the latex is dry, then carefully pick out loose hairs.
4. Repeat for the next section, and the next, and the next until you've created the new piece, picking out loose hairs before moving on to each new section of hair.

5. Trim the beard as before and you're ready to remove the new piece from the lifecast.

6. Powder the exposed edge and carefully lift off the beard, powdering the back so that the latex doesn't stick to itself. If you need to trim the latex, try to keep the blending edge as thin as possible. When you glue the hair appliance onto your subject's face, you might find it necessary to add thin hairs along the top edge of the moustache and beard to help conceal the edge. The bottom edge under the chin and upper lip should not be visible.

To remove the hand-laid beard and moustache, use the appropriate adhesive remover, being careful not to get any in your subject's mouth, and work in small sections just as you did to apply the hair. Brush on a small amount of remover along the top edge of the beard or moustache and, as the solvent loosens the adhesive, gently pull the hair off and continue. When all the hair has been removed, cleanse the skin and apply a moisturizer to the skin.

Eyebrows can also be hand-laid using crepe hair—or yak hair, or human hair, but again, if you are going to use human hair for eyebrows, I think the best way is to ventilate the real hair into fronting lace. One method for applying crepe eyebrows is to attach the crepe to the skin just above the natural eyebrows and comb the crepe down into the natural hair, *or* glue the crepe directly onto the natural brows. However, you might find it necessary to completely cover the natural eyebrows. The consideration here is, will the eyebrows have to match up over several shooting days? In addition, how long will it take to do it every time? If speed and repetition are the order of the day, then by all means, ventilated eyebrows are the way to go. It still might be necessary to block to the original eyebrows, however. This is all essentially moot, of course, if your subject is wearing prosthetics in which eyebrows become part of the makeup. The eyebrows will most likely be ventilated pieces or punched—or not.

Let's move on.

TIP

Blocking eyebrows with Telesis® 5: Telesis® 5 is great for gluing hair down flat. Brush a tiny bit of full-strength Telesis® 5 into your subject's eyebrows, pressing the hair down flat as you brush. Full-strength adhesive is not as runny as thinned adhesive, but still, be careful so none drips near your subject's eyes. When the glue is dry, powder and apply a skin-safe silicone such as Alcone's 3rd Degree, Smooth-On's Skin Tite®, or Mould Life's Sculpt Gel. Silicone can be smoothed with 99 percent alcohol while the silicone is still uncured; once the silicone has begun to kick—that is, while it is still soft but has begun to form a skin—a small piece of plastic wrap can be laid on top of the silicone and the edges pressed smooth and invisible. Once the silicone has fully cured, the plastic wrap can be carefully removed and the edges will be seamless.

FIGURE 8.17
John Blake creating a beard template with plastic wrap, tape, and marker. Photo by the author.

FIGURE 8.18
Veg net, caul net, and power net. Photos by the author.

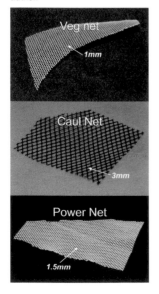

VENTILATING HAIR

Hand-knotting, or ventilating, hair is a skill not easily acquired but one that if mastered could find you in rather high demand. Only the best and finest wigs and hairpieces are completely hand ventilated. Even machine-ventilated pieces that can be purchased from any number of makeup effects suppliers are better than the best wefted ones. (I've never seen a wefted beard or moustache; only wigs.)

The first step in ventilating a beard, moustache, or eyebrow is to have the proper tools and materials on hand, not the least of which is a good lighted magnifier. Even a young Turk with 20/20 vision will go wonky in the head trying to focus on individual hairs through a 1 mm hole in fronting lace and then tie a knot in it with a microscopic fishhook on a stick.

But before ventilation can logically begin, you need to have a pattern for a hair appliance to create. Right? Right.

Using a piece of clear plastic wrap, place it over your subject's face, being careful not to obstruct breathing, and shape it to conform to your subject's facial structure. Once the plastic wrap is in place, proceed to cover it with pieces of Scotch tape; the form will become somewhat rigid and will hold its shape. Then you can draw on the tape the shape of the beard and/or moustache you will create. This pattern can then be cut out with scissors and placed on a chin block or a cast of your subject's face. A piece of fronting lace or foundation (opera) lace can then be laid on top of the pattern.

There are different types of netting used for wig making, beards, and moustaches. Veg net, caul net, and power net are too heavy for beard or moustache work and are best for making wig foundations. Veg net has the smallest holes but does not stretch in any direction. Caul net has the largest holes and stretches horizontally but not much vertically. Power net has small holes and stretches considerably in all directions.

Foundation or opera lace and fronting lace are the two varieties best suited for beard and moustache work. Foundation or opera lace has small holes but very little stretch in any direction. Fronting lace is about half the weight of foundation or opera lace and is virtually invisible when applied to the skin as a foundation for a beard or moustache. Because it is so delicate, it is a bit more flexible in stretch than foundation or opera lace but is more apt to tear as well.

The lace should be at least 1 inch (2.5 cm) longer than the pattern; it will be trimmed later. The pattern should be pinned down with dressmaker pins (on a malleable block) or with transparent tape if you're using a cast of your subject or if you're using a plaster or wood chin block. Position the lace so that the holes are running in a vertical pattern.

1. Place a pin in the top center of the lace, about .25″ (6 mm) from the edge of the pattern.
2. Put another pin in the bottom center of the lace, opposite the top pin, pulling slightly to eliminate any slack in the lace.
3. Do the same for the left and right sides of the lace.
4. Fill in the perimeter of the lace with pins placed no more than .25 to .5 inches (6–12 mm) apart.

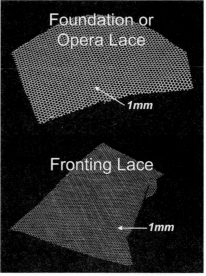

FIGURE 8.19
Foundation/opera lace and fronting lace are good for beard and moustache ventilating. Photo by the author.

Ventilating needles come in several sizes, beginning with the smallest: #00. The bigger the number, the larger the needle. The #00 will grab one hair at a time, whereas #1 or #2 will snag several hairs at a time. As you might suspect, knotting several hairs at once will result in a larger knot, so the larger needles are only to be used where the knots will be covered by subsequent layers of hair. For a moustache, you probably don't want to pull more than two or three hairs at a time, and for edges, a needle that will pull only single hairs should be used.

Preparation

Knowing which end of the hair is the tip and which end is the root is more important for tying wigs than for facial hair, but if you hold a single strand and run your fingers along the shaft you can (usually) tell which end is which. The hair shaft should feel smooth going toward the tip and rough toward the root because of the cuticle direction.

FIGURE 8.20
Ventilate with the lace pattern running vertically. Photo by the author.

Some hair is coarser than others and it's easier to tell which end is which. Even when I know which end is which, I have trouble telling the difference; I guess my fingertips just aren't that sensitive anymore.

I am going to assume you will practice hair tying for a while before you attempt to ventilate a moustache, beard, or wig. Learning how to ventilate on a real piece is likely to be a recipe for disaster. Practice first! It is not as easy as it sounds, I promise. Before you can begin ventilating hair, you will need a few things, not to mention the hair you'll be tying:

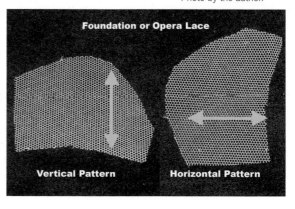

FIGURE 8.21
Hair shaft. Illustration by the author.

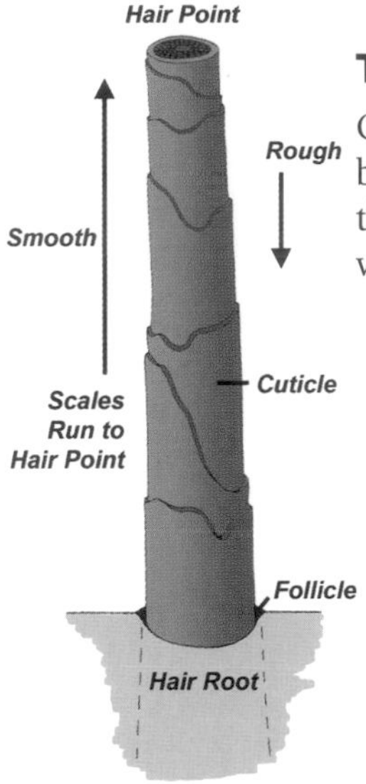

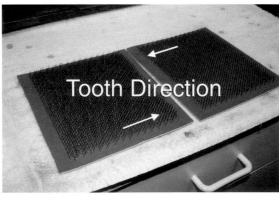

Hair Point

Rough

Smooth

Scales Run to Hair Point

Cuticle

Follicle

Hair Root

Drawing mats
Canvas head block
Pins

Ventilating handle and needle(s)
Foundation lace

Technique

Okay, you've already pinned a piece of practice foundation lace onto a malleable head block, just as described a few paragraphs ago. Now it's time to prepare the hair in the drawing mats. Drawing mats resemble really large pet brushes without handles.

1. Lay one side of the drawing mats (they come in pairs) on a surface in front of you with the bent teeth facing *away* from you.
2. Next, put a small amount of hair on the mat with about 2–2.5 inches (5–6.5 cm) of the root end toward you, hanging over the edge of the mat.
3. Put the other mat on top of the first mat also with the teeth facing away from you, and press down on the mats so the teeth are meshed together, with the hair between them.
4. Now you will be able to *draw* the amount of hair you want from the mats, hence their name…wow.
5. If you haven't done so already, put a ventilating needle into the handle and then practice holding the way you hold a pencil or pen, rolling the needle's hook toward you and away from you. Then find a safe place for the needle to rest so it won't roll off your work surface and break. I use one of my brush holders.
6. If you have a wig clamp with which to mount your canvas block, use it; otherwise you can hold the block in your lap or support it on your work surface with rolled towels to keep it from rolling. However you work, you are almost certainly going to need a lighted magnifier to see what you're doing and not strain your eyes.

238

FIGURE 8.22
Place the drawing mat with teeth facing *away* from you. Photo by the author.

FIGURE 8.23
Put a small amount of hair on the mat with 2 inches hanging over the edge. Photo by the author.

FIGURE 8.24
Hair between drawing mats. Photo by the author.

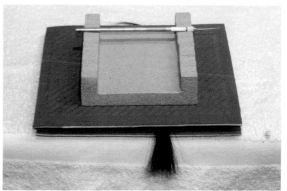

FIGURE 8.25
Ventilating needle and brush holder. Photo by the author.

7. Pull a small amount of hair from the mats and about 2 inches from the root end of the hair, bend it into a loop called the *turnover* and pinch the loop between your thumb and index finger.

For a skill like this I am ambidextrous, so it wouldn't matter which hand the hair was in for me, but you should hold the turnover in whichever hand will not be your needle hand.

FIGURE 8.26
Pull a small amount of hair from the mats and about 2 inches from the root end of the hair, bend it into a loop called the *turnover*, and pinch the loop between your thumb and index finger. Photo by the author.

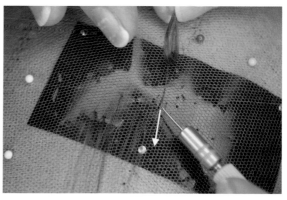

FIGURE 8.27
Pulling a few hairs with a ventilating needle from the turnover through the lace. Photo by the author.

8. With the needle in your hand, slip it through a hole in the lace mesh, passing under the separating fiber and coming out/up through the next hole. Catch a few hairs (which will depend on the size of the needle) from the loop and pull them out just a bit. Moving both hands together, pull the hair back through the holes and out the original hole; be careful not to catch the hook on the lace. If you roll the needle slightly in a counterclockwise direction while also lifting the needle slightly upward against the lace, the needle hook and hair will slide out without becoming caught. Yes, this is easier said than done, but to become good at anything takes practice. Fortunately, this task gets easier quickly. If I can do it, so can you. *You must keep even tension between both hands so that the hair doesn't go slack and slip off the hook!* It will also take practice to find just the right amount of force for the tension.

9. Pull the hook back enough to comfortably be clear of the lace but not so far as to pull the short (root) end of the hair out of the loop between your fingers.

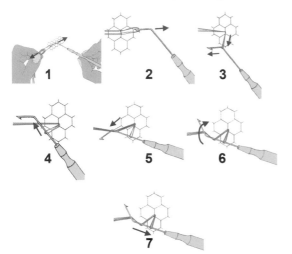

10. With the loop of hair attached to the needle, move the needle forward so that the hair catches in the neck; roll the hook away from you so that the hair wraps around the neck of the needle. Using both hands together to maintain tension, pull the hair and needle toward you, rotating the needle so that the hair is caught by the hook.

11. Turn the needle clockwise; keep the turnover hand still and pull the hooked hair back through the loop of hair that is still on the needle. Pull it all the way so that the hair comes free of the turnover hand. If you maintain tension with both hands, the knot will tighten on the lace. Always pull with the needle hand in the direction you want the hair to lay.

FIGURE 8.28
Hair-ventilating sequence. Illustrations by the author.

FIGURE 8.29
Final step; pull the hair through the loop to form a knot in the hair. Illustrations by the author.

Practice, practice, practice! It's a relatively easy skill to develop. It is not relatively difficult for an artist like you to master, but it is time consuming and potentially monotonous. This is most definitely a repetitive-motion activity, so I strongly suggest taking regular breaks and developing a therapeutic routine to alleviate stress and tension in your wrists and hands. Listen to music.

PUNCHING HAIR

Punching in hair by hand is no less tedious than hand ventilating a lace foundation piece, but it is considerably easier in that there is no lace through which to maneuver an angled needle with a hook at the end. So, what is hair punching?

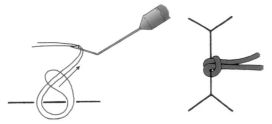

Hair punching involves taking individual strands of hair and pushing them into foam latex, silicone, gelatin, and so on. Hair punching is *not* to be done on an actual person; this technique is reserved solely for prosthetic appliances, masks, or dummies. The actual technique itself does not differ fundamentally from ventilating hair into lace; the difference is that you're not tying knots but planting hairs into a material's surface. You still want to create a mixture of hair colors to create a more natural look just as for hand-ventilating or hand-laying hair. You can even use a ventilating handle for the punching needle.

You can purchase hair-punching needles and holders from various suppliers (see the appendix at the back of this book), but it is also quite easy to make your own, much more inexpensively (no offense to retailers!). I find it easiest to hold a sewing needle with a pair of pliers and cut off part of the eye at an angle with a Dremel cutting wheel, creating a *U* or a *V*, and with the same tool, sharpen the edges to points. If the needle is a long one, you might want to shorten it a bit to give it a bit little of rigidity when you push the needle into the surface to which you are adding hair. Sometimes the material, particularly latex rubber (not foam latex) and silicone, can be a bit stubborn, like real skin.

Technique

Do you recall that there is a pattern to follow when hand laying facial hair? Do you recall that there is a pattern to follow for ventilating hair? Well, there is for punching hair, too, with the front hairline being the last to go in. Otherwise, already punched hairs will be in the way when you put in more; the needle must be inserted at the angle at which you want the hair to lie or else you'll have a head of hair standing on end, straight up.

To save yourself a considerable amount of time, however, consider hand laying the body of the hair (if it's on a head) with adhesive and only punching the hairline at an inch or so (2.5 cm) beyond.

1. Pull a small amount of hair from the drawing mats (yes, they'll come in handy here, too); about 2 inches (5 cm) from the root end of the hair, bend it into a loop and hold it between your thumb and index finger.
2. Holding the needle in your other hand, snag a hair or five and simply inject the needle into the surface, just deep enough for the hairs to remain embedded. Angle the needle to give the hair a "growing" direction.
3. As you move closer to the outer hairline, switch to a lighter hair color. You can also angle the hair direction slightly to help blend lines so the hair "growth" appears to be more random. By the time you reach the hairline, you should be punching only one hair at a time because only one hair grows out of each follicle. For this you will also need to be snagging each hair very near the end so it will be punched into the surface, leaving only a single hair strand sticking out.
4. If you feel that there are too many hairs making up your hairline, you can pull hair out (and punch it back in) to give you the best look.

Can you do facial hair by punching? Sure. What about beard stubble? Absolutely. Ordinarily, for beard stubble you need to use real hair or crepe hair cut into very tiny pieces, the size of shaved whiskers, and attached with adhesive to achieve the unshaved look. Before describing the punched stubble technique, here's how to do that. This can be done to an appliance, mask, or dummy or directly onto an actor's face. No poking or stabbing is involved.

1. Make sure the surface is clean; if the skin beneath the stubble will be visible, use transparent liquid makeup, preferably alcohol-based foundation and color such as Temptu, WM Creations, or Skin Illustrator®. (You might use whatever you choose so long as it is not an oil-based makeup; that will inhibit the adhesive from working properly.)

2. Choose the hair color or colors you want to use, cut tiny pieces onto a flat surface you can control, such as a piece of palette paper.

3. Working in small sections at a time so you don't waste adhesive, cover a small area with adhesive (Pros-Aide® is great for doing this; it dries sticky and is clear when dry, so you know when it's okay to apply the hair).

4. Use a dry rouge brush or similar brush; you probably won't want to use a good brush for this, or at least not one you'll use for rouge or other makeup again, because it'll be full of tiny bits of hair. Dab the brush into the cut hair. The brush will be a surprisingly effective pickup tool. Carefully transfer the hair to the face. Spread the hairs evenly to avoid clumps that will look fake. A second brush would be good for this.

This might not be the best way to do beard stubble, but if it doesn't have to read believably in a tight close-up, it will be fine. This technique should also read well in almost every theater environment, from intimate to substantial.

In his outstanding "how-to" book *Grand Illusions II*, Tom Savini talks about threading a hypodermic needle with a long strand of hair and punching it in loops into the face or facial part of an appliance, until the entire area of beard growth is punched. Then either insert small, sharp scissors into each loop (this could take a while) and cut them individually or take hair clippers or an electric beard trimmer and shave off the tops of the loops, leaving the face with beard stubble just like the real thing! Brilliant!

Another method that I will discuss in a bit more detail in the next chapter is using an electrostatic flocking device. You can use real hair, not just flocking, and you can use it on a real person, not just masks, dummies, and prosthetics. The drawback is that electrostatic flocking guns (they look nothing like a gun, per se) are rather expensive to purchase and are somewhat difficult to find for rental (see the appendix at the back of this book).

A company in Lawrence, Massachusetts, called National Fiber Technology (NFT), specializes in the manufacture of custom-made hair, wigs, and fur fabrics for the entertainment industry, including TV commercials, theme parks, movies, theater, opera, taxidermists, special effects, costumes, mascots, museums, and

FIGURE 8.30
Punching beard stubble into a dummy head. Don't try this on someone's face! Images reproduced by permission of Tom Savini.

242

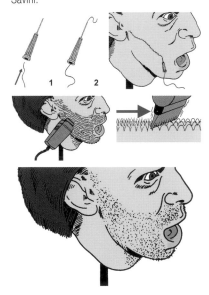

ballet. And, though much of what NFT makes and sells could be considered the domain of costumers and wardrobe people, there's definitely an overlap area that spills over into the realm of makeup effects and hair and makeup. NFT is a terrific resource that has saved my bacon more than once. Put them on speed dial.

CHAPTER SUMMARY

From this chapter you should now have a better understanding of:

- The types and varieties of hair
- The tools and materials needed to create postiche
- Wefted wigs and knotted wigs
- Laying on hair
- Ventilating hair
- Punching hair

243

CHAPTER 9

Other Makeup Effects

Key Points

- How to make Pros-Aide® bondo or Cabo patch
- Uses of plastic bald cap material
- How to make and apply a bald cap
- Simple buildup of ears and nose
- Tuplast
- Sculpting with nose and scar wax
- Making rigid collodion scars
- Airbrush stipple
- Brush spatter/stipple
- 3D transfers
- Stencil tattoos and paint accents
- Electrostatic hair flocking
- Applying wrinkle/age stipple
- Creating trauma, wounds, and bruises
- How to create a nosebleed on demand
- Creating burns, blisters, and skin diseases
- Using skin: safe silicone and gelatin

INTRODUCTION

Wow, that's a lot of stuff to cover, so let's get to it!

In addition to the prosthetics covered throughout the rest of this book, there are other materials that can be used both in conjunction with and separately from prosthetic appliances. Just as a wig can be used without any other makeup or makeup effects, a rigid collodion scar, airbrush tattoo, or any of the items described in the Objectives can be used separately or in combination to create character and creature makeup that is still considered special makeup effects. Some of the items and techniques that are the focus of this chapter have been mentioned already earlier in this book—for example, *bondo*.

What you will also find about this chapter is that is it less detailed in many ways than the previous chapters. Not because I'm running out of steam—no way. I'd happily keep going if I didn't have to be concerned with page count. No, this chapter is less detailed because this is not the focus of the book; this chapter is supplemental and could even have been part of the DVD. Some of the topics in this chapter are beautifully covered in the Makeup Designory (MUD) book *Character Makeup*, by Paul Thompson.

BONDO

Not to be mistaken for its polyester resin car repair namesake from the Bondo® Corporation, our *bondo* is a versatile material made from mixing Pros-Aide® and Cab-O-Sil® (a trademark of the Cabot Corporation), hence its other name, *Cabo patch*. We call it bondo because it is used in much the same way body shops use it to repair dings and dents in cars. By mixing Pros-Aide® adhesive and Cab-O-Sil® together until you have a paste, either thin or thick, with which you can fill holes in prosthetics caused by defects during the casting process or during seaming, and you can use it to blend off edges during application. When the bondo is still wet, the edges can be further smoothed using a brush dipped in water or 99 percent alcohol.

Cab-O-Sil® is fumed silica (silica being the second most common mineral in the world) used as a thickener in food products such as ketchup, pharmaceuticals, and cosmetics. Fumed silica is nontoxic when ingested, but prolonged exposure by inhalation can result in silicosis, which is the most common occupational lung disease worldwide. Fumed silica is very fine, and care should be taken to minimize its dust when mixing with Pros-Aide®.

Bondo has also recently begun to be used to create 3D prosthetic transfers, similar to temporary tattoo transfers. Christien Tinsley won a 2007 Technical Achievement Academy Award for developing the process (Tinsley Transfers), for which he was also nominated in 2004 (Oscar® for Best Achievement in Makeup, shared with Keith VanderLaan) for Mel Gibson's *The Passion of the Christ*. I'll get into some specifics of making your own 3D transfers in a later section of this chapter.

CAP MATERIAL

Cap material comes in two varieties: acetone-based plastic (vinyl) and water-based plastic (vinyl). Michael Davy Film & TV Makeup makes and sells a water-based cap plastic called Water-Melon® that can be dissolved with alcohol; New-Baldies® and Mould Life, both in the U.K., make acetone-based cap material that is also available in the U.S.

Plastic cap material can be used for a variety of applications, not the least of which is making bald caps; hence the name. It can also be used to seal molds or sculpture prior to molding and as an encapsulating layer for gel-filled appliances (GFAs). Cap material is an excellent encapsulating material for silicone GFAs because the edges can so easily be blended off instead of fighting them. Silicone will not dissolve away once it's cured, but the cap material will, with either 99 percent IPA or acetone, though the less acetone comes in direct contact with skin, the better.

Cap plastic can also be used to make thin appliances to cover eyebrows or to make other small prosthetic appliances such as eye bags or built-up ears instead of using slush, or slip latex.

FIGURE 9.1
Richard Snell applying a custom bald cap at IMATS LA, 2004. Photo by the author.

Bald Caps

Bald caps are a specialty in and of themselves, and for a long time demonstrating that you could apply one was a requirement for membership into any of the makeup guilds. From start to finish, the application of a bald cap, including makeup, can realistically be expected to take from 2 to 3 hours. Bald caps can be made generically and fit just about anyone, or they can be completely custom made for a specific head. Generic caps are usually made from either latex or vinyl, whereas custom jobs can be foam latex or even silicone. The late

Richard Snell, who showed me how to apply a bald cap, was the best and could put a bald cap on someone with hair down to her waist and make it look as though he'd shaved her head. I don't have a photo of that, unfortunately, but I do have one taken by one of my former students at IMATS, the International Makeup Artist Trade Show, in Pasadena, California, in 2004. It shows Richard applying one of the custom silicone caps he was known for. He was an amazing guy.

Making a Bald Cap

You can certainly buy ready-made bald caps that are quite good. There are several choices of premade caps. Michael Davy Film & TV Makeup sells Water-Melon® caps. Woochie® caps are ones I've used a lot; they're latex, and Kryolan sells Glatzan L caps. But where's the fun in buying something premade?!

The first thing you need to have before you can make your own bald cap is something to make the cap on. You can purchase a plastic bald cap head form made of polyethylene from Alcone for about $35 (£19). See the appendix at the back of this book for contact details. Or you can try your hand at making your own bald cap form from one of the full-head lifecasts you no doubt have by now. You know you want to! For material, Kryolan makes an acetone-based vinyl cap plastic called Glatzan L and Glatzan L matte, and I already mentioned New-Baldies®,

Mould Life, and Michael Davy's Water-Melon®. You can also use slip latex, mold latex, or Pliatex® mold rubber (which is latex) or you could try stippling on silicone that has had a thixotropic agent added to it so it won't be runny. I'd hold off on this last one until you feel really comfortable working with silicones. Foam latex bald caps are also commonly used. Keep in mind that if you make a latex cap, you will not be able to use platinum silicone such as Alcone 3rd Degree or Smooth-On Skin-Tite® to create any kind of build-up effects or wounds, or if you are doing a platinum silicone lifecast with Smooth-On's Body Double® or Mould Life's Life Form because latex will inhibit the cure of platinum silicone and leave you with a gooey mess.

MATERIALS

Polyethylene bald cap head form	1-inch chip brushes
Misc. rubber sponges	Latex rubber or cap plastic
Petroleum jelly	Powder and brush
Plastic wrap	Clear tape
Sharpie marker	Scissors
China marker	Eyebrow pencil

TWEEZERS

There are two ways to approach making your own bald caps: (1) Make a one-size-fits-all cap, or (2) make a custom cap for a specific individual. I'll start off describing how to make a custom cap for a specific head and then describe the actual cap process, which is the same for both caps. Foam latex caps are also custom jobs but require sculpting, mold making, and an oven heat cure.

The steps:

1. With a roll of cling wrap, wrap the plastic fairly tight around your subject's head (the part with hair on it) and then cover the plastic wrap with the clear tape. Use small pieces that will be easier to manage (you did trim the plastic off from the rest of the roll, right?). The tape will make the shell you are creating rigid enough to be manageable.

FIGURE 9.2
Measuring for a custom bald cap with plastic wrap, tape, and a marker. Photo by the author.

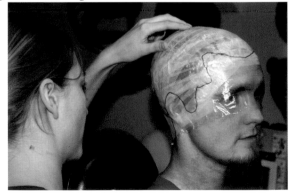

FIGURE 9.3
When the tape has been applied, draw an outline of your subject's hairline all the way around, adding about ½ inch (1.25 cm). Photo by the author.

2. When the tape has been applied, draw an outline of your subject's hairline all the way around, adding about ½ inch (1.25 cm).
3. Carefully lift off the shell and trim it with scissors along the drawn line.
4. Place the shell on the plastic head form and trace the edge with the china marker.

The following steps are the same even if you are making a generic one-size-fits-all bald cap.

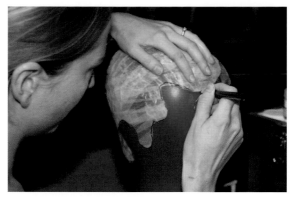

FIGURE 9.4
Place the shell on the plastic head form and trace the edge with the china marker. Photo by the author.

> **NOTE**
> If you are going to make a bald cap using acetone-based plastic cap material, make sure you have good ventilation, wear a respirator, or both.

5. Remove the clear shell and rub a very light layer of petroleum jelly on the surface of the head.
6. Pour a small to moderate amount of the bald cap material of your choice (cap plastic or latex) into a small shallow cup and stipple a thin layer over the cap area on the plastic head with a piece of rubber sponge.
7. When the first layer is dry, stipple on another layer over the first one; repeat this step until you have five thin layers.

If you made a vinyl cap, it can be powdered and removed when the final layer is completely dry; if the cap is latex, let it sit for 24 hours to fully cure. Otherwise, it could tear because it is thin and weak. Powder both the outside and the inside, being very careful not to let the edges roll, because the material, both vinyl and latex, will stick to itself and could be difficult to separate.

FIGURE 9.5
Stippling latex or bald cap plastic onto the head form. Photo by the author.

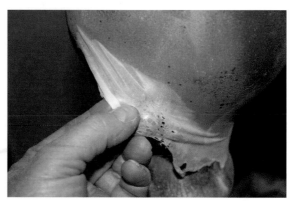

FIGURE 9.6
Powder the cap as you remove it from the form to prevent edges from sticking together. Photo by the author.

249

Applying a Bald Cap

Applying a bald cap is not as easy as making one, but like many aspects of this field, applying a bald cap is not necessarily difficult, but it requires patience and concentration to do it well. Depending on the amount of hair an individual has to hide beneath a bald cap, an application can realistically take anywhere from 1 to 3 hours, including paint and makeup. I think 1½–2 hours is doing pretty well.

1. Have your subject sit comfortably in a chair that is at a height at which it will be comfortable for you to work. Your subject should wear a loose-collared shirt or a robe that will give you good access to the neck.

2. The next step is to flatten your subject's hair as flat as possible to her head. The longer or thicker the hair, the more difficult this will be to accomplish. However, there are a few things you can try:
   Simply wetting the hair with water might be good enough for applying a bald cap prior to lifecasting, but it's not always good for a cap that will be part of a makeup. Whatever you use on the hair, make sure it's not a greasy product that will interfere with the adhesive you use or with the bald cap itself. Some hair gels have alcohol in them, which will begin to dissolve a vinyl bald cap and throw off your whole makeup. A product called Gafquat, which is a copolymer widely used in hairstyling products and is soluble in both water and alcohol, is frequently used to flatten the hair for a bald cap application. When it dries, it forms a film that will hold the hair firmly in place. Richard Snell used to literally glue the hair down with Telesis® 5 silicone adhesive: a rather expensive way to ensure that the hair would lie flat and stay in place, but it sure did work!

3. Make sure the inside of the bald cap is clean—no powder residue to hamper the adhesion. A bit of alcohol on a cotton pad will wipe away any excess powder; if you're using a vinyl cap, be careful because alcohol can easily damage the cap. It won't affect a rubber cap.

4. A cap that is a bit small is preferable to one that's too large, because it will not fit the crown of the head properly or lie correctly against the nape of the neck. A cap that is too small will result in stretching the skin like a bad facelift if you try to make it fit, so try to have one that will fit well without a lot of effort.

5. Make sure that your subject's face is clean, especially around the perimeter of the hairline. Clean the skin with an astringent or with 99 percent IPA.

6. Ask your subject to help with the initial placement if you are unable to stretch the cap sufficiently yourself to get it onto the head.

7. With your subject holding a finger on the front edge of the cap, position it so that there are no wrinkles.

8. Telesis® 5 or Pros-Aide® are both good adhesives. With Telesis®, the cap (non-latex) needs to be placed with the adhesive still wet and can be a bit dodgy if you are pulling slightly to keep wrinkles out. Pros-Aide® works best as a contact cement, with the adhesive applied to both surfaces, skin and cap, and allowed to dry before pressing them together.

9. Start at the front of the bald cap. Apply adhesive to the forehead (center) and to the underside of the bald cap in about a 2-inch (5 cm) strip; allow both surfaces to dry (clear) and then press the cap to the forehead. This will serve as an anchor as you the glue the back of the neck.
10. Fold back the bottom of the bald cap and apply some adhesive; tilt your subject's head back slightly and apply adhesive to the back of your subject's neck.
11. With your subject's head still tilted back slightly, pull the cap down and press the cap to the skin. This will ensure a tight fit and no wrinkles once your subject's head is straightened again.
12. Next, pick a side, and stretch the cap into position over the ear; with the eyebrow pencil, make a mark above the ear and draw down just behind the ear, following the curve of the helix—the outer flap of the ear.

FIGURE 9.7
Ask your subject to help with the initial placement if you are unable to stretch the cap sufficiently yourself to get it onto the head. Photo by the author.

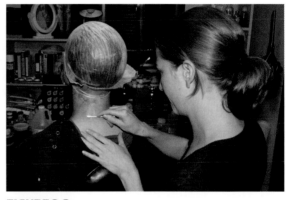

FIGURE 9.8
Fold back the bottom of the bald cap and apply some adhesive; tilt your subject's head back slightly and apply adhesive to the back of your subject's neck. Photo by the author.

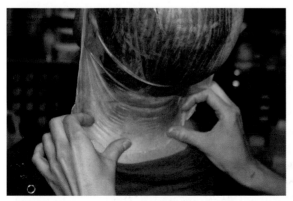

FIGURE 9.9
With your subject's head still tilted back slightly, pull the cap down and press the cap to the skin. This will ensure a tight fit and no wrinkles once your subject's head is straightened again. Photo by the author.

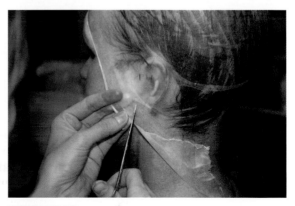

FIGURE 9.10
Next, pick a side, and stretch the cap into position over the ear; with the eyebrow pencil, make a mark above the ear and draw down just behind the ear, following the curve of the helix—the outer flap of the ear. Photo by the author.

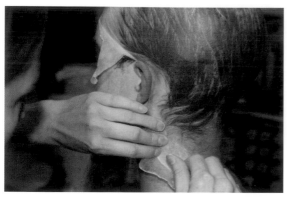

FIGURE 9.11
When both surfaces are dry, have your subject's head tilt a bit toward the side you've just glued, then pull the cap into place and press it to the skin behind the ear down to the neck. Photo by the author.

252

FIGURE 9.12
When the glue is dry, pull the cap down and forward to remove any wrinkles, and then press the cap to the skin. Photo by the author.

This drawn line is where you will make a cut to place the cap around the ear. You will most likely need to do some trimming to fit the cap cleanly behind the ear.

13. Apply adhesive about ½-inch (1 cm) wide to the skin behind the ear and down along the hairline to where the cap is attached to the neck and to the cap; when both surfaces are dry, have your subject's head tilt a bit toward the side you've just glued, then pull the cap into place and press it to the skin behind the ear down to the neck.

14. Next, affix the cap in front of the ear by applying glue from the skin at the top of the ear, down in front of the ear, and around the sideburn to where the cap is attached on the forehead. Apply the glue along the hairline about ½ inch (1 cm) wide. When the glue is dry, pull the cap down and forward to remove any wrinkles, then press the cap to the skin.

15. Repeat steps 12–14 on the other side of the head.

Once the cap has been applied, it must be trimmed of loose and rolled edges. With a good pair of tweezers, lift up the edges that need trimming and cut away the excess, then lay the cap smoothly back into the adhesive. Do this all the way around the cap; don't cut perfect straight lines—vary the cut so the edges will be easier to blend.

Blending the bald cap edges can be done one of four ways: Naphtha, acetone, 99 percent IPA, or bondo (Cabo patch). Naphtha, essentially lighter fluid, will dissolve the edges of a latex cap, but it's a bit harsh on the skin and can cause irritation. Acetone won't dissolve latex, but it'll go through vinyl cap material like nobody's business. It's also likely to cause some skin irritation, so you might want to use 99 percent IPA on a vinyl cap. It also works very well dissolving edges. For a latex cap, though, what is the other option? Oh, yes. Bondo. Of course you remember that bondo is a mixture of Cab-O-Sil® (fumed silica) and Pros-Aide® adhesive.

If you can't get the edge down to the level of the skin, build up the skin to the level of the edge. You don't want to apply the bondo to the cap but to the skin and fill the gap between the skin and the cap.

You can apply the bondo with a small dental spatula or palette knife or even with a small brush. A piece of damp sponge can be used to further blend and texture the bondo to match the skin and the cap. When the bondo has dried, stipple a layer or two of latex over the edges all the way around the cap onto the cap and the skin, using the same kind of sponge you used to make the cap.

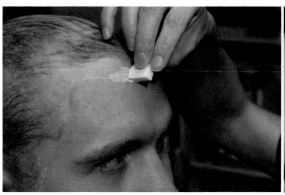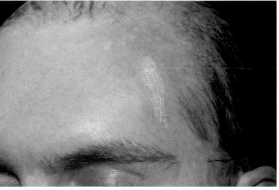

FIGURE 9.13
Apply bondo to blend cap edges. If you can't get the edge down to level of the skin, build up the skin to the level of the edge. You don't want to apply the bondo to the cap but to the skin and fill the gap between the skin and the cap. Photos by the author.

When the latex is dry, powder it. Now it's ready to paint as described in Chapters 6 and 7.

BUILDING UP EARS AND NOSE

This is not rocket science but prosthetics at about their most primitive. Even so, the results can be very good. Full, over-the-ear appliances can be made by building up layers of latex rubber or plastic cap material (or both) onto a positive of the ear.

FIGURE 9.14
Positives for Bat Boy latex build-up ears. Photo by the author.

It is important when building each layer to be cognizant of the edge thickness because it will have to be blended to seal the illusion of reality. How many layers will you need? At least six and perhaps 10 or 12, depending on the needed rigidity of the appliance. When I made rather large ears a few years ago for a production of *Bat Boy: The Musical*, I think there were 10 thin layers of latex plus a very thin foam insert up into the pointy helix to hold the ear upright and still be very light.

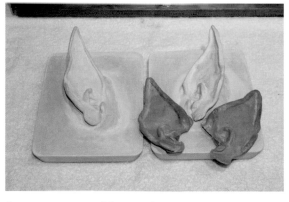

For a nose, instead of a positive, you'll need a negative; you could use a positive, I suppose, but the reason a positive works for an ear and not so much for a nose is that ears don't really have much texture detail, whereas noses often do. Try it both ways and see which you prefer and which looks better. In either instance, blending off the edges and matching the coloration will be the deal breakers.

Before starting any of these tasks, give the positives and the negatives a release of a very thin layer of petroleum jelly to ensure an easier removal of the appliance.

TUPLAST

Tuplast is a liquid plastic material from Kryolan. It comes in a tube and can be useful in creating small flexible cuts, scars, blisters, and the like. It can be applied to the skin directly from the tube and can be sculpted on a piece of glass or placed into a stone plate mold that has been sealed and released with a very thin coat of petroleum jelly or vegetable oil. Or you can use a small silicone mold in the same way, but you really don't need to release it; I'd still give it a thin coat of Epoxy Parfilm. If you intend to apply Tuplast directly to the skin (it is actually pretty decent for creating some burn effects and for creating raised scars), I suggest a barrier layer of PPI's Top Guard® or Pros-Aide® to make adhesion and removal of the Tuplast easier. Kryolan also makes a remover called Old Skin Plast Remover that will facilitate removing the Tuplast.

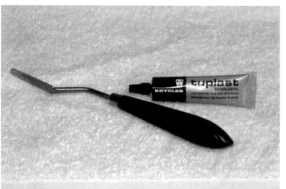

FIGURE 9.15
Tuplast from Kryolan.
Photo by the author.

Tuplast is not my favorite material to work with, maybe because I have few occasions to use it, but you should know what's available in the marketplace. Your kit ought to have a little bit of everything in it; you never know when something could come in handy at just the right time. A lot of material is available for creating the same type of makeup effects that can be done with Tuplast, such as gelatin or skin-safe silicone, which I find much easier to work with and to apply.

NOSE AND SCAR WAX

More for theatrical use than for film and television applications, nose and scar wax (also Derma Wax, Naturo Plasto Mortician's Wax, Bone Simulation Wax, Nose Putty, etc.) is primarily for facial applications to the bony parts of the face: nose, cheeks, chin, and the like. In many ways, theater can be more forgiving than film or television, mostly because in theater we see everything in a wide shot. Unless a character makeup is being seen in an intimate theater setting where the audience is mere feet away from the performers, lighting and distance can help sell a makeup effect that would not fly in a close-up on screen.

When it comes to subtle facial changes, nothing can alter someone's face as dramatically as the nose. An upturn or downturn of the tip or a bump on the bridge can often change a person's face enough to make them literally become someone else.

Working with nose wax is not difficult, but like all makeup effects, it should not be rushed or your results could suffer. Be patient and work diligently. You should definitely experiment with this material because, as with everything else, proficiency comes with practice. Once you have a design in mind, whether it's a new nose, a puffy eye, or some sort of horrific wound, the less material you need to use, the better; it will be easier to shape and blend.

Materials

Nose and scar wax	99% IPA or astringent
Clear latex	Rubber makeup sponges (triangles)
Castor sealer or plastic sealer	Pros-Aide®
Small palette knife or dental spatula	Cotton balls
Applicators (Q-tips, small brushes)	K-Y® lubricant
Stipple sponge	

- Ninety-nine percent IPA or astringent is for cleaning the skin before application.
- K-Y® is for your fingers so that the wax won't stick to you and make application difficult—*if* you're using your fingers for application. It can also be used to help smooth and blend the wax edges.
- Applicators are for applying Pros-Aide®.
- Pros-Aide is to provide a surface for the cotton fibers (only a few!) to adhere to.
- Cotton balls are to provide a few fibers for the wax to grab; dab the cotton into dry Pros-Aide®, then pick off most of the cotton, leaving only a few fibers.
- Clear latex can be used as a sealer over the wax, as can plastic sealer. Your choice. If you use latex, castor sealer will help makeup adhere better and blend well. Makeup or paints can go directly over plastic sealer.
- Rubber sponges can be used to stipple latex or plastic sealer over the wax.
- The stipple sponge can be used to create skin texture if needed.

RIGID COLLODION

Rigid collodion is a solution of nitrocellulose in acetone, sometimes with the addition of alcohols. For makeup effects, it is used to create indented scars on the skin. When the acetone evaporates, it pulls and puckers the skin, creating very realistic-looking scars. Michael Davy Film & TV Makeup makes a tinted rigid collodion called Collodacolor that comes in translucent red, blue, and yellow.

FIGURE 9.16
Rigid collodion scar.
Photo by the author.

Before applying rigid collodion (RC), make sure the skin is clean so the RC will stay on the skin without beginning to peel up at the edges. If applied well, RC should stay on the skin for quite some time. After the skin has been cleaned with alcohol or astringent, apply a thin layer of either Top Guard® or Pros-Aide® to help the RC adhere to the skin better. Pros-Aide® might be preferable because of its flexibility when dry. After the RC has been applied over the adhesive where you want the scar to be, let it dry; the skin around it will pucker as the RC shrinks from the evaporation of the acetone. Then stipple a thin layer of Pros-Aide® over the RC to encapsulate it. Powder the adhesive to remove its stickiness. Powdering will also remove some of the shininess of the RC.

STENCILS

Stencils are a great way to add both accent and detail to a character or creature makeup. Stencils for all sorts of tattoos are available from Temptu and other sources, as well as stencils for creating shapes and patterns to mimic alien skin textures. Zazzo's Character Troupe® templates designed by Brad Look are a great series of stencils that can be used for both beauty and alien character makeups.

Tattoos and Character/Creature Textures

Of course, you can always try your hand at original tattoo artwork by tracing your design onto newsprint using an inkblot pencil—*A Bottle of Ink in a Pencil.* This will result in a temporary tattoo similar to those you can get through Reel Creations, Temptu, or Tinsley Transfers. You will most likely need or want to augment the tattoos with additional color from a source like Skin Illustrator® palettes.

Sponge

Stencils can be used with either an airbrush or by hand using a sponging technique. Vittorio Sodano used stencils to sponge paint patterns on actors in *Apocalypto*, which saved considerable time by not using an airbrush...though that probably would have been nearly impossible on location in the jungle. In using the sponge technique, it is important that the stencil be flush with the skin and that the sponge not be too saturated with color lest it run and seep between the stencil and the skin, bleeding all over and ruining the stenciled pattern.

Temptu carries a spray called Stencil Tack that helps hold the stencil against the skin without transferring any of the tackiness to the skin.

There is another way, and it's using an inkjet printer, Photoshop®, temporary tattoo transfer, and adhesive paper. Kits are available in different paper sizes so that you can create custom temporary tattoos of varying sizes from small to rather large.

Airbrush

An airbrush is a wonderful tool and can create amazing makeup effects in the hands of a skilled user. Airbrushing is not something you can simply become instantly good at; it requires lots of practice, and it requires the right equipment: a dual-action airbrush that allows you to control both airflow and the amount of pigment mixing with the air, and a compressor that's quiet, consistent, and allows you to regulate the amount of air pressure, from just a few pounds per square inch (psi)—say, maybe 3 psi to at least 10 psi.

More than 10psi will put almost as much pigment into the air around you as on your subject. You don't want to get a lot of paint or makeup pigment in the air—that's the same air you're breathing, so that's not really good, and you don't want much air pressure when painting around someone's face (eyes, ears, nose, and mouth). Think of sticking your head out the window of a car going 20 mph

(32 kph). Airbrushing requires a controlled environment with excellent ventilation. And it's almost imperative that you have more than one airbrush to use so that you aren't stopping and starting frequently to refill the brush, clean it, change color, and so on. If you're working on a show, time is money, and the longer you take … well, you get the picture.

If airbrushing is something you'd like to give a whirl, and I know you do, take a class. There is too much to know about how airbrushes work and what safety precautions you need to know to keep a safe and healthy working environment. You'll find some resources in the appendix at the back of this book.

SPATTER AND STIPPLE

You can use an airbrush to create a spatter or stipple effect if the pressure is sufficiently low and you remove both the needle cap and nozzle cap of the airbrush. If you're painting directly on someone (or even if you're not), *be careful*, because the needle point is exposed, and airbrush needles are very sharp and pointy. With little air pressure coming from the compressor, you will get even less by not fully pressing down on the trigger; pull back to let the pigment flow and you will get a spatter. The more air you introduce into the mix, the finer the spatter. Trust me when I tell you that this requires a good bit of practice to master. I've been airbrushing since the 1970s, but if I don't do it for a while, sometimes months, it takes a little refreshing to get the feel back.

FIGURE 9.17
Neill Gorton painting a makeup appliance with a cut-down chip brush and spatter technique with Skin Illustrator®. Photo by the author.

257

This effect can also be achieved very effectively using cut down 1-inch chip brushes. It also creates a somewhat more random pattern as well, though I'm sure that point is arguable. By cutting down the brush, lightly swirling it in your color, and then flicking the bristles with your finger, you will flick the pigment.

Moving the brush closer and farther away from your subject and/or using varying pressure will ensure that the randomness of the spatter will continue. Don't forget to move the brush to new areas, too. This technique is discussed in Chapters 6 and 7.

3D PROSTHETIC TRANSFERS

Christien Tinsley's need for time management, ease of application, and continuity in large numbers led to the development of first 2D, then 3D prosthetic transfers, first for the 2001 film *Pearl Harbor* and then for 2003's *Master and Commander: The Far Side of the World*. Prosthetic transfers have been used extensively since, on such projects as *The Passion of the Christ*, *Find Me Guilty*, *The Cinderella Man*, *Nip/Tuck*, *Grey Gardens*, *Pirates of the Caribbean*, *The Fallen*, and many more.

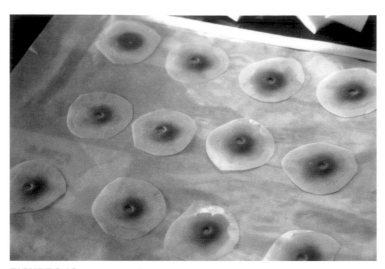

FIGURE 9.18
3D prosthetic transfers made by Tinsley Transfers, Inc., for *The Enemy God*. Photo by the author.

Making 3D Transfers

The following is not exactly Christien Tinsley's recipe; Christien's a great guy, but he's not going to give away the proprietary formula and process for an innovation that won him a 2007 Scientific and Technical Academy Award. But it is one that works; Oscar nominee Vittorio Sodano used it for the 2006 Mel Gibson epic *Apocalypto* and he shared it with me.

You can try your own, too. The technical and creative proclivity of this industry only advances by curious experimentation and discovery, so go experiment and discover.

Materials

Silicone mold rubber	Silicone release (Frekote® 1711)
Silicone parchment paper	Transfer paper (white or blue)
.002 mm acetate sheets	Krylon Dulling Spray
Small (dental) spatula	Latex makeup sponges
Pre-colored bondo	Flat straight-edge scraper
Scissors	Modeling clay or modeling wax
Final Seal or Blue Aqua Sealer	Q-tips®

Remember that bondo is a mixture of Pros-Aide® and Cab-O-Sil®; you can color it with a bit of flocking material, pigment, or both—it depends largely on what the end result is supposed to be. With pigment, the appliance may become opaque, but with flocking, there will be translucency and visible variation in the surface coloration.

1. Once the lifecast has been made of the body part needed for the 3D transfer, cast a silicone positive because this is what you will sculpt the prosthetic on.

For silicones, the higher the Shore A number, the harder the cured silicone. For example, Smooth-On's Dragon Skin® has a Shore A hardness of 10, which is pretty soft. Polytek's Plat-Sil Gel 10 has a Shore A hardness of —you guessed it—10; also soft, which is why it's good for prosthetic appliances, but not for this. Smooth-On's Mold Max 30 has a Shore A hardness of 30, which is fairly stiff and should be sufficient for this process.

2. Sculpt the appliance with either modeling clay (such as Chavant® Le Beau Touché) or modeling wax.

When you're done with the sculpture, put the silicone positive in the freezer until the piece freezes.

FIGURE 9.19
Wound sculpt on a silicone positive. Photo by the author.

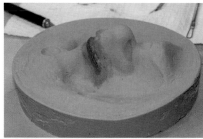

3. Carefully remove the clay piece (or pieces) from the silicone positive; the silicone will still be pliable even if the clay is very firm from being frozen. Press against the silicone to help separate it from the clay, being careful not to disturb the edges more than necessary.

4. Lay the clay onto an 8½ × 11-inch sheet of silicone parchment paper (a larger sheet if necessary). Gently press it down with a soft sponge until the clay bottom is in complete contact with the parchment, especially the edges. Make sure you are doing this on a completely flat surface.

5. Retexture if necessary.

6. Build a clay flashing channel and a low retaining wall; you're creating a box mold. Use foam-core strips or flexible rubber molding, depending on the shape you need for the new mold, and hot-glue the wall (low temp so you don't melt the acetate) so that it won't leak.

7. Mix enough Hard Shore A silicone to rise ½ inch (1 cm) above the highest point of the clay. When the silicone has fully cured, peel the clay out of the mold and clean any residue with 99 percent IPA and a Q-tip®.

259

8. Release the negative mold with silicone release—Mann's Ease 200 or Ease 800, Loctite's Frekote® 1711, or Smooth-On's Universal Mold Release will each work—and then add the precolored bondo, making sure to get into every part of the mold.

9. Cut and place a piece of the silicone parchment paper across the top of the negative

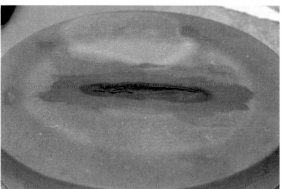

FIGURE 9.20
Place sculpt on a perfectly flat surface, redo the edges, and retexture if necessary. Photo by the author.

TIP
You can follow the instructions here, or you can sculpt your piece directly on a smooth surface that you can then make a silicone mold of, complete with flashing channel. Simply begin at step 6 instead of step 1. Personally, I prefer to sculpt the appliance on a smooth, flat surface.

mold. Make sure the flat scraper is wider than the mold and then use it to squeegee the excess bondo into the flashing channel, taking care not to press hard enough to remove any material from the negative itself.

10. Now place this mold in the freezer until the bondo is frozen and then carefully peel out the prosthetic and the silicone parchment paper from the mold.

TIP
If you use the silicone parchment, you will notice that moisture from the bondo will cause the paper to buckle somewhat. Don't worry, this will not affect the application of the piece. You might want to try using the .002 mm acetate in place of the parchment; it will not buckle and you will get a perfectly uniform contact with the bondo. However, you must properly release the acetate before using it or you will never get it off the appliance when you attach the transfer paper. A thin layer of Frekote® 1711 applied first, followed by a thin layer of Krylon Dulling Spray, will allow the acetate sheet to easily peel away from the appliance after you've attached it to the transfer paper.

This is what has happened to the bondo: When the adhesive freezes, it becomes polymerized (becomes plastic) but remains soft and rubbery and still a bit tacky. Why? Near as I can figure it, it's because Pros-Aide® is a water-based acrylic adhesive; when it freezes, the water is drawn out of the acrylic, allowing it to plasticize and become rubbery. When it thaws, the water begins to evaporate, leaving just the plasticized bondo. I'm not a chemist and haven't asked one about this because it's only occurring to me now as I'm writing it.

11. Allow the prosthetic to dry. You might want to hit it with a hair dryer for a few minutes to help it along. It could take as long as an hour or more to dry if allowed to just sit. It is partly dependent on the size of the appliance.

12. Powder the appliance to remove the tackiness and store it safely covered until you're ready to use it.

13. When you are ready to use it, stipple a light coat of Pros-Aide® over the surface of the prosthetic transfer all the way to the edges using a small piece of latex makeup sponge or a Q-tip® and let the adhesive dry until it's clear.

14. Place the prosthetic face-down onto the shiny side of the transfer paper.

15. Press the appliance firmly onto the transfer paper, paying close attention to the edges. *This is the most important part of the process.*

16. Trim the paper as close to the edge of the prosthetic as you can.

17. *Slowly* peel off the silicone parchment (or acetate). If any part of the prosthetic starts to pull away from the transfer paper, carefully press the whole appliance back onto the paper and repeat until the silicone parchment or acetate comes away cleanly.

Now the transfer is ready for application.

18. Make sure the skin is clean, dry, and oil/makeup-free.
19. Carefully position and place the appliance face down onto the skin and press firmly.
20. Wet the back of the prosthetic—the transfer paper—with a moist paper towel, powder puff, cotton pad, or the like and hold it firmly to the paper for about 30 seconds.
21. Peel or slide the paper carefully off the prosthetic. Smooth the transfer with a bit of water and let it dry. Again, you can use a hair dryer to help. Any visible edges can be blended off easily with a small brush and 99 percent IPA.
22. Seal with Pros-Aide® (dry it first, then powder) or powder with translucent setting powder and then seal with Final Seal or Blue Aqua Sealer. Tinsley recommends Final Seal from Ben Nye®. FYI, Blue Aqua Sealer from Reel Creations is water-based acrylic and Final Seal is alcohol based.

Then apply makeup or paint as necessary. Matthew Mungle also uses bondo appliances for his award-winning makeup work, but foregoes the transfer paper route. His process is:

261

1. Two coats W. M. Creations Soft Sealer in a silicone mold.
2. Pros-Aide® Bondo spatulated into the mold. Dried.
3. One coat of Soft Sealer.

Take some time and try these and variations. Always remember: There is never one and only one way to do anything in our field. Removing bondo appliances is easy using Super Solv®, Bond Off!®, or Isopropyl Myristate, dampened on a powder puff, and so on.

ELECTROSTATIC FLOCKING

This stuff is cool! I mentioned this process earlier in the book, but it bears repeating here. Outside of Los Angeles, these devices are not very easy to find for makeup use. You might want to consider purchasing one (they're somewhat pricey—over $1,000) and making it available for rental when you are not using it; it is not a tool that is likely to get a lot of regular use unless you also are a mask, costume, prop, or puppet maker, taxidermist, or Furry enthusiast. However, I suspect that having one could inspire lots of uses within the makeup effects craft for both stage and screen. I want one!

FIGURE 9.21
Electro-Static Flocking Gun from Minke-Props, Germany. Image reproduced by permission of Gernot Minke.

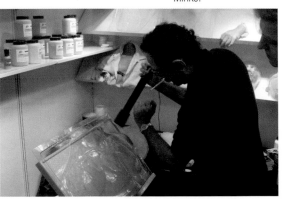

FIGURE 9.22
Tiger head was flocked with 2, 3, 4, 6, and 10 mm flock and then punched to blend. Image reproduced by permission of Esteban Mendoza.

262

The way it works is this: The device is charged with high-voltage electricity—70 kv *but* with *very* low amperage so that there is no health or safety risk. The principle is that two poles of opposite polarity attract each other and the field lines always hit the surface vertically. So, if a hair (fiber) is charged at one pole, it will fly according to the field lines directly at the opposite pole. Now, presume that the surface at the opposite pole is coated with adhesive; the fiber will embed vertically in the adhesive. The flocking gun should be no more than about 8–12 inches (20–30 cm) from the subject.

Varying lengths of flocking material can be used to simulate bottom and top hairs, and depending on the adhesive used, low pressure compressed air can be used to direct hairs in a particular direction or pattern to mimic the reality of growth patterns.

One fairly obvious note of caution: During application, which should occur in brief stages when applied directly to a subject's face and head, keep your subject's eyes closed and have her hold her breath for a moment, since the flocking can and will enter the eyes, nose, and mouth if they're open during application.

FIGURE 9.23
Adding different hair after a bald cap application using electrostatic flocking instead of a wig. Photo by the author.

WRINKLE (AGE) STIPPLE

This is an easy way to age someone either subtly or dramatically. There are a variety of methods for creating age-simulating wrinkles, too. However, trying to age someone in their late teens to late 20s might be ineffective with this technique because for it to work well there needs to be some stretch and pliability to the skin. Young skin is often too firm and taut to stretch enough for the stipple technique to be noticeable. However, combined with more traditional makeup techniques of highlight and shadow, and with prosthetics, aging can be convincingly achieved.

The most common aging stipple technique involves using latex; it can be done in 16 stages, with each stage involving five steps, or it won't work. Remember that skin stretches perpendicular to the pull of the muscle beneath it. Also, only do those parts of the face that require aging for the particular makeup.

The stages:

1. The eyelid—pull up at the eyebrow. Stipple carefully on the upper eyelid with the eyes closed.
2. The other eyelid—pull up at the eyebrow.
3. Under the eye—pull down and away from the eye.
4. Under the other eye—pull down and toward the center of the face.
5. Temple—pull up above the temple and pull down below to create crow's feet outside the eye.
6. Temple—pull up above the other temple and pull down below to create crow's feet outside the eye.
7. Nasolabial fold—lift area away from center of face or have the subject puff area to be aged.

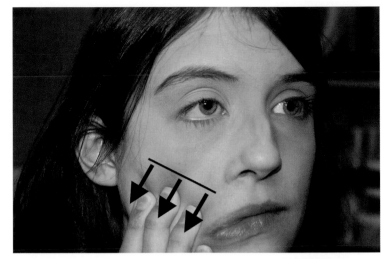

FIGURE 9.24
Under the eye—pull down and away from the eye. Photo by the author.

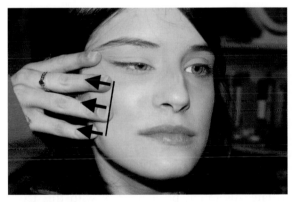

FIGURE 9.25
Nasolabial fold—lift area away from center of face or have subject puff area to be aged. Photo by the author.

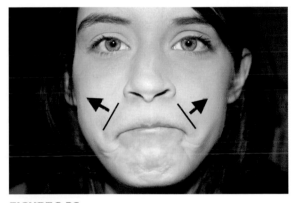

FIGURE 9.26
Upper lip—have subject puff entire area to be stippled. Photo by the author.

8. Nasolabial fold (other side) —lift area away from center of face or have subject puff area to be aged.
9. Upper lip—have subject puff entire area to be stippled.
10. Chin—with neck arched, pull the side of the chin away from the center of the face.

NOTE

Latex may have strong ammonia smell, so be prepared to use a fan of some sort.

FIGURE 9.27
Chin—with neck arched, pull the side of the chin away from the center of the face. Photo by the author.

FIGURE 9.28
Cheek—using a large craft stick (tongue depressor), have your subject carefully reach deep into the cheek inside the mouth and push out. Photo by the author.

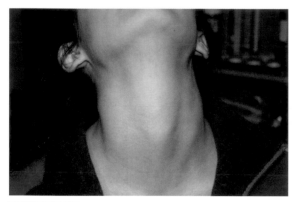

FIGURE 9.29
Neck—begin with the head tilted back to stipple the throat first. Photo by the author.

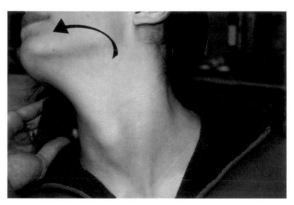

FIGURE 9.30
Neck—now with the head turned one way, then the other. Photo by the author.

264

11. Chin—with neck arched, pull the other side of the chin away from the center of the face.
12. Cheek—using a large craft stick (tongue depressor), have your subject carefully reach deep into the cheek inside the mouth and push out. This will help tie the nasolabial folds and under-eye areas together.
13. Cheek—have your subject carefully reach deep into the other cheek and push out.
14. Neck—begin with the head tilted back to stipple the throat first.
15. Neck—now with the head turned one way.
16. Neck—now with the head turned the other way.

Again, the steps:

1. Stretch the skin.
2. Apply the latex. It does not have to be applied heavily; apply it thinly. Two layers are often enough.

3. Dry the latex.
4. Powder the latex.
5. Release (unstretch) the skin.

Excess powder should be removed with a small amount of water-soluble lubricant (such as K-Y® jelly) on a small brush. To color the latex, you can use RMGP, but it is not absolutely necessary. If you first brush a thin layer of castor sealer over the latex, you can use regular crème colors to paint the latex; if you don't use the castor sealer, the latex will absorb the carrier vehicle of the crème makeup and result in a discoloration of the latex that won't match the rest of the skin.

Latex can be used as a contact adhesive and acts as such. If latex dries on the applicator you are using to add age stipple and dries on the skin, when the two come in contact with one another they will bond and you will either pull up the latex from your subject's face or your subject will have an applicator stuck to her face.

There are several additional techniques for aging that involve latex and other materials, but I list merely some of them here. These provide more extreme effects, each with its own unique characteristics:

- Latex and tissue
- Latex, tissue, and adhesive
- Latex, cotton, and adhesive
- Latex, cornmeal, wheat germ, or bran and adhesive
- Green Marble SēLr® and Attagel

TRAUMA, WOUNDS, AND BRUISES

This is definitely the realm of the well-rounded makeup effects artist but not the focus of this book. So this will be merely a glancing blow. Much of what you'll create to simulate trauma and various wounds is approached from the same direction as much of the work in this book: Know the type of makeup you need to create, research it and gather photos, sculpt it on a cast of the "victim," mold it, cast it, paint it, and apply it. Then add blood. Or pus. Or both. For really excellent "how-to" information on this stuff, it's hard to beat Tom Savini's *Grand Illusions* and *Grand Illusions Book II*. Tom's work is as much about special effects as it is makeup effects.

Bruises

Bruises are the result of internal bleeding, when capillaries near the skin's surface break:

- First is redness as blood spills from the broken vessels.
- Next comes maroon as the blood begins to coagulate, then turns bluish purple over time, maybe even black.
- As the bruise begins to heal, it will change to a brownish green and then to yellow as everything is gradually reabsorbed back into the body.

FIGURE 9.31
Small sponge balls for the nosebleed-on-command effect. Photo by the author.

Nosebleed on Demand

I'll share one trick I use because it is really effective and quite low tech, as many great effects can be. This gag requires a piece of porous rubber sponge, a piece of latex makeup sponge, a pair of tweezers, and some stage blood. And a performer with clear nasal passages.

1. With small, sharp scissors, form each of the sponge pieces into balls about ¼–½ inch (.5–1 cm).
2. Saturate the porous sponge with stage blood and place it into one of your subject's nostrils with the tweezers, just out of sight. You might want to test first to ensure that the sponge doesn't flare the nostril unnaturally. Clean off any blood with a Q-tip.
3. Place the latex sponge into the other nostril, also out of sight. Make sure it doesn't flare the nostril either. Because the latex sponge is dense, it will prevent your subject from passing air through that nostril.
4. The other nostril has a porous sponge that will allow air through as air forces the blood out. You with me?

Your performer will need to be a mouth breather for a bit or the effect will be premature. At the appropriate time—say, when your subject gets punched in the face (but not really) —your subject breathes out through the nose; all the air is channeled into one nostril and blood begins to trickle or run out of the nostril, just as if he'd been actually hit.

Of course, breathing out too hard may expel the sponge, so there's that to keep in mind.

FIGURE 9.32
Everything in place for the nosebleed effect. Photo by the author.

FIGURE 9.33
Somebody get a tissue! Photos by the author.

Burns

Tuplast and gelatin make great herpes blisters, burn blisters, and any other sort of gross pus-filled lesions you might be called on to create for a character. Again, you need examples from reality for what you are creating. There are forensic books and medical books available as reference with all the pictures you could want and then some. Some of them are listed in the appendix at the back of this book. Be forewarned: Some of the images contained in these books might be quite disturbing to look at and should definitely be kept away from impressionable eyes.

SKIN CONDITIONS

The best preparation for simulating skin diseases is reference images, unless it's some sort of alien crud that nobody's ever seen before. Go back to Chapter 2 and look at the section on surface anatomy and skin, and you might come up with some ideas.

SKIN-SAFE SILICONE AND GELATIN

These two materials are absolute essentials for an artist's kit. Skin-safe silicones are two-part (A–B) components that are mixed 1:1 by volume and can be applied directly to the skin, sculpted into a wound, burn, or the like, powdered, and then painted. These silicones set up in minutes and can feasibly be peeled off and used again later. There are three that I know of on the market currently, from Alcone, Smooth-On, and Mould Life, called Third Degree, Skin Tite®, and Sculpt Gel, respectively.

Gelatin is easy to use as an out of the kit material. It needs to be heated so that it will melt and can then be applied directly to the skin; make sure that it's not too hot. It will burn if it's heated too much. You can also damage the gelatin itself by too much heat. Warm it just enough for it to melt. Blisters, scars, and the like are easy to create. When the gelatin is set, powder it to remove the stickiness. If you're using gelatin blood,

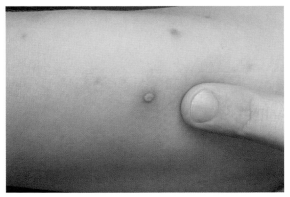

FIGURE 9.34
Chickenpox. Image reproduced by permission of Wikipedia/GNU Free Documentation License.

FIGURE 9.35
Skin-Safe silicone. Photo by the author.

TIP
Pick up an electric coffee mug warmer at Target®, Brookstone®, or wherever you can find one. By keeping your skin, scar, and blood gelatin in small glass jars, you can keep them placed on the warmer and ready to use at a moment's notice. And a coffee mug warmer is a lot easier to schlep around than a microwave.

powdering it will remove the glossiness that wet blood would have, so don't powder blood.

Before applying gelatin, apply a layer of Top Guard® or Pros-Aide® as a barrier layer to prevent perspiration from causing the gelatin to loosen. Refer back to Chapter 6 for more information on working with gelatin.

CHAPTER SUMMARY

After reading this chapter, you should now know more about:

- Making bondo and its use as a prosthetic transfer material
- How to make and apply a bald cap and some other uses for the different types of bald cap plastic material
- Making built-up ears and noses out of latex or plastic cap material
- What Tuplast is
- Using nose and scar wax
- Making scars with rigid collodion
- Tattoo and creature texture stencils
- Why you should take an airbrush class
- Making and using 3D prosthetic transfers
- How to incorporate electrostatic flocking into your work
- Applying latex age stipple
- Collecting reference images for creating trauma, wounds, burns, and skin conditions
- Working out of the kit with skin-safe silicone and gelatin

Appendix A
Your Kit

You will find some discrepancies among makeup artists about what is absolutely essential to have in your kit or at least in your possession. I have kits for different gigs as well as chests, cases, and bags of differing sizes, from countertop oak behemoths to over-the-shoulder canvas on-set bags and everything in between.

Gerstner & Sons of Dayton, Ohio, make well-crafted oak machinist chests that I've found to be excellent units for holding many of the items I use. They are available in numerous sizes and configurations, but they can be quite expensive. Harbor Freight carries a machinist chest that is also oak, versatile, and much less expensive than a Gerstner chest. RCMA used to sell nice makeup cases like these; I'm not sure if they still do or not.

FIGURE A.1
A Gerstner & Sons Machinist chest makes a great makeup storage chest.

Here is a partial list of items you will want to have in your kit; with them you will be armed with the tools to create virtually anything you are asked to create right out of the kit.

269

- Makeup case
- On-set bag
- Brush holders
- Brush roll
- Misc. brushes
- Latex triangle sponges
- Orange sponge (porous synthetic rubber sponges might even be yellow)
- Palette knife (plastic and metal)
- Tissues
- Misc. clips
- Stipple sponges
- Velour powder puffs
- Tweezers (several sizes)
- Hand mirror
- Small sharp scissors
- Utility scissors
- Misc. combs; rattail comb
- Misc. hair brushes
- Cotton pads
- Cotton balls
- Cotton swabs (Q-tips®)—round end, point end, flat end

FIGURE A.2
Harbor Freight carries a machinist chest that is also oak, versatile, and much less expensive than a Gerstner chest.

FIGURE A.3
Misc. brush holders (these are homemade).

FIGURE A.4
A typical brush roll by Crown Brushes.

- Long cotton swabs
- Bald cap head form
- Brush cleaner (Parian Spirit) and container
- Misc. plastic containers
- 1 oz. and 2 oz. plastic cups for adhesives, etc.
- Hair hackle
- Drawing mats
- Breath mints (seriously; I'm not kidding)
- Purell or other hand sanitizer
- Work towels
- Paper mats
- Makeup cape or cover cloth
- Misc. spray bottles
- Misc. hairclips
- Misc. hair bands
- Airbrush and compressor
- Pipe cleaners
- Misc. tooth brushes
- Hair-thinning scissors
- Small blow dryer
- Misc. curling irons
- Misc. flattening/straightening iron
- Disposable lip gloss applicators
- Disposable mascara brushes
- Misc. syringes (without needles)
- Nail clippers
- Setting powder
- Ninety-nine percent isopropyl alcohol
- Telesis® 5 adhesive

- Telesis® 5 thinner
- Telesis® Super Solv®
- Pros-Aide® adhesive
- Isopropyl Myristate
- Blood
- Misc. gelatin
- Rigid collodion
- Collodion remover
- Crepe hair (wool)
- Coffee mug warmer
- Makeup sealer
- Plastic cap material
- Latex stipple
- Misc. crème foundations
- Styptic pencil
- Eye drops
- Makeup pencil sharpener
- Disposable razors
- Shaving cream
- Skin moisturizer
- Skin cleanser
- Telesis® Top Guard®
- Ben Nye® Bond Off!
- Orangewood stick
- Misc. craft sticks
- Toothpicks
- Tuplast
- Skin-safe silicone (3rd Degree; Skin Tite®, Sculpt Gel)
- Disposable eyeliner brushes
- Misc. eyebrow pencils
- Skin Illustrator or Stacolor palettes
- Bondo (Pros-Aide® and Cab-O-Sil®)
- Cab-O-Sil®
- Glycerin
- K-Y® lubricant
- Castor sealer
- Latex, vinyl, or nitrile gloves
- Nose and scar wax

FOAM LATEX
GM Foam/Monster Makers Foam/Burman Foam

A typical batch of foam latex consists of:

- 150 grams of high grade latex base
- 30 grams of foaming agent
- 15 grams of curing agent
- 14 grams of gelling agent

There are other ingredients and quantities that can be added for different foam characteristics, but this is a good place to begin. As I mentioned in the text, this operation is time and temperature sensitive as well as humidity sensitive; optimal conditions would be in a room 69–72°F (20.6-22°C) with 45–55 percent humidity. I am based in Colorado, so I have humidity (rather, the lack of humidity) to contend with, as well as a higher elevation air pressure that also affects what I do. The "optimal" conditions are based on mixing at sea level; I'll show a schedule for both sea level and high altitude, though most of you will probably be working at lower elevations.

Foam latex can be cured in molds made of a variety of materials, including Ultracal 30, dental stone, fiberglass, epoxy, silicone, aluminum, or even steel, and should only be mixed and cured in rooms with good ventilation; foam latex gives off unpleasant and unhealthy fumes.

Weigh the first three components—the latex base, the foaming agent and the curing agent—and add them to the mixing bowl. It would be great if you have an accurate digital gram scale. Weigh out the gelling agent into a small cup and set it aside. We won't add that until we're almost done mixing. If you're adding pigment, put a few drops of your color into the bowl, too. Then place the mixing bowl into position and you are ready to begin. This first description will be a 12-minute mix. A timer that will count down is a plus, but if you can tell time and count, a clock or a watch will suffice.

1. For the first minute, mix the ingredients on speed 1.
2. For the next 4 minutes, whip the ingredients on speed 10. This will froth the foam and increase the volume (and lower the foam density) in the bowl. Gil Mosko, GM Foam's founder, says to not be a slave to the schedule. All mixers run differently, and many conditions can affect how the foam will rise in the mixer. Once you understand how foam latex works, you will be able to adapt to any situation.

Whipping the latex to a high volume lowers the foam's density, which will result in a lighter foam and creates a foam that can be difficult (near impossible) to pour. This foam is more apt to trap air when transferring it into molds; this can be especially true when injecting the foam. All three latex manufacturers have a flow enhancer that makes it easier to pour high-volume foam with little or no effect on the gelling process.

What the high-speed mixing does in addition to creating high-volume foam is de-ammoniate the latex. Too much ammonia loss and your foam will gel too quickly; not enough ammonia loss and your foam might not gel at all. It might seem like you need a degree in chemistry to run foam (it certainly wouldn't hurt), but that is why there is a mixing guideline to follow, so you don't have to know specific pH values and other scientific-type stuff. Simply understanding the function of the ingredients and the stages of the process should be enough information to do some experimentation. Such as:

- The *foaming agent* is a soap that bonds to the cells of the latex, lowering the surface tension of the latex and allowing it to froth and rise more easily.
- The *curing agent* contains sulfur to help vulcanize—strengthen and add elasticity—the latex;
- The *gelling agent* creates a reaction that changes the foam from a liquid into a solid.

Okay, back to the process:

3. Now, turn the speed down to 4 for 1 minute. This stage will begin to refine the foam, breaking up the biggest bubbles.
4. Turn the speed down to 1 for the last 4 minutes to further refine the foam. When there are 2 minutes left, begin adding the gelling agent and continue mixing until 12 minutes. It is critical that the gelling agent be mixed well, and depending on what mixer you use, the methods of assuring that the gelling agent is sufficiently mixed might vary.
5. At 12 minutes, turn off the mixer, remove the bowl, and you are ready to carefully fill your molds. Once the foam has gelled (you can tell by gently pressing on the foam; it should give a little, and bounce back) you can place the molds in the oven and heat them until the foam is fully cured.

NOTE

This recipe is the general one recommended by GM Foam *at sea level*. I suspect Monster Makers and Burman would concur. Check with each manufacturer to be certain.

I have had good results with these times, but I have also had disastrous results with these times; a movie I did recently in Colorado required numerous foam appliances, and the following mixing times worked beautifully every time and has become my high-altitude schedule with a KitchenAid mixer. It is a 9-minute schedule instead of a 12-minute schedule:

09:00   Speed 1
08:00   Speed 10
07:00   Speed 4
05:30   Speed 1
03:00   Speed 1—*add gelling agent*
00:00   Stop

The oven you cure the foam in should be capable of reaching 185°F (85°C). Small molds will most likely need only 2–2½ hours; larger molds might need three to four hours. However, if the mold is thin—say, ¼-inch (5 mm) fiberglass—it can be baked at a much lower temperature for a longer period of time—140°F (60°C) for four to five hours. Even thicker gypsum molds will benefit from lower temperatures and longer times; for one thing, it's less stressful on the molds, and you'll get the added benefit of softer foam (without having to deal with a high-volume, nonpourable foam from the mixing stage). Monster Makers suggests trying a typical gypsum mold at 140°F (60°C) for 10 hours and comparing the feel of the resulting foam with foam run at a higher temperature for a shorter time using the same mold.

Once you determine that your foam is fully cured, turn off the oven and let the mold begin to cool. If you try to cool the molds too rapidly, they will crack and break; you do not want to rush the process! When the molds are still warm to the touch, you can carefully demold your appliances; they will come out more easily when warm rather than if you let the molds cool completely. Carefully pry the mold halves apart and help remove the appliance with the use of a blunt wooden tool (so you don't scratch the mold's surface detail), powdering as you go to keep the thin foam edges from sticking together.

After you've removed the appliance from the mold, it must be gently washed in warm water containing only a few drops of dishwashing liquid (I use either Ivory or Palmolive soap) to remove any residual sulfur from the curing agent. Repeat this procedure until there is no more visible residue in the water, then rinse until all the soap is gone, and gently squeeze out the water; you might want to use two towels to press the appliance between, then allow it to dry completely on the lifecast so that it will maintain its shape. When your appliance is completely dry, it is ready to paint and apply or be stored in an airtight plastic bag for future use.

GELATIN

Just as there are different recipes for foam latex—though I only provided one in this appendix—there are also a number of gelatin recipes. Some include Sorbitol, some don't; Sorbitol will add to the tear strength of the gelatin. I've seen a recipe that added Elmer's Glue (white school glue), presumably for strength and stability; however, the more glue you use, the less elastic the gelatin will become.

Here's Matthew Mungle's recipe:

- 100 grams sorbitol (liquid)
- 100 grams glycerin
- 20–30 grams 300-bloom gelatin (the higher the bloom, the greater the tear resistance; the gelatin you can buy at your local supermarket has a bloom factor of 250–275)
- Flocking or pigment for internal coloration

Procedure:

1. Mix the ingredients together in a microwave-safe bowl and let them sit, preferably overnight.
2. Heat in a microwave for approximately 2 minutes, mixing several times. Do not allow the mixture to bubble or foam, because that's an indication that it's about to burn. It will change color and leave undesirable bubbles in your finished appliance.
3. You can either fill a mold and cast your appliance, or pour the gelatin into a form and let it cool and cure for later use. Powder when it's fully set.

Now Kevin Haney's recipe:

- 21 grams sorbitol (liquid)
- 20 grams glycerin
- 9–11 grams 300 bloom Gelatin

Up to ¼ gram (¼ tsp.) zinc oxide powder (zinc oxide will cause the opacity of the gelatin, as well as the tear resistance, to increase)

- Flocking or pigment for internal coloration

Procedure:

1. Mix the ingredients together in a microwave-safe bowl and let sit, preferably overnight.
2. Heat in a microwave for approximately 2 minutes, mixing several times. Do not allow the mixture to bubble or foam, because that's an indication that it's about to burn. It will change color and leave undesirable bubbles in your finished appliance.

NOTE

You can double or triple this formula. Very small or large batches aren't as easy to mix up as a medium-sized one.

Thea's recipe:

- 80 grams sorbitol (⅛ cup)
- 80 grams glycerin (⅛/ cup)
- 40 grams 300-bloom gelatin (⅛ cup)
- Up to ½ gram (½ tsp.) zinc oxide powder

Add flocking to desired effect, about ½ tsp. or less if mixing colors. Add cosmetic pigment in your choice of flesh color. (You can also use cake makeup ground up finely.)

In a microwave-safe bowl, mix most of the sorbitol and glycerin. Leave a small amount of the sorbitol out so you can mix the zinc oxide into it before adding it all together.

Slowly add the gelatin to the sorbitol and glycerin mixture. Then add the zinc oxide mixed in the small amount of sorbitol and some flocking. If you are adding flesh pigment or red blood pigment (you can use any color), mix the pigment into a small amount of sorbitol before adding to the batch. Heat it in the microwave for another minute or two, stirring frequently, but be careful it doesn't bubble over the container.

FOAMING GELATIN

Any of preceding above recipes will work for making the base gelatin for a foamed version of gelatin. You will notice that Kevin Haney's recipe is about ½ of the other two, so take that into account.

- 160 grams (¼ cup) glycerin
- 40 grams (⅛ cup) 300-bloom gelatin
- ½ gram (½ tsp.) zinc oxide
- ½ gram (½ tsp.) tartaric acid
- ½ gram (½ tsp.) baking soda

The tartaric acid in Cream of Tartar is what adds volume to egg whites when they're beaten. Baking soda reacts with the heat and with the tartaric acid to create carbon dioxide.

1. Mix the ingredients together (minus the tartaric acid and baking soda) in a microwave-safe bowl and let sit, preferably overnight.
2. Heat in a microwave for approximately 2 minutes, mixing several times. Do not allow the mixture to bubble or foam, because that's an indication that it's about to burn.
3. Add the tartaric acid and stir briskly.
4. Add the baking soda and stir again briskly, then let the gelatin mixture rise for about 30 seconds without stirring, until it stops rising.
5. Stir the foamed gelatin to refine it, heating a little if needed.

The foamed gelatin is ready to be poured into a prepared mold.

BONDO

Mixing up a batch of bondo is about as easy as things get, but you do need to be mindful of working with Cab-O-Sil®; it is extremely light and will get airborne easily.

- Pour Pros-Aide® adhesive into the container you will be using to mix bondo.
- Carefully spoon a small amount of Cab-O-Sil® from its container into the Pros-Aide®.
- Slowly stir with a small craft stick (popsicle stick) until the Cab-O-Sil® and Pros-Aide® are thoroughly mixed.
- Add more Cab-O-Sil® and stir.
- Repeat until it reaches the thickness that you want.
- Cover to prevent the bondo from drying out.

If you are making bondo for 3D transfer or bondo appliances, you can add flocking or pigment along with the Cab-O-Sil®.

AGE STIPPLE

If you'd like to try your hand at something a little different than simply stretching the skin and stippling on latex, here are a couple of recipes you can try for variety in your repertoire.

Premiere Products

PPI's Green Marble SēLr® is one way to approach subtle aging, but achieving the finished result also requires subtle painting. To turn Green Marble SēLr® into an aging material, you must use the concentrate and not the spray; added to the Green Marble SēLr® is Attagel, a very fine clay powder used as a thixotropic agent in cosmetics.

Ratio (oz) of Attagel to Green Marble SēLr®:

- 1 oz. to 3 oz. heavy ager on most skin types
- 1 oz. to 4 oz. medium–heavy ager
- 1 oz. to 5 oz. medium–light ager
- 1 oz. to 6 oz. light ager on most skin types

A 1:6 Attagel:Green Marble SēLr® ratio will work as a fine-line wrinkle texture when used very lightly. Without affecting large wrinkles, this 1:6 formula changes the texture of the skin, which is excellent for subtle, closeup aging. The application technique works the same as with latex for stretch and stipple.

REPAIRS AND QUICK FIXES

Depending on the thickness and placement of the ager, some areas of the face may crack or flake. This usually happens around the mouth, but repairs can be done quickly and easily using any of the following three methods:

- Paint 99 percent alcohol in the direction of the wrinkles.
- Apply Telesis® thinner and/or acetone (faster) with a brush. Then apply only Green Marble Sēlr® (use a brush, sponge or spray).
- Reapply some of the original ager material.

TEMPORARY PATCHING

This technique is useful when you don't have time to do a thorough repair. Temporary patching media include:

- Oil-free sodium-based moisturizers
- K-Y® jelly
- 99 percent pure clear aloe.

REMOVAL

The best removal technique to dissolve Green Marble materials involves the use of isopropyl myristate or IPM gel, massaged with the fingers, into the skin. In addition, the finger-massage technique works exceptionally well around the eyes and is more comfortable for the actor.

Pros-Ager

I made up that name (at least I've never seen or heard it anywhere else before), but I didn't make up the formula; it comes from Richard Corson. It's a mixture of Pros-Aide® adhesive, acrylic matte medium (I use Liquitex liquid), and either pure talc or Cab-O-Sil® to thicken the mixture slightly. Too much of either talcum or Cab-O-Sil® will cause the mixture to remain white after it dries. You want it to dry relatively transparently so that it can be used over set foundation for a more natural aging technique.

Try mixing Pros-Aide® and Matte Medium 1:1 by volume. Thinner mixtures will result in finer wrinkles, whereas thicker mixtures will produce thicker, deeper wrinkles. Because Pros-Aide® is part of the solution, it will dry somewhat tacky, so it will need to be powdered.

Dick's Ager

Years ago makeup pioneer Dick Smith created a latex wrinkle stipple formula that almost everybody has used at one time or another. It's a mixture of high-grade foam latex base, pure talc, pulverized cake makeup foundation, gelatin, and water. Yum! Here's the recipe from Richard Corson and James Glavan's book, *Stage Makeup*:

- 90 grams (100 ml) foam latex base
- 10 grams (5 tsp.) pure talc U.S.P.
- 6 grams (2 tsp.) loose powdered cake foundation (or pigmented powder)
- 2 grams (½ tsp.) Knox® unflavored gelatin (or 300-bloom gelatin if you have it)
- 32.ml (3 Tbsp.) boiling distilled water
- Acrylic gel medium (for medium stipple recipe)
- Pliatex Casting Filler from Sculpture House (for heavy stipple)

Once this mixture is prepared, it must be stored in a refrigerator between uses. Because it contains gelatin, it must be heated until it liquefies for application. This recipe can be modified to create a light wrinkler, medium wrinkler, or heavy wrinkler. When you need something that will have a bit more sticking power, mix 1:1 Pros-Aide® and foam latex base.

Light recipe:

1. Mix talc, powdered foundation, and gelatin in small mixing bowl.
2. Add 3 Tbsp. boiling distilled water to the powders. Be sure to use distilled water; some tap water will change the pH of the latex and cause it to curdle. Add the water *1 Tbsp. at a time*, stirring after each, until the mixture is smooth.
3. Strain the latex through tulle or cheesecloth to remove lumps.
4. Slowly add the dissolved powder mixture to the latex, stirring quickly to avoid lumps.
5. Pour the mixture into 2 oz. or 3 oz. jars (plastic or glass); label them, including the date.

Medium recipe:

1. Combine the light recipe with either 60 grams of acrylic gel medium or 50 grams of gel medium and 3 Tbsp. of Cab-O-Sil®.
2. Stir small amounts of the light stipple into the gel medium until they are thoroughly mixed.
3. Pour into small jars and label with the date.

Heavy recipe:

1. Combine one part medium recipe by volume with one part Sculpture House Pliatex Casting Filler.
2. Pour into jars and label with the date.

These should all be refrigerated after pouring into jars and sealed. Application of these formulas follows the same procedures and steps as for regular latex stipple.

H-10

I'm not sure what H-1 through H-9 were like, but H-10 is pretty cool. H-10 is a mixture of Gaf Quat and moustache wax heated and blended, then mixed with 70 percent isopropyl alcohol (rubbing alcohol); it's used to flatten hair around the hairline for bald cap applications. Here's how to make it:

1. Heat 1 part moustache wax with 1 part Gaf Quat until both are melted. If you use a microwave, be careful not to overheat; the Gaf Quat will bubble and expand. Heat gradually.
2. When both the wax and the Gaf Quat are mixed completely, slowly add 1 part alcohol (all parts are by volume, not weight) until thoroughly mixed.
3. Before the mixture sets up, pour it into a small container with a lid.

The H-10 can then be applied with a small dental spatula, old toothbrush, or your fingers. This stuff will hold hair in place in a typhoon; it'll sure as heck keep hair in place for a bald cap application.

PAX Paint & PAX Medium

I know *pax* is Latin for peace, but does anyone know what PAX stands for other than perhaps Pros-Aide®/Acrylic MiX? Works for me, but I'm just guessing. Whatever the acronym, it's good stuff and has been around for a while. It can be purchased in ready-made colors matched to William Tuttle and RCMA foundation shades, but it's really easy to make yourself, too.

PAX paint can be used directly on the skin, but is best used for painting appliances prior to application. Use good judgment regarding use on someone's skin. To make your own opaque, flexible PAX paint, mix Pros-Aide® and acrylic artist paint (e.g., Liquitex) 1:1. Because it is a mixture of acrylic paint and a strong prosthetic adhesive, it can be somewhat stubborn to remove, so be careful about using it near sensitive areas of skin, such as around the eyes. PAX Paint can be altered and modified for considerable versatility by doing one or more of the following:

- Mix acrylic matte medium with Pros-Aide® to create what is called PAX Medium, a liquid that dries clear and somewhat flat. When PAX Medium is added to PAX Paint in varying amounts, it creates varying layers of transparent color that will aid in creating more realistic skin coloration.
- Add distilled water to make a thinner, more transparent paint. Thinning can be by as much as 24:1 (24 parts water to 1 part PAX Paint). A mixture this thin becomes a wash that can add very subtle color tints.
- Thinned PAX Medium can be used as a makeup sealer.
- Adding additional Pros-Aide® (i.e., 2:1) will make the paint stick better, but it will be harder to remove; less adhesive will make a weaker bond and be easier to remove.
- Makeup can be applied over PAX paint; in fact, just about anything (except acetone) can be applied to PAX.

Whether you use PAX Paint, PAX Medium, or both, it dries with a bit of a shine and remains a bit tacky to the touch. It is a good idea to powder it with a translucent setting powder.

281

9 MM SPECIAL EFFECTS

832 E. Main St. Ste. 4
Medford, OR 97504
Phone: 1-866-826-9696 or 541-608-7412
www.9mmsfx.com
Custom contact lenses

ADMTRONICS

224 Pegasus Ave.
Northvale, NJ 07647
Phone: 201-767-6040
www.admtronics.com
Pros-Aide water-based adhesive

A FOX INTERNATIONAL

G3426 Beecher Rd.
Flint, MI 48532
Phone: 810-732-8861
http://afoxintl.com
Wigs, hair extensions, and accessories

BEN NYE

3655 Lenawee Ave.
Los Angeles, CA 90016
Phone: 310-839-1984
www.bennyemakeup.com
Professional makeup

BRICK IN THE YARD MOLD SUPPLY

521 Sterling Dr.
Richardson, TX 75081
Phone: 214-575-5600
http://brickintheyard.com
Mold making, casting, sculpting supplies, and tools

BURMAN INDUSTRIES

13536 Saticoy St.
Van Nuys, CA 91402
Phone: 818-782-9833
http://burmanfoam.com/
Silicones, latex, sculpting, and mold-making supplies

CAISSON LABORATORIES

1740 N Research Park Way
North Logan, UT 84341-1977
Phone: 877-840-0500
http://caissonlabs.com
Sorbitol powder, etc.

CHARLES H. FOX LTD.

22 Tavistock St.
Covent Garden
GB-London WC2 E7PY
Phone: +44 207 / 240 31 11
www.charlesfox.co.uk
Professional makeup supplies

CHEAP CHEMICALS

P.O. Box 480-C
Round Hill, VA 20142-0480
Phone: 540-338-3877
www.cheap-chemicals.com
Cab-O-Sil, sorbitol, zinc oxide

CINEMA SECRETS

4400 Riverside Dr.
Burbank, CA 91505
Phone: 818-846-0431
www.cinemasecrets.com
Professional makeup supplies

COLORADO SCIENTIFIC

95 Lincoln St.
Denver, CO 80223
Phone: 303-777-3777
www.sciencecompany.com
99% isopropyl alcohol, laboratory supplies, containers, scales, etc.

COMPLEAT SCULPTOR, THE

90 Vandam St.
New York NY 10013
Phone: 212-243-6074
http://sculpt.com/
Mold making, casting, sculpting supplies, and equipment

COMPOSITE STORE, THE

Phone: 1-800-338-1278
www.cstsales.com/
Fiberglass, mold-making products, and epoxy

CROWN BRUSHES

3 North Court St., B354
Crown Point, IN 46307
Phone: 219-791-9930
http://crownbrush.com/
Cosmetic brushes

CHAVANT, INC.

5043 Industrial Rd.
Wall Township, NJ 07727-3651
Phone: 1-800-CHAVANT
www.chavant.com
Modeling clay, sculpting tools, and accessories

CUSTOM COLOR CONTACTS

55 W. 49th St.
New York, NY 10020
Phone: 800-598-2020
www.customcontacts.com
Special FX, prosthetic, and cosmetic lenses

CYBERGRAPHIC DESIGNS MAKEUP EFFECTS & SUPPLY CO.

3202 Center Dr.
Cleveland, OH 44134
Phone: 440-888-8548
www.getspfx.com
Professional makeup effects supplies

DAVIS DENTAL SUPPLY

7347 Ethel Ave.
North Hollywood, CA 91605
Phone: 1-800-842-4203 or 818-765-4994
www.davisdentalsupply.com
Dental molding and casting supplies

DE MEO BROS.

129 W. 29th St., 5th Floor
New York, NY 10001
Phone: 212-268-1400
Hair and wig supply, wig lace, wig-making supplies

ENVIRONMOLDS

18 Bank St.
Summit, NJ 07901
Phone: 1-866-278-6653
www.artmolds.com
www.environmolds.com
Mold making, lifecasting, sculpting supplies and tools

FACTOR II, INC.

P.O. Box 1339
Lakeside, AZ 85929
Phone: 928-537-8387
www.factor2.com
Prosthetic silicone and adhesives, etc.

FANGS F/X, LTD.

The Studio, Sheepcote Dell Rd.
Beamond End, Amersham
Bucks HP7 0QS
Phone: +44 (0) 1494 713 807
www.fangsfx.com
Specialized teeth and dental appliances for film and television

FIBERGLASS WAREHOUSE

8250 Commercial St.
La Mesa, CA 91942
Phone: 619-270-9541
www.fiberglasswarehouse.com
Fiberglass, mold-making products, mold release and epoxy

FIBRE GLAST DEVELOPMENTS CORP.

385 Carr Dr.
Brookville, OH 45309
Phone: 1-800-330-6368
www.fibreglast.com
Fiberglass, foam, resins, and reinforcements

FREEDOM OF TEACH

1912 Stanford St.
Alameda, CA 94501
Phone: 510-769-1828
http://freedomofteach.com/
*Anatomy figures, DVDs, artist busts,
    armatures, and wall charts for artists*

FRENDS BEAUTY SUPPLY

5270 Laurel Canyon Blvd.
North Hollywood, CA 91607
Phone: 818-769-3834
Cosmetic supplies for FX artists

FX WAREHOUSE

2090 S. Nova Rd.
South Daytona, FL 32119
Phone: 386-322-5272
www.fxwarehouse.info *online sales only*
Supplies for FX artists and scenic studios

GEORGE TAUB PRODUCTS & FUSION CO.

Phone: 1-800-828-2634
Email: sales@taubdental.com
www.taubdental.com
Minute Stain Acrylic Resin Stains

GM FOAM, INC.

14956 Delano St.
Van Nuys, CA 91411
Phone: 818-908-1087
www.gmfoam.com
Foam latex and pigments

GRAFTOBIAN

510 Tasman St.
Madison, WI 53714
Phone: 608-222-7849
www.graftobian.com
Professional makeup supplies, makeup effects

GRAPE AND GRANARY, THE

915 Home Ave.
Akron, OH 44310
Phone: 1-800-695-9870
http://thegrape.net
Tartaric acid

HAIRESS CORPORATION

880 Industrial Blvd.
Crown Point, IN 46307
Phone: 219-662-1060
http://hairess.com/
Manufacturer, importer, distributor of hair care products and supplies

HIS & HER HAIR GOODS CO.

5525 Wilshire Blvd.
Los Angeles, CA 90036
Phone: 1-800-421-4417
http://hisandher.com/
Hair and wig supply, human hair wigs, tools, and accessories

IASCO

5724 West 36th St.
Minneapolis, MN 55416
Phone: 888-919-0899
www.iasco-tesco.com/oldsite/
Plastics, mold making, casting

JAMESTOWN DISTRIBUTORS

17 Peckham Dr.
Bristol, RI 02809
Phone: 1-800-497-0010 or 401-253-3840
www.jamestowndistributors.com
Fiberglass, adhesives, and epoxy

KAB DENTAL

34842 Mound Rd.
Sterling Heights, MI 48310
Phone: 586-983-2502 or 1-800-422-3520
www.kabdental.com
Dental supplies

K&J MAGNETICS, INC.

2110 Ashton Dr., Suite 1A
Jamison, PA 18929
Phone: 1-888-746-7556 or 215-766-8055
www.kjmagnetics.com
Magnets

KEN'S TOOLS

Phone: 951-943-1217
www.drbanksensteinfx.com
www.kenstools.com
Sculpting tools

KOSMETECH CORP.

26 Delavan St.
Brooklyn, NY 11231
Phone: 718-858-7000
www.kosmetech.com
Makeup applicators and storage

KRYOLAN

132 Ninth St.
San Francisco, CA 94103
Phone: 415-863-9684
www.kryolan.com
Professional makeup

LAGUNA CLAY

14400 Lomitas Ave.
City of Industry, CA 91746
Phone: 1-800-4-LAGUNA or 626-330-0631
www.lagunaclay.com
Sculpting supplies

LONDON WIGS

Unit 107
156 Blackfriars Rd.
London SE1 8EN U.K.
Phone: 0207 7217095
www.wigslondon.com
Wigs and wig-making supplies

MAC COSMETICS

Phone: 1-800-387-6707
www.maccosmetics.com
Cosmetics, makeup products

MAKE UP MANIA

Headquarters:
4407 Lowell Blvd.
Denver, CO 80211
Phone: 800-711-7182
Make Up Mania @ The Make Up Trailer
182 Allen St.
New York, NY 10002
Phone: 212-380-1090
www.makeupmania.com
Cosmetics, makeup effects products

MAKE UP STORE

Southlands Mall
6205 E. Main St., Suite 101
Aurora, CO 80016
Phone: 303-563-2123
www.makeupstore.se
Cosmetics, makeup products

MASTERPAK

145 E 57th St., 5th Floor
New York, NY 10022
Phone: 1-800-922-5522
www.masterpak-usa.com/
Silicone parchment paper

MILE HI CERAMICS

77 Lipan
Denver, CO 80223
Phone: 303-825-4570
www.milehiceramics.com
WED Clay, Ultracal, Hydrocal, plaster

MINKE - PROPS

Cecilienstraße 31
D-47051 Duisburg
Phone: +49-(0)203-28101-0
www.minke-props.com
Special effects supplies, electrostatic
  flocking gun

M. J. GORDON COMPANY

255 North St.
P.O. Box 4441t
Pittsfield, MA 01201
Phone: 413-448-6066
www.mjgordonco.com
Mold release

MOTION PICTURE F/X COMPANY

123 S Victory Blvd.
Burbank, CA 91502
Phone: 818-563-2366
www.monsterclub.com
Chemicals, dental supplies,
  latex, silicones, sculpting tools

MOULD LIFE

Tollgate Workshop
Bury Road
Kentford, Suffolk CB8 7PY
Phone: +44(0)1638-750679 (U.K.)
949-923-9583 (U.S.)
www.mouldlife.co.uk
Casting and moulding supplies for
  special makeup effects

MOUNTAIN ROSE HERBS

P.O. Box 50220
Eugene, OR 97405
Phone: 1-800-879-3337
www.mountainroseherbs.com
Makeup ingredients

MUDSHOP

129 S. San Fernando Blvd.
Burbank, CA 91502
Phone: 818-557-7619
375 W. Broadway #202
New York, NY 10012
Phone: 212-925-9250
www.makeupdesignory.com
*Cosmetics, tools, brushes, cases,
    skin care, books*

NAIMIE'S BEAUTY CENTER

12640 Riverside Dr.
Valley Village, CA 91607
Phone: 818-655-9933
www.naimies.com
Cosmetics, tools, and makeup cases

NATIONAL FIBER TECHNOLOGY

300 Canal St.
Lawrence, MA 01840
Phone: 1-800-842-2751
www.nftech.com
*Custom-made hair, wigs
    and fur fabrics*

NIGEL'S BEAUTY EMPORIUM

11252 Magnolia Blvd.
North Hollywood, CA 91601
Phone: 818-760-3902
www.nigelsbeautyemporium.com
*Supplier to the beauty, film, television,
    fashion, and media industries*

NORCOSTCO

4395 Broadway St.
Denver, CO 80216
Phone: 1-800-220-6928, 303-620-9734
www.norcostco.com
Professional makeup supplies

NOTCUTT

Homewood Farm
Newark Lane
Ripley, Surrey GU23 6DJ
Phone: +44 (0)1483 223311
www.notcutt.co.uk
Mold-making materials and casting resin specialists

PEARSON DENTAL SUPPLIES CO.

Phone: 1-800-535-4535, 818-362-2600
www.pearson-dental.com
Dental molding and casting supplies

PINK HOUSE STUDIOS

35 Bank St.,
St. Albans, VT 05478
Phone: 802-524-7191
www.pinkhouse.com
Lifecasting, mold-making and casting supplies

PLASTICARE

4211 South Natches Court, Unit K
Englewood, CO 80110
Phone: (303) 781-1171
http://plasticareinc.com/
Mold-making, casting, reinforcement supplies and equipment

POLYTEK DEVELOPMENT CORP.

55 Hilton St.
Easton, PA 18042
Phone: 610-559-8620, 1-800-858-5990
www.polytek.com
Mold-making and casting materials

RAY MARSTON WIG STUDIO, LTD.

No. 4 Charlotte Rd.
London EC2A 3DH
Phone: 020 7739 3900
www.raymarstonwigs.co.uk
Specialized hair work to the film, television, and theater industry

REEL CREATIONS

7831 Alabama Ave., Suite 21
Canoga Park, CA 91304
Phone: 818-3-GO-REEL (818-346-7335)
www.reelcreations.com
Professional makeup effects supplies

REEL EYE COMPANY, THE

365–367 Watling St.
Radlett, Hertfordshire WD7 7LB
Phone: +44 (0)1923 850207
www.reeleye.co.uk
Special effects contact lenses

REINKE BROS

5663 S. Prince St.
Littleton, CO 80120
Phone: 303-795-5006
www.reinkebrothers.com
Professional makeup supplies

SALLY BEAUTY

15091 E. Mississippi Ave.
Aurora, CO 80012
Phone: 303-750-5593
www.sallybeauty.com
Professional makeup, hair and nail supplies

SCREENFACE

20 Powis Terrace
Westbourne Park Rd.
Notting Hill, London W11 1JH
and:
48 Monmouth St.

Covent Garden
London WC2 9EP
Phone: 020 7221 8289, 020 7836 3955
www.screenface.co.uk
Professional makeup supplies

SCULPTURE HOUSE

405 Skillman Rd.
P.O. Box 69
Skillman, NJ 08558
Phone: 609-466-2986
www.sculpturehouse.com
Professional modeling, molding and casting supplies

SEPHORA

8505 Park Meadows Center Dr.
Littleton, CO 80124
Phone: 303-799-4800
www.sephora.com
Professional makeup supplies

SILICONES, INC.

211 Woodbine St.
P.O. Box 363
High Point, NC 27261
Phone: 336-886-5018
www.silicones-inc.com
Silicone for mold making and prosthetics

SILPAK, INC.

470 E. Bonita
Pomona, CA 91767
Phone: 909-625-0056
www.silpak.com
Molding and casting supplies

SMOOTH-ON, INC.

2000 Saint John St.
Easton, PA 18042
Phone: 1-800-762-0744
http://smooth-on.com/
Foams, liquid rubber, and plastics

SPECIAL EFFECTS SUPPLY CORP.

543 W. 100 North, Suite 3
Bountiful, UT 84010
Phone: 801-298-9762
www.xmission.com/~spl_efx/
Foams, liquid rubber, and plastics

TEMPTU

26 W. 17th St., Suite 503
New York, NY 10011
Phone: 212-675-4000
www.temptu.com
Cosmetic and special FX makeup and tools

THREEWIT-COOPER

2900 Walnut St.
Denver, CO 80205
Phone: 303-296-1666
Dental impression plaster, lab dental plaster, Ultracal, Hydrocal

TIRANTI

3 Pipers Court
Berkshire Drive
Thatcham, Berkshire RG19 4ER
and:
27 Warren St.
London W1T 5NB
Phone: +44 (0)845 123 2100
+44 (0)20 7380 0808
www.tiranti.co.uk
Sculptors' tools, materials, and studio equipment

VAN DYKE'S

Orders 1-800-843-3320
Customer Service 1-800-787-3355
www.vandykestaxidermy.com
Glass eyes, animal forms

VARAFORM

U.S. distributors:
Douglass & Sturgess, San Francisco; www.artstuff.com
The Compleat Sculptor, NYC; www.sculpt.com
U.K. distributors:
Bentley Chemicals, Worcestershire; www.bentleychemicals.co.uk
Flint Hire & Supply, London; www.flints.co.uk
Thermoplastic impregnated cotton mesh for mold making

WESTERN SCULPTING SUPPLY

2855 W. 8th Ave.
Denver, CO 80204
Phone: 303-623-4407
www.westernsculptingsupply.com
Sculpting supplies and tools

WILSHIRE WIGS

5241 Craner Ave.
North Hollywood, CA 91601
Phone: 1-800-927-0874 or 818-761-9447
http://wilshirewigs.com/
Wigs, hair extensions, and accessories

WHIP MIX CORPORATION

361 Farmington Ave.
P.O. Box 17183
Louisville, KY 40217
Phone: 1-800-626-5651 or 502-637-1451
www.whipmix.com
Dental molding and casting supplies

W.M. CREATIONS, INC.

5755 Tujunga Ave.
North Hollywood, CA 91601
Phone: 1-800-454-8339 or 818-763-6692
http://matthewwmungle.com
EZ Scar kits, professional specialty cosmetic supplies

ZELLER INTERNATIONAL

Phone: 607-363-2071
http://zeller-int.com/
Makeup effects and special effects, casting, mold-making supplies

The following tables show some of the more common measures and the conversion between larger and smaller units. The Imperial (U.K.) and U.S. systems have the same definition of the pound and the same definition of the ounce. There are 16 ounces in 1 pound; 453.60 grams in one pound. However, the Imperial system uses the *stone*, which is not used in the U.S. system; 1 stone = 14 pounds.

In the Imperial systems a *hundredweight* is not a hundred pounds but is equal to 8 stones, giving a weight of 112 pounds (8 × 14 pounds). Likewise, the Imperial ton is defined as 20 *hundredweight*, given a weight of 2,240 pounds (20 × 112 pounds), whereas the U.S. ton is a weight of 2,000 pounds. Therefore, when speaking of a hundredweight or a ton, you need to know whether it is the Imperial version of these measures or the U.S. version. I'm just throwing that in for you; it's unlikely that you will be working with measurements that large in your makeup effects work, but it's possible—if you're casting a large creature, say, a *Thestral* for a Harry Potter movie.

WEIGHT

Imperial/U.S. Unit	Metric (SI) Unit	Metric (SI) Unit	Imperial/U.S. Unit
1 ounce (weight)	28.35 grams	1 gram	0.035 ounces
1 pound	0.45 kilograms	1 kilogram	2.21 pounds
1 inch	2.54 centimeters	1 centimeter	0.39 inches
1 foot	30.48 centimeters	1 meter	3.28 feet
1 yard	0.91 meters	1 meter	1.09 yards

TEMPERATURE

The U.S. and Imperial systems measure temperature using the Fahrenheit system. The metric (SI) system originally used the Celsius temperature system but now officially uses the Kelvin temperature system. However, few people aside from brainiacs have switched to the Kelvin system, and the Celsius system is almost always used by most people for nonscientific purposes—unless, of course, you live and work in the United States. The following points compare the Fahrenheit and Celsius systems:

- The freezing point of water in Fahrenheit is 32 degrees; in Celsius it is 0 degrees.
- The boiling point of water in Fahrenheit is 212 degrees; in Celsius it is 100 degrees.
- Consequently, the difference between freezing and boiling is 180 degrees Fahrenheit (212 – 32) or 100 degrees Celsius (100 – 0). This means that a 180-degree change in Fahrenheit is equal to a 100-degree change in Celsius, or more simply, 1.8 degrees Fahrenheit equals 1.0 degrees Celsius.

This gives rise to the following equations to convert between Celsius and Fahrenheit:

$$°C = (°F - 32) \div 1.8 \text{ For example: } (68°F - 32) \div 1.8 = (36) \div 1.8 = 20°C$$
$$°F = (°C \times 1.8) + 32 \text{ For example: } (20°C \times 1.8) + 32 = (36) + 32 = 68°F$$

Some common examples are:

- Freezing = 0°C, 32°F
- Room temperature = 20°C, 68°F
- Normal body temperature = 37°C, 98.6°F
- A very hot day = 40°C, 104°F
- Boiling point of water = 100°C, 212°F

AREA CONVERSION

Imperial/U.S. Unit	Metric (SI) Unit	Metric (SI) Unit	Imperial/U.S. Unit
1 square inch	6.45 square cm	1 square cm	0.16 square inches
1 square foot	0.09 square meters	1 square meter	10.76 square feet
1 cubic inch	16.39 cubic cm	1 cubic cm	0.06 cubic inches
1 cubic foot	0.028 cubic meters	1 cubic meter	35.23 cubic feet

VOLUME CONVERSION (CAPACITY CONVERSION)

Imperial/U.S. Unit	Metric (SI) Unit	Metric (SI) Unit	Imperial/U.S. Unit
1 teaspoon (U.K.)	5.92 milliliters	1 milliliter	0.17 teaspoons (U.K.)
1 teaspoon (U.S.)	4.93 milliliters	1 milliliter	0.20 teaspoons (U.S.)
1 tablespoon (U.K.)	17.76 milliliters	10 milliliters	0.56 tablespoons (U.K.)
1 tablespoon (U.S.)	14.79 milliliters	10 milliliters	0.68 tablespoons (U.S.)
1 fluid ounce (U.K.)	28.41 milliliters	100 milliliters	3.52 fluid ounces (U.K.)
1 fluid ounce (U.S.)	29.57 milliliters	100 milliliters	3.38 fluid ounces (U.S)
1 pint (U.K.)	0.57 liters	1 liter	1.76 pints (U.K.)

Imperial/U.S. Unit	Metric (SI) Unit	Metric (SI) Unit	Imperial/U.S. Unit
1 pint (U.S.)	0.47 liters	1 liter	2.11 pints (U.S.)
1 quart (U.K.)	1.14 liters	1 liter	0.88 quarts (U.K.)
1 quart (U.S.)	0.95 liters	1 liter	1.06 quarts (U.S.)
1 gallon (U.K.)	4.55 liters	1 liter	0.22 gallons (U.K.)
1 gallon (U.S.)	3.79 liters	1 liter	0.26 gallons (U.S.)

Measures of volume are different for the two systems due to the Imperial ounce being slightly smaller than the U.S. equivalent (which affects all multiples of the ounce) and also due to the U.K. pint having 20 ounces whereas the U.S. pint has only 16 ounces.

The sizes of the smaller Imperial measures (teaspoon and tablespoon) are open to interpretation.

CUBIC VOLUME

Volume of a cube:

Width × Length × Height = Cubic volume

Volume of a cylinder:

To calculate the volume of a cylinder, we need to know the radius of the circular cross-section of the cylinder; this is the measurement from the center of the circle to the outer-edge, or ½ the diameter (outer edge to outer edge). A cylinder with radius r units and height h units has a volume of V cubic units given by $V = \pi r^2 h$; $\pi = 3.142$.

Volume of a cone:

$V = 1/3\pi r^2 h$

Volume of a sphere:

$V = 4/3\pi r^3$

Anatomy for the Artist, by Sarah Simblet; ISBN 0-7894-8045-X

The Art and Science of Professional Makeup, by Stan Campbell Place; ISBN 0-87250-361-9

Atlas of Anatomy, by Giovanni Iazzetti; ISBN-10: 190232840X, ISBN-13: 978-1902328409

Atlas of Human Anatomy for the Artist, by Stephen Rogers Peck; ISBN-10: 0195030958, ISBN-13: 978-0195030952

Behind the Mask: The Secrets of Hollywood's Monster Makers, by Mark Salisbury and Alan Hedgcock; ISBN 1-85286-488-5

Cinefex Magazine; www.cinefex.com/store/subs.html

The Complete Make-up Artist, by Penny Delamar; ISBN 0-8101-1969-2

Designing Movie Creatures and Characters, by Richard Rickitt; ISBN 978-0-240-80846-8, ISBN 0-240-80846-0

Dick Smith's Do-It-Yourself Monster Makeup, by Dick Smith; ASIN B000VJ5U64

Fangoria Magazine; www.fangoria.com

Forensic Art and Illustration, by Karen T. Taylor; ISBN 0-8493-8118-5

Forensic Pathology, by David J. Williams, Anthony J. Ashford, David S. Priday, and Alex S Forrest; ISBN 0-443-05388-X

Grande Illusions: A Learn-by-Example Guide to the Art and Technique of Special Make-Up Effects from the Films of Tom Savini, by Tom Savini, ISBN-10: 0911137009, ISBN-13: 978-0911137002

Grande Illusions: Book II, by Tom Savini; ISBN-10: 0911137076, ISBN-13: 978-0911137071

Gray's Anatomy, by Henry Gray; ISBN-10: 0517223651, ISBN-13: 978-0517223659

How to Draw the Human Head, by Louise Gordon; ISBN 0-14-046560-X

Human Proportions for Artists, by Avard T. Fairbanks and Eugene F. Fairbanks; ISBN 0-9725841- 1-0

Kryolan Makeup Manual, by Arnold Langer; ASIN: B000BWPGVA

The Makeup Artist Handbook, by Gretchen Davis and Mindy Hall; ISBN 978-0-240-809410

Makeup Artist Magazine; 4018 NE 112th Ave. D-8, Vancouver, WA 98682; http://makeupmag.com/subscribe.htm

Makeup Designory's Character Makeup, by Paul Thompson; ISBN 0-9749500-0-9 LCCN 2004091103

Making Faces, Playing God: Identity and the Art of Transformational Makeup, by Thomas Morawetz; ISBN-10: 0292752474, ISBN-13: 978-0292752474

Men, Makeup & Monsters: Hollywood's Masters of Illusion and FX, by Anthony Timpone; ISBN-10: 0312146787

The Monster Makers Mask Makers Handbook, by Arnold Goldman; ISBN-10: 0977687007, ISBN-13: 978-0977687008

One Hundred Over 100, by Jim Heynen; ISBN 1-55591-052-1

The Professional Makeup Artist's Resource Guide, by Shauna Giesbrecht; ISBN 0-9755912-0-7

The Prop Builder's Molding & Casting Handbook, by Thurston James; ISBN-10: 1558701281, ISBN-13: 978-1558701281

Special Effects Makeup, by Janus Vinther; ISBN-10: 087830178X, ISBN-13: 978-0878301782

Special Makeup Effects, by Vincent J-R Kehoe; ISBN-10: 0240800990, ISBN-13: 978-0240800998

Stage Makeup, by Richard Corson and James Glavan; ISBN-10: 0136061532, ISBN-13: 978-0136061533

Stage Makeup Step-by-Step, by Rosemary Swinfield; ISBN-10: 155870390X, ISBN-13: 978-1558703902

Stage Makeup: The Actor's Complete Guide to Today's Techniques and Materials, by Laura Thudium; ISBN-10: 0823088391, ISBN-13: 978-0823088393

The Technique of the Professional Makeup Artist, by Vincent J-R Kehoe; ISBN-10: 0240802179, ISBN-13: 978-0240802176

Techniques of Three-Dimensional Makeup, by Lee Baygan; ISBN 0-8230-5260-5, ISBN 0-8230-5261-3

Wigs & Make-up for Theatre, Television and Film, by Patsy Baker; ISBN 0-7506-0431-X

The Winston Effect: The Art & History of Stan Winston Studio, by Jody Duncan; ISBN-10: 1845761502, ISBN-13: 978-1845761509

DVDS AND VIDEOS

Mark Alfrey's Sculpting the Human Head, DVD
Mark Alfrey's Ultimate Lifecasting, DVD and Video
Mark Alfrey's Sculpting Movie Monsters, DVD
Mark Alfrey's Standard Molds and Castings, DVD
Mark Alfrey's Prosthetic Makeup for Beginners, DVD
Mark Alfrey's Sculpting the Nude Figure, DVD
Mark Alfrey's Sculpting with Water Clay, DVD
Michael Pack's Bite Me: The Video, video
Neill Gorton Studios' Creating Character Prosthetics in Silicone (Series in 4 Parts), DVD
The Special Makeup Effects Artist's Guide to Using GM Foam, video

2.5D *Two-and-a-half dimensional* is an informal term used to describe visual phenomena that are considered "between" 2D and 3D. This is also called *pseudo-3D*.

3D Three-dimensional; usually short for *3D computer graphics*.

3D makeup Dimensional makeup, which includes prosthetic appliances.

3D Studio Max® A leading 3D modeling and animation software package from Autodesk.

3D transfers Small prosthetic appliances that are applied in the same manner as temporary tattoos.

Acetone A solvent. Acetone is the active ingredient in nail polish remover and is also used to make plastics. Acetone is mixable with water, alcohol, ether, and other liquids.

Acrylic A versatile polymer (type of plastic) used in paints, sealers, molds, textiles, *etc.*

Actors' Equity Actors' Equity Association (AEA) is the labor union representing U.S. actors and stage managers in the theater.

AD Abbreviation for *assistant director*. The duties of an AD include setting the shooting schedule, tracking daily progress against the filming production schedule, arranging logistics, preparing daily call sheets, checking the arrival of cast and crew, maintaining order on the set, rehearsing cast, and directing extras.

Addition-cure silicone Also known as *platinum-cure silicone*; widely used as a material for making prosthetic appliances. Cures by a self-contained chemical reaction.

ADR *Additional* (or *automated*) *dialogue recording* (or *replacement*); when location audio is unusable due to uncontrollable factors such as traffic or animal noise, actors will rerecord their dialogue tracks in a studio at a later time, lip syncing while listening to their performance through headphones and watching a video playback. Also known as *dubbing* or *looping*. In the U.K. it is called *post-synchronization* (or *post-sync*).

Airbrush A small, air-operated tool that sprays various media, including ink and dye but most often paint, by a process of atomization. Used extensively today for the application of makeup.

Alginate Derived from seaweed and giant kelp, alginate absorbs water quickly and is used extensively as a mold-making material in dentistry, makeup effects and prosthetics, lifecasting, and textiles. It is also used in the food industry as a thickening agent and in various medical products, including burn dressings.

Algislo® A product of EnvironMolds, Algislo® is an alkaline (base) solution designed to retard the set of alginate, bond set alginate with fresh alginate, and soften freshly set alginate to allow the application of fibers to hold a rigid support mold.

Anaplastology The art and science of restoring a malformed or absent part of the human body through artificial means. An anaplastologist makes prosthetic devices. From the Greek *ana*, again, + *plastos*, formed. See also: *Appliance, Prosthetic, Prosthetist*.

Angora hair Also *angora wool*. The hair of the angora goat or of the angora rabbit.

Animatronics The technology connected with the use of electronics to animate puppets or other figures, as for motion pictures.

Anthropometry The study of human body measurement for use in anthropological classification and comparison.

Appliance Another name for a prosthetic device. See also: *Prosthetic*.

Armature In sculpture, a skeletal framework built as a support on which a clay, wax, or plaster figure is constructed.

Articulation 1. The act of properly arranging artificial teeth; 2. the action or manner in which the parts come together at a joint.

Astringent A cosmetic liquid that cleans the skin and constricts the pores.

Attagel A clay mineral used as a thixotropic agent; the active ingredient of fuller's earth. When mixed with PPI's Green Marble SēLr,® can be used as stipple ager.

Bald cap A flexible cap, often made of latex or vinyl but can also be made of foam latex or silicone, for creating the appearance of baldness.

Biomechanical engineering *Biomechanics* is mechanics applied to biology; it is the engineering of a living body, especially of the forces exerted by muscles and gravity on the skeletal structure.

Bleeder An escape hole for air trapped inside a mold; it fills with excess casting material as the mold is filled.

Blend line The point at which any prosthetic appliance tapers off into real skin. The blend between appliance and skin must be invisible.

Block mold Often a two-piece rubber mold that doesn't need a rigid mother mold due to the thickness of the rubber. Casting material is poured through a sprue hole. See also: *Box mold*.

Boardwork A word used to describe the act of making postiche.

Bondo A mixture of Pros-Aide® water-based acrylic adhesive and Cab-O-Sil® (fumed silica) to create a paste used to blend seams and edges of prosthetic appliances. See also: *Cabo patch*.

Box mold A type of mold made by creating a box form and filling it with mold rubber, covering the model to be reproduced. Box molds can be one or two pieces. One-piece box molds are open faced and used for reproducing objects such as medallions, whereas two-piece box molds can be used to reproduce more complex shapes. See also: *Block mold*.

Breakdown makeup The opposite of beauty makeup.

Brush coat The first, thin coating of material brushed into a mold or onto a sculpture to pick up details before building up reinforcing layers. See also: *Brush-up layer, Detail layer, Print coat*.

Brush-up layer – The first coat of material that is applied by brush to pick up detail. See also: *Brush coat, Detail layer, Print coat*.

Buck Another name for the stone positive of a face from a lifecast.

Burlap Bought by the yard or in rolls, burlap is a loose-weave fabric used as a reinforcing material in the outer layers of gypsum molds, making the stone stronger and less susceptible to cracking.

Cabo patch An acrylic adhesive paste used to blend thick edges on foam latex appliances or reused bald caps. Useful in patching foam latex appliances. Apply with a spatula and blend with a wet sponge. See also: *Bondo*.

Cab-O-Sil® Untreated fumed silica used as an inert filler to thicken thin liquids. Cab-O-Sil® is a registered trademark of the Cabot Corporation.

Case mold A rigid multipiece mold that encases a sculpture when closed and clamped together. A *matrix mold* is a type of case mold.

CGI Computer-generated imagery.

Cholesterol cream A hair-conditioning cream that is an excellent release used on hair in lifecasting, to prevent alginate from sticking to it.

Cinema 4D A commercial cross-platform high-end 3D graphics and animation application.

Cold foam Soft or rigid two-part urethane foam that does not require the application of heat to cure. See also: *Poly foam, Soft foam, Urethane*.

Collagen A fibrous structural protein extracted from the bones and connective tissue of animals that when partially hydrolyzed (broken down by water) becomes gelatin.

Collodion A solution of nitrocellulose in acetone, sometimes with the addition of alcohols. In makeup, it is used to create scars on the skin. When the acetone evaporates, it pulls and puckers the skin, creating realistic-looking scars.

Condensation-cure silicone Also known as *tin-cure silicone* and *room-temperature vulcanization*, or RTV, silicone. Used extensively for mold making but sometimes also used for prosthetics.

Core The interior positive portion of a multipiece mold. If a character makeup requires a full-head cowl, for example, the front and back negative parts of the mold hold the detail of the makeup that will be outward while the interior positive, or core, holds the detail of the head the appliance will be attached to.

Craniofacial implant Usually, titanium anchors surgically implanted to hold medical prostheses in place for individuals with catastrophic injuries, allowing people to improve their quality of life.

Cream time For 1:1 2-part urethane foam, cream time is the working time to mix the liquid before it begins to foam. See also: *Pot life, Working time.*

Critical corner Area where the dividing wall meets the sculpture. It is considered critical because it is an area of the sculpture that is subject to trapping air when the mold is being made.

Crystalline silica A basic component of quartz, soil, sand, granite, and many other minerals. Found in many types of alginate. Respirable crystalline silica is a known carcinogen and can also cause silicosis.

Cure The chemical reaction that causes materials such as silicone, urethane, and Ultracal to set up, or harden.

Cyberscan Method of transcribing a real object into a digital model by accurately measuring it with a laser. Normally used to create a scan of an actor or maquette to produce a 3D copy for sculpting purposes.

Decalcification The loss of calcium or calcium compounds, as from bone or teeth.

Dental acrylic powder Acrylic powder available in various colors; when mixed with a liquid acrylic monomer, becomes a plastic liquid used for making false teeth and gums.

Dental impression plaster A very low expansion plaster used for dental impressions; also makes very strong mother mold as a substitute for using plaster bandages.

Dental stone Very hard, low-expansion gypsum for casting dental models. See also: *Die stone.*

Dental tray Plastic upper and lower trays for making dental impressions with dental alginate.

Detail layer The first, thin coating of material brushed into a mold or onto a sculpture to pick up details before building up reinforcing layers. See also: *Brush-up layer, Brush coat, Print coat.*

Die stone Very hard, low-expansion gypsum for casting dental models. See also: *Dental stone.*

Dividing wall A temporary wall made with WED clay or other water clay to create a separation between the front half and the back half of a case mold. See also: *Mold wall.*

Dremel® Versatile electric and battery-operated rotary tool used extensively by model makers and sculptors.

Dressing Refers to trimming, curling, and setting postiche—wigs, moustaches, and beards—for a more natural appearance when they are applied.

Drip coat The gypsum stone applied immediately after the brush coat using the remainder of the first batch of stone. Usually built up to a thickness of ½–1 inch. See also: *Splash coat*.

Ectomorphic A human build with little fat or muscle but with long limbs.

Emollient Having the power of softening or relaxing, as a medicinal substance; soothing, especially to the skin.

Endomorphic A squat and fleshy human build.

Epicanthic fold A fold of skin of the upper eyelid that partially covers the inner corner of the eye. Common in many people of Asian decent, American Indians, and American Eskimos.

Ester A compound produced by the reaction between an acid and an alcohol with the elimination of a molecule of water.

Extrinsic coloration External coloration. Appliance materials such as foam latex may be initially colored intrinsically with a base color but are then usually colored extrinsically to add detail and a sense of depth.

Fiberglass A material consisting of extremely fine glass fibers suspended in a polymer resin, used in making various products, such as yarns, fabrics, insulators, and structural objects or parts. An excellent mold material; extremely strong and very lightweight.

Fibonacci series A sequence of numbers named after Leonardo of Pisa, known as Fibonacci; after two starting values, each number is the sum of the two preceding numbers: 0, 1, 1, 2, 3, 5, 8, 13, 21, 34, 55, 89, 144, 233, 377, 610, 987, 1597, 2584, 4181, 6765, 10946, 17711, 28657, 46368, 75025, 121393, ….

Flange A projecting rim, collar, or ring on a mold that gives additional strength, stiffness, or support and provides an area for clamping or bolting mold sections together.

Flashing Excess casting material in a prosthetic mold that is separated from the appliance by the cutting edge of the mold. Also, the area of a mold where overflow collects.

Flocking Usually synthetic material used for coloring gelatin or silicone prosthetics intrinsically (internally).

Foam latex Very soft, lightweight, spongy material used to create prosthetics. An actor's physical expressions are very easy to project through foam latex. Liquid latex is mixed with various additives and whipped into a foam, then poured or injected into a mold before being placed in a oven to cure. In addition to prosthetic appliances, foam latex is also used to make rubber body suits and skins for animatronic (mechanical) characters.

Forensic Relates to the use of science or technology in the investigation and establishment of facts or evidence.

Forton MG Though technically a gypsum product, (Hydrocal is the main ingredient), it is considered a resin casting material because it incorporates plastics and fiberglass.

Foundation Base makeup applied before highlight and shadow. Used to cover or blend blotchy or uneven skin tones.

Fuller's earth Calcium bentonite is known as *fuller's earth,* a term that is also used to refer to *attapulgite. Pascalite* is another commercial name for the calcium bentonite clay. It is used in special effects for simulating explosions. Fine-grained fuller's earth makes a much larger plume than ordinary dirt, suggesting a larger explosion and allowing use of a smaller, safer charge, sometimes only compressed air. It is also used in breakdown makeup to add dirt and smudges.

Fumed silica Silicon dioxide; has unique properties and is commonly added to liquids or coatings and solids to improve various properties. Fumed silica is used frequently as a thixotropic additive that, when dispersed into liquids, increases viscosity; when mixed with powders it prevents caking. Cab-O-Sil® is fumed silica.

Galloon A braided silk lace ribbon used to frame a wig foundation.

Gel coat A thick polymer resin coat used in fiberglass fabrication; the gel coat is used as a detail or brush-up layer before applying resin and fiberglass mat or fiberglass cloth as strength layers.

Gelatin Extracted from collagen; when mixed with various ingredients, gelatin is commonly used as a prosthetic appliance material. It is widely considered to be hypoallergenic.

GFA Gel-filled appliance; a silicone gel often encapsulated by a thin envelope of silicone or plastic (vinyl) bald cap material.

Glycerin A colorless, odorless, thick liquid widely used in pharmaceutical formulations; it is a sugar alcohol and is sweet-tasting and of low toxicity. In makeup effects, glycerin is a component of gelatin used for prosthetics. It is also used to simulate tears and sweat because of its viscous nature and low evaporation. It is also found in WED clay and helps it remain moist for longer periods than normal water-based clays.

Gnomatic growth A process that leaves the resultant features of an individual similar to the original. Although our faces undergo enormous growth from youth to adulthood, there is a constancy of appearance; the face of a man remains recognizably the same, regardless of age.

Golden Ratio Can be expressed as a mathematical constant, usually denoted by the Greek letter φ (phi). The figure of a golden section illustrates the geometric relationship that defines this constant. Expressed algebraically:

$$\frac{a+b}{a} = \frac{a}{b} = \varphi.$$

This equation has as its unique positive solution the algebraic irrational number:

$$\varphi = \frac{1+\sqrt{5}}{2} \approx 1.6180339887...$$

Go off To set up. See also: *Kick.*

Green Marble SēLr® Created as a makeup sealer for Premiere Products by Kenny Myers and Richard Snell.

Gypsum A common mineral, hydrated calcium sulfate, used to make Plaster of Paris, Ultracal, Hydrocal, dental stone, etc.

H-10 A material used to flatten hair at the hairline to eliminate the "bump" under a bald cap and to control hair around the ears and at the nape of the neck. Made from a mixture of moustache wax, Gaf Quat, and 70 percent alcohol. Great for keeping a Mohawk haircut stiff, too.

Hackle A metal plate with rows of pointed needles used to blend or straighten hair. The hackle is clamped to a table with a C-clamp.

Hair lace Very fine, flexible netting material similar to tulle; often made of silk and used for creating wigs and hairpieces. See also: *Wig lace*.

Hair punching The process of adding hairs to a prosthetic appliance one at a time using a special needle, putting it over a strand of hair and pushing it into the surface of the appliance in the direction the hair is "growing."

Hair tying A very tedious process of knotting hairs into wig lace one-by-one with a special needle that resembles a very small, fine fish hook (called a *ventilating needle*). See also: *Ventilating*.

Hexane A petroleum distillate used as a solvent; Bestine® Rubber Cement Thinner is hexane. Hexane is flammable and is a known carcinogen.

HSE Health and Safety Executive, responsible for health and safety regulation in Great Britain; the U.K.'s equivalent to OSHA in the U.S.

Hydrocal® A white gypsum plaster.

Hygroscopic Absorbing or attracting moisture from the air.

Hypoallergenic Designed to reduce or minimize the possibility of an allergic response by containing relatively few or no potentially irritating substances.

Ichabod Crane Ichabod Crane is a fictional character in the Washington Irving short story, *The Legend of Sleepy Hollow*, made into a film by director Tim Burton.

Incisal Relating to the cutting edges of the incisor and cuspid teeth.

Intrinsic coloration Internal coloration. Often silicone and gelatin appliances are colored intrinsically with different-colored flocking material to more closely mimic the appearance of real human skin.

IPA Isopropyl alcohol.

IPM Isopropyl myristate.

Isopropyl alcohol Also isopropanol; rubbing alcohol. Sometimes sold as isopropyl rubbing alcohol, 70%, and isopropyl rubbing alcohol, 99%, the latter of which is frequently used in makeup effects. See also: *IPA*.

Isopropyl myristate An ester of isopropyl alcohol and myristic acid. Used as an emollient and nongreasy lubricant. Also used in topical medicinal preparations where good skin absorption is needed. An effective makeup remover and Pros-Aide® bondo remover, it is the mildest of the adhesive removers. See also: *IPM*.

Jacket mold A combination mold made with a registered/keyed silicone or urethane rubber interior and a registered/keyed support mold that is registered/keyed to the rubber interior for extremely precise casting; a type of case mold. See also: *Matrix mold.*

Jowls Folds of flesh hanging from the lower jaw in older and overweight people.

Key An indentation or protrusion to aid in precise alignment of mold parts. See also: *Mold key, Registration key.*

Kick Sometimes referred to as *kick time*, the amount of time it takes for a material to begin to set up during its curing phase. Example: "Plat-Sil Gel 10 will kick faster if you apply heat." See also: *Go off.*

Latex As found in nature, the milky sap of Pará rubber trees. Used extensively in creating makeup effects and prosthetics, especially in making foam latex. See also: *Slip latex, Slush latex.*

Laying on hair The process of applying hair by hand (with hair and glue), a small amount at a time, to create a head of hair, eyebrows, moustache, or beard.

Lesion An injury or wound; in pathology, any localized, abnormal structural change in the body.

Lifecasting The process of creating a three-dimensional copy of a living human body or body parts through the use of alginate molding and casting techniques.

Lightwave 3D® A leading 3D modeling and animation software from Newtek.

Maquette French word for scale model, sometimes referred to by the Italian name *bozzetto*. In makeup effects, it is a scale model of a finished sculpture for a character design or makeup. Often used as a guide for a larger sculpture.

Matrix mold A combination mold made with a registered/keyed silicone or urethane rubber interior and a registered/keyed support mold that is registered/keyed to the rubber interior for extremely precise casting. See also: *Jacket mold.*

Maxillofacial prosthetics Prostheses made for patients with acquired, congenital, and developmental defects of the head and neck. Common maxillofacial prosthetics include auricular prostheses (ears), nasal prostheses (noses), and ocular prostheses (eyes). Made by prosthetists and anaplastologists.

Maxillofacial prosthetist A highly specialized physician or technician who helps restore a sense of normalcy to cancer, trauma, and congenital defect patients. There are only about 500 of these specialists in the U.S. and they are dedicated to restoring the health and dignity of thousands of people who live with severe facial deformities.

Maya® A leading 3D modeling and animation software from Autodesk.®

Melanin In humans, melanin is the polymeric pigmentation found in our skin and hair. Produced by melanocytes, melanin is the primary determinant of human skin color.

Mesomorphic A human structure that is naturally muscular with a trim waist and that can easily lose and gain fat and muscle weight.

Mold key An indentation or protrusion to aid in precise alignment of mold parts. See also: *Key, Registration key.*

Mold negative In making a casting of a three-dimensional object (the positive), the resulting mold is the opposite or inverse of that object, or a mold negative. See also: *Negative.*

Mold positive The resulting cast of an object when material is put into a negative mold. See also: *Positive.*

Mold wall A temporary water clay wall used to form a divider between the front and back halves of a case mold. See also: *Dividing wall.*

Mother mold The rigid support shell of a soft inner mold.

MSDS Material safety data sheets, required by law on some products. All makeup effects artists should have MSDS sheets available for all materials in their makeup kits and should also be familiar with properties of all materials being used in the workshop.

MudBox® A high-resolution brush-based 3D sculpting software owned by Autodesk.®

Negative The mold surface that contains a reverse three-dimensional imprint of the positive sculpture. See also: *Mold negative.*

Nevus The medical term for growths or lesions of the skin commonly known as birthmarks and moles.

New-Baldies® The first bald cap plastic to be medically approved; it is completely free from phthalate softeners.

Nitrile Nitrile or nitrile rubber is a synthetic rubber copolymer generally resistant to oil, fuel, and other chemicals. Its resilience makes it the perfect material for disposable lab, cleaning, and examination gloves. These gloves, along with vinyl gloves, are ideal for working with platinum-addition RTV silicone because they will not react negatively with it.

No. 1 Pottery Plaster Made by U.S. Gypsum (USG), this plaster is excellent for mold making and casting.

Occlusal Related to the fitting together of the teeth of the lower jaw with the corresponding teeth of the upper jaw when the jaws are closed. See also: *Occlusion.*

Occlusion Fitting together of the teeth of the lower jaw with the corresponding teeth of the upper jaw when the jaws are closed. See also: *Occlusal.*

Ocularistry The field of designing, fabricating, and fitting artificial eyes and the making of ocular prostheses associated with the appearance or function of human eyes.

Oil clay Oil-based modeling clay; the clay is mixed with oil to prevent it from drying out or shrinking.

Orthotics The field of application and manufacture of devices that support or correct human function. Many professionals use the adjective *orthotic* as a noun, usually to describe a foot-supporting device or shoe insole.

OSHA Occupational Safety and Health Administration, the main federal agency charged with the enforcement of safety and health legislation.

Overflow Excess appliance material in a mold; flashing is added to a mold to allow overflow someplace to collect without damaging the mold or the casting.

Parting edge The parting edge or parting line of a mold determines how and where the pieces of a mold will fit together and come apart.

Pax paint Acrylic paint mixed with Pros-Aide adhesive for painting prosthetic appliances.

Photoshop® Image manipulation software from Adobe.®

Pigmentation Coloration; in skin, it is the coloration by pigment cells called *melanin*. In prosthetics, pigmentation can be achieved by various shades and tints of flocking or by adding solid pigments.

Plaster bandage Plaster of Paris-impregnated cloth bandages used for making support shells for alginate molds.

Plaster of Paris A white gypsum used for mold making and casting that starts as a dry powder that is mixed with water to form a paste that liberates heat and then hardens. Named for a large gypsum deposit found at Montmartre in Paris, France.

Plasticize To render or become plastic. See also: *Polymer, Polymerization*.

Plastiline A type of oil-based modeling clay

Plate mold In makeup effects, a plate mold is a flat mold with a negative impression, frequently used for making generic wounds or 3D prosthetic transfers. Can be either a one-piece or two-piece mold.

Polyfoam Urethane foam that can be either soft or rigid, usually soft, and can be mixed in a 1:1 ratio by either volume or weight. See also: *Cold foam, Soft foam, Urethane*.

Polymer A compound of high molecular weight derived either by the addition of many smaller molecules, as polyethylene, or by the condensation of many smaller molecules with the elimination of water, alcohol, or the like, as nylon. See also: *Plasticize, Polymerization*.

Polymerization The bonding of two or more monomers to form a polymer. See also: *Plasticize, Polymer*.

Positive Any sculpture or model used to create the mold negative. See also: *Mold positive*.

Postiche A French word used to describe any article of hair work, which can be as small as a false eyelash or as large as a wig.

Pot life Term for the working time of a material before it begins to cure. See also: *Working time, Cream time*.

PPI Premiere Products, Inc., maker of Telesis® products and Skin Illustrator® palettes.

Print coat The first, thin coating of material brushed into a mold or onto a sculpture to pick up details before building up reinforcing layers. See also: *Detail layer, Brush-up layer, Brush coat.*

Pros-Aide® A very popular water-based prosthetic adhesive made by ADM Tronics.®

Prosthetic A device, either external or implanted, that substitutes for or supplements a missing or defective part of the body. Also called an *appliance;* used for special makeup effects, the basis of this book. Usually made of silicone, foam latex, or gelatin. See also: *Appliance.*

Prosthetist A professional who makes prosthetic devices. See also: *Anaplastology.*

PSI Pounds per square inch, a measure of pressure.

Pull Term for mask or appliance making using a mold. Each time a prosthetic appliance is removed from a mold, it is known as a *pull.* Well-maintained molds should allow many pulls before breaking down.

Quik-Tube® A cylindrical prefab product manufactured by Quikrete® that is well suited to some lifecasting applications.

Registration key A drilled or carved indentation or a protrusion made of clay, rubber, or resin that is used to precisely align parts of a mold when held together. See also: *Key, Mold key.*

Relative density The ratio of the mass of a solid or liquid to the mass of an equal volume of distilled water at 4°C (39°F) or of a gas to an equal volume of air or hydrogen under prescribed conditions of temperature and pressure. See also: *Specific gravity.*

Release agent Release agents are materials that allow you to separate cast objects from molds. There are two categories for most release agents: barrier and reactive, or chemically active release agents.

Rigid foam Rigid urethane foam mixed in a 1:1 ratio by either volume or weight. It is available in varying densities.

RTV silicone Most commonly a tin-cure condensation silicone, though there are platinum room-temperature vulcanization (RTV) silicones.

Rubber mask greasepaint RMGP is makeup for use over foam latex and slush latex appliances. Creates washes of color by adding a couple of drops of 99 percent isopropyl alcohol to the makeup and then applying with a sea sponge for dimensional texture.

Running foam The term for processing a batch of foam latex.

Sculpt Used by makeup effects artists, *sculpt* is just another name for the sculpture.

Sealer Liquids or sprays that are absorbed into porous surfaces to seal against moisture, making the surface essentially no longer porous; they can act as both a seal and a release for some materials.

Seaming Removing and cleaning up surface blemishes and flashing on prosthetic seams.

Shell Support mold; mother mold; the rigid outer part of a matrix mold.

Shim Material, often thin wood or metal, used as a dividing wall in mold making.

Silicosis Sometimes called grinder's disease or potter's rot; a disabling, nonreversible, and sometimes fatal lung disease caused by overexposure to respirable crystalline silica, the second most common mineral on earth.

Slip latex Liquid latex that will air-dry and does not need a heat cure like foam latex. Used most often for making rubber masks. See also: *Latex, Slush latex.*

Slush latex Liquid latex used for build-up appliances or rubber masks. Called *slush* because the latex is poured into a mask mold and sloshed around, forming a skin that will become the mask. See also: *Latex, Slip latex.*

Soft foam Soft urethane foam mixed in a 1:1 ratio by either volume or weight. It is also available in varying densities. See also: *Cold foam, Polyfoam, Urethane.*

Softimage XSI® High-end 3D software for gaming, film, and television; a subsidiary of Avid Technology, Inc.

Somatotype A term for human body shape and physique type.

Special effects SFX or SPFX for short; traditionally practical or physical effects usually accomplished during live-action shooting. This includes the use of mechanized props, scenery and scale model miniatures, and pyrotechnics.

Specific gravity The ratio of the mass of a solid or liquid to the mass of an equal volume of distilled water at 4°C (39°F) or of a gas to an equal volume of air or hydrogen under prescribed conditions of temperature and pressure. See also: *Relative density.*

Spirit gum Also called Mastix; a natural gum resin commonly used as a theatrical adhesive for lace wigs and beards.

Splash coat The gypsum stone applied immediately after the brush coat using the remainder of the first batch of stone. See also: *Drip coat.*

Sprue In mold making, the passage through which casting material is poured into a mold. The term can also refer to the excess material on a rough casting that solidified in the sprue hole.

Stipple The technique of using small dots to simulate varying degrees of solidity, or shading, such as beard stipple, or lightly applying latex for an aging, wrinkled effect. Usually created with a coarse stipple sponge.

Stipple sponge A rough, open-weave synthetic sponge used for old-age stippling, beard stippling, bruises, and adding a hint of capillary coloring to produce a natural flesh-tone makeup.

Straight makeup Can incorporate corrective makeup and camouflage makeup; it can overlap into beauty and fashion makeup, but its function is to correct and define a person's face, not to change it. Straight makeup, in general, should be understated and imperceptible.

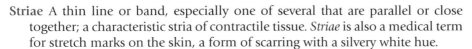

Striae A thin line or band, especially one of several that are parallel or close together; a characteristic stria of contractile tissue. *Striae* is also a medical term for stretch marks on the skin, a form of scarring with a silvery white hue.

Suppurate To produce or discharge fluid, as with severe burns.

Telesis® Telesis® products from Premiere Products are a line of adhesives, thinners, removers, solvents, skin preps, and conditioners that are used extensively by medical professionals (maxillofacial prosthetists) and makeup effects artists.

Terra alba Dried, powdered cured plaster; as an additive to fresh plaster, will cause it to kick, or begin to set, in a fraction of its normal time.

Texture stamp A flexible stamp that is pressed into the clay sculpture to add texture during final detailing.

Thixotropic An example of an application for thixotropic properties is the thickening of silicone so it won't be runny; it becomes more of a paste. Cab-O-Sil® added to Pros-Aide® adhesive becomes a thixotropic paste that can be used to patch appliance seams and the like.

Tincture of Green Soap Also Green Soap Tincture; it isn't necessarily green. A medicinal topical detergent used for surgical prep; also an excellent release agent. Contains 30 percent alcohol.

Tulle A fine, often starched net of silk, rayon, or nylon, used especially for veils, tutus, or gowns.

Ultracal 30® Super-strength gypsum cement recommended where extreme accuracy and greater surface hardness are required. Ultracal 30® has the lowest expansion of any rapid-setting gypsum cement available. Captures very high detail in lifecasting or sculpture.

Undercut Any area of a positive or negative that creates a locking state between the mold and the core.

Urethane Also polyurethane, a family of rubbers and plastics materials that are used for making molds. Widely known for its tough properties, urethane also refers to soft or rigid foam that is used for casting in molds. See also: *Cold foam, Polyfoam, Soft foam.*

Vascularity Pertaining to vessels or ducts that convey fluids such as blood, lymph, or sap.

Ventilating Hand-tying hair with a ventilating needle into wig lace. See also: *Hair tying.*

Visual effects VFX for short; visual effects usually involve the integration of live-action footage with CGI or other elements (such as pyrotechnics or miniatures) to create realistic environments. *Visual effects* predominantly refers to post-production, whereas special effects refers to on-set mechanical effects.

Vulcanization The process of improving the strength, resiliency, and freedom from stickiness and odor (of rubber, for example) by combining with sulfur or other additives in the presence of heat and pressure.

Water clay A modeling clay suspended in water; like WED clay but without glycerin. Used by sculptors and mold makers.

WED clay A water-based clay great for large sculptures; it has a smooth, fine grain. This clay has been specially formulated to be a very smooth, slow-drying clay for modeling; it stays moist longer because it contains glycerin. It is used primarily by design studios and the entertainment industry for modeling, design, mockup, and tooling. Named for Walter Elias Disney (WED).

Weft As it pertains to hair, a bundle of hair that is sewn together at one end (root end) for easier manipulation during the wig-making process.

Wig block Also called a *malleable*; used for dressing pastiche (wigs and hairpieces).

Wig lace A very fine, flesh-colored, four-way stretch mesh used to blend off hairlines where they meet the skin to give the impression of a natural hairline effect of a wig or hairpiece. See also: *Hair lace*.

Witch hazel Used medically as a lotion for treating bruises and insect bites, it is also an effective topical astringent used on the skin prior to applying a prosthetic appliance.

Working time The amount of time to mix, pour, brush, or otherwise apply a material before it begins to kick, or set. See also: *Pot life; Cream time*.

Wrinkle stipple Often made of thin specialty liquid latex that dries nearly transparently; ideal for creating facial wrinkles and crow's feet.

Yak hair Coarse hair often used for makeup effects postiche.

ZBrush® A digital sculpting tool that combines 3D/2.5D modeling, texturing, and painting.

Index

321

323

Top Guard®, 268
Torso muscles, 37–38
Triceps, 38
Tucker, Christopher, 206–207
Tulle, 317
Tuplast, 254
2.5D, 305

U

Ultracal 30®
    definition, 317
    lifecasting, 72, 88–89, 98–99,
        102–103
Undercut, 317
Urethane, 317
    cold foam appliance casting
        appliance removal, 179
        materials, 176–177
        mold
            filling, 178–179
            preparation, 177–178
        painting, 199–200
        quirks, 177
        safety, 176
    gelatin
        appliance removal, 184–186
        makeup application to
            appliances, 218–219

materials, 180–181
mold filling, 182–184
overview, 179–180
painting, 199–200
quirks, 181–182
seaming, 192
mold, 156–158

V

Varicose veins, 44
Vascularity, 317
Vellus hair, 46
Ventilating hair, 236–240, 317
Ventilating needle, 224–225
Ventilation, workspace, 13–14
Visual effects, 1, 317
Volume, conversion charts,
    300–301
Vulcanization, 317

W

Wade, Brian, 25–27
Walken, Christopher, 16
Walker, Brian, 224
Water, 318
WED clay, 88, 115, 318
Weft wig, 225–226, 318

Weight, conversion charts, 299
Wig block, 225, 318
Wig lace, 318
Wigs
    knotted wigs, 226
    placement
        lace wig, 229
        preparation for donning
            long hair, 228
            medium hair, 227–228
            short hair, 227
        technique, 228
    postiche tools and materials,
        224–225
    weft wigs, 225–226
Witch hazel, 318
Working time, 318
Workspace, 12–13
Wrinkle stipple, 262–265, 318

Y

Yak hair, 224, 318

Z

ZBrush®, 24–25, 29, 118, 318

Special Makeup Effects for Stage and Screen

Todd has worked as a professional makeup artist and as a professional teacher, and it really shows in this book's detailed, clear, concise and no-nonsense approach to the art and craft of special mak eup effects. I'm now insanely jealous of all the people who will learn from this book because this is the book I would have killed to have had when I was starting out....... IT'S NOT FAIR!!!

–Neill Gorton, BAFTA winner for Best Makeup and Hair Design, *Help* (2005), nominee for Best Makeup and Hair Design, *The Catherine Tate Show* (2007), Royal Television Society (UK) winner for Best Makeup Design, *Help* (2005), and nominee for Best Makeup Design, *Doctor Who* (2005, 2006)

Among the most exhaustive and thorough tomes on the subject of special effects makeup there is, written with a likable and easy-to-understand style that is accessible to all ages.

–Jordu Schell, creature and character designer

The artistry of makeup has been a lifelong passion of mine and hope it will be to everyone who purchases this book. This book will inspire future makeup artists and novices to continue the art and discover newer, more innovative materials and procedures to work with. The techniques and education in this book are inspiring. To create believable character makeups on human faces is a challenging, rewarding art form which will continue to evolve and inspire those who study this book.

–Matthew W. Mungle, Oscar® winner and BAFTA nominee for Best Makeup, *Dracula* (1992), Oscar® nominee for Best Makeup, *Ghosts of Mississippi* (1996), and Oscar® and BAFTA nominee for Best Makeup, *Schindler's List* (1993)

I highly recommend Todd's Book as a must *for everyone involved and interested in special prosthetic makeup effects. Crammed with cutting-edge information on materials and techniques, formulas, suppliers, how-to's, and more, this is a book I wish I had when I first started! Every student, beginner, and makeup artist for film, TV, theater, video, and commercials should not hesitate to pick up a copy of this book— don't leave home without it! Make sure it's part of your kit!*

–Christopher Tucker, BAFTA winner for Best Makeup Artist, *Quest for Fire [La Guerre du feu]* (1981), BAFTA nominee for Best Special Visual Effects and Best Makeup Artist, *The Company of Wolves* (1984), and Emmy nominee for Outstanding Achievement in Makeup for a Miniseries or a Special, *War and Remembrance* (1988)